STRUCTURAL PRINCIPLES OF EU LAW

This book provides the first comprehensive treatment of the principles shaping EU law: autonomy, conferral, equality, national identity, loyalty, solidarity, supremacy and effectiveness.

Much has been written about principles of EU law inspired by national law, such as fundamental rights, but what of the principles that are specific to EU law? The book discusses the origins of the EU's structural principles, where they are located, and how they are applied in practice. The author proposes that these principles are deeply interrelated and ensure the legal unity and uniformity of EU law. Their role in the EU's external relations is also explored.

This book brings a much-needed focus to the network of structural principles upholding the EU's constitutional order.

Volume 135 in the Series Modern Studies in European Law

Modern Studies in European Law

Recent titles in this series:

Free Movement and Welfare Access in the European Union: Re-Balancing Conflicting Interests in Citizenship Jurisprudence
Victoria Hooton

EU Trade and Investment Treaty-Making Post-Lisbon: Moving Beyond Mixity
Gesa Kübek

The Normative Foundations for EU Criminal Justice: Powers, Limits and Justifications
Jacob Öberg

EU Neighbourhood Law: Wider Europe and the Extended EU's Legal Space
Alessandro Petti

The Dynamics of Powers in the European Union
Edited by Christina Eckes, Päivi Leino-Sandberg and Anna W Ghavanin

The European Convention on Human Rights and Private Law: Comparative Perspectives from South-Eastern Europe
Edited by Mateja Durovic and Cristina Poncibò

Judging Composite Decision-Making: The Transformation of European Administrative Law
Filipe Brito Bastos

EU Diplomacy in Multilateral Fora
Edited by Christine Kaddous and Frank Hoffmeister

The Market Citizenship Illusion: Free Movement Rights for Atypical Workers
Alice Welsh

Actors and Roles in EU Disability Law
Edited by Delia Ferri and Eva S Krolla

The Impact of War (in Ukraine) on the EU
Edited by Inge Govaere, Sacha Garben and Eleanor Spaventa

The European Judiciary: A Community of Law and a Community of Judges
Edited by Alejandro Saiz Arnaiz and Joan Solanes Mullor

Dissensus over Liberal Democracy: Insights from European Judges
Edited by Ramona Coman, Viktor Kazai, Leonardo Puleo and Andrew Bradley

Structural Principles of EU Law
Marcus Klamert

For the complete list of titles in this series see www.bloomsbury.com/uk/series/modern-studies-in-european-law/

Structural Principles of EU Law

Marcus Klamert

• H A R T •
OXFORD • LONDON • NEW YORK • NEW DELHI • SYDNEY

HART PUBLISHING

Bloomsbury Publishing Plc

Kemp House, Chawley Park, Cumnor Hill, Oxford, OX2 9PH, UK

1385 Broadway, New York, NY 10018, USA

Bloomsbury Publishing Ireland Limited, 29 Earlsfort Terrace, Dublin 2, D02 AY28, Ireland

HART PUBLISHING, the Hart/Stag logo, BLOOMSBURY and the Diana logo are trademarks of Bloomsbury Publishing Plc

First published in Great Britain 2025

A catalogue record for this book is available from the British Library.

A catalogue record for this book is available from the Library of Congress.

Library of Congress Control Number: 2025942510

ISBN: HB: 978-1-50997-952-3
ePDF: 978-1-50997-954-7
ePub: 978-1-50997-953-0

Typeset by Compuscript Ltd, Shannon

For product safety related questions contact productsafety@bloomsbury.com

To find out more about our authors and books visit www.hartpublishing.co.uk. Here you will find extracts, author information, details of forthcoming events and the option to sign up for our newsletters.

FOREWORD

There is nothing quite like this book by Marcus Klamert. There are several books, and many journal articles, dealing with *general* principles of EU law, but the principles examined by Klamert are something else – they are *structural* principles. That term has been used in the title of a recent collective volume edited by Marise Cremona, but that volume dealt with structural principles of EU *external* relations law, whereas Klamert's book studies the structural principles of EU law as a whole.

The ambition of this book is to present a new perspective on what makes the distinctiveness of the European Union's legal order. This idea of distinctiveness is a true *leitmotiv* of this book, and it serves to distinguish the structural principles examined here from the more familiar concept of general principles of EU law. Indeed, the general principles of EU law have principally served, especially in pre-Charter times, as a way to provide for the protection of fundamental rights and norms of good governance in the EU legal order, in the absence of a clear basis for them in the text of the Treaties. The general principles therefore served to make EU constitutional law more similar to the constitutional law of a state, where the protection of rights traditionally occupies a prominent position. The structural principles identified in this book serve, on the contrary, to affirm the distinctiveness and special legal nature of the European Union.

This book builds on an earlier monograph from 2014 in which Marcus Klamert examined in detail the many dimensions and many roles played by the principle of loyalty in the EU legal order. Loyalty is, not surprisingly, one of the structural principles examined in the new book, but it is now accompanied by a number of others, namely: autonomy, conferral, equality, solidarity, national identity, effectiveness and primacy/direct effect. Some of these may sound familiar, as they figure prominently in many EU law textbooks. Some choices may seem more surprising, most of all perhaps the principle of national identity. Klamert spends many pages of his study in showing how the structural principles are related to each other, so as to form a network that buttresses the EU legal order. So, for example, loyalty relates to conferral but also to supremacy and to effectiveness, and understanding these relationships helps to understand the overall architecture of EU constitutional law.

There is, in my view, a double interest in the approach taken in this book, of identifying and discussing the structural principles of EU law. On the one hand, it helps us to understand better the special nature of the EU legal order and thereby contributes to the literature dealing with the theory and nature of EU law. On the other hand, Klamert also shows that the structural principles play a practical role in the case law of the European Court of Justice. They have been the object of creative interpretation by the Court. Even though many of the principles (such as conferral, autonomy, primacy and direct effect) had antecedents and a conceptual basis in public international law (and sometimes also in national constitutional law), the Court chose to 'camouflage' those origins, emphasizing rather their autonomous meaning as principles of EU law, and only of EU law, so as to better advance the project of European legal integration.

Reading this book allows for a stimulating reconsideration of some of the key elements of the EU legal order as it developed over the years and it offers new perspectives. The author should be complimented for having undertaken this project and executing it so competently.

Bruno De Witte
July 2025.

PREFACE

This book has been a while in the making. It took time to write, but, more importantly, I have thought and written about some of the principles in this book for a long time now. This not only concerns the principle of loyalty but also the principle of solidarity, on which I first gave a talk in 2012 on recommendation by Stefan Griller, laying the groundwork for some of the considerations that have informed this book.

Without a doubt, this book could have been approached in many alternative ways: more historically, more theoretically, or more comparatively. I have written it the best way I can and hope that the outcome will benefit the discussion about the European Union and EU law.

Writing for this book has ended at a time when chaos and lawlessness seem to take hold of the world. I sincerely hope that I am not overestimating the resilience of EU law, which I have in this book also attributed to its structural principles.

My thanks go to (in alphabetical order) Christian Breitler, Cristina Contartese, Christoph Krenn, Stefan Mayr, and Lorin-Johannes Wagner for their invaluable comments and advice. Christine Pesendorfer has been an inspiration and a wonderful person to work with. I am grateful to Takis Tridimas for his encouragement and to Sinead Moloney, Sasha Jawed and Tom Adams at Hart Publishing for taking this project on board and being generally so supportive. I am honoured that Bruno De Witte has written a foreword.

Last but not least, I am thankful to my wife Anna for her patience and support.

CONTENTS

TABLE OF CASE LAW

International Courts and Tribunals

Court of Justice of the European Union

General Court/Court of First Instance

Court of Justice

National Courts

German Federal Constitutional Court

Austrian Constitutional Court

Introduction: How to Think about European Union Law

When we think about and discuss European Union (EU) law, where do we start? Judging by some textbooks on European law, it is either with the history of European integration and the succession of Treaty changes or with the EU's institutional set-up.[1] This basic layout of the law of the European Union is used even in books claiming to take a more 'constitutional' approach.[2]

Both starting points are fine and reflect two important facts about the European Union: it is, from the perspective of international law in particular, an International *Organisation*, which means that the way it is organised is an essential characteristic of its nature. Secondly, the European Union is a 'community of law', as it is commonly stated, which means that it is shaped and developed by legal instruments, ie, the integration Treaties. Different from nation states, the European Union is, historically, in a permanent state of 'constitutional' development, which makes the succession of Treaty changes more topical and relevant compared to nation-states that tend to change their constitutions less often.

This book suggests thinking about EU law in terms of the legal principles that are characteristic of it, that make it special. Most textbooks do discuss such principles but it is done at a later stage, such as with principles of direct effect and supremacy (or primacy) in chapters explaining the relationship between national law and Union law or in the context of EU administrative law.[3] Readers could indeed be overwhelmed if complex principles such as autonomy or loyalty are discussed before they are conveyed a grasp on the EU institutions or its legislation. As this book also shows, EU law viewed through its underlying principles is

[1] See, eg, D Chalmers et al, *European Union Law: Text and Materials*, 5th edn (Cambridge, Cambridge University Press, 2024); A Dashwood et al, *Wyatt and Dashwood's European Union Law*, 6th edn (Oxford, Hart Publishing, 2011). See, by contrast, E Muir, *An Introduction to the EU Legal Order* (Cambridge, Cambridge University Press, 2023), who writes about equality, sincere cooperation and values on the first pages. See also the first chapters in PJ Kuijper et al (eds), *The Law of the European Union*, 5th edn (The Hague, Kluwer Law International, 2018), such as B de Witte, 'Structure and Evolution of Union Law' 43.

[2] See R Schütze, *European Constitutional Law*, 3rd edn (Oxford, Oxford University Press, 2021). See, by contrast, A Rosas and L Armati, *EU Constitutional Law: An Introduction*, 3rd edn (Oxford, Hart Publishing, 2021).

[3] See M Bobek, 'The Effects of EU Law in the Legal Systems' in C Barnard and S Peers (eds), *European Union Law*, 4th edn (Oxford, Oxford University Press, 2023) 140; H Hofmann, 'General Principles of EU Law and EU Administrative Law' in C Barnard and S Peers (eds), *European Union Law*, 4th edn (Oxford, Oxford University Press, 2023) 212.

indeed challenging and sometimes confusing. So this is not a critique of textbooks presenting EU law in an orthodox manner. The point I want to make is that this should be a conscious choice and should not lead to a presentation of EU law where principles are sidelined.

The approach suggested here does not necessarily negate the importance of the EU's organisational set-up because this can equally be analysed against the background of principles such as conferral and institutional balance. However, an orthodox, history and/or institution-centred presentation of the law of the European Union arguably obstructs a clear view of the centrality of certain overarching principles. A case in point is the principle of autonomy. It is hardly discussed in leading EU law textbooks.[4] This cannot be because it is not mentioned in the text of the EU Treaties. After all, primacy and direct effect are discussed extensively in textbooks and are equally not provided in the Treaties. Another case in point is the principle of solidarity, which is widely discussed in the literature but, reading some textbooks, would seem to be of peripheral relevance.[5]

Integrating principles more comprehensively is challenging to the way we commonly think about EU law because types and hierarchies of norms in EU law are most often discussed either in the context of Union legislation, thus in terms of the relation between primary law, secondary law and delegated legislation,[6] or are discussed in terms of the relation of Union law with the laws of the Member States. This means that the former discussion will centre on conferral and institutional balance and the latter on primacy and effectiveness. This, conversely, means that the relationship between written primary law and unwritten EU law principles is not so much in focus in EU law. Even when the unity of the legal order of the European Union is discussed, this is largely (again) done in terms of the relation of EU law with the legal orders of the Member States and thus again in terms of primacy and national identity.[7] While these are important questions, they arguably neglect that there equally is a claim to legal unity about the EU law order per se.

If presentations of EU law in terms of its development by Treaties and its institutional set-up are indicative of the peculiar 'integration process' and it being an *organisation* with *organs*, a presentation of the European Union and EU law in terms of principles would arguably be indicative of a more 'constitutional' perspective on EU law. In constitutional laws, it would seem common to emphasise its

[4] There is no such index entry in Dashwood et al, *Wyatt and Dashwood's European Union Law* (n 1). Schütze, *European Constitutional Law* (n 2) has one index entry on autonomy which refers the reader to 'national procedural autonomy, principle of', which is something different from the principle of autonomy discussed in this book. In Chalmers et al, *European Union Law* (n 1) autonomy is discussed at 193–94.

[5] Compare Schütze, *European Constitutional Law* (n 2).

[6] See KStC Bradley, 'Legislating in the European Union' in C Barnard and S Peers (eds), *European Union Law*, 4th edn (Oxford, Oxford University Press, 2023) 100.

[7] See N Walker, 'The Philosophy of European Union Law' in D Chalmers and A Arnull, *The Oxford Handbook of European Union Law* (Oxford, Oxford University Press, 2015) 3.

fundamental principles.[8] Most textbooks on Austrian Constitutional Law start with discussing the *Baugesetze*, thus the 'building laws' underlying the legal order.[9] Focusing on the principles essential to the EU legal order would thus also rather emphasise the 'constitution' or 'construction' of EU law as it stands now instead of how it was created or the institutions applying it. It would mean focusing on the qualities and peculiarities of EU law as a legal *order*. It would discuss the principles governing its interrelation with national law but would equally deal with other principles shaping EU law itself.

Counterintuitively, for making this claim for a more constitutional perspective on EU law, we will rely heavily on public international law. When writing this book, it has become increasingly clear that almost all principles discussed can be traced back to international law. This may seem to undermine the *sui generis* view on the European Union and EU law, but as I will explain, it is not, quite to the contrary. It could also be seen to militate against a constitutional law perspective on EU law.[10] This, as well, is unfounded because we will show how the European Court of Justice (ECJ), despite obvious parallels with public international law, has always chosen to frame EU law in distinctive or constitutional terms.[11] However, it is not within the purview of this book to comprehensibly define the nature of the European Union or EU law.

Often, the EU's values enshrined in Article 2 of the Treaty on European Union (TEU) are also seen as principles and it has been suggested that it is them that should be put front and centre when thinking about EU law and there is a whole new legal 'ecosystem' built around them.[12] We do not dispute the centrality of the EU's values and it certainly is worthwhile exploring their relevance for the understanding of the EU legal regime. However, it is submitted that the approach in this book is a comparably less far-reaching one: we do not aim at 'reconfiguring' EU law but want to lay bare the construction that is already here but is perhaps not very visible for a variety of reasons mentioned above.

[8] See the examples by LD Spieker, *EU Values Before the Court of Justice: Foundations, Potential, Risks* (Oxford, Oxford University Press, 2023) 94, who, however, discusses them in a values context.

[9] See, eg, T Öhlinger and H Eberhard, *Verfassungsrecht*, 13th edn (Vienna, Facultas, 2022) chapter III, 54 et seq.

[10] See A von Bogdandy and J Bast, 'Die Systematik des Verfassungsrechts der europäischen Gesellschaft' in A von Bogdandy and J Bast (eds), *Unionsverfassungsrecht – Eine Neubestimmung anhand der Grundlagen im EU-Vertrag* (Baden-Baden, Nomos, 2025) 39, as well as J Bast and A von Bogdandy, 'The constitutional core of the Union: On the CJEU's new, principled constitutionalism' (2024) 61 *CML Rev* 1471, 1479–84, arguing for a constitutional approach as opposed to public international law perspectives such as would be represented by J Klabbers, *An Introduction to International Organizations Law* (Cambridge, Cambridge University Press, 2022).

[11] Compare M Rasmussen, 'The Origins of a Legal Revolution: The Early History of the European Court of Justice' (2008) 14 *Journal of European Integration History* 77, 98: 'The early history of the European legal order is thus one of federalist political and legal forces promoting, through different actors at different points in time, a particular constitutional thinking about the Treaties and the ECJ'.

[12] See, especially, now von Bogdandy and Bast, *Unionsverfassungsrecht* (n 10); Spieker, *EU Values Before the Court of Justice* (n 8).

Chapter one, after laying some groundwork regarding legal theory and international law, suggests making a distinction between those principles that have been called 'systemic' or 'constitutional' principles, underpinning the constitutional structure of the Union and defining its nature, and the 'general principles of the Union's law' referred to in Article 6 TEU, such as proportionality, legal certainty, or fundamental rights. Thus, this book will discuss, among others, autonomy, supremacy, direct effect, loyalty, solidarity, effectiveness, conferral, and non-discrimination based on nationality as a structural variant of equality in EU law. As much has been written about the origin and effect of the general principles of Article 6 TEU, as little has been said about the 'other' proposed category of principles of Union law. However, it is these other principles, referred to here as 'structural principles', which determine the nature of the Union legal order and which need to be understood in order to grasp Union law as a whole.

Chapter two will explore whether and to what extent EU law is indeed a 'structured' legal *order* as it has been put by the ECJ. We will discuss different conceptions of 'order', such as the 'network' concept also mentioned by the Court, and we will discuss the interrelations between values, objectives and principles in EU law. It will be submitted that, while there are some connections between these three categories of norms, they do not structure EU law in a very coherent manner.

Chapter three will deal with the interrelations and dependencies between the principles mentioned above. While there is an understanding that Union law principles, of which most are not explicitly provided in the EU Treaties and are still being developed in the case law of the European courts, are interconnected and somehow related to each other, the nature of these interrelations and what they would mean for the roles and functions of principles have often remained unclear. While some structural principles have been discussed in the more narrow context of external relations[13] or in contributions to edited books,[14] this book takes a more holistic and cross-cutting perspective. It will be shown that, indeed, structural principles are connected in manifold ways, creating a 'network' of principles structuring EU law itself and in its relation with Member State laws.

Chapter four looks at the relevance and application of the principles covered in this book in the law of external relations of the European Union. It is submitted that as much as EU law cannot be fully understood without exploring its interrelation with national law, it cannot be fully understood without exploring the specific area of the Common Foreign and Security Policy and the other, often interlinked, areas of external action of the European Union. It will be shown that,

[13] M Cremona (ed), *Structural Principles in EU External Relations Law* (Oxford, Oxford University Press, 2018).

[14] KS Ziegler, PJ Neuvonen and V Moreno-Lax (eds), *Research Handbook on General Principles in EU Law: Constructing Legal Orders in Europe* (Cheltenham, Edward Elgar, 2022); R Schütze and T Tridimas (eds), *Oxford Principles Of European Union Law: The European Union Legal Order: Volume I* (Oxford, Oxford University Press, 2018).

while structural principles apply in these areas, they often apply in a different, stronger or weaker manner.

Chapter five will show that the Court has reasoned in an autonomous and often highly self-referential manner with structural principles. Finally, chapter six will take a step back and try to see 'the wood for the trees'. It will be explained that, in our view, it would be difficult to rank structural principles according to their importance. Exploring what we call 'grand narratives' about EU law, we will suggest that the rule of law and the unity and the uniformity of EU law are important values respectively concepts of EU law, but that they should not be seen as self-standing structural principles.

This book is an attempt to bring some order to the 'jungle of principles' within Union law. Not only for the sake of order, but also to better understand the relationships between individual principles and how they work, and thus to better understand the Union legal order itself. It will be shown that, if the values including fundamental rights are the EU's foundation, the structural principles are the pillars that give shape to Union law and to the European Union as an organisation.

There are two seemingly contradictory risks with the approach taken in this book, which should not be underestimated. On the one hand, it could be accused of overstating the relevance of international law for the understanding of EU law and thus relitigating an issue that has seemed to be settled for a long time. At the same time, it could be seen as falling into the trap of 'overconstitutionalisation' by seeing a (constitutional) order and a legal structure where there is none or very little in primary law and thus provide backing for attempts by the ECJ to 'construct' EU law in that mould. We will revert to these points in the Final Remarks. Suffice to note here that if indeed both criticisms were made, on average, it would not seem such a bad outcome.

I

Categories and Functions of Principles

1. Introduction

Union law is rich in principles.

'General principles' are mentioned in Article 6 of the Treaty on European Union (TEU) concerning fundamental rights and in Article 340 of the Treaty on the Functioning of the European Union (TFEU) on extra-contractual liability of the Union. Part One of the TFEU has the heading 'Principles' and covers rules on competences in Articles 2–6 TFEU and the mainstreaming provisions in Articles 7–17 TFEU. The rules contained therein, however, are usually not called (general) principles. The Treaty also provides the 'principle of conferral' and the 'principles of subsidiarity and proportionality' in Article 5 TEU. Article 194 TFEU has been said to contain a 'principle of energy solidarity' that is 'like general principles'.[1] State liability would be a 'principle' of Union law,[2] and there would also exist a 'principle of autonomy' in EU law.[3] Other provisions in the Treaty that do not expressly mention principles have also been referred to as containing 'general principles', such as sincere cooperation in Article 4(3) TEU.[4]

It is well known that discussions on the nature and functions of principles as a legal source have a long and celebrated history. In the following, we do not want to relitigate these discussions but merely provide a brief background as far as is useful for this book. It will be shown that there are lessons to be learned for understanding EU law both from legal theory and from public international law. The focus on public international law in this chapter does not ignore the relevance of a (federal) constitutional law perspective on EU law as it stands today as well as the relevance of that perspective for analysing some principles discussed in chapter three.

Against this background, we will explain why we should distinguish between different categories of principles within EU law, and, more specifically, why we propose to distinguish the principles falling under Article 6 TEU on the one hand from what we suggest to call structural principles on the other. We will, moreover, discuss the role of principles of international law within EU law, first

[1] Case C-848/19 P, *Germany v Poland (OPAL)*, ECLI:EU:C:2021:598, para 45.

[2] See, eg, Joined Cases C-6/90 & C-9/90, *Francovich*, ECLI:EU:C:1991:428, para 37.

[3] Case C-612/18 P, *Client Earth*, ECLI:EU:C:2020:223, para 42.

[4] Case C-429/07, *X*, ECLI:EU:C:2009:359, para 21.

for the sake of completeness, and secondly because their role will be instructive for discussing the case law of the CJEU in chapter three where these principles were *not* applied.

2. Lessons from Legal Theory and Public International Law

1. Introduction

Interestingly, the focus of the discussions in legal theory has been quite different from that in international law. While the main discussion in legal theory has, famously, revolved around the distinction between rules and principles, the discussion in (public) international law has rather focused on distinguishing two categories of principles. The reason for this might be that the existence of legal principles as legal sources is a given in international law because of their inclusion in Article 38(1) of the Statute of the International Court of Justice. Fewer differences seem to exist between the views in legal theory and international law concerning the functions of legal principles.

2. On the Distinction between Rules and Principles

In legal theory, famously, it has been stipulated that 'the difference between legal principles and legal rules is a logical distinction'.[5] Rules would apply in an all-or-nothing fashion, meaning that when the facts that a rule establishes as a condition are fulfilled, the answer it provides must be accepted.[6] If two rules are in conflict, one of them would have to be invalid.[7] According to the same theory, principles would differ from rules in that they do not make a certain decision mandatory but merely suggest reasons that speak in favour of a certain decision.[8] If two principles collide with each other, the principle with the relatively greater weight would be decisive, without the principle with the lesser weight becoming invalid.[9]

This seminal distinction between rules and principles has been further developed by arguing that principles are norms that require that an objective should be

[5] See R Dworkin, *Taking Rights Seriously*, 2nd edn (Cambridge, MA, Harvard University Press, 1978) 40. On the following, see also M Potacs, *Rechtstheorie*, 2nd edn (Vienna, Facultas, 2019) 106–08; A von Bogdandy, 'Founding Principles of EU Law: A Theoretical and Doctrinal Sketch' (2010) 12 *European Law Journal* 95.

[6] See Dworkin, *Taking Rights Seriously* (n 5) 41.

[7] See R Dworkin, 'The Model of Rules' (1967) 35 *University of Chicago Law Review* 14, 27.

[8] See Dworkin, *Taking Rights Seriously* (n 5) 42.

[9] See Dworkin, 'The Model of Rules' (n 7) 27.

realised to the greatest extent possible ('optimization').[10] A balancing, weighing form of application including an assessment of proportionality would be characteristic of principles, and principles would above all be fundamental rights.[11]

Others, by contrast, have claimed that there is no fundamental difference in nature between rules and principles at all.[12] Principles should be conceived to mean simply a 'very important rule', making any differentiation purely rhetorical in nature.[13] This would make principles very important (or fundamental, or basic), general (ie, indeterminate in content) rules, and thus structural decisions (*Strukturentscheidungen*).[14] They could be rules of conduct but, because of their usually very general nature, would mostly apply indirectly as guidelines for the interpretation of concrete rules.[15]

3. On the Distinction between Different Principles

In legal theory, it has been distinguished between substantive principles, which dictate a goal to be pursued or a value to be protected, and principles of discretion, which guide discretion by stipulating what types of goals and values the judge may take into account.[16] It has also been distinguished between formal principles and substantive principles, which would differ only as regards the object of optimisation with substantive principles pertaining to certain contents such as life, freedom of speech, or protection of the environment, while the optimisation objects of formal principles would be legal decisions regardless of their content.[17] The latter categorisation seems somewhat similar to the distinction between formal and axiological principles, with the first category comprising principles such as *lex superior*, *lex specialis*, or *pacta sunt servanda*, and the latter value-related principles such as good faith, legal certainty, or human rights.[18]

In public international law, according to Article 38(1) of the Statute of the International Court of Justice (ICJ), the ICJ shall apply international conventions, customary international law, and 'the general principles of law recognized by civilized nations'. This triad of legal sources has invited debates both on their

[10] See A Jakab, *European Constitutional Language* (Cambridge, Cambridge University Press, 2016) 368–71 with further references. See also R Alexy, 'Zur Struktur der Rechtsprinzipien' in B Schilcher, P Koller and B-C Funk (eds), *Regeln, Prinzipien und Elemente im System des Rechts* (Vienna, Verlag Österreich, 2000) 31, 32–35.

[11] See Potacs, *Rechtstheorie* (n 5) 106–08.

[12] See S Griller, 'Der Rechtsbegriff bei Ronald Dworkin' in S Griller and H-P Rill (eds), *Rechtstheorie: Rechtsbegriff – Dynamik – Auslegung* (Vienna, Springer, 2011) 57, 64–70.

[13] See Jakab, *European Constitutional Language* (n 10) 369.

[14] See Jakab, *European Constitutional Language* (n 10) 377.

[15] See Jakab, *European Constitutional Language* (n 10) 381.

[16] See J Raz, 'Legal Principles and the Limits of Law' (1972) 81 *Yale Law Journal* 823, 841.

[17] See R Alexy, 'Formal principles: Some replies to critics' (2014) 12 *International Journal of Constitutional Law* 511.

[18] See A von Arnauld, 'Harmonisation through general principles of law' in KS Ziegler, PJ Neuvonen and V Moreno-Lax (eds), *Research Handbook on General Principles in EU Law: Constructing Legal Orders in Europe* (Cheltenham, Edward Elgar, 2022) 40, 43–44.

precise meaning as well as on the relations among them.[19] While different categories of general principles of international law have been suggested in the literature, broad consensus has been lacking for a long time.[20] In 2018, the International Law Commission (ILC) decided to approach the topic of 'general principles of law' and appointed a special rapporteur. The Report of the Special Rapporteur with draft conclusions was provisionally adopted by the ILC on its first reading in 2023.[21]

In the First Report by the Special Rapporteur, it is stated that general principles of law, 'in addition to serving as a direct source of rights and obligations, may serve as a means to interpret other rules of international law or as a tool to reinforce legal reasoning'.[22] Moreover, it found 'A more abstract role is sometimes attributed to them, such as that they inform or underlie the international legal system, or that they serve to reinforce its systemic nature'.[23]

The Report has also made a distinction that is instructive for the arguments made in this book. Within the category in Article 38(1) of the ICJ Statute of 'the general principles of law recognized by civilized nations', the Report distinguishes general principles of law 'derived from national legal systems' on the one hand from general principles 'formed within the international legal system' on the other.[24]

It has been noted that principles formed within international law were always a part of Article 38(1)(c) of the ICJ Statute with that provision not referring to the possible origins of general principles.[25] The practice of international Treaties and tribunals would be evidence of the existence of such principles. Principles such as the independence and territorial integrity of states or the solution to the question of whether provisions of municipal law can prevail over those contained in international Treaties could, by their very nature, not have been derived from national legal systems.[26]

Paragraphs 1 and 2 of Draft Conclusion 7 of the Second Report by the Special Rapporteur state the following:

> To determine the existence and content of a general principle of law that may be formed within the international legal system, it is necessary to ascertain that the community of nations has recognized the principle as intrinsic to the international legal system.

[19] See, eg, C Redgwell, 'General Principles of International Law' in S Vogenauer and S Weatherill (eds), *General Principles of Law: European and Comparative Perspective* (Oxford, Hart Publishing, 2017) 5; J Ellis, 'General Principles and Comparative Law' (2011) 22 *European Journal of International Law* 949; R Kolb, 'Principles as Sources of International Law (With Special Reference to Good Faith)' (2006) 53 *Netherlands International Law Review* 1; and the contributions in M Andenas et al (eds), *General Principles of Law and the Coherence of International Law* (Leiden, Brill, 2019).

[20] See G Gaja, 'General Principles of Law' in *Max Planck Encyclopedia of Public International Law* (Oxford, Oxford University Press, 2012).

[21] See ILC, Report of the International Law Commission, UN Doc A/78/10. See also ILC, Second report on general principles of law by M Vázquez-Bermúdez, Special Rapporteur, UN Doc A/CN.4/741, 53.

[22] See ILC, First report on general principles of law of the Special Rapporteur M Vázquez-Bermúdez, UN Doc A/CN.4/732, para 26.

[23] See ILC, First report, UN Doc A/CN.4/732 (n 22) para 26.

[24] See ILC, Report, UN Doc A/78/10 (n 21) 14 et seq.

[25] See E Bjorge, 'General Principles of Law Formed Within The International Legal System' (2023) ICLQ 845, 852.

[26] See Bjorge, 'General Principles of Law' (n 25) 857.

> Paragraph 1 is without prejudice to the question of the possible existence of other general principles of law formed within the international legal system.[27]

According to the Draft Conclusion, in this case, the required 'recognition' can be achieved where a principle: (1) 'is widely recognized in treaties and other international instruments'; (2) 'underlies general rules of conventional or customary international law'; or (3) 'is inherent in the basic features and fundamental requirements of the international legal system'. Whereas there is agreement by and large about the first and second categories, the third category has been disputed among states by pointing to the risk of confusion with customary international law in particular.[28] They were considered an 'innovation' of the ILC without 'any real practice in support of such a category'.[29]

At the same time, general principles formed within the international legal system are considered to be deduced from international legal materials or 'the structure of the international legal system', to answer questions that cannot be resolved by treaty or customary rules.[30] It has also been observed that states have often referred to either 'generally recognised principles of international law' or 'general principles of law' instead of referring to customary international law because they wanted to emphasise the fundamental importance of a norm as compared to the many rules of customary international law which are of lesser weight.[31] Moreover, it has been argued that the 'only difference between general principles derived from domestic legal systems and those formed within the international legal system would lie in whether the issue the general principle seeks to address is unique to international law or it has an analogous counterpart in domestic legal systems'.[32]

The term 'structural principles' has been used in international law on the one hand for referring to structural aspects that would not form part of international law but 'explain and underlie it', and on the other hand for referring to legal principles important for a certain field.[33]

4. On the Functions of Principles

In legal theory, it has been submitted that specialised regulations must be interpreted in conformity with general regulations.[34] Thus, where two interpretations

[27] ILC, Second report, UN Doc A/CN.4/741 (n 21) 53.

[28] See X Shao, 'What We Talk about When We Talk about General Principles of Law' (2021) 20 *Chinese Journal of International Law* 219, 221 with further references.

[29] Quoted in Bjorge, 'General Principles of Law' (n 25) 848.

[30] See Shao, 'What We Talk about' (n 28) 254.

[31] See Bjorge, 'General Principles of Law' (n 25) 856–57.

[32] See Shao, 'What We Talk about' (n 28) 232.

[33] See, respectively, R Kolb, *Theory of International Law* (Oxford, Hart Publishing, 2016) 157 et seq, and D Shelton (ed), *The Oxford Handbook of International Human Rights Law* (Oxford, Oxford University Press, 2013).

[34] See Raz, 'Legal Principles and the Limits of Law' (n 16) 839.

of a law are possible, preference must be given to whichever is (more) compatible with legal principles as the more general norms.[35] Interpreting other norms in the light of principles would also seem to be the logical consequence when principles are considered very important norms or structural decisions, as mentioned above. In that sense, principles would determine the meaning of other norms because of their weight.

The same logic cannot automatically be applied to the question of whether legal principles also have a function as a standard for assessing the validity of other norms. Giving such a role to a norm because it is more general than another norm would contradict the conflict resolution or interpretative principle of *lex specialis derogat legi generali*.[36] There must thus be another explanation why principles could have a role as standards of validity. It has been suggested that principles would have such a function because they have or are assumed to have a higher rank than other norms.[37] Thus, the function of principles as standards of validity is dependent on whether they have a higher rank than the norm that is assessed in their light.

Legal principles have also been seen 'as grounds for making new rules', thus for developing respectively changing the law.[38] It has been observed that this function is characteristic in particular where a legal order is underdeveloped and, thus, more dependent on the borrowing of solutions already existing in other legal orders.[39] This, thus, refers to the gap-filling function of legal principles.

General principles have been considered relevant for the interpretation of conventional and customary international law including for developing and modifying these categories of sources.[40] They have been used by international courts to fill gaps in treaty and customary international law, which would arise where conventions and customs fail to address particular legal issues in dispute.[41] In other words, general principles formed within the international legal system are considered to be required to answer questions that cannot be resolved by treaty or customary rules.[42] It is because of general principles that the ILC could claim that international law would be 'a complete system' in the sense that 'every international legal situation is capable of being determined as a matter of law', and international adjudicators are capable of avoiding declaring *non liquet*.[43]

[35] See S Vogenauer, *Die Auslegung von Gesetzen in England und auf dem Kontinent* (Tübingen, Mohr Siebeck, 2001) 1257 ff.

[36] On this, see E Vranes, 'Lex Superior, Lex Specialis, Lex Posterior – Rechtsnatur der "Konfliktlösungsregeln"' (2005) 65 *ZaöRV* 391.

[37] See A Jakab, 'Re-Defining Principles as "Important Rules". A Critique of Robert Alexy' in M Borowski (ed), *On the Nature of Legal Principles*, ARSP Beiheft 119 (Stuttgart, Steiner, 2009) 145.

[38] See J Esser, *Grundsatz und Norm in der richterlichen Fortbildung des Privatrechts* (Tübingen, Mohr, 1956); Raz, 'Legal Principles and the Limits of Law' (n 16) 841.

[39] See, eg, JA Usher, *General Principles of EC Law* (London, Longman, 1998) 123 f.

[40] See MC Bassiouni, 'A Functional Approach to "General Principles of International Law"' (1990) 11 *Michigan Journal of International Law* 768, 775–76.

[41] See Bassiouni, 'A Functional Approach' (n 40) 800–01.

[42] See Shao, 'What We Talk about' (n 28) 233.

[43] ILC Conclusions of the Work of the Study Group on the Fragmentation of International Law: Difficulties Arising from the Diversification and Expansion of International Law (2006) A/61/10, para 251.

Finally, when general principles have been seen as not being fundamentally different in nature from (other) legal norms, they have been seen as the normative basis for formulating an operable rule in a given case.[44] Thus, in the EU law context (general) principles have been deemed fundamental propositions 'from which concrete rules or outcomes may be derived'.[45]

On a more systemic level, it has been submitted that the preservation of unity 'in a legal order … is the function of the overarching principles that sustain its normative edifice and keep it together'.[46] Principles such as good faith would instil some order into the 'naturally chaotic environment' that is international law, countering tendencies for internal fragmentation in international law.[47] It has also been noted that the effect of framing international law as a system would have allowed courts 'to develop international law beyond the intention of governments' because judges could draw on 'the basic principles of the system and its underlying norms'.[48]

5. Interim Conclusions

The principles discussed in this book can be considered fundamental, largely indeterminant 'structural decisions' (*Strukturentscheidungen*), in line with the definition mentioned above. A strict distinction between principles and rules is not useful in the context of EU law.[49]

For the purposes of this book, moreover, we will distinguish principles according to their object of reference on the one hand, and according to where they are derived from on the other.

Thus, in line with legal theory, we will distinguish principles that are (more) formal from principles that are (more) substantive or axiological.

In line with public international law, we will distinguish principles derived from Member State legal systems (those resulting 'from the constitutional traditions common to the Member States' as stated in Article 6 TEU), on the one hand,

[44] See M Herdegen, 'The Origins and Development of the General Principles of Community Law' in U Bernitz and J Nergelius (eds), *General Principles of European Community Law* (The Hague, Kluwer, 2000) 3, 17.

[45] See T Tridimas, *General Principles of EU Law*, 2nd edn (Oxford, Oxford University Press, 2006) 1.

[46] See G Abi-Saab, 'Fragmentation or Unification: Some Concluding Remarks' (1999) 31 *New York University Journal of International Law and Politics* 919, 926.

[47] See Kolb, *Theory of International Law* (n 33) 159.

[48] See E Benvenisti, 'The Conception of International Law as a Legal System' (2007) 50 *German Yearbook of International Law* 393, 396. Compare also I Saunders, *General Principles as a Source of International Law: Art 38(1)(c) of the Statute of the International Court of Justice* (Oxford, Hart Publishing, 2022) 213.

[49] See also PJ Neuvonen and KS Ziegler, 'General principles in the EU legal order: Past, present and future directions' in in KS Ziegler, PJ Neuvonen and V Moreno-Lax (eds), *Research Handbook on General Principles in EU Law: Constructing Legal Orders in Europe* (Cheltenham, Edward Elgar, 2022) 7, 11.

from those formed within EU law deduced from the structure of the EU legal system, on the other. Paraphrasing the Special Rapporteur cited above, this book is concerned with principles that are 'widely recognized' in EU primary law, underlie EU Treaty rules or are 'inherent in the basic features and fundamental requirements' of the EU law system.

As is the case in legal theory and international law, these distinctions are not clear-cut in EU law as will be shown. While the EU's values are often called (substantive or axiological) principles, especially one value in Article 2 TEU, the rule of law, overlaps in many ways with principles that are also considered as being formal, such as the principle of loyalty that is an expression of *pacta sunt servanda*, as will be discussed in chapter three. It will also be shown in chapter three that principles that are important for the structure of EU law, such as effective legal protection, can be derived from Member State legal systems.

While many principles discussed in this book share the (interpretative and gap-filling) functions of principles established in legal theory and international law, some qualifications must be made. We will show in chapter five that developments based on the principles explored in this book cannot 'merely' be considered gap-filling in a technical sense and can also not be attributed to avoiding a *non-liquet* situation. In this context, we will, in chapter six, discuss unity as one 'grand narrative' in EU law for which its structural principles play a central role. However, the 'push for unity' in EU law is predicated by a context that is different from 'normal' international law. Some principles in EU law, as will be shown, have a unifying function, not only to avoid fragmentation within one legal order (as could be seen as being the case with international law), but also and more importantly to bring about legal unity in the interaction between different legal orders, those of EU law and its Member States.

3. Why We should Distinguish Principles in EU Law

1. Introduction

It has been remarked that there is widespread agreement that there is no sound analytical framework for general principles of EU law,[50] and that there is no doctrinal consensus on an overall dogmatic of general principles of EU law.[51] It has been considered regrettable that Article 6 TEU would leave undefined the relationship between the Charter and the principles mentioned in its paragraph 3, much like

[50] See Neuvonen and Ziegler, 'General principles' (n 49) 9–10.

[51] See E Castellarin, 'General Principles of European Union Law and General International Law' in M Andenas et al (eds), *General Principles of Law and the Coherence of International Law* (Leiden, Brill, 2019) 131, 133. Compare also C Semmelmann, 'General Principles of EU Law: The Ghost in the Platonic Heaven in Need of Conceptual Clarification' (2013) 2 *Pittsburgh Papers on the European Union* 1.

the Treaties would generally be silent as to their relationship with the general principles of EU law.[52] For some time now, it has been wondered whether principles in EU law should not be distinguished by their origin between those stemming from the legal heritage of the Member States and those derived from the nature of EU law.[53]

In the following, we will argue that such a distinction should indeed be made, for three reasons discussed below. First, to provide the analytical framework that is found missing and which has likely contributed to the prevailing terminology not being very useful. Secondly, because Article 6(3) TEU *does* provide a definition for one category of principles, which allows us to compare and distinguish. The third reason is that the extensive discussion about general principles in the mould of Article 6(3) TEU seems to have stymied a comprehensive treatment of the principles in this book.

2. On Terminology

It has been noted that there is no clear terminology and also that the Union courts have referred to principles very inconsistently.[54]

It is submitted that the term 'principles' by itself is not useful. It implies that all principles are either of the same nature or so different as to defy categorisation. However, as will be shown below, the principles in EU law do not all operate in the same manner.[55]

Similarly, there is little to be gained by using the term 'constitutional principles'.[56] The same can be said for the term 'fundamental principles', sometimes used by the Court such as in relation to solidarity.[57] The EU Treaties are commonly seen as the constitution of the European Union, which means that all primary law principles are at the same time constitutional and therefore fundamental principles. It would again imply that all these principles are the same or, conversely, all different.

[52] See T Lock, 'Commentary on Article 6 TEU' in M Kellerbauer, M Klamert and J Tomkin (eds), *The EU Treaties and the Charter of Fundamental Rights: A Commentary*, 2nd edn (Oxford, Oxford University Press, 2024) para 22; M Klamert, 'Commentary on Article 1 TEU' in Kellerbauer, Klamert and Tomkin (eds), *Commentary*, para 17.

[53] See X Groussot and HH Lidgard, 'Are There General Principles of Community Law Affecting Private Law?' in Bernitz and Nergelius, *General Principles of European Community Law* 155, 157 with references to the works of Schermers and Boulouis.

[54] See Neuvonen and Ziegler, 'General principles' (n 49) 7, 9 ff with further references.

[55] See also A von Bogdandy, 'Grundprinzipien des Unionsrechts – eine verfassungstheoretische und -dogmatische Skizze' (2009) *Europarecht* 749, 760. Compare also W Schroeder, *Das Gemeinschaftsrechtssystem* (Tübingen, Mohr Siebeck, 2002) 262 ff, on the function of principles in Union law.

[56] See, eg, K Lenaerts and P van Nuffel, *European Union Law*, 3rd edn (London, Sweet & Maxwell, 2011) 851, who distinguish between principles of proper administration such as legal certainty and protection of legitimate expectations and constitutional principles such as fundamental rights, proportionality, subsidiarity and non-discrimination.

[57] Case C-123/22, *Commission v Hungary*, ECLI:EU:C:2024:493, para 116.

Using the label 'general principles' is also not very evocative if it infers that principles apply generally within Union law.[58] Do the principles governing the internal market such as the prohibition of restrictions apply generally in Union law? Does it make a difference that this prohibition is not only applicable in the internal market but also to measures impeding Union citizenship?[59] Is it relevant for that label whether principles apply also to the Common Foreign and Security Policy (CFSP), as discussed in chapter four? It is suggested that emphasising that principles are 'general' in the sense that they apply widely within EU law is only useful with regard to the principles under Article 6 TEU when making the point that fundamental rights apply in all areas of EU law.[60] If 'general', by contrast, is used to emphasise that principles are indeterminate norms, it is a pleonasm as principles are inherently indeterminate, as discussed earlier.[61]

3. On the Relevance of Article 6(3) TEU

There is (only) one provision in the Treaties that defines (a certain category of) principles. Article 6(3) TEU has the following wording:

> Fundamental rights, as guaranteed by the European Convention for the Protection of Human Rights and Fundamental Freedoms and as they result from the constitutional traditions common to the Member States, shall constitute general principles of the Union's law.

Thus, 'general principles of the Union's law' are fundamental rights and fundamental rights are 'general principles of the Union's law' according to Article 6(3) TEU. The principles discussed in this book predominantly are not fundamental rights. As will be shown in chapter three, principles such as autonomy, conferral, or supremacy are neither guaranteed by the European Convention on Human Rights (ECHR) nor do they 'result from the constitutional traditions common to the Member States'.[62] It is therefore submitted that it is not advisable to refer to these principles as 'general principles' without inviting some unnecessary confusion.

[58] See RA Wessel, 'General Principles in EU Common Foreign and Security Policy' in Ziegler, Neuvonen and Moreno-Lax (eds), *Research Handbook* 607, 609, who argues for 'general' to mean that princples are not confined to particular treaty articles, and apply across the Union legal order.

[59] See, eg, Joined Cases C-11/06 & 12/06, *Morgan*, ECLI:EU:C:2007:626, para 30.

[60] Compare, however, B de Witte, 'The Role of Institutional Principles in the Judicial Development of the. European Union Legal Order' in F Snyder (ed), *The Europeanisation of Law: The Legal Effects of European Integration on General Institutional Principles of EU law* (Oxford, Hart Publishing, 2000) 83, 84, for other examples of non-general principles.

[61] Compare J Bengoetxea, 'General Legal Principles Navigating Space and Time' in U Bernitz, X Groussot and F Schulyok (eds), *General Principles of EU law and European private law* (The Hague, Kluwer Law, 2013) 45, 48: 'all principles tend to be general, or at least rather general as compared to rules'.

[62] For supremacy, the difference to general principles of law is also emphasised by C Rauchegger, 'Four functions of the principle of primacy in post-Lisbon case law in Ziegler, Neuvonen and Moreno-Lax (eds), *Research Handbook* 157, 159.

It seems that the definition in Article 6(3) TEU is often not taken very seriously. This may be because the literature has found the methodology it alludes to and that is discussed below as not fully reflecting the (more autonomous) practice of the Court. Nonetheless, we arguably should take Article 6(3) TEU for what it is: a primary law statement about the origin and status of (a category of) EU law principles.

Discussing *all* Union law principles under the impression of this definition has obstructed a clear view of the principles discussed in this book, which can be illustrated by the following observations.

There seems to be agreement that Article 6 TEU is *not* the provision where the principles discussed in this book can be located. No legal commentary of the EU Treaties, to my knowledge, discusses autonomy, supremacy, or solidarity under the purview of Article 6 TEU. Indeed, Article 6 TEU is too evidently concerned with nothing else but fundamental rights/rule of law principles for that to make sense. In general, when principles of Union law are discussed in the literature, this mostly concerns the principles of Article 6(3) TEU and possible differences between them and other Union principles are not dealt with, or only in passing.[63]

Moreover, definitions of EU law principles suggested in the literature often appear not very clear in what they should encompass, arguably because these definitions try to capture too much. General principles have been defined as 'fundamental propositions of law which underlie a legal system',[64] and respectively as 'having a dimension of weight and importance'.[65] Founding principles have been defined as 'those norms of primary law having a normative founding function for the whole of the EU's legal order; they determine the relevant legitimating foundations given the need to justify the exercise of public authority'.[66] In particular, the last part of this definition points at principles like those covered by Article 6(3) TEU. It seems misleading to consider that supremacy of EU law would justify the exercise of the EU's *public* authority.

It is also not helpful for present purposes to place importance on whether principles specify 'legal consequences that follow automatically in certain defined

[63] See K Lenaerts and JA Gutiérrez-Fons, 'The Role of General Principles of EU Law' in A Arnull, C Barnard, M Dougan and E Spaventa (eds), *A Constitutional Order of States: Essays in EU Law in Honour of Alan Dashwood* (Oxford, Hart Publishing, 2011), 179, who focus exclusively on fundamental rights, with the exception of the principle of state liability. See S Weatherill, 'From Myth to Reality: The EU's "New Legal Order" and the Place of General Principles Within It' in Vogenauer and Weatherill (eds), *General Principles of Law* 21, who discusses direct effect and primacy, but largely as a background for the introduction of fundamental rights into the Union legal order. See also JP Terhechte, '§ 14 Prinzipienordnung der Europäischen Union' in A Hatje and P Müller-Graff (eds), *Europäisches Organisations- und Verfassungsrecht*, 2nd edn (Baden-Baden, Nomos, 2022) 773, who does distinguish general principles of law from 'general principles' such as direct effect and primacy but then develops an 'order of principles' in which this distinction is barely reflected. See also the examples by de Witte, 'The Role of Institutional Principles' (n 60) 84.

[64] See Tridimas, *General Principles* (n 45) 1.

[65] See J Wouters, D Coppens and D Geraets, 'The Influence of General Principles of Law' in SE Gaines, B Egelund Olsen and K Engsig Sørensen (eds), *Liberalising Trade in the EU and the WTO: A Legal Comparison* (Cambridge, Cambridge University Press, 2012) 43, 44.

[66] See von Bogdandy, 'Founding Principles of EU Law' (n 5) 105; Wessel, 'General Principles in EU Common Foreign and Security Policy' (n 58) 611.

circumstances'.[67] That may be true for loyalty and supremacy, but it is less so for solidarity, effectiveness, or national identity. Moreover, a distinction between written and unwritten principles may be useful for Article 6 TEU principles, but not so much for the principles in this book.[68] Some principles discussed in this book, such as conferral, are explicitly provided in primary law while others, such as autonomy and direct effect, are not.

4. On Categorisations

There have been suggestions in the literature for distinguishing categories of principles in EU law that are largely in line with the approach in this book.

It has been differentiated between general principles of the rule of law such as fundamental rights, equality and proportionality, general principles of substantive Union law such as fundamental freedoms, and systemic principles such as primacy, division of competences, subsidiarity and direct effect.[69] Moreover (vertical and horizontal) 'institutional principles' have been proposed as a sub-category of general principles that would not serve to protect individuals, but would rather concern the relations between the institutions, such as institutional balance, subsidiarity, or sincere cooperation.[70]

In the German literature, principles discussed in this book have sometimes been called structural principles and would include primacy and direct effect of Union law,[71] state liability,[72] conferral[73] and the principle of solidarity.[74] In the context of external relations, in addition, the principles of loyalty, institutional balance and autonomy have been considered systemic and relational structural principles.[75]

[67] See Wouters, Coppens and Geraets, 'The Influence of General Principles of Law' (n 65) 44.

[68] Compare Wessel, 'General Principles in EU Common Foreign and Security Policy' (n 58) 609, who discusses what we call structural principles and who considers them being 'general principles' despite the fact that they are not 'unwritten'.

[69] See Tridimas, *General Principles* (n 45) 6.

[70] See de Witte, 'The Role of Institutional Principles' (n 60) 84. See also M Wimmer, 'The Dinghy's Rudder: General Principles of European Union Law through the Lens of Proportionality' (2014) 20 *European Public Law* 331; M Claes, 'The equality of the Member States' in Ziegler, Neuvonen and Moreno-Lax (eds), *Research Handbook* 99, 110.

[71] See W Schroeder, 'Art 288 TFEU' in R Streinz (ed), *EUV/AEUV*, 3rd edn (Munich, Beck, 2018) para 36.

[72] See B Wegener, 'Art 267 TFEU' in C Calliess and M Ruffert (eds), *EUV/AEUV*, 6th edn (Munich, Beck, 2022) para 1.

[73] See S Schill and C Krenn, 'Artikel 4 EUV' in E Grabitz, M Hilf, and M Nettesheim (eds), *EU-Kommentar* (Munich, Beck, 2023); T von Danwitz, 'B. II. Rechtsetzung und Rechtsangleichung' in M Dauses and M Ludwigs (eds), *Handbuch des EU Wirtschaftsrechts* (Munich, Beck, 58th supplement, 2023) para 3. C Calliess, 'Art 13 EUV' in Calliess and Ruffert (eds), *EUV/AEUV*, para 18, mentions the objective of the separation of powers, understood as a means of preserving democratic freedom and the rule of law as a structural principle of Union law.

[74] See M Ruffert, 'Art 3 EUV' in Calliess and Ruffert (eds), *EUV/AEUV*, para 41.

[75] See M Cremona, 'Structural Principles of External Relations Law' in M Cremona (ed), *Structural Principles in EU External Relations Law* (Oxford, Oxford University Press, 2018) 3. See also L Azoulai, 'Structural Principles in EU Law: Internal and External' in Cremona (ed), *Structural Principles* 31, 36,

In the following, we will propose to differentiate between those principles falling under Article 6 TEU on the one hand, and what we call structural principles on the other. We will not deal with what has been called general principles of substantive Union law such as the fundamental freedoms. We will show that indeed all principles discussed in this book are systemic, not substantive (in the sense that they pursue a certain policy objective such as with the fundamental freedoms), and generally do not empower individuals but govern the relations between the Member States or between them and the European Union.

While such categorisation is useful for the reasons mentioned above, we will show that there are also (normative) communalities between some principles discussed in this book and general principles under Article 6 TEU, and that some principles can be assigned to both categories.[76]

4. 'General Principles of the Union's Law' under Article 6 TEU

1. Introduction

The existence of general principles in EU law more broadly can be traced back to the phrase 'any rule of law relating to application' in Article 33 of the European Coal and Steel Community (ECSC), which was later carried over to Article 173 TFEU, what is now Article 263 TFEU, as a grounds of judicial review.[77]

The EEC Treaty referred to the 'general principles common to the laws of the member States' in what is now Article 340 TFEU on the tort liability of the Union institutions. A fundamental right was only provided in what is now Article 157 TFEU on equal pay.[78] The European Court of Justice (ECJ) introduced a much broader range of general principles including especially fundamental rights starting in 1969 by relying on its mandate to 'ensure that in the interpretation and

who mentions 'principles of non-discrimination, free movement, primacy, effet utile, judicial review, institutional balance and loyal cooperation'.

[76] The following builds upon M Klamert, 'Was sind Strukturprinzipien des Unionsrechts?' (2024) *Europarecht*, Special Issue No 1, 9. See, for a different perspective, B Bertrand, 'Retour sur un classique: quelques remarques sur catégorie des principes généraux du droit de l'Union européenne' (2013) 29 *Revue française de droit administratif* 1217, who makes a categorical distinction between general and structural principles.

[77] Article 33 ECSC Treaty: 'The Court shall have jurisdiction over appeals by a member State or by the Council for the annulment of decisions and recommendations of the High Authority on the grounds of lack of legal competence, substantial procedural violations, violation of the Treaty or of any rule of law relating to its application, or abuse of power'. See P Craig, 'General principles of law: treaty, historical, and normative foundations' in Ziegler, Neuvonen and Moreno-Lax eds), *Research Handbook* 25, 27, also mentioning Article 19 TEU as a basis for general principles.

[78] We will explain later why what is now Article 18 TFEU should not be considered a fundamental right in a narrow sense.

application of the Treaties the law is observed'.[79] Until the Treaty of Lisbon, which made the Charter binding, general principles were the only sources of fundamental rights protection in EU law. It has been noted that this is the most striking contribution by the ECJ to the development of the EU's system of legal sources.[80] Article 6(3) TEU now speaks of 'general principles of the Union's law', as mentioned above.

General principles that have been introduced by the Court include the right of defence, the principle of proportionality, the principle of non-discrimination, the right to be heard, the principle of effective judicial protection of the rights of individuals under Union law, the principle of *non bis in idem*, the obligation to state reasons, the duty of the competent institution to establish the facts, the principle of legal certainty, and the protection of legitimate expectations.[81]

While most general principles falling under Article 6(3) TEU embody fundamental rights, especially when considering the broad scope of the Charter of Fundamental Rights (CFR), there are principles such as the right to the protection of trade secrets that have an even broader scope than those covered by the Charter (in this case Article 7 CFR).[82] This observation can also be made regarding the relation between Article 47 CFR and Article 19 TEU.[83]

2. How Article 6 TEU Principles are Established

As mentioned above, Article 6(3) TEU provides that fundamental rights as guaranteed by the ECHR and 'as they result from the constitutional traditions common to the Member States' shall constitute general principles of the Union's law. Both sources of inspiration mentioned in Article 6(3) TEU were already established in the early case law of the ECJ.[84] It has been noted that this approach was not comparable to the practice of any international court, but rather to the case law of the French Conseil d'Etat.[85] It is thus characteristic of the general principles under Article 6(3) TEU that they can be found in the same or a similar form in national

[79] Case 29/69, *Stauder*, ECLI:EU:C:1969:57. See also, eg, Case 44/79, *Hauer*, ECLI:EU:C:1979:290; Case C-112/00, *Schmidberger*, ECLI:EU:C:2003:333; Case C-438/05, *Viking*, ECLI:EU:C:2007:772.

[80] See B de Witte, 'Sources and the subjects of international law' in S Besson and J D'Aspremont (eds), *The Oxford Handbook on The Sources of International Law* (Oxford, Oxford University Press, 2017) 769, 775.

[81] See Lock, 'Commentary on Article 6 TEU' (n 52) paras 21–25. See the Opinion of AG Trstenjak in Case C-101/08, *Audiolux*, ECLI:EU:C:2009:410, para 71; Opinion of AG Trstenjak in Case C-282/10, *Dominguez*, ECLI:EU:C:2011:559, para 96.

[82] Case C-927/19, *Klaipėdos regiono atliekų tvarkymo centras*, ECLI:EU:C:2021:700, para 132. See Lock, 'Commentary on Article 6 TEU' (n 52) para 25.

[83] See M Klamert and B Schima, 'Commentary on Article 19 TEU' in Kellerbauer, Klamert and Tomkin (eds), *Commentary*, para 4.

[84] See Case 11/70, *Internationale Handelsgesellschaft*, ECLI:EU:C:1970:114, para 4 on Member State traditions; Case 4/73, *Nold*, ECLI:EU:C:1974:51 on the ECHR as a Treaty; Case C-13/94, *P v S and Cornwall County Council*, ECLI:EU:C:1996:170, on the case law of the ECtHR.

[85] See de Witte, 'Sources and the subjects of international law' (n 80) 775.

constitutions or the ECHR. This does not mean that the ECJ simply transplants (or adopts to use monist language) principles from either Member State law or the ECHR into EU law.[86] It rather 'imports' them into the Union legal order by taking specific Union interests into account.[87] The interpretation of those fundamental rights is ensured 'within the framework of the structure and objectives of the EU'.[88]

Nonetheless, the establishment of general principles under Article 6(3) TEU can be called derivative or deductive in the sense that there is a strong 'extra-Union' element in the process. They are established by 'evaluative comparison' of the legal orders of the Member States,[89] even if this is not always done with the same level of rationality.[90] The connection between national regimes and fundamental rights is also acknowledged for the rights codified in the Charter by Article 52(4) CFR, which states that in so far as the Charter 'recognises fundamental rights as they result from the constitutional traditions common to the Member States, those rights shall be interpreted in harmony with those traditions'. While it is not clear which Charter rights are covered by this provision, the duty should avoid a situation where the national understanding of a right in one Member State comes to dominate the interpretation of the Charter or where a 'lowest common denominator' approach prevails.[91]

It has been noted that the development of general principles of law 'served to reassure Member States and national courts that the rapidly growing Community power would be subject to proper legal scrutiny, in accord with principles analogous to those in national legal orders'.[92] The legitimacy of the Article 6 TEU principles is thus grounded on the presumption that they are also recognised in other (national, read Member States, and international, read ECHR) legal regimes that are deemed to share the same value system as the European Union. Thus, it could be said somewhat poignantly that when it comes to fundamental rights including the rule of law, the European Union *wants* to be like a state. The whole point of having a fundamental rights regime in EU law, it is submitted, is to show that the protection of individual rights in EU law is equivalent to the protection offered by its Member States. Thus, the affirmation of fundamental rights in the European

[86] See, eg, M Herdegen, 'The Methodological Challenge' in U Bernitz, J Nergelius and C Cardner (eds), *General Principles of EC Law in a Process of Development* (The Hague, Kluwer, 2008) 343, 343 and 346–49.

[87] See R Streinz, 'Art 6 EUV' in Streinz (ed), *EUV/AEUV*, para 25.

[88] Opinion 2/13, *ECHR II*, ECLI:EU:C:2014:2454, para 170.

[89] Opinion of AG Kokott in Case C-550/07 P, *Akzo Nobel*, ECLI:EU:C:2010:229, para 94.

[90] See Case C-144/04, *Mangold*, ECLI:EU:C:2005:709. See, among many others, Weatherill, 'From Myth to Reality' (n 63) 35.

[91] See CFR Explanations. See T Lock, 'Commentary on Article 52 CFR' in Kellerbauer, Klamert and Tomkin (eds), *Commentary*, para 30.

[92] See Craig, 'General principles of law' (n 77) 38. Compare also G Delledonne and F Fabbrini, 'The Founding Myth of European Human Rights Law: Revisiting the Role of National Courts in the Rise of EU Human Rights Jurisprudence' (2019) 44 *EL Rev* 178, with a replique by W Phelan, 'The role of the German and Italian constitutional courts in the rise of EU human rights jurisprudence: A response to Delledonne and Fabbrini' (2021) *EL Rev* 175.

Union has the purpose of affirming not the distinctiveness of the European Union as a legal regime, but, to the contrary, its likeness to the Member States.

3. How Article 6 TEU Principles are Applied

General principles are not subordinate to Charter rights and can provide further-reaching protection though a gap-filling function.[93] The Court of Justice of the European Union (CJEU) applies them as self-standing unwritten norms, alongside the written norms of the Treaties, with the same rank as the Charter and primary EU law.[94]

General principles now regulated under Article 6(3) TEU have been considered 'unwritten principles, recognised by the European Court of Justice, which possess a higher law status by the fact that they may be invoked as a standard for the review of Community acts (and, in addition, of Member State acts falling within the scope of Community law)'.[95] They are, as a rule, directly applicable.[96] They are also, as a rule, standards of interpretation and standards of legality for secondary Union law.[97]

According to Article 51(1) CFR, violations of Charter rights are established by applying a traditional three-step test, involving the scope of the respective right, interference with the right, and the absence of justification under Article 52(1) CFR. Assessment of justification again has three limbs, namely that the limitation must be provided for by law, that it must respect the essence of the right restricted, and that it must be proportionate. This also applies and has already been developed concerning the general principles under Article 6(3) TEU.[98]

The principle of proportionality is itself a general principle of EU law derived from German constitutional law.[99] In theory, its application requires a four-stage test, involving the pursuit of a legitimate goal, suitability to attain that goal, whether a measure is the least restrictive measure available to achieve the aim equally well as the measure chosen, and whether the competing interests have been balanced correctly.[100]

Where several fundamental rights are at issue in a case, 'the assessment of observance of the principle of proportionality must be carried out in accordance with the need to reconcile the requirements of the protection of those various rights, striking a fair balance between them'.[101] Thus, because fundamental rights are all on the same (primary law) rank, the solution to any conflict between them is balancing.

[93] See Lock, 'Commentary on Article 6 TEU' (n 52) para 24.
[94] See de Witte, 'Sources and the subjects of international law' (n 80) 775–76.
[95] See de Witte, 'The Role of Institutional Principles' (n 60) 83.
[96] See Case C-645/18, *Bezirkshauptmannschaft Fürstenfeld*, ECLI:EU:C:2019:110, para 3 on the principle of proportionality. See C Breitler, 'Die unmittelbare Wirkung des Verhältnismäßigkeitsgrundsatzes zwischen Rechtsanwendung und Rechtsetzung' (2023) *Europarecht* 270.
[97] See *Germany v Poland (OPAL)* (n 1) para 45.
[98] See, eg, Case 5/88, *Wachauf*, ECLI:EU:C:1989:321, para 18.
[99] See Lock, 'Commentary on Article 52 CFR' (n 91) para 10.
[100] See Lock, 'Commentary on Article 52 CFR' (n 91) para 10.
[101] Case C-752/18, *Deutsche Umwelthilfe*, ECLI:EU: C:2019:1114, para 50.

5. Structural Principles of EU Law

1. Introduction

We have seen above that there are voices in the literature that consider some principles of Union law to be structural or systemic principles that would underlie the constitutional order of the European Union. We prefer the term *structural* principles for the principles discussed in this book. It is true that, in legal theory, as mentioned, principles in general have been defined as being structural decisions, so this term may seem a pleonasmus. However, in EU law, it arguably makes sense to emphasise this quality because Article 6 TEU principles are not structural in the meaning advocated in this book, as explained below. The notion of *systemic* principles, by contrast, would seem to allude to a notion of a 'legal system' often linked to considerations of hierarchy and a Kelsenian order of legal sources (*Stufenbau*), which is not our focus here.[102]

Recall that, in the context of international law, it would be the function of overarching principles to preserve unity in a legal order, to 'sustain its normative edifice and keep it together'.[103] Thinking in terms of principles, it has also been suggested, would convey an idea of 'the whole' and would make it possible to understand the constitutional structures of the European Union.[104] Former ECJ judge Pescatore emphasised the importance of what he called 'structural principles' and wrote extrajudicially: 'Before one can talk of the substance of legal norms, one must see what the structure into which these norms are integrated is'.[105]

We think that the metaphor of a legal structure is an apposite one for the European Union. Construction is a frequently used term with the process of European integration.[106] It emphasises the role of actors such as the CJEU in shaping EU law.[107] It has, however, been argued that the building metaphor would be ill-suited to describe the overlapping of EU and Member State legal orders because buildings cannot overlap and it would recall theories focused on *Stufenbau* and the ranking of norms according to their validity.[108] Indeed, we will in the next chapter suggest seeing EU law as governed by a network of interwoven legal principles. We do not need to think of buildings or houses to emphasise that EU law itself and in

[102] Compare Schroeder, *Das Gemeinschaftsrechtssystem* (n 55).

[103] See Abi-Saab, 'Fragmentation or Unification' (n 46) 926.

[104] See von Bogdandy, 'Grundprinzipien des Unionsrechts' (n 55) 753 f. See also C Calliess, 'Art 1 AEUV' in Calliess and Ruffert (eds), *EUV/AEUV*, para 10.

[105] Cited in Azoulai, 'Structural Principles' (n 75) 32.

[106] See, eg, ME Bélanger, 'Europeanization as a Foundation of the European Construction' in R Coman, T Kostera and L Tomini (eds), *Europeanization and European Integration* (London, Palgrave Macmillan, 2014) 29. See also the references and discussion by J van de Beeten, 'On Metaphor and Meaning: The Autonomy of EU Legal Order Through the Lens of Project and System' (2023) 8 *European Papers* 1441, 1450–51.

[107] See K Lenaerts et al (eds), *Building the European Union: The Jurist's View of the Union's Evolution* (Oxford, Hart Publishing, 2021).

[108] See P Westerman, 'Weaving the Threads of a European Legal Order' (2023) 8 *European Papers* 1308, 1307.

relation to national law is subject to a certain normative structure, which, as will be shown, safeguards unity and uniformity.

This understanding of the term 'structural principles' is not always shared. Thus, it has been mentioned that the general principles under Article 6(3) TEU would also include principles which are closely connected with and may be derived from the structural principles of the European Union, 'such as liberty, democracy, respect for human rights and fundamental freedoms, and the rule of law'.[109] Except for the rule of law discussed in chapter six, these are not principles that are the focus of this book. Also, the Court has stated in two judgments on the primacy of Union law that 'the validity of a Community measure or its effect within a Member State cannot be affected by allegations that it runs counter to either fundamental rights as formulated by the constitution of that State or the principles of a national constitutional structure'.[110] This has been taken to imply, in the context of national identity under Article 4(2) TEU discussed in chapter three, that the legal systems of the Member States (also) comprise structural principles.[111]

2. Defining Structural Principles

It has been noted that the principles discussed in this book (including some not discussed here) cover a 'vast array of heterogeneous issues'.[112]

In an external relations context, structural principles have been defined as 'principles which have been drawn from the Treaties and elaborated by the Court to establish [the] institutional space … within which policy may be formed, in which the different actors understand and work within their respective roles'.[113] Structural principles have been categorised as 'relational' governing relations between actors in the European Union and 'systemic' and would not be concerned 'with the substantive content of policy, but rather with process and the relationships between actors in those processes'.[114] This definition would include the duty of sincere (and close) cooperation, the principles of conferral and institutional balance, mutual solidarity, subsidiarity, and the principle of autonomy.[115]

[109] Opinion of AG Trstenjak in *Audiolux* (n 81) para 70; Opinion of AG Trstenjak in *Dominguez* (n 81) para 95.

[110] *Internationale Handelsgesellschaft* (n 84) para 3. See also Case C-409/06, *Winner Wetten*, ECLI:EU:C:2010:503, para 61; Case C-399/11, *Melloni*, ECLI:EU:C:2013:107, para 59. The reference to 'principles of a national constitutional structure' has only been repeated by the Court once, in Case C-97/87, *Dow Chemical Ibérica*, ECLI:EU:C:1989:380, para 38. See, however, the Opinion of GA Szpunar in Case C-33/22, *Austrian Data Protection Authority*, ECLI:EU:C:2023:397, para 138.

[111] See Schill and Krenn, 'Artikel 4 EUV' (n 73) para 18, and Streinz, 'Art 4 EUV' (n 87) paras 21, 23.

[112] See Castellarin, 'General Principles' (n 51) 132.

[113] See Cremona, 'Structural Principles of External Relations Law' (n 75). See also Wessel, 'General Principles in EU Common Foreign and Security Policy' (n 58) 609.

[114] See Cremona, 'Structural Principles of External Relations Law' (n 75) 12. Compare also the use of these notions by C Contartese, *The Principle of Autonomy in EU External Relations Law.* (Milan, Wolters Kluwer, 2025).

[115] See Cremona, 'Structural Principles of External Relations Law' (n 75) 12.

While this definition might align with the role of structural principles in external relations law, where actorness is a pivotal issue as we will discuss in chapter four, we will show that structural principles are always equally relational and systemic, when we take a broader perspective. We will show that structural principles define the nature of the European Union as an organisation and of EU law as a legal order. They make the European Union the legal order that it is, characterise it and arguably also make it unique. This includes the principles mentioned above, thus autonomy, conferral including subsidiarity and institutional balance, loyalty, and solidarity, and in addition, supremacy/primacy and direct effect, national identity, equality including Member State equality, and effectiveness.

We do not insist that these principles must be called structural principles or that this list is exhaustive. We will, however, show in the next chapter (three) that they all have elements in common, despite their heterogeneity, which is in itself setting them apart from the homogenous general principles under Article 6 TEU. They are not substantive in the sense that they are applied for fulfilling policy objectives such as under the internal market. In most cases, they do not involve balancing with other principles, the consideration of Member State interests, or a proportionality assessment, all typical of fundamental rights. Sometimes, as with the principle of supremacy of EU law, this denial of balancing (such as with the principle of national identity) is even a central quality of the principle. We will also show that they are not principles guaranteed by the ECHR and mostly are not derived from national constitutional traditions.[116] Because they are not meant to protect individuals, they mostly also lack direct effect, again different from fundamental rights.[117] They are general in the sense that they apply within the entire EU legal order (including the CFSP, as is shown in chapter four), and they are to a lesser degree general in the sense of being indeterminate.

3. Why Some Principles are not Considered Structural Principles

State liability has been deemed 'inherent' in Union law and it seems to have no parallels in other legal systems by including liability for acts of the legislature, both of which would argue in favour of considering it a structural principle. At the same time, it was not qualified by the ECJ as an 'essential characteristic' of Union law (see later on this term) and the majority of the literature does not mention it as being a structural/systemic principle, as shown above. Moreover, state liability differs from structural principles in so far as the ECJ has relied on legal comparison

[116] Similarly, W Kahl, 'Art 4 EUV' in Calliess and Ruffert (eds), *EUV/AEUV*, para 97 on the principle of loyalty, and Terhechte, '§ 14 Prinzipienordnung der Europäischen Union' (n 63) 779 on primacy and direct effect.

[117] Compare also de Witte, 'The Role of Institutional Principles' (n 60) 83.

for developing it.[118] However, state liability will be discussed in chapter five as an example of the reasoning of the ECJ using structural principles.

Another principle that some might miss and therefore deem neglected in this book is mutual trust. It has so far been applied predominantly, but not exclusively, in the area of freedom, security and justice.[119] It has been argued in the literature that it cannot be considered a self-standing principle but rather 'is a principle that operates exclusively through the legislative provisions that variously implement it', consisting 'of a bundle of interpretive doctrines triggered by legislation'.[120] While we will not devote a separate section to mutual trust, we will discuss it where appropriate, especially in the context of loyalty, solidarity and the equality of Member States (chapter three).

As also mentioned earlier, we do not claim to discuss all principles of EU law, and notably those dealt with in the context of European private law are not fully reflected in this book.[121]

4. Why Most Fundamental Rights are not Considered Structural Principles

The Union's fundamental rights are undoubtedly a central part of Union law and the identity of the European Union as an organisation. According to the ECJ, fundamental rights recognised by the Charter are 'at the heart of' the EU's legal structure.[122] It has been shown that the Union's fundamental rights are based on the principle of human dignity and therefore present themselves in a certain structure.[123] Moreover, structural issues discussed in chapter two such as legal unity, EU law as a network of principles, and coherence have all been explored from the perspective of the fundamental rights regime of the European Union.[124] It would therefore seem counterintuitive to claim that fundamental rights should not be discussed in a book about structural principles.

[118] See Lenaerts and Gutiérrez-Fons, 'The Role of General Principles of EU Law' (n 63) 279 with further references.

[119] See Joined Cases C-187 & 385/01, *Gözütok and Brügge*, ECLI:EU:C:2003:87; Case C-159/02, *Turner*, ECLI:EU:C:2004:228; Joined Cases C-411 & 493/10, *NS*, ECLI:EU:C:2011:865. But see, for an application in other contexts, Case C-64/16, *Associação Sindical dos Juízes Portugueses*, ECLI:EU:C:2018:117; Case C-284/16, *Achmea*, ECLI:EU:C:2018:158; Case C-34/17, *Donnellan*, ECLI:EU:C:2018:282.

[120] See F Maiani and S Migliorini, 'One principle to rule them all? Anatomy of mutual trust in the law of the Area of Freedom, Security and Justice' (2020) 57 *CML Rev* 7, 10, 44.

[121] J Basedow, *EU Private Law: Anatomy of a Growing Legal Order* (Cambridge, Intersentia, 2021); J Basedow, 'General Principles of European Private Law and Interest Analysis: Some Reflections in the Light of Mangold and Audiolux' (2016) 24 *European Review of Private Law* 331.

[122] *ECHR II* (n 88) para 169.

[123] Compare P Gragl, 'Die strukturierende Wirkung der Unionsgrundrechte: Dreidimensionalität und Föderalisierung' (2024) *Europarecht*, Special Issue No 1, 89.

[124] See X Groussot, J Hettne and GT Pétursson, 'General Principles and the Many Faces of Coherence: Between Law and Ideology in the European Union' in Vogenauer and Weatherill (eds), *General Principles of Law* 77.

However, as explained, fundamental rights can also be found in the same or a similar form in national law. Thus, the pronouncement of fundamental rights in the European Union has the purpose of affirming not the distinctiveness of the European Union, but to the contrary, its likeness to the Member States. The argument that individual fundamental rights are not what we call here structural principles can be illustrated by the right of every worker to an annual period of paid leave under Article 31(2) CFR. Without doubt, this is an important fundamental right and has been deemed mandatory and unconditional, because of which it has also been granted direct effect between private parties by the ECJ.[125] This however, it is submitted, does not make it essential to the nature of the Union or Union law.

The only fundamental right that will be discussed in this book is the principle of effective (judicial) protection. A distinction is therefore suggested between the protection of individual fundamental rights and the protection of Union fundamental rights *in toto*.[126] As will be explained in chapter three, the principle of effective judicial protection is not only recognised as a fundamental right under Article 47 CFR, but is also provided by Article 19(1) TEU. Different from other fundamental rights, this principle is interrelated in manifold ways with other principles discussed in this book, above all with the principle of effectiveness but also with supremacy and direct effect.

Suffice it to note at this point that we also do not consider the prohibition of discrimination based on nationality in Article 18 TFEU a fundamental right in the meaning of Article 6 TEU, despite it being also provided in Article 21(2) CFR, for reasons explained in chapter three.

6. On the Relevance of (Principles of) International Law

1. Introduction

There are two reasons for discussing the role of principles of (customary) international law in EU law.

First, it has been argued that in some instances principles of international law would be transformed into primary EU law and applied as general principles of EU law. If this were true, and as explained below we do not think that is the case, there would be another category of principles of EU law we would have to look at for the present purposes.

Secondly, it is useful to explore why the Court has in some cases applied principles of international law instead of applying principles of EU law. We will suggest that the reason can mainly be seen in what we, in this context, call the EU's actorness.

[125] Case C-569/16, *Bauer*, ECLI:EU:C:2018:871.
[126] See also Gragl, 'Die strukturierende Wirkung der Unionsgrundrechte' (n 123) 89.

2. The European Union as an International Actor Bound by International Law

Article 3(5) TEU is the part in the provision on the EU's objectives that requires the European Union to contribute to 'the strict observance and the development of international law'. This is understood by the Court as requiring Union institutions to observe international law in its entirety, including principles of international law.[127]

Already before the Treaty of Lisbon, it was settled case law that EU law must be interpreted in the light of the relevant rules of international law.[128] I have explained elsewhere that the Court relied on good faith and *pacta sunt servanda* as principles of public international law when determining how international Treaties concluded by the European Union must be interpreted and applied.[129] Other international law principles applied by the Court in cases with an international law context are the principle of *rebus sic stantibus*, the principle of the relative effect of Treaties (also known as *pacta tertiis nec nocent nec prosunt*),[130] and the principle of self-determination as 'one of the essential principles of international law'.[131] In these constellations, it is submitted, the European Union is bound to apply international law because of its role as an international actor engaging with third states or international organisations.

Until recently it was not clear whether general principles of international law could invalidate secondary Union law such as the Council decisions taken under Article 218 TFEU.[132] It has now been clarified in *Front Polisario* that, while the review of validity technically concerns the Council decision concluding an international agreement, it 'is capable of encompassing the legality of that act in the light of the actual content of the international agreement in question'.[133]

[127] Case C-366/10, *Air Transport Association of America and Others*, ECLI:EU:C:2011:864, para 101; Case C-363/18, *Organisation juive européenne*, ECLI:EU:C:2019:954, para 48.

[128] Case 98/78, *Racke*, ECLI:EU:C:1979:14, paras 45–46; Joined Cases C-402/05 P & C-415/05 P, *Kadi*, ECLI:EU:C:2008:461, para 291.

[129] Case C-308/06, *Intertanko*, ECLI:EU:C:2008:312, para 52; Case C-15/17, *Bosphorus Queen Shipping*, ECLI:EU:C:2018:557, para 45; Case C-203/07 P, *Greece v Commission (Project Abuja)*, ECLI:EU:C:2008:606. See M Klamert, 'Loyalty and Solidarity as General Principles' in Ziegler, Neuvonen and Moreno-Lax (eds), *Research Handbook* 118; G de Baere and T Roes, 'EU Loyalty as Good Faith' (2015) *ICLQ* 829.

[130] Case C-386/08, *Brita*, ECLI:EU:C:2010:91, para 44; Joined Cases C-779/21 P & C-799/21 P, *Front Polisario*, ECLI:EU:C:2024:835, para 131.

[131] Case C-104/16 P, *Council v Front Polisario ('Fisheries Agreement')*, ECLI:EU:C:2016:973, paras 88–89; Joined Cases C-779/21 P & C-799/21 P, *Front Polisario* (n 130) para 131.

[132] See M Klamert, 'Commentary on Article 3 TEU' in Kellerbauer, Klamert and Tomkin (eds), *Commentary*, para 20.

[133] Joined Cases C-779/21 P & C-799/21 P, *Front Polisario* (n 130) para 174.

3. International Law Applied in 'Internal' Cases

General principles of international law have also been applied between the Member States in cases without an external relations context.

In *Van Duyn*, the Court held regarding the refusal of entry of a Union citizen into the United Kingdom under the previous Citizens' Rights Directive, Council Directive 64/221/EEC:

> Furthermore, it is a principle of international law, which the EEC Treaty cannot be assumed to disregard in the relations between Member States, that a State is precluded from refusing its own nationals the right of entry or residence.
>
> It follows that a Member State, for reasons of public policy, can, where it deems, necessary, refuse a national of another Member State the benefit of the principle of freedom of movement for workers in a case where such a national proposes to take up a particular offer of employment even though the Member State does not place a similar restriction upon its own nationals.[134]

In *Hungary v Slovakia*, the status of a Head of State was deemed to have a 'specific character, resulting from the fact that it is governed by international law, with the consequence that the conduct of such a person internationally, such as that person's presence in another State, comes under that law, in particular the law governing diplomatic relations'.[135] This would justify a limitation, based on international law, to the exercise of the right of free movement under Article 21 TFEU.

Thus, in both cases international law was applied to interpret Union law, viz primary law in *Hungary v Slovakia* and secondary law in *Van Duyn*. What was decisive in both cases, it is submitted, was that the issues concerned (the status of Heads of State outside their role within the EU institutions, the refusal of entry for a Member State's own citizens) did not fall under Union law. In these cases, thus, international law was applied as a subsidiary legal source.[136]

This must be distinguished from case law where the Court referred to a principle of good faith in cases involving the implementation of Union secondary law.[137] In these cases, good faith arguably was not applied as a principle of international law but in order to add more weight to the EU loyalty principle, discussed in chapter three. This is illustrated by the well-known *Tafelwein* case, where the Court held:

[134] Case 41/74, *Van Duyn*, ECLI:EU:C:1974:133, paras 22, 23.

[135] Case C-364/10, *Hungary v Slovakia*, ECLI:EU:C:2012:630, para 49.

[136] See also Case 244/80, *Foglia*, ECLI:EU:C:1981:302, para 24 on the principle of territority.

[137] See Case C-217/88, *Commission v Germany (Market in Wine)*, ECLI:EU:C:1990:290. Compare also the *Opel Austria* case, where the General Court applied an EU law principle of legal certainty and legitimate expectations that would be the 'corollary' of the principle of good faith under customary international law to justify imposing obligations of abstention. See, further, M Klamert, 'Legal Certainty and Customary International Law: Opel Austria' in G Butler and R Wessel (eds), *EU External Relations Law: The Cases in Context* (Oxford, Hart Publishing, 2022) 367.

> It ought to be added that when a Member State in implementing a Commission regulation encounters unforeseeable difficulties which make it absolutely impossible to carry out the obligations imposed by that regulation, it must submit those problems to the Commission and suggest to it appropriate solutions. In such a case, the Commission and the Member State are obliged, by virtue of the reciprocal duties of genuine cooperation imposed on them in particular by Article 5 of the EEC Treaty, to work together in good faith in order to overcome those difficulties while complying in full with the provisions of the Treaty.[138]

It has been suggested that in cases such as *Van Duyn* and *Hungary v Slovakia*, principles of international law would be transformed into primary EU law and applied as general principles of EU law through 'systemic integration'.[139] However, there seems to be no good reason to assume that principles of international law in the above cases are not applied as sources of international law but as *doppelgänger* EU law norms.[140] This is different with international agreements, which are not only binding on the Union according to Article 216(2) TFEU, but also form an integral part of EU law, thus becoming sources of EU law with their conclusion under Article 218 TFEU.

7. Conclusions: Sameness, Otherness, Actorness

We have shown that there is ample reason to claim that it is not useful to always speak of 'general principles' when this could refer to so varied norms such as fundamental rights, conferral, or supremacy. Indicating, by this term, that such principles would apply generally in EU law is possibly the least informative point one can make in this respect, as few of these principles would be confined to apply *not* generally. When we refer to the principles under Article 6 TEU, we will therefore always make this clear.

We have suggested distinguishing the principles defined by and covered under Article 6 TEU from what we call structural principles. Notably, this does not mean that structural principles cannot apply generally or cannot have functions that are usually ascribed to principles under Article 6 TEU, such as applying as a standard of review for Union measures. This will be explored in the following chapter, when we discuss structural principles individually and in their relation with each other.

The principles discussed in this book can be considered fundamental norms which are inherent in or derived from EU law and which are not informing policy decisions. They are also largely formal rather than axiological. It is submitted that it is helpful to understand the development of general principles under

[138] *Commission v Germany (Market in Wine)* (n 137) para 33.
[139] See Castellarin, 'General Principles' (n 51) 140.
[140] Compare Kolb, *Theory of International Law* (n 33) 180: 'For customary rules, all the world's systems are monistic'.

Article 6 TEU as driven by a strive for 'Sameness'. They are an expression of the objective of the European Union to be more like a nation state, to provide the protections that are common in its Member States. By contrast, structural principles represent a strive for 'Otherness'. Their development is driven by the aim to be different both from Member States and from international organisations. We will see in chapter three that these two orientations can come into conflict such as with accession to the ECHR, which would have served Sameness but where the Court insisted on Otherness through the principle of autonomy in Opinion 2/13.[141]

International law is applied over EU law, it has been shown, in situations when the European Union acts on the external sphere by engaging with international actors. The application of international law within EU law can therefore be seen to represent the 'Actorness' of the European Union. This Actorness will be important when we discuss the role of structural principles in external relations in chapter four. By contrast, in the following chapter three, we will see that principles of international law have often *not* been applied in situations governed exclusively by EU law, involving only Member States without any 'external' context.

[141] *ECHR II* (n 88). See also B de Witte, 'The Relative Autonomy of the European Union's Fundamental Rights Regime' (2019) 88 *Nordic Journal of International Law* 65, 73: 'The Court emphatically does not define itself as a participant in an international human rights community but rather as the guardian of the separateness of the EU legal order'.

II

Premise: The EU Legal Order has a Structure that Involves Principles

1. Introduction

National legal systems are usually characterised as being free from contradictions.[1] More than that, there is the assumption of a meaningful relationship between individual norms of a legal order which, among others, provides the basis for the method of systematic interpretation of the law. This is itself based on the presumption that the actors involved in drafting the law are acting rationally and are able to see individual norms as a part of a larger regime.

While this assumption of order is hardly ever disputed in national law contexts, the sources of international law are diverse and involve a large number of actors, whose actions are not always coordinated, lest centrally governed. The ILC Study Group on Fragmentation of International Law has thus felt the need to affirm the following:

> [I]nternational law is a legal system. Its rules and principles (i.e. its norms) act in relation to and should be interpreted against the background of other rules and principles. As a legal system, international law is not a random collection of such norms. There are meaningful relationships between them.[2]

With EU law, no one arguably would claim that the EU Treaties are a random collection of provisions. Yet, EU primary law never had a reputation for being well organised, something the Treaty of Lisbon has attempted to improve.[3] Under the current EU Treaties, at least the European Court of Justice (ECJ) now sees a structure and thus an order on constitutional, primary law level within Union law. In Opinion 2/13 on accession of the European Union to the European Convention on Human Rights (ECHR) alone, the ECJ sitting as Full Court has referred to a 'structure' or 'structured' no less than 10 times in relation to the European Union

[1] See D Felix, *Einheit der Rechtsordnung: zur verfassungsrechtlichen Relevanz einer juristischen Argumentationsfigur* (Tübingen, Mohr Siebeck, 1998) 146 f.

[2] ILC Conclusions of the Work of the Study Group on the Fragmentation of International Law: Difficulties Arising from the Diversification and Expansion of International Law (2006), A/61/10, para 251.

[3] See, eg, P Craig, 'Competence: Clarity, Conferral, Containment and Consideration' (2004) 29 *EL Rev* 323.

and EU law: 'a particularly sophisticated institutional structure';[4] 'the constitutional structure of the EU';[5] 'a structured network of principles, rules and mutually interdependent legal relations';[6] 'legal structure';[7] 'within the framework of the structure and objectives of the EU';[8] 'the structure of the EU';[9] 'provisions, which are part of the framework of a system that is specific to the EU, are structured in such a way';[10] 'the Court's powers are structured' by the Treaties.[11]

In the following, we will begin by discussing conceivable forms of structure or order that could be ascribed to EU law. We will then examine whether the Treaty of Lisbon brought a certain order to (parts of) primary law and will conclude the chapter by discussing whether there is a discernible order with structural principles based on primary law.

2. Conceptions of Order in EU Law

1. Union Law as a Hierarchical System

It has been argued that the EU legal order was conceived by the Court of Justice of the European Union (CJEU) 'as a structured legal order comprising a clear hierarchy of sources that departs from the traditional "horizontal" nature of international law where the main sources of law do not stand in a hierarchical relationship with each other'.[12] The development of an 'idiosyncratic system of sources' in EU law especially by the creation of a 'differentiated and subtle system of instruments of secondary EU law', and by the great importance assumed by the general principles of EU law as an unwritten source, has also been noted.[13] At the top of the legal hierarchy in EU law would be the Treaty on European Union (TEU) and the Treaty on the Functioning of the European Union (TFEU) as well as the EU Charter of Rights and Freedoms together with the unwritten general principles of EU law, followed by international agreements concluded by the European Union, secondary law, and finally EU 'soft law'.[14] Thus, there is a hierarchy between primary law on the one hand, and secondary (and tertiary) EU law on the other, the former being superior to the latter, for which reason the latter must be interpreted in the light of the former.[15]

[4] Opinion 2/13, *ECHR II*, ECLI:EU:C:2014:2454, para 158.
[5] *ECHR II* (n 4) para 165.
[6] *ECHR II* (n 4) para 167.
[7] *ECHR II* (n 4) paras 168, 169.
[8] *ECHR II* (n 4) para 170.
[9] *ECHR II* (n 4) para 171.
[10] *ECHR II* (n 4) para 172.
[11] *ECHR II* (n 4) paras 253, 257.
[12] B de Witte, 'Sources and the subjects of international law' in S Besson and J D'Aspremont (eds), *The Oxford Handbook on The Sources Of International Law* (Oxford, Oxford University Press, 2017) 769, 771–72.
[13] de Witte, 'Sources and the subjects of international law' (n 12) 771–72.
[14] de Witte, 'Sources and the subjects of international law' (n 12) 772.
[15] See M Nettesheim, 'Normenhierarchien im EU-Recht' (2006) 6 *Europarecht* 737, 753.

Despite the name of the TFEU, which suggests subordination to the TEU, the Treaties (and the Charter of Fundamental Rights (CFR)) are of equal legal value.[16] Most would therefore see no legal hierarchy between TEU, TFEU, the Charter, and the provisions contained therein. However, one could mention that Article 48 TEU makes a distinction between the Treaties in so far as large parts of the TFEU can be changed under the simplified revision procedure.[17] Moreover, a 'substantive hierarchy' has been suggested with Article 2 TEU at the top containing the Union's founding principles and outlining the basic tenets of the Union's constitution, the provisions giving expression to these values coming second, and the rest of primary law, including large parts of what has been termed the EU's 'economic constitution', forming a third level.[18] This is not the place to engage with this theory. Suffice it to note that it would seem that the case law involving Article 2 TEU can also be rationalised by a 'simple' systemic interpretation of primary law.

The relationship of EU law with the legal orders of the Member States is commonly not discussed in terms of hierarchy. This is also the case when the point is made that Union law can have direct effect in national law and can, therefore, conflict with national law in specific situations.[19] We will discuss in chapter three how the literature and probably also the Court prefer the terms 'primacy' or 'precedence' over the term 'supremacy' to avoid conveying that there is a strict hierarchy between Union law and national law. Such a non-hirarchical narrative is also at the core of the different concepts of pluralism that have been proposed but have also (often strongly) been disputed in the literature.[20]

2. Union Law as a Network

In public international law, it has been argued that there would be 'fragmentary constitutional law elements' situated both '"horizontally" (sectorally) and "vertically" (encompassing both the international and the national level)' that may

[16] Article 1(2) TFEU, Article 1(3) TEU, Article 6(1) TEU.

[17] See Opinion of AG Kokott in Case C-370/12, *Pringle*, ECLI:EU:C:2012:675, para 60.

[18] See LD Spieker, *EU Values Before the Court of Justice: Foundations, Potential, Risks* (Oxford, Oxford University Press, 2023) 100.

[19] R Schütze, *European Constitutional Law*, 2nd edn (Cambridge, Cambridge University Press, 2016) 117–18. See also H Hofmann, 'Conflicts and Integration: Revisiting *Costa v ENEL* and *Simmenthal II*' in MP Maduro and L Azoulai (eds), *The Past and Future of EU Law: The Classics of EU Law Revisited on the 50th Anniversary of the Rome Treaty* (Oxford, Hart Publishing, 2010) 60.

[20] See D Sarmiento, 'Review Article – Making Sense of Constitutional Pluralism: A Review of Klemen Jaklic's *Constitutional Pluralism in the EU*' (2015) 40 *EL Rev* 110; M Claes, 'Primacy of EU Law in European and National Law' in A Arnull and D Chalmers (eds), *The Oxford Handbook of European Union Law* (Oxford, Oxford University Press, 2015) 178, 202; and J Baquero Cruz, *What's Left of the Law of Integration? Decay and Resistance in European Union Law* (Oxford, Oxford University Press, 2018) 27–52: 'Indeed, in prescriptive terms constitutional pluralism is a deeply disturbing doctrine regarding the way in which Union law and the laws of the states should interact, because it undermines the main objective of integration and the basic social function of law'.

complement and support each other.[21] This has been called a 'constitutional network', describing 'relationships and interaction of norms and of their users', which 'cannot be aligned in an abstract hierarchy'.[22]

The CJEU has (repeatedly) held that the essential features of EU law discussed above have led to a 'structured network' of interwoven principles, rules and legal relationships linking the European Union and its Member States and the Member States to each other.[23] This can be understood to make two different assertions: one about the relation between the EU (legal order) and (the legal orders of) the Member States; and another about the relations between the Member States themselves.

A good example of the former is the fundamental rights regimes of the European Union and of the Member States discussed above. Both regimes are separate yet interlocked and are strongly reliant upon each other in their respective development. Another example of the interwoven legal relationship between the European Union and Member States is the preliminary reference procedure under Article 267 TFEU as 'an instrument of cooperation between the Court of Justice and national courts'.[24] It has been suggested that Article 267 TFEU could have given rise to a hierarchical model, in which the ECJ would have tried to affirm its own superiority, but it has relied instead on the goodwill of national courts and an emphasis on cooperation.[25] It has also been noted that the network that is established thereby involves many actors by conferring on them powers they would not have enjoyed without EU law.[26]

For Union law-based networks between Member States and their actors, we can mention the various cooperation mechanisms established under secondary law, which the ECJ regularly qualifies as manifestations of the principle of loyalty.[27] Thus, Council Regulation 1/2003 created the European Competition Network (ECN), a forum for cooperation and coordination between the EU competition authorities on enforcement. The Market Surveillance Regulation 2019/1020 established an EU Product Compliance Network, containing national and Commission representatives and experts.[28] Council Decision 2001/470 established a European

[21] See A Peters, 'Compensatory Constitutionalism: The Function and Potential of Fundamental International Norms and Structures' (2006) 19 *Leiden Journal of International Law* 579, 601.

[22] See Peters, 'Compensatory Constitutionalism' (n 21) 601.

[23] *ECHR II* (n 4) paras 166–67; Case C-621/18, *Wightman and Others*, ECLI:EU:C:2018:999, para 45; Opinion 1/17, *CETA*, ECLI:EU:C:2019:341, para 109; Case C-573/17, *Popławski II*, ECLI:EU:C:2019:530, para 52.

[24] Case C-231/89, *Gmurzynska-Bscher*, ECLI:EU:C:1990:386, para 18.

[25] See R Dehousse, *The European Court of Justice: The Politics of Judicial Integration* (New York, Springer, 1998) 136–137.

[26] See P Westerman, 'Weaving the Threads of a European Legal Order' (2023) 8 *European Papers* 1308, 1311, also pointing to direct effect in this context.

[27] Case C-304/02, *Commission v France*, ECLI:EU:C:2005:444; Case C-326/00, *IKA*, ECLI:EU:C:2003:101. See Case C-429/07, *X*, ECLI:EU:C:2009:359, para 20 f on Chapter IV of Council Regulation 1/2003 on the implementation of the rules on competition laid down in Articles 81 and 82 of the Treaty [2003] OJ L1/1.

[28] See Regulation (EU) 2019/1020 [2019] OJ L169/1.

Judicial Network (EJN) in civil and commercial matters for facilitating contacts between the authorities of the Member States on judicial cooperation in civil and commercial matters.[29]

It is submitted that by using the concept of a network linking the European Union and its Member States and the Member States to each other, the Court strives to steer these relationships conceptionally away from a framing in terms of hierarchy and systemic competition. Speaking of a network arguably does not make a ranking judgement about the relations between EU and national law, but rather emphasises that EU and national legal orders have become so intertwined that the functionalities of one are also reflected in the other and that the one does not function without the other. It would seem like an attempt to give the primacy principle with its implications of a hierarchical superiority of EU law a different, less confrontational narrative. Talking about a network stresses the togetherness instead of the differences between the legal systems of the European Union and the Member States, putting a focus on their co-dependence and not on who has the final say. When we recall the discussion in international law mentioned above, it would also seem to make a *constitutional* argument about the nature of EU law.

We will show in chapter three that there is indeed a network made up of structural principles that involves EU law, its interaction with the laws of the Member States, and also the legal relations between the Member States themselves. We will also show that these principles interact, among others, to foster legal unity within EU law and in its relation to the laws of the Member States, which is a conception of order introduced in the following.

3. Union Law and Legal Unity

3.1. Introduction

It has been suggested that the unity of a legal system can be based on sociology, legal theory, or legal policy postulates, among others.[30] It would involve a system of legal norms that is characterised by freedom from contradiction.[31] Conflict of laws rules are therefore hardly required within national (non-federal) legal orders. The principle of the unity of legal language, according to which identical terms in a legal system generally must be deemed to have the same content, applies without any question.[32]

In federal states, it has been observed, another dimension is added because the question arises how federal and sub-federal levels should interact with each other,

[29] Council Decision 2001/470 [2001] OJ L174/25, amended by Decision No 568/2009/EC of the European Parliament and of the Council of 18 June 2009 [2009] OJ L168/35.

[30] See K Röhl and HC Röhl, *Allgemeine Rechtslehre*, 3rd edn (Cologne, Heyman, 2008) § 56 I, 451.

[31] See Felix, *Einheit* (n 1) 146 f.

[32] See M Potacs, *Rechtstheorie*, 2nd edn (Vienna, Facultas, 2019) 165.

whereby the classic conflict of laws rules of *lex specialis* and *lex posterior* were of no help.[33] In federal states, there would therefore be a whole ring of homogeneity-securing rules.[34] While conflicts of norms between the federal and the state level in such orders may occur, it is more important to have rules and techniques that prevent such conflicts from arising in the first place.

In international law, by contrast, fragmentation is a perennial concern and homogeneity-securing rules are scarce.[35] Fragmentation is generally understood as the emergence of specialised and (relatively) autonomous partial legal orders, the extent to which these conflict with each other, how such a conflict is to be resolved and whether the general rules of international law apply to them.[36] WTO law, the ECHR, international environmental law, and international investment protection law have been analysed against this backdrop.[37]

In EU law, discussed in the following, concepts of unity are varied.

3.2. *Different Concepts of Unity in EU Law*

In EU law, the concepts of uniformity and unity are most commonly discussed in the context of so-called variable geometry or differentiated integration.[38] It has been noted that the terminology in this respect is very inconsistent and also strongly politicised, including concepts with different and sometimes not so positive connotations such as core Europe, Europe of concentric circles, multi-speed Europe or 'Europe à la carte'.[39] Thus, one could say that unity and uniformity are not always considered a good thing in the discussion about the European Union and about EU law.

Another form of legal unity that is more closely related to the subject matter of this book is the unity of Union law in the sense of the intrasystemic or internal unity of the body of Union law itself. A panoply of concepts exists in EU law meant to ensure this form of unity, such as homogeneity, coherence and consistency.[40]

[33] See H Dreier, 'Einheit und Vielfalt der Verfassungsordnungen im Bundesstaat' in K Schmidt (ed), *Vielfalt des Rechts – Einheit der Rechtsordnung? Hamburger Ringvorlesung* (Berlin, Duncker & Humblot, 1994) 113, 118.

[34] See Dreier, 'Einheit und Vielfalt' (n 33) 119.

[35] Compare G Teubner and A Fischer-Lescano, 'Regime-Collisions: The Vain Search for Legal Unity in the Fragmentation of Global Law' (2004) 25 *Michigan Journal of International Law* 999.

[36] See J Pauwelyn, 'Fragmentation of International Law' in *Max Planck Encyclopedia of Public International Law*, 2nd edn (Oxford, Oxford University Press, 2012).

[37] See S Griller, 'Fragmentations in Public Law: Discourse Comparison in International and National Law' (2018) *Veröffentlichungen der Vereinigung der Deutschen Staatsrechtslehrer* (*VVDSTRL*) 238, 266 with further references.

[38] See G de Búrca and J Scott (eds), *Constitutional Change in the ECLI:EU: From Uniformity to Flexibility?* (Oxford, Hart Publishing, 2000) 133; M Ruffert, 'Art 20 EUV' in C Calliess and M Ruffert (eds), *EUV/AEUV*, 6th ed (Munich, Beck, 2022) para 1 et seq; B de Witte, 'An undivided Union? Differentiated integration in post-Brexit times' (2018) 55 *CML Rev* 227.

[39] See M Pechstein, 'Art 20 EUV' in R Streinz (ed), *EUV/AEUV*, 3rd edn (Munich, Beck, 2018) para 3 f.

[40] See M Klamert, 'Einheit und Fragmentierung im Unionsrecht' (2019) *Europarecht* Special Issue No 2, 133, with further references to legal theory. See also SEM Herlin Karnell and T Konstadinides, 'The Rise and Expressions of Consistency in EU Law: Legal and Strategic Implications for European

It is in this vein that Article 256(2) TFEU allows the General Court to refer a case to the ECJ for a ruling where it considers that the case requires a decision of principle likely to affect the 'unity or consistency of Union law'. Similarly, Article 256(3) TFEU puts certain decisions by the General Court to review by the ECJ 'where there is a serious risk of the unity or consistency of Union law being affected'.[41] Moreover, identical or similar legal concepts in different legal texts of Union law must be interpreted consistently, unless there are good reasons against such a systematic interpretation.[42]

Another variation of legal unity, and the one that interests us most here, is the unity of Union law with the legal systems of the Member States, which could be called composite legal unity. Unity in this sense has often been a cipher for a discussion of this relation in terms of monism and dualism.[43] That is not the focus we will have when discussing legal unity in connection with EU and national law. This form of legal unity can refer to cases where the ECJ has invoked unity and coherence to argue that the conditions for the non-contractual liability of the Union must be the same as those for the state liability of Member States,[44] regarding the system of interim relief between the Court of Justice and national courts as functional Union courts,[45] and concerning the system of judicial protection provided for by EU law.[46] As we will see in chapter five, this unity topos has also frequently appeared to frame the relationship between EU law and national law in 'positive', non-hierarchical terms, and without allusions to the theoretical 'baggage' that comes with a discussion in terms of monism and dualism.

3. The Order Introduced by the Lisbon Treaty

1. Introduction

According to the ECJ, '[The EU] legal structure is based on the fundamental premise that each Member State shares with all the other Member States, and recognises

Integration' (2012–13) *Cambridge Yearbook of European Legal Studies* 139 with further references to the literature on coherence in external relations and under the fundamental freedoms.

[41] See also Articles 62 and 62b of the Statutes of the ECJ. See S Hummelbrunner, 'The Unity and Consistency of Union Law' (2018) 73 *Zeitschrift fur Offentliches Recht* (*ZoR*): *Journal of Public Law* 295.

[42] See also Felix, *Einheit* (n 1) 157 f on unity of the legal system as a requirement for uniform terminology within the overall legal system.

[43] Compare, among others, P Eleftheriadis, 'The Structure of European Union Law' (2010) 12 *Cambridge Yearbook of European Legal Studies* 121, 148; S Griller, 'International Law, Human Rights and the European Community's Autonomous Legal Order: Notes on the European Court of Justice Decision in Kadi' (2008) 4 *European Constitutional Law Review* 528.

[44] Case C-352/98 P, *Bergaderm*, ECLI:EU:C:2000:361, para 41.

[45] eg, Joined Cases C-143/88 & C-92/89, *Süderdithmarschen*, ECLI:EU:C:1991:65, para 18.

[46] Case C-351/22, *Neves 77 Solutions*, ECLI:EU:C:2024:723.

that they share with it, a set of common values on which the EU is founded, as stated in Article 2 TEU'.[47] This implies that there is not only a network of norms and principles in EU law as mentioned above, but that there would be a 'legal structure' that has a certain foundation, which, in the view of the ECJ, lies in the EU's values.

In the following, we will discuss the interrelations between the EU's values in Article 2 TEU, its objectives listed in Article 3 TEU, and the principles provided in Articles 4, 5 and 6 TEU.

2. On the Interrelation between Values and Objectives

Article 2 TEU merges what formerly was provided in several Articles to create one single 'homogeneity' clause. Article F(1) of the Treaty of Maastricht introduced democracy as a basis of the Union. The Treaty of Amsterdam included a reference to the rule of law and human rights. The Treaty of Lisbon added minority protection and rebranded the newly codified principles as 'values'. Now, according to Article 2 TEU, the Union 'is founded on the values of respect for human dignity, freedom, democracy, equality, the rule of law and respect for human rights, including the rights of persons belonging to minorities'. These values would be 'common to the Member States in a society in which pluralism, non-discrimination, tolerance, justice, solidarity and equality between women and men prevail'. It has been noted that the values would be substantive norms.[48]

Article 3 TEU (following the approach of Article I-3 of the Constitutional Treaty) merges the objectives of the TEU with those of the former EC Treaty, adding the promotion of peace, cultural and linguistic diversity, and cultural heritage. Summarily, the objectives in Article 3 TEU concern: (1) the area of freedom, security and justice; (2) the internal market; (3) social affairs and equal treatment; (4) cohesion; (5) culture; (6) economic and monetary union; and (7) external action. These objectives clearly also have substantive content as they determine in which (policy) fields the European Union can act.

There arguably is no ranking between the individual objectives in Article 3 TEU.[49] Moreover, there is no reason to assume that Union objectives that are not mentioned in Article 3 TEU, such as the 'mainstreaming' objectives set out in the provisions in Title II of Part One TFEU (Articles 8–17 TFEU), are less important

[47] *ECHR II* (n 4) para 168. See also Case C-455/14 P, *EUPM in Bosnia and Herzegovina*, ECLI:EU:C:2016:569, para 41, and Case C-483/20, *Commissaire général aux réfugiés et aux apatrides*, ECLI:EU:C:2022:103, para 27.

[48] See Spieker, *EU Values Before the Court of Justice* (n 18) 4.

[49] See J-P Jacqué, 'Art 3 EUV' in H von der Groeben, J Schwarze and A Hatje (eds), *Europäisches Unionsrecht*, 7th edn (Baden-Baden, Nomos, 2015) para 3. On possible conflicts between objectives, see Case 139/80, *Maizena v Council (Isoglucose)*, ECLI:EU:C:1980:250, para 23, and Case 9/56, *Meroni*, ECLI:EU:C:1958:7, on the ECSC.

for the Union than the objectives in Article 3 TEU. As has been argued, '[a]ll these objectives are to be treated on equal footing with the objectives set for the Union in other specific provisions of the Treaties'.[50]

It would seem that not all values laid down in Article 2 TEU (such as freedom) can be assigned to objectives in Article 3 TEU, nor are Union values necessarily corresponding with objectives (such as cultural policy). Thus, it is unlikely that one can (still) speak of a system of 'cascades of concretisation'[51] concerning the relationship between Article 2 TEU on the values of the Union and Article 3 TEU on its objectives. However, values and objectives are intertwined in so far as Article 3(1) TEU defines the goal of promoting the values of the Union, and some values in Article 2 TEU (freedom, non-discrimination, justice, solidarity, equality of women and men) are also objectives in Article 3 TEU. Article 3(5) TEU on the Union's objectives states that in its relations with the wider world, the Union shall uphold and promote its values and interests.[52]

3. On the Interrelation between Values and Structural Principles

It is obvious that there are overlaps between the values in Article 2 TEU and the general principles under Article 6 TEU.[53] The picture is more opaque when we look at the principles that are the focus of this book.

Often, the values in Article 2 TEU are referred to as principles.[54] Thus, it has been argued that Article 2 TEU would contain principles, which, despite certain interplays, could be distinguished from structural principles 'such as autonomy, primacy, direct effect, the principles of conferral, subsidiarity, mutual loyalty, or national identity'.[55] Also the Court speaks of 'the principle of solidarity, mentioned

[50] See K Lenaerts, P van Nuffel and T Corthaut, *EU Constitutional Law* (Oxford, Oxford University Press, 2021) para 5.007.

[51] See F Reimer, 'Ziele und Zuständigkeiten: Die Funktionen der Unionszielbestimmungen' (2003) *Europarecht* 993.

[52] See also the CFSP 'convergence clause', Article 32 TEU, and Article 42(5) TEU on the common security and defence policy.

[53] See M Klamert and D Kochenov, 'Commentary on Article 2 TEU' in M Kellerbauer, M Klamert and J Tomkin (eds), *The EU Treaties and the Charter of Fundamental Rights: A Commentary*, 2nd edn (Oxford, Oxford University Press, 2024) para 6, with further references. See also LS Rossi, 'La valeur juridique des valeurs. L'article 2 TUE: relations avec d'autres dispositions de droit primaire de l'Union européenne et remèdes jurisdictionnels' (2020) *Révue trimestrielle de droit européen* 639, 653 f.

[54] See, eg, C Calliess, 'Art 1 EUV' in Calliess and Ruffert (eds), *EUV/AEUV*, para 1, who, in addition to the principles of 'integration', transparency, proximity to citizens and subsidiarity in Article 1 TEU, also declares the values of Article 2 TEU to be structural principles. On conceptual matters regarding Article 2 TEU, see, eg, JP Terhechte, '§ 14 Prinzipienordnung der Europäischen Union' in A Hatje and P Müller-Graff (eds), *Europäisches Organisations- und Verfassungsrecht*, 2nd edn (Baden-Baden, Nomos, 2022) 773, 779.

[55] See Spieker, *EU Values Before the Court of Justice* (n 18) 4.

in Article 2 TEU'.[56] While they have been called as such before the Treaty of Lisbon, it would seem that there was a conscious decision to now refer to them as values. Moreover, as we have shown above, there is an abundance of 'principles' in the Treaties and case law. At the same time, when we define principles (broadly) as very important norms that can be more formal or more axiological, as suggested in chapter one, it is indeed apposite to also refer to the values in Article 2 TEU as principles. It should then however be clarified that the values in Article 2 TEU do not have the same normative function as, for example, the 'principle of conferral' in Article 5 TEU. We will discuss in chapter five whether the rule of law can be seen as a distinct principle of EU law.

It is submitted that there are several direct and more indirect connections between structural principles and values.

Mutual trust is the principle with perhaps the most direct connection to the Union's values. Starting with Opinion 2/13, the Court held that the European Union is built on the 'fundamental premise' that each Member State shares these values with all the other Member States, and recognises that they share them with it, which would imply and justify the existence of mutual trust between the Member States 'that those values will be recognised and, therefore, that the law of the EU that implements them will be respected'.[57] As we will see in chapter three, mutual trust in turn has several interrelations with other principles discussed in this book such as, especially, Member State equality, loyalty, and solidarity and will be further discussed in this context.

Effective judicial protection will be discussed in this book as part of the structural principle of effectiveness and is a hallmark of the value of the rule of law. Solidarity can also be assigned to the values of Article 2 TEU, if alone for the fact that solidarity is mentioned in Article 2 TEU.

With some principles, a more indirect, implicit connection with values can be made. Thus, the principles of state liability and supremacy/primacy could be seen as expressions of the value of the rule of law. It has also been argued that competences can be understood as a manifestation of the rule of law, and respectively a 'principle of constitutional legality'.[58] Moreover, the democracy value undoubtedly stands in relation to the principle of conferral including the principle of institutional balance.

There is an indirect connection between Article 2 TEU and Article 4(2) TEU on the national identities of the Member States.[59] In 2022, the Full Court held that the

[56] Case C-157/21, *Poland v Parliament and Council (Conditionality mechanism)*, ECLI:EU:C:2022:98, para 147; Case C-156/21, *Hungary v Parliament and Council (Conditionality mechanism)*, ECLI:EU:C:2022:97, para 129.

[57] *ECHR II* (n 4) para 168; Case C-284/16, *Achmea*, ECLI:EU:C:2018:158, para 34; Joined Cases C-83/19 et al, *Asociația 'Forumul Judecătorilor din România'*, ECLI:EU:C:2021:393, para 160, and Joined Cases C-357/19 et al, *Euro Box Promotion*, ECLI:EU:C:2021:1034, para 160. See Klamert and Kochenov, 'Commentary on Article 2 TEU' (n 53) para 8; K Lenaerts, 'La vie après l'avis: Exploring the Principle of Mutual (Yet Not Blind) Trust' (2017) 54 *CML Rev* 805.

[58] A von Bogdandy and J Bast, 'The Federal Order of Competences' in A von Bogdandy and J Bast (eds), *Principles of European Constitutional Law*, 2nd edn (Oxford, Hart Publishing, 2009) 275, 278.

[59] See A Haratsch, 'Nationale Identität aus europarechtlicher Sicht' (2016) 51 *Europarecht* 131, 142.

values contained in Article 2 TEU 'define the very identity of the European Union as a common legal order'.[60] Article 2 TEU can thus be seen as an expression of an 'EU identity', outlining the constitutional core of the Union as a legal–political system.[61] In that sense, Article 4(2) TEU would represent the 'other side', a distinct identity of the Member States that is however embedded within EU law and couched in the values Article 2 TEU proclaims to be common to the Member States. Thus, it has been argued that Article 4(2) TEU cannot protect the 'national constitutional space' if this would weaken the EU's values.[62]

The Full Court has also held that, for this reason, the European Union must be able to defend those values, within the limits of its powers as laid down by the Treaties.[63] Thus, values (in that case the rule of law), in accordance with the principle of conferral and the principle of consistency, can constitute 'the basis of a conditionality mechanism covered by the concept of 'financial rules' within the meaning of Article 322(1)(a) TFEU'.[64] Short of constituting a fully-fledged legal basis, values can thus influence what can be enacted based on legal bases in the Treaties.

Case law on the principle of autonomy, discussed in chapter three, suggests that the ECJ might see that principle as linked with values in the sense that it serves the aim of their protection.[65] In that vein, values would represent substantive meta-characteristics of EU law, which are safeguarded through the principle of autonomy. However, as we will discuss in chapter three, the case law of the Court is more nuanced and more circumspect and does not (yet) make such a clear connection.

There is, in any case, a commonality between the values in Article 2 TEU and structural principles in how they function. Both transcend the scope of application of Union law as well as the scope of the competences of the European Union.[66] Starting with the *Portuguese judges (ASJP)* case, the ECJ established that violations by Member States of the principle of judicial independence, a core part of the rule of law value, fall within the scope of EU law, irrespective of whether the European Union has competence for these matters.[67] A similar claim could be made for loyalty or non-discrimination based on nationality.

Despite these interrelations and commonalities, we do not think that it would be accurate to say that values and structural principles are systematically linked.

[60] *Hungary v Parliament and Council (Conditionality mechanism)* (n 56) para 127.

[61] Compare now A von Bogdandy, *The Emergence of European Society through Public Law: A Hegelian and Anti-Schmittian Approach*, Collected Courses of the Academy of European Law (Oxford, Oxford University Press, 2024). Compare also the perspective of Rossi, 'La valeur juridique' (n 53) 642–46.

[62] See Lenaerts, van Nuffel and Corthaut, *EU Constitutional Law* (n 50) para 5.041.

[63] *Poland v Parliament and Council (Conditionality mechanism)* (n 56) para 145.

[64] *Poland v Parliament and Council (Conditionality mechanism)* (n 56) para 146.

[65] Compare K Lenaerts and JA Gutiérrez-Fons, 'Epilogue. High Hopes: Autonomy and the Identity of the EU' (2023) 8 *European Papers* 1495. Critical of this is J van de Beeten, 'On Metaphor and Meaning: The Autonomy of EU Legal Order Through the Lens of Project and System' (2023) 8 *European Papers* 1441.

[66] See M Hilf and F Schorkopf, 'Art 2 EUV' in E Grabitz, M Hilf and M Nettesheim (eds), *EU-Kommentar* (Munich, Beck, 2020) para 18.

[67] Case C-64/16, *Associação Sindical dos Juízes Portugueses*, ECLI:EU:C:2018:117, para 29.

Structural principles could (and mostly did) exist without (and before) the values. It would thus seem challenging to conceive the structure of EU law alone through the lens of values. While they can explain many characteristics of EU law and can also be connected to a number of structural principles, it is submitted that a principle such as autonomy or loyalty in all its manifestations cannot fully be explained as giving expression to the values in Article 2 TEU.[68]

4. On the Interrelation between Objectives and Structural Principles

The objectives laid down in Article 3 TEU generally do not have an independent function in EU law, they 'merely lay down a programme', with their implementation to be achieved through the policies and actions of the Union as well as those of the Member States.[69] The pursuit of the objectives of Article 3 TEU 'is entrusted to a series of fundamental provisions, such as those providing for the free movement of goods, services, capital and persons, citizenship of the Union, the area of freedom, security and justice, and competition policy'.[70] They cannot, therefore, 'unlike the specific provisions of the TEU Treaty that implement the general objectives which it sets out and govern the matter in question, form part of the parameters for assessing the conformity with primary law of a provision of secondary legislation'.[71]

Thus, the objectives in Article 3 TEU as well as those in other provisions of the Treaties are not general principles in the sense that they are a standard of review for secondary law.[72] They are concretised by substantive principles of EU law such as the fundamental freedoms.

There are some explicit connections made in primary law between objectives and structural principles.

Objectives are linked with conferral through Article 1 TEU which states that the Member States 'confer competences to attain objectives they have in common' on the Union, as is also discussed in chapter three. The objectives of Article 3

[68] Compare Spieker, *EU Values Before the Court of Justice* (n 18) 97: 'On the one hand, one could reject the inclusion of these principles into the proposed scheme as they are either a premise or – concerning the latter three – an effect of EU law but not part of EU constitutional law itself'.

[69] Case C-149/96, *Portugal v Council*, ECLI:EU:C:1999:574, para 86. See also Case C-304/21, *Ministero dell'Interno (Limite d'âge pour le recrutement des commissaires de police)*, ECLI:EU:C:2022:897, para 34: 'Article 3 TEU merely sets out the objectives of the Union, which are made explicit by other provisions of the Treaties'.

[70] *ECHR II* (n 4) para 172.

[71] See Joined Cases C-541/20 to C-555/20, *Mobility Package*, ECLI:EU:C:2024:818, para 424. See Case 6/72, *Europemballage*, ECLI:EU:C:1973:22, para 23.

[72] See however K-P Sommermann, 'Art 3 TEU' in H-J Blanke and S Mangiameli (eds), *The Treaty on European Union (TEU): A Commentary* (New York, Springer, 2013) paras 9–11 (p 157 (162–64)) who argues for a categorical equivalence of objectives and principles such as equal treatment.

TEU would therefore express 'the common European interest'.[73] We will return to this common interest in chapter three when we discuss the nature of conferral in EU law.

For the assessment of subsidiarity, the qualitative added value of EU action must be assessed in the light of the Union's objectives (and its values).[74] At the same time, neither are all competences of the European Union reflected in the objectives nor can all objectives mentioned in Article 3 TEU be achieved by the European Union (alone).[75] The second subparagraph of Article 3(3) TEU mentions promoting 'social justice and protection', the solidarity between generations, and the protection of the rights of the child, all of which are hard to assign to Union competences.[76]

The Union's objectives are also referred to in Article 4(3) TEU on the principle of loyalty, according to which the Member States 'shall facilitate the achievement of the Union's tasks and refrain from any measure which could jeopardise the attainment of the Union's objectives'.[77] Notably, ex Article 5 EC in conjunction with the Treaty objective for transport policy played an important role in establishing exclusive external competence in *ERTA*.[78] However, in some cases, the Court has explicitly refused to attach legal effects to a combination of objectives and what is now Article 4(3) TEU.[79]

Article 3(3) TEU states that the Union shall promote 'solidarity among Member States'. This is one of the many cases where a positive notion of solidarity (not towards Union citizens but) between the Member States is mentioned in the Treaties. As an objective, there is no clear-cut competence norm to achieve this, but some Treaty provisions allow for secondary law to this end, as discussed in chapter three.

According to the fourth subparagraph of Article 3(3) TEU, the Union shall respect its rich cultural and linguistic diversity and shall ensure that its cultural heritage is safeguarded and enhanced.[80] This can be seen in connection with the principle of national identity, which concerns the protection of a state's official national language, among others, as also discussed in chapter three.

[73] Opinion of AG Kokott in Case C-358/14, *Poland v Parliament and Council*, ECLI:EU:C:2015:848, para 164.

[74] AG Kokott in *Poland v Parliament and Council* (n 73) para 165. See M Klamert, 'Commentary on Article 5 TEU' in Kellerbauer, Klamert and Tomkin (eds), *Commentary*, paras 28–29.

[75] See J Larik, 'From Speciality to a Constitutional Sense of Purpose: On the Changing Role of the Objectives of the European Union' (2014) 63 *ICLQ* 935, 936, making the point that 'more objectives do not equal more power'.

[76] See M Klamert, 'Commentary on Article 3 TEU' in Kellerbauer, Klamert and Tomkin (eds), *Commentary*, para 16.

[77] Case 22/70, *Commission v Council (ERTA)*, ECLI:EU:C:1971:32, para 22.

[78] *ERTA* (n 77) para 22. See Klamert, 'Commentary on Article 3 TEU' (n 76) para 17.

[79] Case 229/83, *Leclerc*, ECLI:EU:C:1985:1, para 20; Case 254/87, *Syndicat des libraires de Normandie*, ECLI:EU:C:1988:413, para 15; Case C-379/98, *PreussenElektra*, ECLI:EU:C:2001:160, para 65. Compare also M Klamert, *The Principle of Loyalty in EU Law* (Oxford, Oxford University Press, 2014) 122–23.

[80] See also Recitals 3–4 of the Preamble to the TEU, Article 107(3d) TFEU, Article 165 TFEU, and Article 207(4) subpara 3(a) TFEU.

Recently, the Court has allowed exceptionally and provisionally maintaining certain effects of an annulled national measure, seeking to reconcile the principles of legality and primacy of EU law, on the one hand, and the necessity of protecting the environment stemming from Article 3(3) TEU and Article 191(1) and (2) TFEU, on the other.[81]

Again, as with values, while there are interrelations between objectives and structural principles, they are not on a scale where one could speak of a structure involving these two sources. It seems unlikely that the drafters of the Treaty made a conscious effort to 'construct' primary law with a view on Article 3 TFEU.

4. Is there an Order among the Principles in the Treaties?

Articles 1–5 TEU contain several structural principles. However, it is submitted that, from the wording and structure of the Treaties, one cannot readily assume that conferral or also loyalty are more important than other principles provided in these provisions, such as subsidiarity. Moreover, none of these principles would seem to be more important than principles *not* (explicitly) provided in the EU Treaties, such as supremacy/primacy or autonomy. Thus, the text of the Treaties does not suggest that structural principles in particular are provided in a certain order of weight, or that certain parts of the Treaties (such as Articles 1–5 TEU) (conclusively) enshrine the structural principles of the Union.[82]

It is more convincing to claim that Articles 1–19 TEU comprise the constitutional core or 'basic part' of EU law, because this takes account of Article 13 TEU on institutional balance and horizontal loyalty and Article 19 TEU on the jurisdiction of the Court, both of which had an important role in case law in the last years.[83] One could also argue that the principle of autonomy can be located in Articles 1 *and* 19 TEU, solidarity in Article 3 TEU, and supremacy in Articles 4(3) and 19(1) TEU, as will be discussed in chapter three.

However, there arguably would still be tension with the fact that structural principles (like general principles) can be unwritten and can even be inherent sources of EU law, which would repudiate the need to locate them in any part of

[81] Case C-41/11, *Inter-Environnement Wallonie and Terre wallonne*, ECLI:EU:C:2012:103, paras 58–63; Case C-379/15, *Association France Nature*, ECLI:EU:C:2016:603, paras 28–43. See M Klamert, 'Commentary on Article 1 TEU' in Kellerbauer, Klamert and Tomkin (eds), *Commentary*, para 36.

[82] Compare, however, Calliess, 'Art 1 EUV' (n 54) para 1, who argues that Article 1 TEU as well as Article 2, Article 4 and Article 6 TEU would express various structural principles constituting the EU, which define the essential legitimising foundations of the Union.

[83] See A von Bogdandy and J Bast (eds), *Unionsverfassungsrecht – Eine Neubestimmung anhand der Grundlagen im EU-Vertrag* (Baden-Baden, Nomos, 2025); J Bast and A von Bogdandy, 'The constitutional core of the Union: On the CJEU's new, principled constitutionalism' (2024) 61 *CML Rev* 1471.

primary law.[84] Such a 'core' claim would also, in our view, be difficult to square with the fundamental, structural relevance of the prohibition of discrimination based on nationality in EU law as explained in chapter three, which is provided in Article 18 TFEU and would then have to be subsumed under 'equality' in Article 2 TEU.

5. Conclusions

While the Treaty of Lisbon has certainly structured primary law better than previous Treaties, the relations between the various types of norms contained in Articles 2–6 TEU comprising values, objectives and principles are not fully coherent. This also concerns the relationship between the principles analysed in this book as it presents itself in the Treaties. In chapter six, we will discuss a possible ranking of structural principles more broadly, and not only in view of how they are or are not presented in primary law.

By insisting that Union law has a 'structure' in cases such as Opinion 2/13, the Court has arguably tried to frame the Union legal order in more constitutional terms. It seems to be an(other) implicit attempt to distance EU law from international law also on this 'structural' account. International law may not be a random collection of norms as discussed above, but it is certainly placed at the other end of the spectrum from nation states in this regard. The more 'structured' and systematic EU law were to be, the more it would resemble a (national) constitution. The more this structure were to be interlinked and interwoven with the laws of the Member States, the stronger would be the legal unity between EU law and national law. We will return to legal unity as a 'grand narrative' about EU law in chapter five.

We have suggested that the metaphor of a network linking the European Union and its Member States (and the Member States with each other) is useful for avoiding a discussion of this relationship in terms of hierarchies and ranked order. Talking about a network/networks is not only a more positive framing of these relationships, it is also familiar from discussions in (international) constitutional law.

In the following, we will explore whether such a network indeed exists and what it tells us about the individual structural principles.

[84] See also M Cremona, 'Structural Principles of External Relations Law' in M Cremona (ed), *Structural Principles in EU External Relations Law* (Oxford, Oxford University Press, 2018) 3. Compare, however, M Ruffert, 'Art 1 AEUV' in Calliess and Ruffert (eds), *EUV/AEUV*, para 10 et seq, who distinguishes from the general principles of law special structural principles, which, however, would not be an independent source of law because such sources must always be traceable to the wording of the Treaties.

III

Deconstructing the 'Structured Network of Principles'

1. Introduction

We will discuss structural principles in the order they appear in the Treaties, assuming that the principle of autonomy can be located under Article 1 of the Treaty on European Union (TEU). This means we will start with autonomy, followed by conferral stated in Articles 3(6) and 4(1) TEU, among other places, equality comprising both Member State equality in Article 4(2) TEU and non-discrimination of individuals in Article 18 of the Treaty on the Functioning of the European Union (TFEU), national identity mentioned in Article 4(2) TEU, loyalty enshrined in Article 4(3) TEU, solidarity first mentioned as a principle in Article 24 TEU, and finally supremacy/primacy as well as effectiveness including effective judicial protection, which cannot be located in the Treaties with certainty. As mentioned, this list is not meant to be definitive. Moreover, it is not the aim of this book to discuss all facets of these different principles, which would exceed the bounds of this study and has already been done elsewhere for most principles.

This chapter follows a certain sequence in analysing structural principles. We will start by laying out the 'origins' of the respective principles, meaning whether they have been derived from international law, national law or whether they are 'unique' to EU law. Note that we will not consider at that point how Union law presents itself *today* (in many respects very differently from the beginning of European integration). Thus, focusing on public international law when discussing the roots of structural principles in this chapter does not ignore that some principles, such as conferral, might today be seen in a much brighter 'constitutional' light. Note further that, when looking at the EU's inception more broadly, a more 'federal' impression may be gained.[1] We will, by contrast, be concerned more narrowly with the origins of structural principles.

It will be discussed where structural principles are currently located in the Treaties if they can be located there at all. This will be followed by an examination of how the principles operate, meaning whether and how they are applied in

[1] Compare, eg, R Schütze, 'On "Federal" Ground: The European Union as an (Inter)national Phenomenon' (2009) 46 *CML Rev* 1069, 1088–89: 'Functionally, then, the European Union is based on a "constitutional treaty" that assumes and stands on federal middle ground'.

a normative way. It is useful to recall that the principles covered by Article 6 TEU are all directly effective and constitute standards for the review and interpretation of EU law. They can also all be balanced with other such principles. It will therefore be one aim of this chapter to see whether that is also true for structural principles.

Last but not least, it will be shown that structural principles are interrelated in many ways with each other. More of these interrelations will be discussed in chapter four in the context of the EU's external relations.

2. The Principle of Autonomy

1. Introduction

It is somewhat surprising that autonomy has never featured prominently among the principles that have been called constitutional, systemic or structural principles, as shown earlier. After all, *Van Gend* and *Costa* are easily the two most famous cases in EU law and both are widely associated with the autonomy of the European Union and EU law.

Not only is autonomy apparently not considered *on a par* with supremacy or loyalty, but, for quite some time, the concept of autonomy has arguably been somewhat under-researched relative to the importance of *Van Gend* and *Costa*.[2] When autonomy was discussed in the literature, it has often been treated as an idiosyncratic notion of EU law rather than as a concern common to all international organisations, as has been stressed recently.[3]

The main problem when discussing legal concepts of autonomy is that there seems to be general agreement that it is enigmatic, or put less positively, confounding. This assessment is true even when discussing autonomy only in the present context, ignoring related concepts of the autonomy of the Member States (from the European Union!) relevant to the indirect enforcement of Union law and 'strategic' autonomy relevant in the context of the common commercial policy.

Unsurprisingly, this is confirmed in the following where we can only try to usefully structure the various manifestations of autonomy, which had already presented themselves at the early stages of European integration. We will in the

[2] As far as we can see, the first monographs on autonomy since R Barents, *The Autonomy of Community Law* (The Hague, Kluwer Law International, 2004) came out only recently. See C Langenfeld, *Die Autonomie des Unionsrechts in der EuGH-Rechtsprechung* [*The Autonomy of EU Law in the Case Law of the European Court of Justice*] (Tübingen, Mohr Siebeck, 2024); AM Könneke, *Unionsrechtsperson – Rekonstruktion der institutionellen Autonomie der Europäischen Union* [*EU Legal Person. A Reconstruction of the Institutional Autonomy of the European Union*] (Tübingen, Mohr Siebeck, 2024); HM Reissner, *Die Autonomie der Unionsrechtsordnung* [*The Autonomy of Union Law*] (Tübingen, Mohr Siebeck, 2023); and C Contartese, *The Principle of Autonomy in EU External Relations Law*. (Milan, Wolters Kluwer, 2025).

[3] M Konstantinidis, 'Demystifying Autonomy: Tracing the International Law Origins of the EU Principle of Autonomy' (2024) 25 *German Law Journal* 94, 94.

following distinguish internal (institutional and substantive) autonomy from external (institutional and substantive) autonomy in a way that might differ from other taxonomies in the literature and does not claim to be fully 'confusion-proof'.[4]

2. Origins

2.1. National Constitutional Law

Autonomy of course is an old concept that translates from Ancient Greek as 'one who gives oneself one's own law'.[5] While nation states are in that sense autonomous by nature because being autonomous entities is inherent in their statehood, this is commonly expressed with the notion of sovereignty.[6]

Yet, it has been noted that also in domestic systems concerns about autonomy regarding the interpretative monopoly of their highest courts and the effectiveness of their legal rules similar to those at issue in the European Union discussed below can exist.[7] While it is true that states can also seek to be independent from international law there is, it is submitted, a crucial difference with international organisations that is greatly exacerbating this autonomy concern.

International organisations are contractual entities created by (autonomous or sovereign) states. Thus, with international organisations autonomy is not only concerned with their independence from (other) international law but perhaps even to a greater extent with independence from their Member States, as will be discussed in the following.

While in federal (German) theory, the terms 'sovereignty' (of the federal level) and 'autonomy' (of the state level) were established, it has been argued that the conceptual origins of EU autonomy would lie in public international law.[8]

2.2. Public International Law

In public international law, different conceptions of autonomy exist, with often unclear delimitations. In an entirely different context, Article 3(a) of the Convention

[4] Compare, eg, T Schilling, 'The Autonomy of the Community Legal Order: An Analysis of Possible Foundations', available at: www.jeanmonnetprogram.org/archive/papers/96/9610-The.html, who distinguishes original, derivative and interpretative autonomy.

[5] See: en.wikipedia.org/wiki/Autonomy.

[6] See V Moreno-Lax and KS Ziegler, 'Autonomy of the EU Legal Order – a General Principle? On the Risks of Normative Functionalism and Selective Constitutionalisation' in KS Ziegler, PJ Neuvonen and V Moreno-Lax (eds), *Research Handbook on General Principles in EU Law: Constructing Legal Orders in Europe* (Cheltenham, Edward Elgar, 2022) 227, 236; Konstantinidis, 'Demystifying Autonomy' (n 3) 94.

[7] See C Krenn, 'Autonomy and Effectiveness as Common Concerns: A Path to ECHR Accession After Opinion 2/13' (2015) 16 *German Law Journal* 147, 162, arguing that any constitutional court would say that its understanding of autonomy, its constitutional principles, and its judicial system are particularly worth preserving.

[8] See Langenfeld, *Die Autonomie des Unionsrechts in der EuGH-Rechtsprechung* (n 2) 30–37.

on the Rights of Persons with Disabilities defines autonomy as including 'the freedom to make one's own choices, and independence of persons'.[9] More pertinently, in a frequently cited contribution, the autonomy of international organisations under international law has been described as 'multifaceted', manifesting itself as 'political', 'institutional', or 'substantive' and 'systemic' autonomy.[10] Political autonomy would involve matters such as whether an organisation can dissolve itself and the question of its joint or concurrent responsibility; institutional autonomy would relate to the extent to which international organisations constitute a legal order distinct from the general international legal order, and 'substantive' and 'systemic' would seem to specifically describe the autonomy of EU law.[11]

According to this theory, political autonomy refers to the ability of an organisation to express a distinct, separate will from its contractual parties.[12] It would also relate to its treaty-making powers and thus its capacity to enter into legal relations with other subjects of international law.[13] In public international law, the autonomy of an international organisation is therefore closely connected to the question of whether it has legal personality.[14] This question would be a 'yes or no question', different from the other questions discussed under autonomy.[15]

Note that all this frames autonomy in a rather positive light.[16] Autonomy, by this understanding, is something an international organisation possesses respectively and is endowed with (a distinct will, treaty-making powers, legal personality). The distinction between political and institutional autonomy seems confusing in cases where international organisations have their own institutions, whose autonomy vis-a-vis the respective organisations' members is thus not only 'political' but always also 'institutional'.

2.3. *Lessons for Discussing the Autonomy of the European Union*

When discussing the European Union below against the background of international law, it seems more useful to distinguish 'internal' from 'external' autonomy,

[9] Resolution adopted by the General Assembly on 13 December 2006, A/RES/61/106.

[10] See J d'Aspremont, 'The multifaceted concept of the autonomy of international organizations and international legal discourse' in R Collins and N White (eds), *International Organizations and the Idea of Autonomy* (London, Routledge, 2011) 63.

[11] See d'Aspremont, 'The multifaceted concept of the autonomy' (n 10) 65–70, 70–76 and 75–76.

[12] See d'Aspremont, 'The multifaceted concept of the autonomy' (n 10) 63–64.

[13] See JE Alvarez, *International Organisations as Law-makers* (Oxford, Oxford University Press, 2005) 129.

[14] See Moreno-Lax and Ziegler, 'Autonomy of the EU Legal Order' (n 6) 237.

[15] See T Gazzini, 'Legal Personality of International Organisations' in J Klabbers and Å Wallendahl (eds), *Research Handbook on the Law of International Organisations* (Cheltenham, Edward Elgar, 2010) 33, 43.

[16] See J Odermatt, 'The Principle of Autonomy: An Adolescent Disease of EU External Relations Law?' in M Cremona (ed), *Structural Principles in EU External Relations Law* (Oxford, Oxford University Press, 2018) 291, 295. See also R Collins and N White, 'International Organizations and the Idea of Autonomy: Introduction and Overview' in Collins and White, *International Organizations* 1, 2.

and not put the focus on what an international organisation wants to possess, but on what it does *not* want, viz internally to be dependent from its Member States and externally to be dependent on other legal regimes.[17]

Internal autonomy of an international organisation would thus relate to the degree it can act independently from the states that have established it.[18] This form of 'internal' autonomy cannot be 'absolute', but remains determined and constrained by the powers conferred upon international organisations to fulfil the functions for which they were constituted and is, therefore, always more limited than that of states.[19] The degree of autonomy is determined by how independent the founding Treaty allows an organisation and its institutions to be, such as by foreseeing veto powers for its members or providing for some form of majority decision.[20] While internal autonomy will commonly be institutional, in EU law this also comprises substantive elements determining how EU law is interpreted.

External autonomy would concern the independence of an international organisation from (broadly speaking) international law and, it is submitted, can also be either institutional or substantive. It is institutional if the autonomy concern relates primarily to the independence of the organisation's institutions from influence by institutions set up under another treaty, such as the autonomy of the jurisdiction of an 'internal' from the jurisdiction of an 'external' court. It is substantive if the autonomy concern relates primarily to the refusal to abide by legal standards imposed by international law, such as with the *lex posterior* principle in *Costa* and the denial of effective judicial protection in *Kadi* discussed below.

The substantive and institutional dimensions of autonomy are closely related both internally and externally because the protection of substantive standards can only be ensured through the final jurisdiction of the European Court of Justice (ECJ).

[17] Other distinctions suggested in the literature are between normative and regulatory autonomy, see C Eckes, 'The Autonomy of the EU Legal Order: The Case of the Energy Charter Treaty' (2023) 8 *European Papers* 1465, and between purposive, substantive and institutional autonomy, see N Nic Shuibhne, 'What is the autonomy of EU law, and why does that matter?' (2019) 88 *Nordic Journal of International Law* 9.

[18] In its Advisory Opinion *Legality of the Use by a State of Nuclear Weapons in Armed Conflict* (1966) ICJ Reports 66, para 19, the ICJ speaks of 'new subjects of law endowed with a *certain* autonomy, to which the parties entrust the task of realizing common goals' (emphasis added).

[19] See B de Witte, 'European Union Law: How Autonomous is its Legal Order?' (2010) 65 *Zeitschrift fur Offentliches Recht* (ZoR): *Journal of Public Law* 141, 142. See also BVerfG, *Lisbon Treaty*, 2 BvE 2/08 et al, para 231, where the German Federal Constitutional Court, while conceding that Union law establishes 'a supranational autonomy which undoubtedly makes considerable inroads into everyday political life', states that such influence would be factually limited and 'autonomy can only be understood – as is usual regarding the law of self-government – as an autonomy to rule which is independent but derived, i.e. is granted by other legal entities'.

[20] See N Blokker, 'International Organisations and its Members' (2004) 1 *International Organisations Law Review* 139; ND White, 'Separate but Connected: Inter-Governmental Organizations and International Law' (2008) 5 *International Organisations Law Review* 175.

2.4. The Early Case Law of the European Courts

2.4.1. Introduction

I have written elsewhere, probably in line with the most commonly held view in the literature, that autonomy was introduced in *Van Gend en Loos* of 1963 and in *Costa* of 1964.[21] Both cases will be discussed later in the context of the principles of direct effect and supremacy. Suffice to note here that in *Van Gend*, the ECJ characterised the (then) European Economic Community as 'constitut[ing] a new legal order of international law for the benefit of which the states have limited their sovereign rights'.[22] In *Costa*, the ECJ explained that '[b]y contrast with ordinary international treaties, the EEC Treaty has created its own legal system' and characterised EU law as 'stemming from … an independent source of law'.[23] In doing so, the Court emphasised the permanence of the European Union ('a Community of unlimited duration'), its personality and capacity of representation, and the independence of its 'own' institutions.[24]

In the literature, there is some disagreement on how predictable this case law had been for the Member States.[25] Two things can be noted with certainty, however. First, neither *Van Gend* nor *Costa* referred (in their English version) to the concept of autonomy. One reason might be that this concept, as shown above, was established in international (organisations) law and the last thing, it is suggested, the Court wanted to do in these two cases was to talk in the 'language' of public international law. Nonetheless, 'autonomy', and even a 'principle' of autonomy, have been referred to in the context of the European Union in the case law of the Court some years before *Van Gend* and *Costa*.

The following also shows how multifaceted the concept of autonomy has been since the beginning of EU integration. All four forms of autonomy have already presented themselves. We will discuss the case law chronologically, and will therefore switch between internal and external and institutional and substantive autonomy.

2.4.2. Internal Institutional Autonomy

According to Article 8 of the European Coal and Steel Community (ECSC), the High Authority was 'responsible for assuring the fulfilment of the purposes stated

[21] Case 26/62, *Van Gend & Loos*, ECLI:EU:C:1963:1; Case 6/64, *Costa/ENEL*, ECLI:EU:C:1964:66. See M Klamert, 'The Autonomy of the EU (and of EU Law): Through the Kaleidoscope' (2017) 42 *EL Rev* 815.

[22] *Van Gend & Loos* (n 21).

[23] *Costa/ENEL* (n 21). The French version of the judgment used the term autonomous: '*issue d'une source autonome*'.

[24] *Costa/ENEL* (n 21).

[25] See the accounts by P Pescatore, 'Van Gend en Loos, 3 February 1963 – A View from Within' in M Poiares Maduro and L Azoulai (eds), *The Past and Future of EU Law: The Classics of EU Law Revisited on the 50th Anniversary of the Rome Treaty* (Oxford, Hart Publishing, 2010) 3 (emphasising precedents) and M Rasmussen, 'From Costa v ENEL to the Treaties of Rome: A Brief History of a Legal Revolution' in Poiares Maduro and Azoulai, *The Past and Future of EU Law* 69 ('accidental' revolution).

in the present Treaty under the terms thereof'. This was read in *Fédéchar* that the High Authority would enjoy 'a certain independence in determining the implementing measures necessary for the attainment of the objectives referred to in the Treaty'.[26]

Article 6(4) of the ECSC Treaty provided that the ECSC 'shall be represented by its institutions, each one of them acting within the framework of its *own* powers and responsibilities'.[27] In *Algera* of 1957, the Court interpreted this provision as follows:

> The institutions are autonomous within the limits of their powers ...
>
> [Article 6(4) ECSC Treaty] applies to all the institutions of the Community without distinction; the fact that the Common Assembly has special powers changes nothing in that respect; its functional autonomy exists only with in the limits of its powers, as laid down by the Treaty (last paragraph of Article 6).[28]

AG Lagrange had the following to say in his Opinion in that case:

> The Member States agreed to give up part of their sovereignty only in favour of institutions functioning under clearly defined conditions, which must be sufficient in themselves. Therefore, none of the institutions can exercise powers other than those conferred upon it by the Treaty, either in relation to the other institutions or in regard to third parties, whether they be States or private persons. On the other hand, each institution, within the limits of its powers, is fully autonomous and cannot be subject to the authority of any other: it exercises its powers spontaneously and directly under the conditions laid down by the Treaty.[29]

However, AG Lagrange continued, 'such 'autonomy' clearly could not be absolute as regards financial matters, since no institution, even a supranational one, can escape the necessity of submitting to a certain amount of supervision in that area', for which reason Article 78 of the ECSC Treaty on drawing up the ECSC's budget would have sought 'to reconcile the principle of the autonomy of the institutions with the unity of the Community'.[30]

Algera and follow-up case law were primarily concerned with the internal autonomy of the institutions of the ECSC, thus what today would be called institutional balance and which is discussed later.[31] However, the statements cited above clearly make a broader claim, it is submitted, namely of the independence of the institutions of (in that case the) ECSC from any other authority, including the Member States.[32] The set-up of the European Commission (and before it the

[26] See Case 8/55, *Fédéchar*, ECLI:EU:C:1956:11, 300.

[27] Emphasis added. Contreast this with Article 13(2) TEU: 'Each institution shall act within the limits of the powers conferred on it in the Treaties, and in conformity with the procedures, conditions and objectives set out in them'.

[28] Joined Cases 7/56 & 3/57 to 7/57, *Algera*, ECLI:EU:C:1957:7, 57–58.

[29] Opinion of AG Lagrange in Joined Cases 7/56 & 3/57 to 7/57, *Algera*, ECLI:EU:C:1957:6, 82.

[30] Opinion of AG Lagrange in *Algera* (n 29) 82–83.

[31] See W Schroeder, *Das Gemeinschaftsrechtssystem* (Tübingen, Mohr Siebeck, 2002) 132–34.

[32] See also Könneke, *Unionsrechtsperson* (n 2) 59–60.

High Authority of the ECSC) show that such institutional autonomy had in fact existed.[33] Notably, the *proviso* for this claim of autonomy is that the institutions act and remain within the framework of their conferred powers, thus respect the principle of conferral discussed later.

Autonomy was mentioned in later yet still early case law such as *Lord Bruce of Donington* of 1981 on the privileges and immunities of Members of the European Parliament. The Court found that an appraisal of the system of allowances by authorities of a Member State instead of the Parliament would be likely 'to impair the effectiveness of the action of the Parliament and be incompatible with its autonomy'.[34]

In this context, we can also mention Opinion 1/76 on a draft agreement establishing a European laying-up fund for inland waterway vessels, best known for introducing one ground for assuming (implied) exclusive competence of the European Union.[35] It also seems to be the first case where the Court safeguarded the institutional autonomy of the Court of Justice.[36] The Court found fault with the composition of the Fund Tribunal that would have the power to give judgments relating to Fund activities as well as issue preliminary rulings regarding decisions adopted by the organs of the Fund. The draft provided that six members of the ECJ would sit on the Fund Tribunal, which the Court found 'might conflict with the obligation on the judges to give a completely impartial ruling on contentious questions when they come before the Court'.[37]

2.4.3. External Substantive Autonomy

Costa not only introduced EU law supremacy discussed later, but also affected how (customary) international law was applied within EU law, thus between the Member States. In *Costa*, the parties had still argued in the 'language' of public international law, relying on the principle of *lex posterior derogat legi priori*.[38] The Court conspicuously did not engage with this argument.

Another noteworthy judgment handed down in the time between *Van Gend* and *Costa* was in an infringement action initiated by the Commission against

[33] See Article 17(3) TEU and Article 130 TFEU, respectively. On the ECB, see M Klamert, 'Loyalty and Solidarity in the Euro-Crisis' (2017) *Zeitschrift fur Offentliches Recht* (ZoR): *Journal of Public Law* 699, 709–11. See also W Schroeder and A Müller, 'Elements of Supranationality in the Law of International Organizations' in U Fastenrath et al (eds), *From Bilateralism to Community Interest: Essays in Honour of Judge Bruno Simma* (Oxford, Oxford University Press, 2011) 358, 362.

[34] Case 208/80, *Lord Bruce of Donington*, ECLI:EU:C:1981:194.

[35] Opinion 1/76, *European laying-up fund for inland waterway vessels*, ECLI:EU:C:1977:63. See P Koutrakos, *EU International Relations Law*, 2nd edn (Oxford, Hart Publishing, 2015) 89 ff.

[36] See HP Hestermeyer, 'European Union Law, Autonomy of' in *Max Planck Encyclopedia of Public International Law* (Oxford, Oxford University Press, 2025) para 13. See also A Rosas, 'EU External Competence in the Absence of Internal Rules, and the Sleeping Beauty: Opinion 1/76 (Laying Up Fund for Inland Waterway Vessels)' in G Butler and RA Wessel (eds), *EU External Relations Law: The Cases in Context* (Oxford, Hart Publishing, 2022) 97, 107–08.

[37] *European laying-up fund* (n 35) para 22.

[38] *Costa/ENEL* (n 21).

Luxemburg and Belgium based on (as in *Van Gend*) Article 12 EEC. The two Member States had imposed a special duty leviable upon the issue of import licences for skimmed-milk powder and had claimed that the Council had failed to act on this matter by not establishing a common organisation of the markets in the milk products sector. In the view of Luxembourg and Belgium, international law would allow a party, injured by the failure of another party to perform its obligations, to withhold performance of its own, for which reason the Commission would have lost the right to plead infringement of the Treaty. The Court in *Dairy Products*, without citing *Van Gend*, held as follows concerning admissibility:

> In fact the Treaty is not limited to creating reciprocal obligations between the different natural and legal persons to whom it is applicable, but establishes a new legal order which governs the powers, rights and obligations of the said persons, as well as the necessary procedures for taking cognizance of and penalizing any breach of it. Therefore, except where otherwise expressly provided, the basic concept of the Treaty requires that the Member States shall not take the law into their own hands. Therefore the fact that the Council failed to carry out its obligations cannot relieve the defendants from carrying out theirs.[39]

This was later, in 1978, also in an infringement case involving Article 12 EEC, rephrased as follows:

> A Member State cannot under any circumstances unilaterally adopt, on its own authority, corrective measures or measures to protect trade designed to prevent any failure on the part of another Member State to comply with the rules laid down by the Treaty.[40]

Thus, again, the Court used the 'new legal order' claim to depart from principles of international law. As, indeed, under international law the principle of retaliation/reciprocity also called the 'self-help' mechanism could have applied here. If we see *Van Gend* as a case on the autonomy of EU law, it is submitted that the *Dairy Products* case should also be seen as such.[41] It is important to note that both cases concerned only the (inter-se) relation between the Member States. As shown in chapter two, in cases with an 'external' context such as an international agreement, the Court has always (more or less faithfully) applied principles of international law.

Even though these cases are not external in the sense of involving third states, they concern the application of principles of international law. Contrary to institutional autonomy, they concern *how* Union law is interpreted and applied, not by

[39] Joined Cases 90–91/63, *Commission v Belgium and Luxemburg (Dairy Products)*, ECLI:EU:C:1964:80, 626. See also W Phelan, 'The Revolutionary Doctrines of European Law and the Legal Philosophy of Robert Lecourt' (2017) *European Journal of International Law* 935, 938–40; W Phelan, *Great Judgments of the European Court of Justice – Rethinking the Landmark Decisions of the Foundational Period* (Cambridge, Cambridge University Press, 2019) 84–122.

[40] Case 232/78, *Commission v France (Mutton and Lamb)*, ECLI:EU:C:1979:215, para 9. While no reference was given in this paragraph, Case C-5/94, *Hedley Lomas*, ECLI:EU:C:1996:205, para 20, shows that *Dairy Products* was the precedence.

[41] See also Contartese, *The Principle of Autonomy* (n 2) ch 1, section 3.1.

whom. We will categorise this case law therefore as external substantive autonomy. Note, however, that cases discussed below under this category will instead concern external regulatory respectively human rights standards.

2.4.4. External Institutional Autonomy

Different from the ECSC discussed above, it was not initially clear that the European Union would have legal personality. In the *ERTA* case of 1971, the Court stated, without further elaboration, that Article 210 EEC, which provided that the EEC 'shall have legal personality' would not only mean such personality within the Member States, but also 'the capacity to establish contractual links with third countries'.[42]

The first ECJ case that connected *Van Gend* (but not *Costa*) with the 'autonomy' of EU law (without speaking of a principle, however) was Opinion 1/91 on the draft agreement between the then European Community and the European Economic Community.[43] In a dispute relating to the interpretation or application of that agreement, the EEA Court could be called upon to interpret whether the expression 'Contracting Party' would mean the Community, the Community and the Member States, or simply the Member States. The Court held as follows:

> It follows that the jurisdiction conferred on the EEA Court … is likely adversely to affect the allocation of responsibilities defined in the Treaties and, hence, the autonomy of the Community legal order, respect for which must be assured by the Court of Justice pursuant to Article 164 of the EEC Treaty. This exclusive jurisdiction of the Court of Justice is confirmed by Article 219 of the EEC Treaty, under which Member States undertake not to submit a dispute concerning the interpretation or application of that treaty to any method of settlement other than those provided for in the Treaty. Article 87 of the ECSC Treaty embodies a provision to the same effect.
>
> Consequently, to confer that jurisdiction on the EEA Court is incompatible with Community law.[44]

Opinion 1/91 was therefore concerned with preserving the monopoly of the Court of Justice of the European Union (CJEU) for deciding upon the division of competences between the EU and the Member States. AG Lagrange in *Algera* had already emphasised that the mandate of the Court to ensure that 'the law is observed' (for that case provided in Article 31 ECSC) was 'an absolutely essential aspect of the Treaty'.[45]

[42] Case 22/70, *Commission v Council (ERTA)*, ECLI:EU:C:1971:32, para 14. Compare the Opinion of AG Dutheillet de Lamothe in *ERTA*, ECLI:EU:C:1971:23, 293–94 on this point, arguing for a narrow interpretation of the Treaty. See J Wouters et al, *The Law of EU External Relations: Cases, Materials, and Commentary on the EU as an International Legal Actor*, 3rd edn (Oxford, Oxford University Press, 2021) 1 et seq.

[43] Opinion 1/91, *EEA I*, ECLI:EU:C:1991:49. See, however, Case 25/70, *Köster*, ECLI:EU:C:1970:115, para 9 discussed below.

[44] *EEA I* (n 43) paras 34–36, and mentioning *Van Gend & Loos* (n 21) in para 21.

[45] Opinion of AG Lagrange in *Algera* (n 29) 83.

Note that, in Opinion 1/91, the Court did not appear to find the draft agreement to conflict with the principle of conferral or a principle of autonomy. While autonomy is mentioned, the default is found in a violation of what is now Article 344 TFEU 'and, more generally, with the very foundations of the Community'.[46] Yet, in the light of later case law discussed, one might entertain the thought that these 'foundations of the Community' are merely another term for autonomy and it thus has indeed operated as a standard of review of the draft agreement in Opinion 1/91.[47]

2.4.5. Internal Substantive Autonomy

In *CILFIT*, the Court in 1982 proclaimed the following as to the interpretation of EU law against the background of several, equally authentic language versions:

> It must also be borne in mind, even where the different language versions are entirely in accord with one another, that Community law uses terminology which is peculiar to it. Furthermore, it must be emphasized that legal concepts do not necessarily have the same meaning in Community law and in the law of the various Member States.[48]

In *Ekro*, decided in 1984 and also discussed in chapter five in respect of uniformity, the Court held that the terms of a provision of Union law making no express reference to the law of the Member States must normally be given an 'independent and uniform interpretation' throughout the Union.[49]

Again, as above, the Court does not place his reasoning in a larger context, does not refer to either the *Algera* case law or to *Van Gend* or *Costa*, and generally does not use the term autonomy (but independent instead).

Nonetheless, the fact that this case law was about autonomy is obvious now. However, as far as we can see, it took the Court until 2003 to make this explicit. In *SENA*, referring to *Ekro* among others (but not to *CILFIT*) and concerning the concept of equitable remuneration in Article 8(2) of Directive 92/100, the Court held that 'Pursuant to the principle of the autonomy of Community law, it is a concept that must be interpreted uniformly in all Member States'.[50]

It is submitted that here the main concern is not the institutional side of autonomy. It was not primarily about protecting some competence of the Court or other Union institutions. What was at stake in these cases was the 'substantive' autonomy of EU law vis-a-vis national law, concerning how Union law is to be

[46] *EEA I* (n 43) paras 46, 71.

[47] See Hestermeyer, 'Autonomy' (n 36) para 22.

[48] Case 283/81, *CILFIT*, ECLI:EU:C:1982:335, para 19. Compare the Opinion of AG Lagrange in Case 10/55, *Mirossevich v High Authority*, ECLI:EU:C:1956:9, 346, 348: 'the independent nature of law arising from the Treaty of course prevents the application of general provisions borrowed from national laws'.

[49] Case 327/82, *Ekro*, ECLI:EU:C:1984:11, para 11. See also Case C-287/98, *Linster*, ECLI:EU:C:2000:468, para 43.

[50] Case C-245/00, *SENA*, ECLI:EU:C:2003:68, paras 23–24.

interpreted rather than by whom. Of course, this does not ignore that these two aspects are interlinked because it is essentially the EU court system with the ECJ as its *apex* that secures that such interpretation and thus application of EU law is realised.

2.4.6. Interim Conclusions

We have shown that autonomy in case law had a very undefined and unsystematic start. In *ERTA*, the 'external' legal personality of the EEC was confirmed, but without any elaboration. In *Algera*, this issue was moot, firstly because it concerned the internal autonomy of the ECSC institutions, but also because the ECSC had been endowed with legal personality in Article 6(1) ECSC Treaty.

The most famous cases associated with autonomy in EU law such as *Costa* and *Van Gend* did not mention *Algera*, institutional autonomy, or even the word 'autonomy' itself (at least in the English version), while lesser-known cases did. Only in lesser-known cases, autonomy was called a principle. Moreover, in none of the cases discussed above was autonomy applied as a general principle of EU law in the traditional sense. However, it could be argued that, in *Algera*, the ECSC Treaty was interpreted in its light and that in Opinion 1/91 it already operated as a concealed standard of review.

3. Applications

3.1. Autonomy as Descriptor

Essentially, the implicit claim for autonomy in *Costa* and *Van Gend* was a positive claim about what makes the European Union, and EU law, special.[51] In a paper, co-authored by the President of the ECJ writing extrajudicially, autonomy was argued to relate to the constitutional framework of the European Union, the nature of EU law, the principle of mutual trust between the Member States, the system of fundamental rights protection provided for by the Charter, the substantive law of the European Union that directly contributes to the implementation of the process of European integration, the principle of sincere cooperation, and the EU system of judicial protection.[52] The ECJ itself has offered that autonomy 'resides in the fact that the Union possesses a constitutional framework that is unique to it'.[53] It has been claimed that '[t]he autonomy of EU law is what makes EU law a legal order'.[54]

[51] See Klamert, 'Autonomy' (n 21) 815.

[52] See K Lenaerts, JA Gutiérrez-Fons and S Adam, 'Exploring the Autonomy of the European Union Legal Order' (2021) 81 *Zeitschrift für ausländisches öffentliches Recht und Völkerrecht* 47, 59.

[53] Opinion 1/17, *CETA*, ECLI:EU:C:2019:341, para 110.

[54] See C Eckes, 'Some Reflections on Achmea's Broader Consequences for Investment Arbitration' (2019) 4 *European Papers* 79, 81.

Such far-reaching and open-ended claims are problematic if they carry normative implications as discussed below.[55] They could, however, also 'merely' be seen as a descriptor for the EU's legal identity. Autonomy in this sense could capture in one word what has been said in many words in *Van Gend* and *Costa* and we would not need to debate whether autonomy is relative or absolute because it would not make precise statements regarding the relation between EU law and national or international law.[56] In legal theory, such use of the concept of a principle has been compared to acronyms being shortcuts that refer to some phenomena, but which do not have any meaning of their own.[57] Indeed, recent studies on autonomy cover a lot of ground and discuss many lines of case law, such as that on the requirements for the independence of national courts, in the light of autonomy.[58]

In that light, it is certainly apposite to recall that

> an examination of the evolution of European law shows that it is more realistic, and legally more appropriate, to propose a more modest reading of the claim for autonomy of the Community legal order: the autonomy of EU law is not absolute but relative; it does not mean that EU law has ceased to depend, for its validity and effective application, on the national law of its member states, nor that it has ceased to belong to international law.[59]

3.2. *Autonomy as Gatekeeper*

Even though this has never been expressly stated in case law it seems, autonomy for the European Union also relates to whether and how international law takes effect within EU law.[60] Starting with *Van Gend*, the Court reserved the right to decide on the (direct) effect of Union law within the national legal orders to itself, at variance with the modus under public international law.[61] While in *Van Gend* the Court reversed the power to decide on how EU law takes effect within *national* law, autonomy for the European Union also means that it needs to have the same control concerning the effects of *international* law within EU law.

Autonomy thus polices the permeability of the EU legal order in all directions, both its effect vis-a-vis national law and the effect of international law vis-a-vis EU law. In Opinion 2/13, the Court held that 'the Member States have … accepted that

[55] See V Moreno-Lax, 'The Axiological Emancipation of a (Non-)Principle: Autonomy, International Law and the EU Legal Order' in I Govaere and S Garben (eds), *The Interface Between EU and International Law* (Oxford, Hart Publishing, 2019) 45, 61, who criticises that 'a (hollow) suprematised "autonomy" has become an end in and of itself, to be cherished and pursued for its own sake'.

[56] Compare Moreno-Lax and Ziegler, 'Autonomy of the EU Legal Order' (n 6) 227: 'descriptive umbrella term'.

[57] See J Raz, 'Legal Principles and the Limits of Law' (1972) 81 *Yale Law Journal* 823, 828–29.

[58] See, critically, Langenfeld, *Die Autonomie des Unionsrechts in der EuGH-Rechtsprechung* (n 2) 349–350 and 397–398, who speaks of a 'chiffre' with regard to the scope of application of autonomy.

[59] See de Witte, 'How Autonomous' (n 19) 142. See also Odermatt, 'An Adolescent Disease' (n 16) 291.

[60] Compare Odermatt, 'An Adolescent Disease' (n 16) 306–08.

[61] *Van Gend & Loos* (n 21) para 3.

relations between them as regards the matters covered by the transfer of powers from the Member States to the European Union are governed by EU law, to the exclusion, if EU law so requires, of *any* other law'.[62] This would explain case law where the Court did not apply public international law between the Member States, what I have called external substantive autonomy above.

Thus, it arguably could be said that autonomy is in a certain sense similar to supremacy. While supremacy can be seen as a 'gatekeeper' in respect of the relation of EU law with the laws of the Member States (in practical terms expressed through primacy as is discussed later), autonomy can be considered both a 'gatekeeper' for this 'internal' relation as well as for the relation of EU law with international law. Autonomy, in this sense, would be similar to so-called 'hinge provisions' (*Scharniernormen*) in the German Basic Law, governing if and how to take international law into account, thus superseding, re-shaping or influencing the provisions of Union law.[63] Because such a provision is missing in the EU Treaties, autonomy can be seen to have a gap-filling function. Moreover, as we will discuss in chapter five, autonomy also informs the understanding of (other) structural principles of EU law such as effectiveness, which recalls the 'classic' interpretative function of principles.

Therefore, this role would make autonomy more than a mere idea or concept, it is submitted.[64] In the following, we will discuss whether autonomy does also operate as a standard of review for EU law or national measures.

3.3. *Autonomy as Standard of Legality*

3.3.1. Introduction

Autonomy has not been referred to as a 'general principle' of EU law as far as can be seen. However, in *Achmea*, discussed below, the Court called autonomy a 'principle' enshrined in particular in Article 344 TFEU.[65] In the literature, it has been considered a (normative) general principle of EU law by some.[66] As discussed above, the Court in Opinion 1/91 applied the standard of the 'foundations of the Community' for the review of an international agreement. We will now discuss whether later case law has been clearer about the quality of autonomy as a standard for the review of legality. Starting with Opinion 1/91, the concept of essential

[62] Opinion 2/13, *ECHR II*, ECLI:EU:C:2014:2454, para 193. Repeated in Case C-28/12, *Commission v Council (Voting Arrangements)*, ECLI:EU:C:2015:282, para 40, discussed below (emphasis added).

[63] Compare PM Huber and AL Paulus, *XVIth Congress of the Conference of European Constitutional Courts in 2014, Cooperation of Constitutional Courts in Europe – Current Situation and Perspectives – National Report Germany*, 2, available at: www.confeuconstco.org/reports/rep-xvi/LB+KF-Allemagne-EN.pdf. See also A Paulus and JR Leiss, 'Constitutionalism and the Mechanics of Global Law Transfers' (2018) 9 *Goettingen Journal of International Law*, Special Edn Holterhus 35, 48.

[64] Compare also G Marti, Les *grandes notions du droit de l'Union européenne* (Paris, PUF, 2023) 55, who speaks of a 'notion structurante'.

[65] Case C-284/16, *Achmea*, ECLI:EU:C:2018:158, para 32.

[66] See Hestermeyer, 'Autonomy' (n 36) para 4.

characteristics of Union law has become central to the reasoning of the Court and is thus explored next.

3.3.2. Developing the 'Essential Characteristics' Doctrine

In Opinion 1/91, the Court had already mentioned 'essential characteristics' of EU law after recalling *Van Gend*, in the following manner:

> The essential characteristics of the Community legal order which has thus been established are in particular its primacy over the law of the Member States and the direct effect of a whole series of provisions which are applicable to their nationals and to the Member States themselves.[67]

This has then, not entirely faithfully, been paraphrased in Opinion 1/00 on a proposed agreement between the European Community and non-Member States on the establishment of a European Common Aviation Area (ECAA) as follows:

> Preservation of the autonomy of the Community legal order requires therefore, first, that the essential character of the powers of the Community and its institutions as conceived in the Treaty remain unaltered (Opinion 1/91, paragraphs 61 to 65, and 1/92, paragraphs 32 and 41).[68]

This paragraph cited above has been deemed the 'minimum core' of the EU's external autonomy.[69] However, as will be shown below, it is equally relevant for the autonomy of the European Union from the Member States, thus 'internal' autonomy.

The Court, in Opinion 2/13 on the accession of the European Union to the European Convention on Human Rights (ECHR), also mentioned 'the constitutional framework and founding principles of the EU, a particularly sophisticated institutional structure and a complete set of legal rules ensuring its functioning'.[70] In *Achmea*, discussed later, it held that the essential characteristics of the European Union and its law would relate 'in particular to the constitutional structure of the EU and the very nature of that law'.[71]

The most elaborate summary of what seem to have become the 'essential characteristics' of EU law can be found in Opinion 1/17 on the draft Comprehensive Economic and Trade Agreement between Canada and the European Union and its Member States (CETA):

> That autonomy accordingly resides in the fact that the Union possesses a constitutional framework that is unique to it. That framework encompasses the founding values set

[67] *EEA I* (n 43) para 21.This has been repeated in Opinion 1/09, *Unified Patents Court*, ECLI:EU:C:2011:123, para 65. See also Case C-573/17, *Popławski II*, ECLI:EU:C:2019:530, para 52.

[68] Opinion 1/00, *ECAA*, ECLI:EU:C:2002:231, para 12.

[69] See E Kassoti and J Odermatt, 'The principle of autonomy and international investment arbitration: Reflections on Opinion 1/17' (2020) 7 *Questions of International Law* 5, 11.

[70] *ECHR II* (n 62) para 158, 164 ff, 172; *Unified Patents Court* (n 67) para 21.

[71] *Achmea* (n 65) para 33.

> out in Article 2 TEU, which states that the Union 'is founded on the values of respect for human dignity, freedom, democracy, equality, the rule of law, and respect for human rights', the general principles of EU law, the provisions of the Charter, and the provisions of the EU and FEU Treaties, which include, inter alia, rules on the conferral and division of powers, rules governing how the EU institutions and its judicial system are to operate, and fundamental rules in specific areas, structured in such a way as to contribute to the implementation of the process of integration described in the second paragraph of Article 1 TEU.[72]
>
> In order to ensure that those specific characteristics and the autonomy of the legal order thus created are preserved, the Treaties have established a judicial system intended to ensure consistency and uniformity in the interpretation of EU law. In accordance with Article 19 TEU, it is for the national courts and tribunals and the Court to ensure the full application of that law in all the Member States and to ensure effective judicial protection, the Court having exclusive jurisdiction to give the definitive interpretation of that law. To that end, that system includes, in particular, the preliminary ruling procedure provided for in Article 267 TFEU.[73]

This means that the 'essential characteristics' of EU law that need to be preserved are really all aspects of primary EU law and it is for the CJEU to preserve them by giving the 'definitive' interpretation of EU law. As we will discuss in the following, their protection has involved both internal and external EU law contexts.

When reading case law such as the one cited above, one comes to think of treaty change and whether it could affect these characteristics. If they are essential, would this not imply that changing or even abolishing them should not be possible? Indeed, an analogy has been made between unwritten 'constitutional values' of the European Union introduced by case law and the 'eternity clause' (*Ewigkeitsklausel*) in Article 79(3) Grundgesetz (German Basic Law).[74] I have argued elsewhere that there is little to indicate that such (broad) limits to treaty change exist.[75]

3.3.3. The Internal Institutional Dimension

The 'essential characteristics' doctrine was invoked by the Court in a case that did not concern external relations. In *Pringle*, the Court reviewed decisions by the European Council adopting simplified Treaty amendments. Referring to Opinions 1/00 and 1/09, among others, the Court held that Member States could entrust tasks to the Commission (and to the ECB) under the (extra-unional) ESM-Treaty in areas not falling under the exclusive competence of the Union if

[72] *CETA* (n 53) para 110.

[73] *CETA* (n 53) para 111.

[74] K Lenaerts, P van Nuffel and T Corthaut, *EU Constitutional Law* (Oxford, Oxford University Press, 2021) para 3.010. Compare also Schilling, 'The Autonomy of the Community Legal Order' (n 4) with further references.

[75] M Klamert, 'Commentary on Article 48 TEU' in M Kellerbauer, M Klamert and J Tomkin (eds), *The EU Treaties and the Charter of Fundamental Rights: A Commentary*, 2nd edn (Oxford, Oxford University Press, 2024) para 26.

those tasks 'do not alter the essential character of the powers conferred on those institutions by the EU and FEU Treaties'.[76]

The *Hybrid Acts* case had an external relations context but mainly concerned decision-making in the Council.[77] The Commission had adopted a proposal for a Council Decision on the signature and provisional application of a mixed air transport agreement. The Council, instead, adopted a hybrid decision, ie a decision emanating both from the Council and from the Representatives of the Governments of the Member States meeting within the Council. The Council had argued that its autonomy would empower it to choose the form in which to grant the necessary authorisations in the procedure for the negotiation and conclusion of international agreements. The Court disagreed and annulled the pertinent decision because it would not conform with the procedural rules under Article 218 TFEU and because it would not be possible to discern which act reflected the will of the Council and which the will of the Member States.[78] The word 'autonomy' does not appear in the body of the judgment but the Court referred to Opinions 1/09 and 2/13 and the keywords above the operative part include 'Autonomy of the EU legal order'.[79] It has been noted that 'a mixed agreement may indeed be hybrid, but comes into being, thrives and perishes in the international legal order; the contested hybrid decision however was an act internal to the autonomous EU legal order'.[80] According to AG Mengozzi in this case, the principle of autonomy of the institutions would mean that

> the institutions must operate, from the internal, organisational point of view, entirely independently of the Member States, which must refrain from interfering in the EU institutions' ability to determine themselves how they are organized and their procedures and functions, within the limits laid down by the Treaties.[81]

Pringle and the *Hybrid Acts* case can also be discussed under the principle of institutional balance.[82] However, they also clearly stand in the line of the (institutional) autonomy case law. The *Hybrid Acts* case recalls the discussion above apropos *Algera* that EU institutions such as the Council have autonomy, but that this autonomy is set limits by the powers conferred on them. In both cases, notably, it was not (a principle of) autonomy that was the ground upon which the respective decisions were reviewed.

[76] Case C-370/12, *Pringle*, ECLI:EU:C:2012:756, para 158.

[77] *Voting Arrangements* (n 62). See C Eckes, *EU Powers Under External Pressure: How the EU's External Actions Alter its Internal Structures* (Oxford, Oxford University Press, 2019) 152.

[78] *Voting Arrangements* (n 62) para 50.

[79] *Voting Arrangements* (n 62) paras 39–40. See also T Verellen, 'On hybrid decisions, mixed agreements and the limits of the new legal order: Commission v. Council ("US Air Transport Agreement")' (2016) 53 *CML Rev* 741.

[80] See M Chamon, 'Constitutional Limits to the Political Choice for Mixity' in E Neframi and M Gatti (eds), *Constitutional Issues of EU External Relations Law* (Baden-Baden, Nomos, 2018) 137, 162.

[81] Opinion of AG Mengozzi in *Voting Arrangements*, ECLI:EU:C:2015:43, para 57.

[82] See PJ Loewenthal, 'Commentary on Article 13 TEU' in Kellerbauer, Klamert and Tomkin (eds), *Commentary*, para 7.

3.3.4. The External Institutional Dimension

In the *ECAA* Opinion 1/00 mentioned above, the Court did not only state that preservation of autonomy requires that the essential character of conferred powers remain unaltered, but also found as follows:

> Second, it requires that the procedures for ensuring uniform interpretation of the rules of the ECAA Agreement and for resolving disputes will not have the effect of binding the Community and its institutions, in the exercise of their internal powers, to a particular interpretation of the rules of Community law referred to in that agreement (Opinions 1/91 and 1/92).[83]

Having another court decide 'on the allocation of responsibilities defined in the Treaties' has been considered a threat to the autonomy of the EU legal order by the Court.[84] This side of autonomy will also be discussed in chapter four on external relations.

Its most prominent application is certainly Opinion 2/13 on the ECHR accession mentioned above. Protocol No 8 to the Lisbon Treaty states that the accession agreement of the European Union to the ECHR under Article 6(2) TEU 'shall make provision for preserving the specific characteristics of the Union and Union law' and shall ensure 'that accession of the Union shall not affect the competences of the Union or the powers of its institutions'.[85] Moreover, Article 3 of the Protocol states that nothing in the accession agreement 'shall affect' Article 344 TFEU. One might say, especially of course with hindsight, that the negotiators were given a nearly impossible task: acceding to the ECHR while preserving the substance of Article 344 TFEU.[86] At the same time, as has been noted, primary law requires, in Article 6(2) TEU, accession to the ECHR and would thereby also require the acceptance of the adjudicative role of the European Court of Human Rights (ECtHR) in respect of EU law.[87]

While references to autonomy abound in Opinion 2/13, it must also be noted that the draft accession agreement in that case was technically not found incompatible with (a principle of) autonomy, but with Article 6(2) TEU and with Protocol No 8 EU. However, it was found incompatible with these provisions because it was, among others, 'liable adversely to affect the specific characteristics and the autonomy of EU law', was liable to affect Article 344 TFEU on the exclusive jurisdiction of the CJEU, 'does not lay down arrangements for the operation of the co-respondent mechanism and the procedure for the prior involvement of the

[83] *ECAA* (n 68) para 13.

[84] *EEA I* (n 43) paras 30–35; *ECAA* (n 68) para 13; *ECHR II* (n 62) paras 183–84, 210; *Unified Patents Court* (n 67) para 76.

[85] Protocol (No 8) relating to Article 6(2) of the Treaty on European Union on the accession of the Union to the European Convention on the Protection of Human Rights and Fundamental Freedoms [2012] OJ C 326/273.

[86] Compare Odermatt, 'An Adolescent Disease' (n 16) 313, who notes that the main fault lay in the fact that the drafters of the accession agreement had treated the EU essentially as a state in all respects.

[87] See B de Witte, 'The Relative Autonomy of the European Union's Fundamental Rights Regime' (2019) *Nordic Journal of International Law* 65, 72.

Court of Justice that enable the specific characteristics of the EU and EU law to be preserved', and 'fails to have regard to the specific characteristics of EU law'.[88] It has been noted that the Court, in Opinion 2/13, referred to the 'specific' characteristics of the Europen Union and EU law instead of the essential characteristics of EU law, the former arguably being broader (and being the wording used in Protocol No 8 EU).[89] It has also been noted that the Court did not only protect the prerogatives of the Court but equally the status of the Member States as parties to the ECHR.[90]

In Opinion 2/15, on the competence for concluding the Free Trade Agreement between the European Union and the Republic of Singapore, the Court spoke of the 'criterion relating to the autonomy of EU law'.[91] In Opinion 1/17 on *CETA*, further discussed in chapter four, the Court seems to be prepared to go one step further and allow for a review of the agreement under a principle of autonomy, even though the Court never uses this exact phrase. It held:

> An international agreement entered into by the Union may, moreover, affect the powers of the EU institutions provided, however, that the indispensable conditions for safeguarding the essential character of those powers are satisfied and, consequently, there is no adverse effect on the autonomy of the EU legal order.[92]

Autonomy in that sense is certainly different from autonomy as a descriptor discussed above. It would have to be understood in absolute legal terms as it would function as a standard of legality for EU law including for agreements submitted to the procedure under Article 218(11) TFEU.[93]

3.3.5. The External Substantive Dimension

Autonomy also played a role with the openness of EU law to 'external' legal standards. In this respect, the essential characteristics doctrine did not seem to play a decisive role, even though the scope of the doctrine as employed in *CETA* quoted above clearly also comprises the safeguarding of substantive standards.

In *Kadi*, the ECJ denied full deference to a sanctions resolution of the UN Security Council. The ECJ recalled that EU law provides a complete system of remedies for the judicial review of Union acts and thus also for the protection of individuals' rights.[94] The Court then recalled 'the autonomy of the Community legal

[88] *ECHR II* (n 62) para 183.

[89] See C Contartese, 'The autonomy of the EU legal order in the ECJ's external relations case law: From the "essential" to the "specific characteristics" of the Union and back again' (2017) 54 *CML Rev* 1627. Compare also Krenn, 'Autonomy and Effectiveness as Common Concerns' (n 7) 163, on an alternative reading of 'specific characteristics' in Protocol No 8.

[90] See Odermatt, 'An Adolescent Disease' (n 16) 313.

[91] Opinion 2/15, *Free Trade Agreement with Singapore*, ECLI:EU:C:2017:376, para 301.

[92] *CETA* (n 53) para 107.

[93] See Eckes, *EU Powers Under External Pressure* (n 77) 31, arguing that the claim to 'normative autonomy' of EU law by the CJEU 'is best understood as absolute … rather than a matter of degree'.

[94] See Joined Cases C-402/05 P & C-415/05 P, *Kadi*, ECLI:EU:C:2008:461, para 281, referring to Case 294/83, *Les Verts*, ECLI:EU:C:1986:166. See also Case C-229/05 P, *Oçalan*, ECLI:EU:C:2007:32, para 109.

system', and continued that 'obligations imposed by an international agreement cannot have the effect of prejudicing the constitutional principles of the EC Treaty, which include the principle that all Community acts must respect fundamental rights', which would be for the Court to review.[95] The review of Union measures in the light of fundamental rights was an expression 'of a constitutional guarantee stemming from the EC Treaty as an autonomous legal system which is not to be prejudiced by an international agreement'.[96]

Kadi thus had an external relations (sanctions) context but did not concern an international agreement or the jurisdiction of another court.[97] In this case, autonomy appears to have been the argument for allowing the Court to review sanctions measures of the European Union implementing a UN Security Council resolution in the light of fundamental rights.[98] The Court also referred to the rule of law in *Kadi*.[99] In that respect, it has been argued that seeing the rule of law through the lens of autonomy would mean shielding EU law from potential internal and external contestation, which would be the opposite of what the classical understanding of the rule of law would imply.[100] However, *Kadi* can also be seen not so much as a defensive application of autonomy but as a positive one, affirming that the autonomy of EU law would necessitate the protection of fundamental rights in the European Union.[101]

Also in Opinion 1/17 on *CETA* discussed above, the Court was not merely concerned with protecting the prerogatives of the ECJ but also with the possible effects of the agreement on substantive, regulatory standards in the European Union. It thus was emphasised by the Court that Article 8.9.1 of the CETA agreement states explicitly that Parties have the right 'to regulate within their territories to achieve legitimate policy objectives, such as the protection of public health, safety, the environment or public morals, social or consumer protection or the promotion and protection of cultural diversity'.[102] This and other provisions in *CETA* would show, according to the Court, that

> the Parties have taken care to ensure that those tribunals have no jurisdiction to call into question the choices democratically made within a Party relating to, inter

[95] *Kadi* (n 94) paras 282–85.

[96] *Kadi* (n 94) para 316 (emphasis added). *ECHR II* (n 62) para 170 rephrases this without the constitutional reference: 'The autonomy enjoyed by EU law in relation to the laws of the Member States and in relation to international law requires that the interpretation of those fundamental rights be ensured within the framework of the structure and objectives of the EU'.

[97] See Klamert, 'Autonomy' (n 21) 828–29 on these differences.

[98] See I Pernice, 'The Autonomy of the EU Legal Order – Fifty Years After Van Gend" in A Tizzano, J Kokott and S Prechal (eds), *50ème Anniversaire de l'arrêt/50th anniversary of the judgment in Van Gend en Loos, 1963–2013* (Luxembourg, Office des publications de l'Union européenne, 2013) 55, 69.

[99] *Kadi* (n 94) para 316. See Pernice, 'The Autonomy of the EU Legal Order' (n 98) 69.

[100] See D Kochenov, 'EU Law without the Rule of Law: Is the Veneration of Autonomy Worth It?' (2015) 34 *Yearbook of European Law* 74; D Kochenov and N Lavranos, 'Achmea versus the Rule of Law: CJEU's Dogmatic Dismissal of Investors' Rights in Backsliding Member States' (2022) 14 *Hague Journal of the Rule of Law* 195.

[101] See Klamert, 'Autonomy' (n 21) 828–29; de Witte, 'The Relative Autonomy' (n 87) 65.

[102] *CETA* (n 53) para 154.

> alia, the level of protection of public order or public safety, the protection of public morals, the protection of health and life of humans and animals, the preservation of food safety, protection of plants and the environment, welfare at work, product safety, consumer protection or, equally, fundamental rights'.[103]

Because of this, the Court found that 'CETA does not adversely affect the autonomy of the EU legal order'.[104]

The main 'autonomy concern' here, I would submit, is again primarily substantive, and only indirectly also institutional. However, the relation to the essential characteristics doctrine that was so prominently laid out in other parts of Opinion 1/17 quoted above, where the Court refers to 'democracy', among others, does not seem clear.[105]

3.3.6. Interim Conclusions

In many important opinions and cases discussed above, the Court relied heavily on autonomy, without ever stating clearly that a certain agreement or Member State measure would infringe a self-standing (general) principle of autonomy. Instead, the Court made 'positive' statements that a certain agreement would 'not adversely affect' the autonomy of the EU legal order or used similar language.[106] While this sidesteps a discussion of the legal quality of autonomy, it arguably cannot be concealed that some essential characteristics apply as a quasi-standard of review when channelled through the principle of autonomy.

Such as with conferral discussed later, it seems inappropriate to say that autonomy has direct effect. It does not aim to protect Union citizens but is geared at defending the EU legal order. But as with conferral, it can of course have indirect implications for individuals when it is applied in preliminary reference proceedings such as *Achmea*. We can also note, for our comparison with general principles under Article 6 TEU, that the ECJ does not take Member State interests into account and there is no weighing with other principles of Union law.[107] As a standard of legality, autonomy thus operates in an absolute, binary manner.

We can note another peculiarity with autonomy. With other principles discussed in this book, we need to and will discuss whether and how they apply in the Common Foreign and Security Policy (CFSP) in chapter four. With autonomy, by contrast, there can be no debate about whether it applies in an area such as the CFSP. Because it claims to protect the (entire) Union legal order, it is a principle that is 'attached' to the (entire) EU legal order as such.

[103] *CETA* (n 53) para 160.
[104] *CETA* (n 53) para 161.
[105] Compare B Daiber, 'Neue Hürden für den EU-Beitritt zur EMRK?' (2021) *Europarecht* 596. Compare also Eckes, 'The Autonomy of the EU Legal Order' (n 17) 1465.
[106] *EEA I* (n 43) para 34; *ECAA* (n 68) para 26; *ECHR II* (n 62) para 183; *CETA* (n 53) para 161.
[107] See Klamert, 'Autonomy' (n 21) 823 ff.

4. Locations

4.1. *Introduction*

Looking at the early case law just discussed, it is no surprise that it has proven difficult to anchor autonomy in the Treaties if this is attempted at all.

Article 1 of Protocol No 8 to the Treaty of Lisbon requires the agreement for accession to the ECHR to 'make provision for preserving the specific characteristics of the Union and Union law'. Article 2 of Protocol No 8 requires that such agreement ensures 'that accession of the Union shall not affect the competences of the Union or the powers of its institutions'. Similarly, the first sentence of the Declaration on Article 6(2) of the Treaty on European Union, annexed to the Final Act of the Intergovernmental Conference which adopted the Treaty of Lisbon, states that accession should be arranged in such a way as 'to preserve the specific features of Union law'. These provisions are certainly relevant for locating autonomy, including of the Union's institutions. However, they only apply with regard to the accession of the European Union to the ECHR.

For locating autonomy more broadly, three Treaty provisions in particular will be discussed in the following.

4.2. *Article 1 TEU*

If we understand autonomy as a descriptor, as suggested above, Article 1 TEU would seem the most suitable place for situating such a broad concept of autonomy. The second paragraph of Article 1 TEU heralds the TEU as a new stage in the process of creating an ever closer union among the peoples of Europe establishing a framework where further and deeper integration is identified as an ultimate objective. It arguably is this provision, in all its opaqueness and lyricism and despite the very much public international law-infused paragraph 1 of Article 1 TEU, which most prominently represents the supranational character of the European Union.[108] Whatever it is worth, it is also the Article where autonomy is discussed in commentaries on the EU Treaties, if it is discussed at all.

4.3. *Article 267 TFEU and Article 344 TFEU*

Article 267 TFEU provides for the preliminary reference procedure. Different from what is now Article 344 TFEU, this procedure has always been strongly relied on by the Court in cases such as *Van Gend*.[109] Thus, in Opinion 2/13, the EU

[108] See M Klamert, 'Commentary on Article 1 TEU' in Kellerbauer, Klamert and Tomkin (eds), *Commentary*, paras 18–28.

[109] *Van Gend & Loos* (n 21).

judicial system, with the preliminary ruling procedure 'as its keystone' was deemed to have the object of securing uniform interpretation of EU law, 'thereby serving to ensure its consistency, its full effect and its autonomy as well as, ultimately, the particular nature of the law established by the Treaties', including its essential characteristics.[110]

The Court declared its jurisdiction as forming part 'of the very foundations of the Community', arguing that the observance of autonomy is entrusted to it under (what is now) Article 344 TFEU.[111] In *Achmea*, the ECJ stated that the principle of autonomy is enshrined in particular in Article 344 TFEU.[112] Article 344 TFEU is, by its wording, concerned with disputes between Member States concerning the interpretation or application of the Treaties, which should only be settled through methods provided by EU law. Thus, it seems to be concerned with only a quite narrow aspect of the jurisdiction of the Court. Therefore, the invocation of Article 344 TFEU in *Achmea* was to some extent surprising because *Achmea* was about disputes between private investors and Member States based on investment treaties concluded (inter se) between Member States.[113] It is suggested that the Court might have wanted to avoid applying autonomy as a fully-fledged legal principle and therefore had to stretch the meaning of primary law provisions to come to its finding.

4.4. Unwritten Principle

Article 267 TFEU and (a broadly construed) Article 344 TFEU can be seen as the seat of all forms of threats to the independence and powers of the CJEU and the national courts as part of the EU judicial system. However, as we have shown, the significance of the principle of autonomy goes beyond the jurisdiction of the Court.[114] For protecting the independence and powers of the other EU institutions, provisions such as Article 218 TFEU can play a role, as seen in the *Hybrid Acts* case. Yet, if there is no clear basis in the Treaties to 'protect' other EU institutions or substantive standards of EU law are concerned, autonomy would have to be considered an unwritten principle of EU law.[115]

[110] *ECHR II* (n 62) para 176, 201. See also *Unified Patents Court* (n 67) paras 67 and 83; *Achmea* (n 65) paras 35–37.

[111] See *Kadi* (n 94) para 282. See also *EEA I* (n 43) paras 35 and 71; *Achmea* (n 65) para 32.

[112] *Achmea* (n 65) para 32; Case C-741/19, *Komstroy*, ECLI:EU:C:2021:655.

[113] See S Hindelang, 'Conceptualisation and Application of the Principle of Autonomy of EU Law: The CJEU's Judgment in Achmea Put in Perspective' (2019) 44 *EL Rev* 383.

[114] See also T Lock, *The European Court of Justice and International Courts* (Oxford, Oxford University Press, 2015) 84–86.

[115] Compare also Hindelang, 'Conceptualisation' (n 113) 386; Kassoti and Odermatt, 'Reflections on Opinion 1/17' (n 69) 15.

5. Interrelations

5.1. *Autonomy and Conferral*

As discussed above, international public law and early case law clarify that the autonomy of the institutions only exists within their conferred powers. This could also be understood by the dictum of the Court in Opinion 2/13 that 'the Member States have … accepted that relations between them as regards the matters covered by the transfer of powers from the Member States to the European Union are governed by EU law, to the exclusion, if EU law so requires, of any other law'.[116] Conversely, however, this notably means that the greater the powers conferred on an organisation such as the European Union, the greater is the remit of its autonomy. There is thus a direct correlation between the degree of conferral and the degree of autonomy.

As also mentioned above, the *Pringle* case concerned the institutional autonomy of the European Commission especially, but has been and could also be discussed under the principle of institutional balance in the sense of whether it would be permissible for the Union organs to delegate tasks to other institutions.[117] Thus, any procedural rule in the Treaties is an expression of the autonomous powers conferred on the institutions, establishing a balance between those institutions.[118] An example of such interrelation can be seen in the *Köster* case of 1970, where the Court confirmed as legal a mechanism allowing the Council to delegate implementing powers to the Commission because it would not have the effect of 'distorting the Community structure and the institutional balance'.[119]

Finally, autonomy is connected with conferral because of the centrality of the CJEU for preserving the essential characteristics of EU law, as shown above. It has thus been noted that Article 23 TEU providing a bridge between the CFSP and the rest of EU law gave the Court the possibility to interpret the scope of its jurisdiction in a broad manner to defend the autonomy of the EU legal order.[120] The relevance of autonomy in the CFSP will be discussed in detail in chapter four.

5.2. *Autonomy and Equality*

We have discussed above 'with internal substantive autonomy' how EU law should be interpreted in relation to Member State law.

More recently, the Court has held that

> the need for uniform application of Community law and the principle of equality require that the terms of a provision of Community law which makes no express reference to the law

[116] *ECHR II* (n 62) para 193. Repeated in *Voting Arrangements* (n 62) para 40.
[117] See Loewenthal, 'Commentary on Article 13 TEU' (n 82) para 7.
[118] See Case C-425/13, *Commission v Council (ETS)*, ECLI:EU:C:2015;483, para 62 on Article 218 TFEU.
[119] See *Köster* (n 43) para 9. This has been noted by Könneke, *Unionsrechtsperson* (n 2) 61.
[120] See T Ramopolous and L Havas, 'Commentary on Article 23 TEU' in Kellerbauer, Klamert and Tomkin (eds), *Commentary*, para 3.

> of the Member States for the purpose of determining its meaning and scope must normally be given an autonomous and uniform interpretation throughout the Community.[121]

It is not clear to which principle of equality the Court refers here. Most likely it is the 'meta-principle' requiring similar situations not to be treated differently discussed below in the context of equality.

Striving for the harmonious interpretation of legal terms in a legal order is nothing peculiar to EU law.[122] The peculiarity of the EU legal order, when compared with the legal orders of nation-states, is that a heterogeneous interpretation will most likely not occur within one legal order (by lower courts to be eventually corrected by the national supreme court) but between at least two different Member State legal orders. If this happens, the discrepancy is not 'merely' a disturbance of theoretical aspirations to legal 'unity' but is likely to lead to a divergent treatment of persons subject to the rules concerned depending on the Member State they find themselves in.

We will return to legal unity and the uniform interpretation and application of EU law and the roles of autonomy and equality in that context in chapter six.

5.3. *Autonomy and Loyalty*

Because external institutional autonomy is enshrined in particular in Article 344 TFEU, as mentioned, there is an obvious link with Article 4(3) TEU. Article 344 TFEU after all is a specific expression of the principle of loyalty enshrined in Article 4(3) TEU.[123] In *Achmea* and in Opinion 2/13, it is thus not surprising to find arguments based on Article 344 TFEU and Article 4(3) TEU next to each other.[124]

Setting out the context of the mutual trust between the Member States that the law of the European Union that implements its values will be respected, the Court in *Achmea* recalls that the

> Member States are obliged, by reason inter alia of the principle of sincere cooperation set out in the first subparagraph of Article 4(3) TEU, to ensure in their respective territories the application of and respect for EU law, and to take for those purposes any appropriate measure, whether general or particular, to ensure fulfilment of the obligations arising out of the Treaties or resulting from the acts of the institutions of the EU.[125]

In Opinion 2/13, the Court held the following, after recalling that the principle of autonomy would notably be enshrined in Article 344 TFEU:

[121] Case C-388/18, *Finanzamt A*, ECLI:EU:C:2019:642, para 30 with further references; Case C-373/00, *Truley*, ECLI:EU:C:2003:110, para 35.

[122] See M Klamert, 'Einheit und Fragmentierung im Unionsrecht' (2019) *Europarecht* Special Issue No 2, 133.

[123] *ECHR II* (n 62) para 202; Case C-459/03, *Commission v Ireland (MOX Plant)*, ECLI:EU:C:2006:345, para 169. See also M Klamert, 'Commentary on Article 4 TEU' in Kellerbauer, Klamert and Tomkin (eds), *Commentary*, para 34.

[124] *Achmea* (n 65) paras 32 and 34; *ECHR II* (n 62) paras 168 and 173. See also *Unified Patents Court* (n 67) para 68.

[125] *Achmea* (n 65) para 34; *ECHR II* (n 62) paras 168 and 173.

> Furthermore, the obligation of Member States to have recourse to the procedures for settling disputes established by EU law – and, in particular, to respect the jurisdiction of the Court of Justice, which is a fundamental feature of the EU system – must be understood as a specific expression of Member States' more general duty of loyalty resulting from Article 4(3) TEU (see, to that effect, judgment in *Commission* v *Ireland*, EU:C:2006:345, paragraph 169), it being understood that, under that provision, the obligation is equally applicable to relations between Member States and the EU.[126]

It has been argued that, in Opinion 2/13, the Court has used loyalty to expand the scope of Article 344 TFEU so that its exclusive jurisdiction would cover not only disputes between Member States but also claims between the European Union and its Member States, thereby reinforcing the autonomous nature of the EU legal order by expanding and clarifying the scope of the EU's exclusive jurisdiction.[127]

There is also a link with the first sentence of Article 19(1) TEU, according to which it is for the ECJ to ensure that the law is observed in the interpretation and application of the Treaties, which has been referred to in *Achmea* as well.[128]

5.4. *Autonomy and Effective Judicial Protection*

In *Kadi*, handed down before the Lisbon Treaty, autonomy was invoked to justify the application of the right to effective judicial protection also for EU measures implementing UN Security Council resolutions, as discussed. Article 47(1) of the Charter of Fundamental Rights (CFR) now provides that everyone 'whose rights and freedoms guaranteed by the law of the Union are violated has the right to an effective remedy before a tribunal in compliance with the conditions laid down in this Article'.

We have argued above that *Kadi* would be an example of external substantive autonomy. This is testimony to the double role of effective judicial protection as both a substantive principle under Article 6 TEU and a structural principle within the remit of this book.

6. Conclusions

It has been argued that EU law has never become autonomous, but rather has from its beginnings been autonomous 'because of its very nature'.[129] However, all organisations are autonomous to some degree by the way they are established, so that claim does not explain the extent and form of the autonomy of the European Union and of EU law. It is noteworthy that the ECJ has not contributed

[126] *ECHR II* (n 62) para 202.

[127] See A Delgado Casteleiro, 'Loyalty in External Relations Law: The Fabric of Competence, Autonomy and Institutional Balance' in Neframi and Gatti (eds), *Constitutional Issues* 385, 394, pointing also to the *Dior* case law in this respect, which is discussed in ch 6.

[128] *Achmea* (n 65) para 36.

[129] See Barents, *The Autonomy of Community Law* (n 2) 254–255.

to clarifying autonomy for the European Union and EU law, for a long time avoiding mentioning this term despite or rather, it has been submitted, *because* of its long-standing use in public international law.

Autonomy correlates with the kinds of powers the European Union has been conferred. Because these powers, especially of the CJEU with its mandatory and broad jurisdiction but also of the Council being endowed with majority voting, were always formidable compared with other organisations, the EU's claim to autonomy is inherently much more robust than it is with other organisations. It is submitted that this also includes a substantive side. Because the European Union has been vested with a fundamental rights regime equal to that of nation-states, the ECJ could well demand that this regime be respected, also in the light of international law. It has thus been noted that 'the more constitutionally mature' the European Union becomes, the more protective its 'shield' must be.[130]

As we have seen, the ECJ seems to 'sell' uniqueness as the new *sui generis*. The relevance of autonomy for this narrative cannot be underestimated. It by far exceeds its external institutional side, which has attracted the most attention lately. Autonomy is therefore not only defensive but also affirmative, it does not only govern *who* should interpret EU law but also *how* this should be done. For that purpose, it strongly interrelates with the principle of equality to secure the uniform application and interpretation of EU law, as will also be explored in chapter six.

We have distinguished between autonomy as a (relative) descriptor and gatekeeper on the one hand, and autonomy as an (absolute, binary) standard of review on the other.[131] The increasing normativity of autonomy is at odds with an ever-expanding and unclear doctrine of essential characteristics it should serve to protect. In addition, autonomy is one of the few principles discussed in this book that also has a substantive side as a gatekeeper vis-a-vis legal concepts derived from Member State laws as well as vis-a-vis regulatory standards imported from international law.

We will come back to autonomy not only when we discuss external relations law in chapter four but also when we discuss the reasoning of the Court based on structural principles in chapter five.

3. The Principle of Conferral

1. Introduction

Conferral is a principle everyone would agree is of central importance to the European Union and to EU law. The ECJ has qualified 'the constitutional framework

[130] See JWC Van Rossem, 'The Autonomy of EU Law: More is Less?' in R Wessel and S Blockmans (eds), *Between Autonomy and Dependence: The EU Legal Order under the Influence of International Organisations* (The Hague, Springer, 2013) 13, 28. See also Odermatt, 'An Adolescent Disease' (n 16) 315.

[131] See Contartese, *The Principle of Autonomy* (n 2) for a similar distinction.

and founding principles of the EU, a particularly sophisticated institutional structure and a complete set of legal rules ensuring its functioning' as essential characteristics of EU law, explicitly mentioning conferral.[132] Above, we have explored the close link between conferral and autonomy that is expressed in this statement.

Conferral is manifested through distinct requirements such as the need for, the choice of and the limits to legal bases for Union measures, the principles of subsidiarity and proportionality all EU measures must comply with, and also the principle of institutional balance. The latter has been considered a distinct (general, structural) principle.[133] Also proportionality as an element of the rules governing the division of competences in the European Union has received more attention recently.[134] While all these issues cannot be discussed here in detail, institutional balance will be dealt with in the section on the interrelations of conferral, and we will deal with subsidiarity and proportionality when we discuss the application of structural principles in the EU's external relations in chapter four.

In the following, we will begin by exploring conferral in a narrow sense as a legal concept and as a legal principle. While all the above-mentioned manifestations of conferral have given rise to a lot of case law and discussion, the nature of conferral as such in terms of *who* confers *what* and *how* on *whom* has been somewhat neglected.[135] While we cannot discuss these questions comprehensively, we will show in the following that, again, as with autonomy, there are obvious yet undisclosed parallels with theorising the endowment of international organisations under international law.

2. Origins

2.1. National Law

States are originary subjects and plenipotentiaries under international law; their powers are therefore inherent in their statehood.[136] Only a federal state is characterised by a division of competences between the federal and the state level, with the powers of the federal level being normally 'enumerated' and hence limited.[137] It has been suggested that the foundations of the authority of EU institutions could be understood based on the principles of federal government, which would mean that 'they have neither the authority to set their own aims nor are they endowed

[132] *ECHR II* (n 62) paras 158, 164 ff, 172; *Unified Patents Court* (n 67) para 21.

[133] See, eg, S Platon, 'The principle of institutional balance: rise, eclipse and revival of a general principle of EU constitutional law' in Ziegler, Neuvonen and Moreno-Lax (eds), *Research Handbook* 136.

[134] Compare now L von Danwitz, *Föderale Verhältnismäßigkeit Bedeutung und Funktion von Art. 5 Abs. 4 EUV im Föderalismus der Europäischen Union* [*Federal Proportionality. Significance and Function of Article 5 (4) TEU in EU Federalism*] (Tübingen, Mohr Siebeck, 2024).

[135] See S Garben, *The Competence Question in the (Con)Federal European Union* (Oxford, Oxford University Press, forthcoming 2025).

[136] See Moreno-Lax and Ziegler, 'Autonomy of the EU Legal Order' (n 6) 236.

[137] See Schütze, 'On "Federal" Ground' (n 1) 1069. Compare also SR Larsen, *The Constitutional Theory of the Federation and the European Union* (Oxford, Oxford University Press, 2021) 101 discussing a federal union of states.

with a set of prerogative powers' but their independence would consist 'in the duty to pursue a constitutionally specified aim without outside influence'.[138]

This is not the place to discuss whether the European Union today is a federation. What we will discuss, by contrast, is how conferral was viewed at the beginning of European integration. The whole concept of conferral most likely has its origins in international law, where it has been discussed extensively, if not always under this term, as will be shown in the following.

2.2. Public International Law

Above, we have discussed that, in public international law, the autonomy of an international organisation is closely connected to the question of its legal personality and the independence of its institutions from the states that have founded it. This translates into the question of the powers that an international organisation has.[139] The more powers, including implied powers it has, the greater the autonomy of an international organisation as an independent subject of international law.[140]

It has been noted that the EEC was conceived as an international organisation holding limited powers.[141] Indeed, the powers of international organisations are derived powers, conferred on them by their constituent states.[142] Already in 1927, the Permanent Court of International Justice made the following clear:

> International law governs relations between independent States. The rules of law binding upon States therefore emanate from their own free will as expressed in conventions or by usages generally accepted as expressing principles of law and established in order to regulate the relations between these co-existing independent communities or with a view to the achievement of common aims. Restrictions upon the independence of States cannot therefore be presumed.[143]

In international law, it is established that the powers of an international organisation are circumscribed under a principle of speciality. In its Advisory Opinion on the legality of *Nuclear Weapons* of 1996, the ICJ held as follows:

> The Court need hardly point out that international organizations are subjects of international law which do not, unlike States, possess a general competence. International organizations are governed by the 'principle of speciality', that is to say, they are invested by the States which create them with powers, the limits of which are a function of the *common interests* whose promotion those States entrust to them.

[138] See Larsen, *Constitutional Theory* (n 137) 101.

[139] See J Klabbers, 'The Transformation of International Organisations Law' (2015) 26 *European Journal of International Law* 9.

[140] See Moreno-Lax and Ziegler, 'Autonomy of the EU Legal Order' (n 6) 239.

[141] See J Weiler, 'The Transformation of Europe' (1991) *Yale Law Journal* 2403, 2433.

[142] Such conferral of powers can take different shapes. See D Sarooshi, *International Organisations and Their Exercise of Sovereign Powers* (Oxford, Oxford University Press, 2005).

[143] Permanent Court of International Justice, *S.S. Lotus (France v Turkey)* (1927) PCIJ (series A) No 10, para 44. Compare S Besson, Sovereignty in *Max Planck Encyclopedia of Public International Law* (Oxford, Oxford University Press, 2011) paras 36–41.

> The Permanent Court of International Justice referred to this basic principle in the following terms: 'As the European Commission is not a State, but an international institution with a special purpose, it only has the functions bestowed upon it by the Definitive Statute with a view to the fulfilment of that purpose, but it has power to exercise these functions to their full extent, in so far as the Statute does not impose restrictions upon it.' (Jurisdiction of the European Commission of the Danube, Advisory Opinion, P.C.I.J., Series B, No. 14, p. 64.)[144]

The powers of international organisations have always been seen to include implied powers.[145] After all, the constituent treaties of international organisations 'shall be interpreted in good faith in accordance with the ordinary meaning to be given to the terms of the Treaty in their context and in the light of its object and purpose'.[146] Thus, the interpretation of the constituent instruments of international organisations, and thus of the powers and objectives conferred therein, can consider the purpose of the respective organisation. It has been noted that the underlying idea would be that an international organisation 'is expected to evolve and adapt to changes on the international plane'.[147]

In its Advisory Opinion of 1949, *Reparation for Injuries*, the ICJ found that international organisations have limited legal personality as their rights and obligations 'depend upon its purposes and functions as specified or implied in its constituted documents and developed in practice'; the UN 'must be deemed to have those powers which, though not expressly provided in the Charter, are conferred upon it by necessary implication as being essential to the performance of its duties'.[148]

This broad understanding of the implied powers of international organisations has later been qualified by the ICJ as follows in the *Nuclear Weapons* Opinion regarding the question of whether the World Health Organization could be seen as possessing the competence to address the legality of the use of nuclear weapons:

> The powers conferred on international organizations are normally the subject of an express statement in their constituent instruments. Nevertheless, the necessities of international life may point to the need for organizations, in order to achieve their objectives, to possess subsidiary powers which are not expressly provided for in the basic instruments which govern their activities. It is generally accepted that international organizations can exercise such powers, known as 'implied' powers.
>
> The Court is of the opinion, however, that to ascribe to the WHO the competence to address the legality of the use of nuclear weapons even in view of their health and environmental effects would be tantamount to disregarding the principle of speciality; for

[144] ICJ Advisory Opinion, *Legality of the Use by a State of Nuclear Weapons in Armed Conflict* (n 18) para 25 (78–79) (emphasis added). See also ICJ Advisory Opinion, *Pulp Mills on the River Uruguay (Argentina v Uruguay)* (2010) ICJ Reports 113, para 89 (43).

[145] See V Engström, *Constructing the Powers of International Institutions* (Leiden, Brill, 2012) 4.

[146] Article 31 Vienna Convention on the Law of Treaties.

[147] See J Crawford, *Brownlie's Principles of Public International Law*, 9th edn (Oxford, Oxford University Press, 2019) 188.

[148] ICJ Advisory Opinion, *Reparation for Injuries suffered in the service of the United Nations* (1949) ICJ Reports 174, 179–82.

> such competence could not be deemed a necessary implication of the Constitution of the Organization in the light of the purposes assigned to it by its member States.[149]

This means that, while not unlimited, the powers of an international organisation correlate with the objectives it has been mandated to fulfil and the duties it has been mandated to perform.

2.3. EU Law

2.3.1. Primary Law

Article 4(1) EEC provided that its institutions 'shall act within the limits of the powers conferred upon it by this Treaty'. In 1992, conferral was included with the Treaty of Maastricht's Article 3b, according to which the Community 'shall act within the limits of the powers conferred upon it by this Treaty and of the objectives assigned to it therein'.

The ECSC Treaty had no comparably broad clause. Article 6 ECSC Treaty, however, stated that the ECSC 'shall be represented by its institutions, each one of them acting within the framework of its own powers and responsibilities', and that, in its international relationships, the ECSC 'shall enjoy the juridical capacity necessary to the exercise of its functions and the attainment of its ends'.[150]

2.3.2. The Early Case Law on Conferral

It is noteworthy how little seems to have been said in case law about conferral as such. Thus, not about individual legal bases, which have always preoccupied the ECJ, but about the nature of the empowerment of the European Union (at the beginning of the EEC) *per se*.[151] It is therefore also not surprising that, in textbooks, there is generally a lot written about (the different kinds of) competences and very little about the nature of conferral.

It appears that the only fundamental discussion of that topic occurred in the *Algera* case of 1957 under the ECSC Treaty, already discussed above under autonomy. AG Lagrange had the following to say in his Opinion, arguably echoing the language and logic of international law as described above:

> The Treaty is based upon delegation, with the consent of the Member States, of sovereignty to supranational institutions for a strictly defined purpose, namely the operation of a common market in coal and steel.

[149] See NM Blokker, 'International Organizations or Institutions, Implied Powers' in *Max Planck Encyclopedia of Public International Law* (Oxford, Oxford University Press, 2021), suggesting four limitations on the existence and scope of implied powers.

[150] Article 95(3) ECSC spoke of 'the powers which are conferred upon' the High Authority.

[151] See, by contrast, Case T-509/21, *International Management Group (IMG)*, ECLI:EU:T:2024:590, para 211.

> The legal principle underlying the Treaty is a principle of limited authority. The Community is a legal person governed by public law, and as such it 'shall enjoy the legal capacity it requires to perform its functions and attain its objectives' (Article 6), but only that capacity: this is the application of the principle of speciality,which is well known in public law. The way in which the functions are to be performed and the determination of the objectives to be attained are precisely fixed by the Treaty. Moreover (same article), 'the Community shall be represented by its institutions, each within the limits of its powers'. Those powers are themselves carefully defined by all the provisions of the Treaty which confer powers, and the principle of limited authority (which is precisely called 'conferred authority') is expressly stated for each institution …
>
> That is an absolutely essential aspect of the Treaty. The Member States agreed to give up part of their sovereignty only in favour of institutions functioning under clearly defined conditions, which must be sufficient in themselves. Therefore, none of the institutions can exercise powers other than those conferred upon it by the Treaty, either in relation to the other institutions or in regard to third parties, whether they be States or private persons.[152]

In *Humblet* of 1960, concerning the question of whether a Belgian tax law violated the privileges and immunities of civil servants of the ECSC, the Court stated that it had no jurisdiction to annul national measures because the ECSC Treaty 'is based on the principle of a strict separation of the powers of the Community institutions and those of the authorities of the Member States'.[153] This, however, must be seen against the specific background of that Community and does not tell us anything about conferral more generally.

In *Costa*, the Court merely speaks of the European Union having 'real powers stemming from … a transfer of powers from the States to the Community',[154] which, it is submitted, is not a very profound way of paraphrasing conferral.

2.3.3. The Early Case Law on Implied Powers

The implied powers doctrine was applied very early in the ECJ's case law. In the well-known *Fédéchar* judgment of 1956, the ECJ held that the High Authority of the Coal and Steel Community must have the power to fix prices even if that power was not expressly provided for in the ECSC Treaty, arguing as follows:

> The Court considers that without having recourse to a wide interpretation it is possible to apply a rule of interpretation generally accepted in both international and national law, according to which the rules laid down by an international treaty or a law presuppose the rules without which that treaty or law would have no meaning or could not be reasonably and usefully applied.[155]

[152] Opinion of AG Lagrange in *Algera* (n 29) 82–83.
[153] Case 6/60, *Humblet*, ECLI:EU:C:1960:48, 568.
[154] *Costa/ENEL* (n 21) 593.
[155] *Fédéchar* (n 26) 299. See also Case 25/59, *Netherlands v High Authority*, ECLI:EU:C:1960:34, 371 f; Case 20/59, *Italy v High Authority*, ECLI:EU:C:1960:33, 335, 336: 'Writers and case-law agree in recognizing

It is noteworthy that we still need to refer to *Fédéchar* as the 'leading' case on implied powers because more recent case law has not added much substantially to the application of this doctrine in EU law. This is despite or perhaps rather because it has always been viewed critically in some quarters.[156]

In 1987, the ECJ emphasised that such implied powers must be necessary to fulfil tasks expressly conferred. It held that where a Treaty Article 'confers a specific task on the Commission it must be accepted, if that provision is not to be rendered wholly ineffective, that it confers on the Commission necessarily and per se the powers which are indispensable in order to carry out that task'.[157] It has remained unclear, for instance, whether implied powers should be conceived as an exception to the principle of conferral. While *Fédéchar* above arguably does not read in that manner, the General Court has qualified implied powers as a derogation from the principle of conferral which must be 'appraised strictly'.[158]

The implied powers doctrine has been especially important for establishing the EU's external competences because few cases of such competence were expressly provided in the EU Treaties until the Treaty of Lisbon. Thus, *ERTA*, discussed below, and Opinion 1/76, discussed earlier under autonomy, have always been seen as concerning implied powers, even though there were no explicit analogies to the international law doctrine as in *Fédéchar* or references to *Fédéchar* itself, for that matter.[159] In *Kramer* of 1976, the Court, to establish in a particular case whether the (then) Community had authority (at all) to enter into international commitments, considered 'the whole scheme of Community law', stating that such authority may arise 'not only from an express conferment by the Treaty, but may equally flow implicitly from other provisions of the Treaty, from the Act of Accession and from measures adopted, within the framework of those provisions, by the Community institutions'.[160] It would follow 'from the very duties and powers which Community law has established and assigned to the institutions of the Community on the internal level that the Community has authority to enter into international commitments for the conservation of the resources of the sea'.[161]

that the rules established by a treaty imply the principles without which these rules cannot effectively or reasonably be applied'. See also Joined Cases 4-13/59, *Mannesmann*, ECLI:EU:C:1960:13, 130 f.

[156] In its *Maastricht* judgment, the German Federal Constitutional Court warned against de facto treaty change by reliance on implied powers and treaty interpretation based on *effet utile*. See BVerfG, 2 BvR 1877/97, *Maastricht Treaty*, ECLI:DE:BVerfG:1998:rs19980331.2bvr187797, para 157.

[157] Case 281/85, *Germany v Commission*, ECLI:EU:C:1987:351, para 28.

[158] Case T-496/11, *UK v ECB*, ECLI:EU:T:2015:133, para 105; Case T-143/06, *MTZ*, ECLI:EU:T:2009:441, para 47.

[159] *ERTA* (n 42). AG Dutheillet de Lamothe had discussed the concept of implied powers but did not recommend the Court to adopt it for external matters. See AG Dutheillet de Lamothe in *ERTA* (n 42) 291–93: 'It appears clear from the general scheme of the Treaty of Rome that its authors intended strictly to limit the Community's authority in external matters to the cases which they expressly laid down'.

[160] Joined Cases 3, 4 & 6/76, *Kramer*, ECLI:EU:C:1976:114, para 19/20.

[161] *Kramer* (n 160) para 30/33.

3. Locations

3.1. Express Conferral in the Treaties

Compared with the beginning of EU law, as shown above, mentions of conferral have mushroomed in the Treaties.

Article 1 TEU states that 'By this Treaty, the HIGH CONTRACTING PARTIES establish among themselves a EUROPEAN UNION, hereinafter called "the Union", on which the Member States confer competences to attain *objectives they have in common*'.[162] Article 3(6) TEU provides that 'The Union shall pursue its objectives by appropriate means commensurate with the competences which are conferred upon it in the Treaties'. Article 5(1) TEU provides that the 'limits of Union competences are governed by the principle of conferral', while its second paragraph specifies that under 'the principle of conferral, the Union shall act only within the limits of the competences conferred upon it by the Member States in the Treaties to attain the objectives set out therein. Competences not conferred upon the Union in the Treaties remain with the Member States'. Article 4(1) TEU also states that 'competences not conferred upon the Union in the Treaties remain with the Member States'. Article 4(2) TEU furthermore specifies that national security remains the sole responsibility of each Member State.

These provisions all concern the 'vertical' dimension of conferral regulating the division of powers between the European Union and the Member States. To take legally relevant measures the Union must have been empowered to do so, which must be observed concerning both the internal and the international action of the European Union.[163] As a rule, therefore, competences are conferred expressly on the European Union by the Treaties.[164]

The central Article 5 TEU states two 'flip-sides' of conferral: while the Union only has those powers it is vested with by the Member States for attaining a set of objectives, all powers not conferred by the Member States remain with them. The Treaties are largely silent on which matters are reserved for the Member States or fall outside Union law.[165] Only a few scattered provisions emphasise the remaining responsibilities of the Member States, such as Article 4(2) TEU discussed later in the context of national identity.[166]

[162] Emphasis added.

[163] Case C-600/14, *Germany v Council (COTIF)*, ECLI:EU:C:2017:935, para 44; Opinion 2/94, *ECHR I*, ECLI:EU:C:1996:140, para 24.

[164] See Article 216(1) TFEU, first alternative as an expression of this principle.

[165] For a distinction between these two concepts, see B de Witte, 'Exclusive Member State Competences – Is There Such a Thing?' in S Garben and I Govaere (eds), *The Division of Competences between the EU and the Member States: Reflections on the Past, the Present and the Future* (Oxford, Hart Publishing, 2017) 59. Compare K Granat, *The Principle of Subsidiarity and its Enforcement in the EU Legal Order: The Role of National Parliaments in the Early Warning System* (Oxford, Hart Publishing, 2018) 172.

[166] See also Article 166(1) TFEU, Article 345 TFEU and Article 17 TFEU.

Article 13(2) TEU provides that each Union institution 'shall act within the limits of the powers conferred on it in the Treaties, and in conformity with the procedures, conditions and objectives set out in them'. This relates to the 'horizontal', procedural dimension of conferral authorising Union institutions to act, stating the specific objectives to be pursued, the form or type of act that is to be adopted, and the procedure to be followed.[167]

Article 7 TFEU moreover provides that the European Union 'shall ensure consistency between its policies and activities, taking all of its objectives into account and in accordance with the principle of conferral of powers'.

3.2. *Implied Conferral*

Implied powers are not expressly provided in the Treaties. However, it could be discussed whether, in EU law, Article 4(3) TEU on the principle of loyalty has not taken over the role of the implied powers doctrine in some cases.

In *ERTA*, establishing the exclusive competence of the European Union to conclude the European Agreement on Road Transport, the Court relied on the objectives of the then EC read together with ex Article 5 EC (now Article 4(3) TEU).[168] It has been noted that in *ERTA*, by establishing implied external exclusive competence, the Court chose a solution in terms of avoidance of conflict between a Member State agreement and Union (secondary) law on competence grounds instead of a solution in terms of conflict of norms.[169] It could, however, equally be said that, in *ERTA*, the Court could have argued based on implied powers but chose not to.[170]

4. Applications

Conferral is without doubt a legal principle, as stated in Article 5(1) TEU and Article 5(2) TEU cited above. It is a general principle in the sense that it applies to any kind of Union measure, be it legislative or non-legislative, be it internal or an agreement with third states, or be it soft law.[171] It is justiciable and can be applied to review the legality of Union measures. Article 263(2) TFEU explicitly mentions lack of competence as a ground for annulment. In Opinion 2/00, the Court clarified:

[167] See Case 68/86, *UK v Council*, ECLI:EU:C:1988:85, para 32; Case C-133/06, *Parliament v Council*, ECLI:EU:C:2008:257, para 54. See also Case C-93/00, *Parliament v Council (Beef labelling system)*, ECLI:EU:C:2001:689, on the powers to amend a regulation.

[168] *ERTA* (n 42).

[169] See L Azoulai, 'Introduction: The Question of Competence' in L Azoulai (ed), *The Question of Competence in the European Union* (Oxford, Oxford University Press, 2014) 1, 4.

[170] Compare also the discussion in Delgado Casteleiro, 'Loyalty in External Relations Law' (n 127) 399–405.

[171] M Klamert, 'Commentary on Article 5 TEU' in Kellerbauer, Klamert and Tomkin (eds), *Commentary*, para 5.

> The choice of the appropriate legal basis has constitutional significance. Since the Community has conferred powers only, it must tie the Protocol to a Treaty provision which empowers it to approve such a measure. To proceed on an incorrect legal basis is therefore liable to invalidate the act concluding the agreement and so vitiate the Community's consent to be bound by the agreement it has signed. That is so in particular where the Treaty does not confer on the Community sufficient competence to ratify the agreement in its entirety, a situation which entails examining the allocation as between the Community and the Member States of the powers to conclude the agreement that is envisaged with non-member countries, or where the appropriate legal basis for the measure concluding the agreement lays down a legislative procedure different from that which has in fact been followed by the Community institutions.[172]

Thus, under the principle of conferral, a legal measure of the European Union can be invalidated because of the lack of competence of the Union (in its 'vertical' relation with the Member States) or because of a wrong legal basis entailing a wrong procedure (regarding the 'horizontal', inter-institutional dimension of conferral). Invalidation, however, is much more common for having identified an incorrect legal base or having exceeded the scope of the action permitted by the legal base, than because of the absence of competence as such.[173]

In this sense, the principle of conferral can be understood as involving a binary, non-balancing assessment of whether a Union institution has a certain power/competence or whether it has not.[174] At this stage, considerations of subsidiarity which would require such balancing are not yet applicable.[175]

As with autonomy discussed earlier, it would not seem to the point to claim that conferral has direct effect. But as with autonomy, it can of course have indirect implications for individuals when it is applied in annulment actions brought forward by non-privileged claimants under Article 267(3) TFEU or when invalidity is asserted by a private party under a preliminary reference proceeding.[176]

Different from international law logic, it would seem that the relevance of the principle of conferral for the application of EU law has its limits. Lack of conferred competence does not mean that national laws do not come within the scope of application of Union law, entailing that Member States must respect and must not be in breach of Union law, in particular, its prohibition of discrimination under

[172] Opinion 2/00, *Cartagena Protocol*, ECLI:EU:C:2001:664, para 5.

[173] An important exception is Case C-376/98, *Germany v Parliament and Council (Tobacco Advertsing I)*, ECLI:EU:C:2000:544. See also, however, S Garben, 'Commentary on Article 153 TFEU' in Kellerbauer, Klamert and Tomkin (eds), *Commentary*, para 11 on the partial annulment of the Working Time Directive in Case C-84/94, *UK v Council*, ECLI:EU:C:1996:431. Compare also Loewenthal, 'Commentary on Article 13 TEU' (n 82) paras 13–16 on conflicts of legal bases.

[174] See C Hillion, 'Conferral, Cooperation and Balance in the Institutional Framework of EU External Action' in Cremona (ed), *Structural Principles in EU External Relations Law* 117, 148–49, contrasting conferral with the principle of institutional balance. See, on the other hand, G de Baere, 'Subsidiarity as a Structural Principle Governing the Use of EU External Competences' in Cremona (ed), *Structural Principles* 93, 115.

[175] Compare, however, M Cremona, 'Structural Principles and their Role in EU External Relations Law' in Cremona (ed), *Structural Principles*: 'not limited to a binary either/or test'.

[176] Compare also Platon, 'The principle of institutional balance' (n 133) 147–50.

Article 18 TFEU as also discussed later.[177] This was explicitly held to also apply to such Treaty provisions already mentioned that could be interpreted as explicit concretisations of the principle of conferral.[178] It was also asserted for requirements set up by the Court for the organisation of national courts, which was criticised as an arrogation of competence by Poland.[179]

5. Interrelations

5.1. Conferral and Institutional Balance

Article 13(2) TEU, as mentioned, lays down the principle of institutional balance, according to which each EU institution shall act within the limits of the powers conferred on it in the Treaties, and in conformity with the procedures, conditions and objectives set out in them. The Treaties 'set up a system of allocation of powers among the EU institutions, assigning to each institution its own role in the institutional structure of the European Union and the accomplishment of the tasks entrusted to the European Union'.[180] As the Union institutions may only act within the confines of the competences conferred on them by the Treaties,[181] any encroachment by one institution on these competences conferred by the Treaties upon another institution is prohibited.[182]

A violation of the principle of institutional balance in case law commonly also constitutes a violation of a provision conferring particular competences upon an institution.[183] It has been argued that, while the approach of the Court would indicate that it is conceptually distinct and entails specific requirements, the two principles would remain deeply intertwined, if not confused, in operational terms.[184]

[177] See S Prechal, 'Competence Creep and General Principles of Law' (2010) 3 *REALaw* 5.

[178] See Klamert, 'Commentary on Article 5 TEU' (n 171) para 17 with references to case law on Article 17 TFEU and Article 345 TFEU. See also K Haraldsdóttir, 'The Nature of Neutrality in EU Law: Article 345 TFEU' (2020) 45 *EL Rev* 3.

[179] Case C-619/18, *Commission v Poland (Independence of the Supreme Court)*, ECLI:EU:C:2019:531, para 52.

[180] Case C-551/21, *Commission v Council (Fisheries Partnership Agreement)*, ECLI:EU:C:2024:281, para 61. See also Case C-70/88, *Parliament v Council (Chernobyl)*, ECLI:EU:C:1990:217, para 21; Case C-687/15, *Commission* v *Council (WRC-15)*, ECLI:EU:C:2017:803, para 40.

[181] Case C-133/06, *Parliament v Council* (n 167); Case C-409/13, *Council v Commission*, ECLI:EU:C:2015:217, para 64; Case C-24/20, *Commission v Council (Accession to the Geneva Act)*, ECLI:EU:C:2022:911, para 83.

[182] *Chernobyl* (n 180) paras 21–22; Case 138/79, *Roquette Freres*, ECLI:EU:C:1980:249, para 33; Case 139/79, *Maizena*, ECLI:EU:C:1980:250, para 34.

[183] See Loewenthal, 'Commentary on Article 13 TEU' (n 82) para 10. See also the discussion by Platon, 'The principle of institutional balance' (n 133) 146–47.

[184] See Hillion, 'Conferral, Cooperation and Balance' (n 174) 126, 147. See also the critique by M Chamon, 'The Institutional Balance, an Ill-Fated Principle of EU Law?' (2015) 21 *European Public Law* 371, 375–78 especially.

However, this does not ignore that the ECJ, as mentioned, has emphasised the 'particularly sophisticated institutional structure and a full set of legal rules to ensure its operation' as an essential characteristic of EU law.[185] This characteristic is very much protected by the principle of institutional balance, which thereby fulfils the role that the principle of separation of powers has in national constitutional law systems.[186] It was the principle of institutional balance principle that has served to interpret the Treaties in such a manner as to award the European Parliament *locus standi* to protect its institutional prerogatives, absent of such right being expressly provided in the Treaties then.[187]

5.2. Conferral and Loyalty

The principle of loyalty resonates in several ways with conferral.

Conferral with an organisation such as the European Union is conceptionally linked to its objectives and tasks and is therefore inherently functional. Loyalty is closely connected to the principle of effectiveness which is discussed later. Both loyalty and effectiveness reinforce this functional nature of conferral. Article 4(3) TEU expressly mentions the fulfilment of EU obligations, the achievement of the Union's tasks, and the attainment of the Union's objectives. Thus, as we have discussed above, Article 4(3) TEU had a similar function as implied powers, especially in *ERTA*.

As the category of shared competences shows, there is no strict division of competences between the EU level and the Member State level. This is especially pertinent in external relations, where the European Union and the Member States act jointly such as through mixed agreements and need to show unity vis-a-vis third states and in international fora, as discussed in chapter four. This absence of clear boundaries explains the importance of the principle of loyalty in Union law, where the policing of the vertical division of competences is to some extent 'outsourced' to the principle of loyalty.[188] Thus, Article 4(3) TEU has been applied in case law to preempt conflicts between Union and Member States measures by barring Member State action following certain manifestations of a Union interest. For these duties, the distinction between shared and exclusive competence is not relevant. As the Court held in the *PFOS* case, the duty of genuine cooperation 'is of general application and does not depend either on whether the Community competence concerned is exclusive or on any right of the Member States to enter into obligations towards non-member countries'.[189] It has been noted that 'even

[185] *ECHR II* (n 62) paras 158 and 164–67; *Unified Patents Court* (n 67) para 21. See also *Pringle* (n 76) para 158. See Klamert, 'Commentary on Article 1 TEU' (n 108) paras 24–26.
[186] See Loewenthal, 'Commentary on Article 13 TEU' (n 82) para 7.
[187] *Chernobyl* (n 180) paras 26–27.
[188] See M Klamert, *The Principle of Loyalty in EU Law* (Oxford, Oxford University Press, 2014) 206.
[189] Case C-246/07, *Commission v Sweden (PFOS)*, ECLI:EU:C:2010:203, para 71.

if the ECJ uses different words, at the end it seems that it continues to speak the language of exclusive competence about the duty of co-operation'.[190]

Moreover, Article 13(2) TEU restates the principle of sincere cooperation in the EU's institutional framework, which had already previously been acknowledged by the ECJ.[191] Article 13(2) TEU seeks to ensure that the EU institutions cooperate with one another in achieving the aims mentioned in Article 13(1) TEU.[192] While this obligation does not go so far as to modify the division of competences conferred, as discussed in chapter five, several specific obligations of EU institutions have been derived from the principle of mutual sincere cooperation laid down in Article 13(2) TEU.[193] Loyalty therefore also assists in securing the horizontal division of competences.

5.3. *Conferral and Effectiveness*

The connection between conferral and effectiveness is reflected in Union law most clearly in the implied powers doctrine as discussed above. There is an explicit link between the effectiveness or 'efficiency' and the question of specific powers granted to the Union to perform its tasks.[194] Thus, there is also a close connection with *effet utile* discussed later under the principle of effectiveness. In *Germany v Commission*, for example, the Court affirmed the Commission's competence to set up organised consultations because, in the absence of any action to initiate them, collaboration 'might remain a dead letter, even though provision is made for it in the Treaty'.[195]

The connection between conferral and an even stronger manifestation of effectiveness can be illustrated by the case law of the ECJ on the competence of the Union to require Member States to provide for effective criminal sanctions that has also been seen in the context of implied powers.[196] The ECJ held that, while, as 'a general rule, neither criminal law nor the rules of criminal procedure fall within the Community's competence', this would

> not prevent the Community legislature, when the application of effective, proportionate and dissuasive criminal penalties by the competent national authorities is an essential measure for combating serious environmental offences, from taking measures which relate to the criminal law of the Member States which it considers necessary in order to ensure that the rules which it lays down on environmental protection are fully effective.[197]

[190] See A Delgado Casteleiro and J Larik, 'The Duty to Remain Silent: Limitless Loyalty in EU External Relations?' (2011) 36 *EL Rev* 524, 539.

[191] Case C-65/93, *Parliament v Council*, ECLI:EU:C:1995:91, para 23.

[192] See Declaration No 3 on Article 10 TEC annexed to the ToN on inter-institutional agreements.

[193] See Loewenthal, 'Commentary on Article 13 TEU' (n 82) para 12.

[194] See Weiler, 'The Transformation of Europe' (n 141) 2415–16.

[195] *Germany v Commission* (n 157) para 29.

[196] See K Lenaerts and P van Nuffel, *European Union Law*, 3rd edn (London, Sweet & Maxwell, 2011) para 7-017.

[197] See Case C-176/03, *Commission v Council*, ECLI:EU:C:2005:542, paras 47–48.

Arguably, it was the requirement of ensuring the effective implementation of Union law that provided the point of reference for establishing competence in this case in the first place. It seems very hard to reconcile this with an orthodox application of the implied powers doctrine as discussed above. It is submitted that what was at play here instead was a (structural) principle of effectiveness discussed later.

Article 83(2) TFEU codified the case law mentioned above, conferring on the European Union the power to enact directives with minimum rules concerning the definition of criminal offences and sanctions if the approximation of criminal laws and regulations of the Member States proves essential to ensure the effective implementation of a Union policy in an area which has been subject to harmonisation measures. The necessity of the effective implementation of a Union policy thus is a precondition for the criminal law competence in Article 83(2) TFEU.[198]

6. Conclusions

We have discussed earlier that the degree of autonomy depends on the extent of powers that have been conferred on an organisation, which in turn depends on the objectives an organisation has been tasked with performing. Conferral therefore is inherently functional, which explains the relevance of the implied powers doctrine and the strong role of effectiveness. As with autonomy, it is noteworthy that the European courts have done very little to clarify this concept such as by putting it in relation to the international law principle of speciality.

The common interest alluded to in Article 1 TEU is a crucial element for conferral in the European Union, it is submitted. While such common interest can also exist under international treaty law,[199] the European Union and its law is based on the presumption that all Member States share not only the values under Article 2 TEU but also a common purpose, expressed through a host of objectives as provided in Article 3 TEU and in many other Treaty provisions, discussed in chapter two. Delegation is thus no longer for a 'strictly defined purpose' of the operation of a sectoral market as with the ECSC, but for a seemingly open-ended range of objectives grounded in values.

This broad mandate of the European Union is controlled by strict and (mostly) narrow procedural norms providing in detail what its institutions can and cannot do. It is also curtailed by the fact that, as discussed in chapter two, not all objectives provided in the Treaties are matched by competences.

[198] See E Herlin-Karnell, 'General principles and EU criminal law' in Ziegler, Neuvonen and Moreno-Lax (eds), *Research Handbook* 513, 524, who notes that effectiveness triggers the EU's *ius puniendi*.

[199] See ICJ Advisory Opinion, *Reservations to the Convention on the Prevention and Punishment of the Crime of Genocide* (1951) ICJ Reports 23. Compare A Peters, 'Compensatory Constitutionalism: The Function and Potential of Fundamental International Norms and Structures' (2006) 19 *Leiden Journal of International Law* 579, 588 with references.

Normatively, conferral in most cases applies through legal bases, respectively the principle of institutional balance. It is directly effective only in a very 'indirect' way and, as concerns the question if EU competence for a certain matter exists, applies in a binary manner. It thus aligns with the way most structural principles discussed in this book function.

4. The Principle of Equality/Non-Discrimination

1. Introduction

Among the fundamental principles of EU law are the principles of equal treatment, equality, or non-discrimination.[200] These terms can be considered as being synonymous,[201] even though the notion of 'equality' arguably has the broadest, most political connotation.

For our discussion, it is important to distinguish on what ground discrimination is prohibited in EU law.

Case law and now Article 21(1) CFR have introduced prohibitions of discrimination on several specific grounds other than nationality such as age, sex, and disability. It is submitted that these so-called special prohibitions of discrimination essentially fall under the Article 6 TEU category of principles being general principles of law that have been established by legal comparison.[202] They have their origins in international human rights law, are not context-specific and thus 'function' in a purely national context just as well as within EU law.

All of this cannot be said of the prohibition of discrimination on the grounds of nationality enshrined mainly in Article 18 TFEU, nor can it be said of the principle of equality between Member States in Article 4(2) TEU. While the prohibition of discrimination on the grounds of nationality is one of the founding principles of EU law anchored in primary law, Member State equality appeared later and until the Treaty of Lisbon only in case law.

We will also discuss a 'meta-principle of equality' underlying both these non-discrimination standards, which is one of the reasons for dealing with both these principles in one section. Another reason is that both interrelate with supremacy, as is discussed below but also in the section on supremacy later. Despite these commonalities, it will be shown that Article 18 TFEU and Article 4(2) TEU are quite different normatively.

[200] Joined Cases 117/76 & 16/77, *Ruckdeschel*, ECLI:EU:C:1977:160, para 7; Case C-442/00, *Rodríguez Caballero*, ECLI:EU:C:2002:752, para 32; Case C-144/04, *Mangold*, ECLI:EU:C:2005:709, para 76.

[201] See Case C-422/02 P, *Europe Chemi-Con*, ECLI:EU:C:2005:56. See J Wouters and P Schmitt, 'Equality Among Member States and Differentiated Integration in the EU' in LS Rossi and F Casolari (eds), *The Principle of Equality in EU Law* (New York, Springer, 2017) 43, 45–47.

[202] However spurious this may have been. See *Mangold* (n 200) on age discrimination. See ch 2.

2. Origins

2.1. Meta-Principle of Equality

A 'meta-principle of equality' according to which similar situations shall not be treated differently and different situations shall not be treated alike goes back to *Aristotle*.[203] As such, it is a 'loose principle that amounts to little more than a general standard of fairness and rationality'.[204] A general (meta) principle of equality has been explicitly recognised as an unwritten general principle of (now) Union law by the Court in 1977 requiring that 'similar situations shall not be treated differently unless differentiation is objectively justified'.[205] This has been applied numerous times since then.[206] However, already in case law from 1959 under the ECSC Treaty, the Court held that discrimination 'consisting of the dissimilar treatment of comparable situations presupposes that there is a duty to treat all interested parties on the same footing'.[207]

2.2. Member State Equality

The roots of Member State equality do not lie in national constitutional law. In public international law, the principle of sovereign equality aims to protect the smaller states from more powerful ones.[208] Article 2(1) UN Charter states that the UN is based 'on the principle of the sovereign equality of all its Members'.[209] However, it has been argued that Member State equality would not have much in common with the sovereignty-centred view on state relations typical of public international law.[210]

Member State equality was first mentioned in 1973, without any references to that concept in public international law, where the Court held the following in an infringement case against Italy:

> In permitting Member States to profit from the advantages of the Community, the Treaty imposes on them also the obligation to respect its rules. For a State unilaterally

[203] See E Muir, 'Pursuing Equality in the EU' in A Arnull and D Chalmers (eds), *The Oxford Handbook of European Union Law* (Oxford, Oxford University Press, 2015) 919, 920.

[204] See M Bell, 'The Principle of Equal Treatment: Widening and Deepening' in P Craig and G de Búrca (eds), *The Evolution of EU Law*, 2nd edn (Oxford, Oxford University Press, 2011) 611, 626.

[205] *Ruckdeschel* (n 200) para 7.

[206] See, eg, Joined Cases C-567/22 P to C-570/22 P, *Dumitrescu*, ECLI:EU:C:2024:336, para 67 with further references.

[207] Case 14/59, *Sociétés des fonderies de pont-à-Mousson*, ECLI:EU:C:1959:31, 231.

[208] See J Kokott, 'States, Sovereign Equality' in *Max Planck Encyclopedia of Public International Law* (Oxford, Oxford University Press, 2015); LS Rossi, 'The Principle of Equality among Member States of the European Union' in Rossi and Casolari (eds), *The Principle of Equality in EU Law* 3, 4–10.

[209] See also the Declaration on Principles of International Law Friendly Relations and Co-Operation among States in Accordance with the Charter of the United Nations, United Nations General Assembly, A/RES/25/2625. See M Claes, 'The equality of the Member States' in Ziegler, Neuvonen and Moreno-Lax (eds), *Research Handbook* 99, 101.

[210] See Rossi, 'The Principle of Equality among Member States' (n 208) 10–15. See, for a different perspective, Wouters and Schmitt, 'Equality among Member States' (n 201) 50–51.

> to break, according to its own conception of national interest, the equilibrium between advantages and obligations flowing from its adherence to the Community brings into question the equality of Member States before Community law and creates discriminations at the expense of their nationals, and above all of the nationals of the State itself which places itself outside the Community rules.[211]

In 1979, the Court held that while it was justified for the original Member States provisionally to accept inequalities caused by exceptions provided in acts of accession for new Member States, 'it would be contrary to the principle of the equality of the Member States before Community law to accept that such inequalities could continue indefinitely'.[212] Recent case law discussed below would suggest that Member State equality is also rooted in the meta-principle of equality.[213]

2.3. Non-Discrimination Based on Nationality

The origins of the prohibition of discrimination based on nationality are more difficult to trace. It could not have been derived from or inspired by national law. We can assume that, initially, because of the narrow economic focus of the EEC, this non-discrimination standard served a market rationale targeting national privileges.[214] In the Treaty of Rome of 1957, 'nationality' and 'sex' were the only two prohibited grounds mentioned in the Treaties in Article 7 EEC (what is now Article 18 TFEU), and in Article 119 EEC (now Article 157 TFEU) respectively, with the latter ground additionally only applying to matters of remuneration.[215]

It was most likely inspired by the General Agreement on Tariffs and Trade (GATT), which had also otherwise served as a model for drafting parts of the EEC Treaty, such as for what is now Article 28 TFEU.[216] It has been noted that the European Union was 'a child of the GATT, a regional integration agreement based on non-discrimination and market access among a number of regionally linked participants'.[217] Thus, Article I GATT on 'General Most-Favoured-Nation Treatment' and Article III GATT on 'National Treatment on Internal Taxation and Regulation' would seem analogue to what is now Article 18 TFEU.[218]

[211] Case 39/72, *Commission v Italy (Premiums for slaughtering cows)*, ECLI:EU:C:1973:13, paras 24–25.

[212] Case 231/78, *Commission v UK (Potatoes)*, ECLI:EU:C:1979:101, para 17.

[213] Case C-601/22, *WWF Österreich*, ECLI:EU:C:2024:595, para 34.

[214] See M Wendel, 'Artikel 18 AEUV' in E Grabitz, M Hilf and M Nettesheim (eds), *EU-Kommentar* (Munich, Beck, 2024) para 12.

[215] See J Tomkin, 'Commentary on Article 18 TFEU' in Kellerbauer, Klamert and Tomkin (eds), *Commentary*, para 1.

[216] See P-C Müller-Graff, 'Protectionism or reasonable national regulation?' in S Griller (ed), *At the Crossroads: The World Trading System and the Doha Round* (Vienna, Springer, 2008) 147, 150.

[217] See M Cremona, 'Neutrality or discrimination? The WTO, the EU and External Trade' in G de Búrca and J Scott (eds), *The EU and the WTO: Legal and Constitutional Issues* (Oxford, Hart Publishing, 2002) 151, 151–52.

[218] See also Article II:1 GATS requiring each Member to 'accord immediately and unconditionally to services and service suppliers of any other Member treatment no less favourable than that it accords to like services and service suppliers of any other country'. See M Klamert, *Services Liberalization in*

However, both the principles of most favoured nation and national treatment in World Trade Organization (WTO) law are, it is submitted, not really comparable to the prohibition of discrimination on grounds of nationality in EU law as it stands today.[219] It has been argued that 'from a jurisprudential point of view, the protection from discrimination on the ground of nationality is the most fundamental principle of Union law, for it accounts for the very authority of supranational law'.[220] Supranationality, put differently, would protect individuals 'against disadvantages arising *systematically* from the co-existence of nation-states' within the European Union.[221]

This makes the prohibition of discrimination based on nationality an idiosyncratic principle of EU law, whose existence is inherent in EU integration.

3. Locations

The meta-principle of equality as such does not seem to be provided in the Treaties. With the Charter of Fundamental Rights, a general principle of 'equality before the law' was added in Article 20 CFR. It however appears that Union law has so far not recognised all-encompassing equality before the law prohibiting discrimination on any conceivable ground and in all instances.[222]

What is now Article 18 TFEU contained and contains a general prohibition of discrimination on the grounds of nationality.[223] Article 45(2) TFEU on the free movement of workers is the only other provision in the Treaties that explicitly prohibits discrimination based on nationality. However, as is well known, the provisions guaranteeing the fundamental freedoms have all been considered specific prohibitions of discrimination on grounds of nationality.[224] Article 107(2) and (3) TFEU, which provide for derogations from the prohibition of State aid in Article 107(1) TFEU, have recently been qualified as 'special provisions' provided for in the Treaties, within the meaning of the first paragraph of Article 18 TFEU.[225]

According to the first sentence of Article 4(2) TEU, the Union is required to respect 'the equality of Member States before the Treaties'. This is embedded in a

the EU and WTO: Concepts, Standards and Regulatory Approaches (Cambridge, Cambridge University Press, 2014) 24.

[219] See Klamert, *Services Liberalization* (n 218) 104.

[220] See A Somek, *Individualism: An Essay on the Authority of the European Union* (Oxford, Oxford University Press, 2008) 215. See also L Azoulai, 'Structural Principles in EU Law: Internal and External' in Cremona (ed), *Structural Principles* 31, 32 f.

[221] See A Somek, 'On Supranationality' (2001) 3 *European Integration Online Papers* 12 (emphasis in the original).

[222] See the discussion by J Tomkin, 'Article 20 CFR' in Kellerbauer, Klamert and Tomkin (eds), *Commentary*, paras 1–10.

[223] The prohibition on grounds of nationality laid down in Article 21(2) CFR corresponds to Article 18(1) TFEU and must be applied in accordance with that Article. See Case C-703/17, *Krah*, ECLI:EU:C:2019:850, para 18.

[224] See, eg, Case C-3/88, *Commission v Italy*, ECLI:EU:C:1989:606, para 8.

[225] Case C-320/21 P, *Ryanair*, ECLI:EU:C:2023:712, para 111.

paragraph that also confirms the Union's respect as regards the national identities of the Member States, their fundamental political and constitutional structures, and the essential state functions they fulfil, discussed later. There is not much else in the Treaties on the equality of Member States.[226]

On the contrary, there are some Treaty provisions which arguably are based on the notion that some Member States can be in a different situation from other Member States, in which case they are not 'equal before the Treaties' to rephrase Article 4(2) TEU. This concerns the rules in the Treaties on qualified majority voting in the Council, which have not been deemed in breach of the principle of equality of Member States by the ECJ.[227] Also, Article 27 TFEU and Article 114(5) TFEU allow for Member State-specific circumstances that can dispose of the requirement of uniformity in applying harmonisation measures. One could moreover point to opt-outs and other forms of differentiated integration to make the case that Member States are not equal before the Treaties.[228] One might say that the extent of how equal a Member State is before the Treaties depends very much on what derogations it could secure at accession.[229]

4. Applications

Article 18 TFEU and Article 4(2) TEU apply very differently in most matters, it is submitted.

Article 18 TFEU has direct effect, including what has been called a 'semi' horizontal direct effect.[230] So far, the Court has only had the opportunity to rule on whether the specific prohibition of discrimination enshrined in Article 45 TFEU produces 'full' horizontal direct effect, thus also applies in litigation between private individuals.[231] It has however been argued that this reasoning should apply similarly as regards the *lex generalis* of Article 18 TFEU.[232] According to the Court, every provision of *EU* law must be interpreted in the light of the general principle of equality, of which Article 18 TFEU is a specific expression.[233] Article 18 TFEU, by contrast, is mainly a standard of review for *Member State* measures. In that respect, it (only) applies to situations falling within the scope of EU law.[234] It

[226] See, however, Article 244(a) TFEU providing that Member States 'shall be treated on a strictly equal footing' regarding the determination of the sequence of, and the time spent by, their nationals as members of the Commission.

[227] Case C-157/21, *Poland v Parliament and Council (Conditionality mechanism)*, ECLI:EU:C:2022:98.

[228] Compare also the discussion by Claes, 'The equality of the Member States' (n 209) 110–12.

[229] See Wouters and Schmitt, 'Equality among Member States' (n 201) 50–51.

[230] See Tomkin, 'Commentary on Article 18 TFEU' (n 215) para 29.

[231] Case C-281/98, *Angonese*, ECLI:EU:C:2000:296, paras 35–36. See M Kellerbauer, 'Commentary on Article 45 TFEU' in Kellerbauer, Klamert and Tomkin (eds), *Commentary*, para 92.

[232] See Tomkin, 'Commentary on Article 18 TFEU' (n 215) para 30.

[233] Case 374/87, *Orkem*, ECLI:EU:C:1989:387; Case C-98/91, *Herbrink*, ECLI:EU:C:1994:24. See Tomkin, 'Commentary on Article 18 TFEU' (n 215) para 2.

[234] See, eg, Case C-581/18, *TÜV Rheinland*, ECLI:EU:C:2020:453, para 29. This includes situations where Member States implement EU rules: Case C-5/88, *Wachauf*, ECLI:EU:C:1989:321. See, for examples, Tomkin, 'Commentary on Article 18 TFEU' (n 215) paras 4–7.

applies to situations in respect of which the Treaties provide no specific rules on non-discrimination in primary law[235] or secondary law.[236] While it has remained unclear whether discrimination based on nationality is open to justification,[237] it allows for weighing qualified interests advanced by Member States as well as for weighing other fundamental rights.[238]

By contrast, the principle of Member State equality has no direct effect because it does not protect individuals. Member State equality arguably could function as a standard of interpretation for Union secondary law, even though this has not happened until now as far as can be seen. It would certainly be true for acts making explicit reference to Member State equality, such as the Conditionality Regulation, which states that 'the Commission must conduct a thorough qualitative assessment, which should be objective, impartial and fair, should respect the principles of objectivity, non-discrimination and equality of Member States before the Treaties and should be conducted according to a non-partisan and evidence-based approach'.[239]

Different from Article 18 TFEU, Article 4(2) TEU is a standard of review not for Member State measures but for *Union law* measures. It has mainly been applied in an accession context, where the Court has held repeatedly that different rules cannot apply for Member States that have become Members earlier and for Member States that have acceded more recently.[240] Absent an accession context, invoking Article 4(2) TEU by claiming that secondary law would fail to consider differences between Member States has not been successful.[241]

There is one commonality in the application of Articles 18 TFEU and 4(2) TEU, it is submitted. In theory, applying prohibitions of discrimination (in any context) would involve an assessment of whether discrimination exists in the first place; only if this is affirmed must it be examined whether the discrimination can be justified.[242] In line with the meta principle of equality, discrimination will

[235] Case 8/77, *Sagulo*, ECLI:EU:C:1977:131. See, eg, *TÜV Rheinland* (n 234); Case C-566/15, *Erzberger*, ECLI:EU:C:2017:562, para 25.

[236] Directive 2004/38/EC [2004] OJ L158/77. See Case C-333/13, *Dano*, ECLI:EU:C:2014:2358 and Case C-709/20, *CG*, ECLI:EU:C:2021:602, para 67.

[237] See Tomkin, 'Commentary on Article 18 TFEU' (n 215) paras 27–28.

[238] See T Lock, 'Commentary on Article 52 CFR' in Kellerbauer, Klamert and Tomkin (eds), *Commentary*, paras 15–17.

[239] Recitals 16 and 26 of that Regulation (EU, Euratom) 2020/2092 of the European Parliament and of the Council of 16 December 2020 on a general regime of conditionality for the protection of the Union budget [2020] OJ L433I, 1, and corrigendum [2021] OJ L373, 94. See *Poland v Parliament and Council (Conditionality mechanism)* (n 227) para 340.

[240] See Joined Cases C-63/90 & C-67/90, *Portugal and Spain v Council*, ECLI:EU:C:1992:381, paras 36–37 and 44. See also, applying pre-Lisbon law, Case C-336/09 P, *Poland v Commission*, ECLI:EU:C:2012:386, paras 36–37.

[241] See Case C-128/17, *Poland v Parliament and Council*, ECLI:EU:C:2019:194. See now also Joined Cases C-541/20 to C-555/20, *Mobility Package*, ECLI:EU:C:2024:818, paras 331–32, 332: finding that even if some Member States are indirectly affected more than others by a certain provision of secondary law, notwithstanding that it applies without distinction, it cannot be considered to be discriminatory, 'as such a harmonisation measure inevitably produces different effects depending on the prior state of the various national law and practices'.

[242] For a comparison with WTO law, see Klamert, *Services Liberalization* (n 218) 145–46, 271–74.

exist when comparable situations are treated differently and different situations are treated in the same way.[243] Comparability must be assessed not globally and abstractly, but in a specific and concrete manner having regard to all the elements which characterise them, determined in particular in the light of the subject matter and purpose of the EU act which makes the distinction in question and also taking into account the principles and objectives of the field to which the act relates.[244]

The importance of a careful application of this test has been demonstrated in *Austria v Germany* concerning a German law according to which everyone using certain roads in Germany had to pay a highway toll, whereas owners of cars registered in Germany were compensated through a car tax reduction.[245] The Advocate General had denied the comparability between owners of cars registered abroad (who do not pay such tax) and owners of cars registered in Germany, thereby denying any discrimination.[246] The Court in contrast correctly looked at the situation of the persons using German highways, finding that it was discrimination if a part of this group effectively did not have to pay taxes because their cars were registered in that Member State. The level of abstraction was thereby determined by the purpose of the German law in question, whose objective primarily lay in introducing a highway toll, as opposed to regulating taxes.

When and how this test of comparability is applied under Article 18 TFEU (and the fundamental freedoms as its *leges speciales*) is often hard to foresee.[247] The only outlier under the fundamental freedoms is the area of taxation, where the Court has regularly considered arguments as to whether different groups of taxpayers are in a comparable situation and, in the absence of such comparability, has denied the existence of discrimination from the outset.[248] This test has now also been applied in a case on a claim by Austria based on Member State equality that it should be exempted from the system of strict protection of wolf populations under the Habitats Directive that was adopted before Austria's accession in 1995.[249] This was not successful because Austria did not express any reservation as to the inclusion of its wolf population nor did it adduce any evidence such as to show that it was in a situation comparable to that of the other Member States whose wolf populations were, on the same date, exempted from the system of strict protection.

[243] *Mobility Package* (n 241) para 308 with further references. See also M Klamert, 'Supremacy, the Uniformity of EU Law, and the Principle of Equality' (2022) *Austrian Law Journal* 82.

[244] *Mobility Package* (n 241) para 309 with further references. See also the Opinion of AG Bobek in Case C-193/17, *Cresco Investigation*, ECLI:EU:C:2018:614, para 35, and the Opinion of AG Bobek, Case C-143/16, *Abercrombie & Fitch*, ECLI:EU:C:2017:235, para 40.

[245] Case C-591/17, *Austria v Germany*, ECLI:EU:C:2019:504.

[246] AG Wahl in Case C-591/17, *Austria v Germany*, ECLI:EU:C:2019:99. On the fallacy of this reasoning, see M Klamert, 'Maut, Diskriminierung und Methode', Editorial (2019) *European Journal of Business Law* 257.

[247] See critically, Klamert, *Services Liberalization* (n 218) 148–51.

[248] See, eg, Case C-279/93, *Schumacker*, ECLI:EU:C:1995:31, para 30; Case C-80/94, *Wielockx*, ECLI:EU:C:1995:271, para 17.

[249] *WWF Österreich* (n 213).

5. Interrelations

5.1. (Member State) Equality, Solidarity and Mutual Trust

Article 4(2) TEU has been seen as having a connection with the principles of solidarity and mutual trust.[250] A straight line can be drawn from the equality of Member States via solidarity and mutual trust to a prohibition of unilateralism. The anchor for the Court seems to be EU membership, holding Member States to their commitment to adhere to Union law when joining the European Union. This logic of course must be qualified with a view to opt-outs and other exceptions that have been agreed on at accession, as mentioned above. The 'balance between the advantages and obligations arising from its membership of the European Union' is not upset when a Member State relies on the derogations granted to it.

The connection with solidarity is obvious from the fact that the *Premiums for Slaughtering Cows* judgment mentioned above is also one of the foundational judgments for the ('negative' side of the) principle of solidarity prohibiting unilateral measures of Member States as discussed later.[251] It has been paraphrased as follows in *Commission v Hungary* of 2024:

> By unilaterally upsetting the balance between the advantages and obligations arising from its membership of the European Union, a Member State calls into question observance of the principle of equality of the Member States before EU law. That failure in the duty of solidarity accepted by the Member States by the fact of their accession to the European Union strikes at the very root of the EU legal order.[252]

As mentioned in chapter two, mutual trust is based on the 'fundamental premise' that each Member State shares the EU's values with all the other Member States, and recognises that they share them with it, which would imply and justify the existence of mutual trust between the Member States 'that those values will be recognised and, therefore, that the law of the European Union that implements them will be respected'.[253] Thus, mutual trust is built on the understanding between the Member States that they are adhering to their obligations under Union law. Prohibiting unilateral measures by Member States therefore provides an essential safeguard to uphold this presumption in the relations between the Member States. Framing this by relying on the 'horizontal' principles of solidarity and Member State equality complements the more 'vertical' approach relying on supremacy discussed below.

While these requirements flowing from Member State equality address the Member States, there is also a side to it more in line with the wording of Article 4(2) TEU, which addresses the Union. It has been noted that to respect the equality of Member States under the Treaties 'a precondition for any serious attempt to pacify

[250] See Rossi, 'The Principle of Equality among Member States' (n 208) 3; Claes, 'The equality of the Member States' (n 209) 114–16.

[251] *Premiums for Slaughtering Cows* (n 211).

[252] See Case C-123/22, *Commission v Hungary*, ECLI:EU:C:2024:493, para 117.

[253] *ECHR II* (n 62) para 168. See, now, in the context of Union citizenship, Case C-181/23, *Commission v Malta*, ECLI:EU:C:2025:283.

Europe was to avoid the mistakes of the past, such as humiliating a country or nation'.[254] It is submitted that this sentiment also translates into an argument that EU law should be applied evenly and with the same rigour to all Member States. Thus, respecting the equality of Member States before the Treaties would mean for the Commission as the guardian of the Treaties to respect a certain equidistance to all Member States unless it would risk undermining the mutual trust between Member States and between Member States and the Union organs.[255] If one or more Member States was under the impression that for instance the European Commission targets them more often or more severely with infringement proceedings than other Member States, the Member State(s) concerned would likely lose confidence in the fairness and objectivity of its relations with the Commission, and would most likely also look at the other 'favoured' Member States with contempt.

5.2. Equality and Supremacy

In *Costa/ENEL*, the Court held that '[t]he executive force of Community law cannot vary from one State to another in deference to subsequent domestic laws, without jeopardizing the attainment of the objectives of the Treaty set out in Article 5(2) [now Article 4(3) TEU] and giving rise to the discrimination prohibited by Article 7 [now Article 18 TFEU]'.[256] There is thus an obvious connection between supremacy and the prohibition of discrimination on grounds of nationality, which, however, has been neglected in the literature for a long time and has not been repeated by the Court until recently.[257]

In the aftermath of the ultra vires decision by the German Federal Constitutional Court in the PSPP/*Weiss* case,[258] the Court of Justice (unusually) issued a press release arguing that Article 4(2) TEU would underpin the supremacy of EU law by requiring equality of Member States 'before the law'.[259] In *Euro Box Promotion*, the Grand Chamber of the Court held in connection with the principle of supremacy that the Union could respect the equality of Member States only if the Member States were unable to rely on unilateral measures.[260] In *Commission v Hungary*, the Grand Chamber of the Court found

> that the deliberate evasion by a Member State of the application of a common policy as a whole constitutes an unprecedented and exceptionally serious infringement of EU

[254] See E Muir, *An Introduction to the EU Legal Order* (Cambridge, Cambridge University Press, 2023) 3.
[255] See Klamert, 'Loyalty and Solidarity in the Euro-Crisis' (n 33) 704.
[256] *Costa/ENEL* (n 21).
[257] Joined Cases C-357/19 et al, *Euro Box Promotion*, ECLI:EU:C:2021:1034, para 246; Case C-430/21, *RS (Effet des arrêts d'une cour constitutionnelle)*, ECLI:EU:C:2022:99, para 48. See, further, Klamert, 'Commentary on Article 1 TEU' (n 108) para 34. See also Claes, 'The equality of the Member States' (n 209) 113.
[258] BVerfG, BvR 859/15 et al, *Public Sector Asset Purchase Programme (PSPP)*, ECLI:DE:BVerfG:2020:rs20200505.2bvr085915.
[259] ECJ Press Release 58/20 of 8 May 2020, available at: curia.europa.eu/jcms/upload/docs/application/pdf/2020-05/cp200058en.pdf.
[260] *Euro Box Promotion* (n 257) para 249.

> law, which represents a significant threat to the unity of EU law and to the principle of equality of the Member States, referred to in Article 4(2) TEU.[261]

We will unpack how supremacy relates to the prohibition of discrimination on grounds of nationality on the one hand and Member State equality on the other hand later in this chapter.

Suffice to note here that Article 18 TFEU has never been applied by the Court or understood in the literature as conferring a right on a national/resident against its 'own' Member State (of residence) concerning the application of EU law.[262] In other words, Article 18 TFEU commonly prohibits the application of the law of Member State X because it would discriminate against a person from Member State Y. In *Costa/ENEL*, by contrast, the idea rather seems to be that a person in Member State X would be discriminated against in Member State X if Member State X does not give precedence to Union law.[263]

Suffice to note furthermore that Article 4(2) TEU, by its wording, would seem to concern only the position of the Union vis-a-vis the Member States but not vice versa.

5.3. *Equality and Judicial Protection*

In the section on the principle of effectiveness, we will discuss the *Rewe* case law, which has introduced a specific principle of effectiveness in the context of the indirect enforcement of Union rights. This *Rewe*-effectiveness is an emanation of the principle of loyalty, as will be explained later. That case law has also introduced a so-called principle of equivalence, which, by contrast, is an expression of the general prohibition of discrimination under Article 18 TFEU.[264]

Already in early case law, the Court held that, when Union law contains no specific provisions relating to supervision by competent national authorities, these authorities are to 'act in this field with the same degree of care as they exercise in implementing their national legislation, so as to prevent any erosion of the effectiveness of Community law'.[265] Moreover, the principle of equivalence requires that the national rule at issue be applied without distinction, whether the infringement alleged is of Union law or national law, where the purpose and cause of action are similar.[266] Thus, actions involving the enforcement of acts of a national public

[261] *Commission v Hungary* (n 252) para 120.

[262] On the irrelevance of 'reverse discrimination', see Case C-251/90, *Wood and Cowie*, ECLI:EU:C:1992:198.

[263] Compare B de Witte, 'Retour à "Costa" – La primauté du droit communautaire à la lumière du droit international' (1984) *Revue trimestrielle de droit européen* 425, 441.

[264] See Case C-34/02, *Pasquini*, ECLI:EU:C:2003:366, para 57. See also F Episcopo, 'The Vicissitudes of Life at the Coalface: Remedies and Procedures for Enforcing Union Law before the National Courts' in P Craig and G de Búrca (eds), *The Evolution of EU Law*, 3rd edn (Oxford, Oxford University Press, 2021) 275, 294.

[265] Joined Cases 146, 192 & 193/81, *BayWa*, ECLI:EU:C:1982:146, para 22.

[266] See Case C-429/15, *Danqua*, ECLI:EU:C:2016:789, para 30; Case C-417/13, *ÖBB Personenverkehr*, ECLI:EU:C:2015:38, para 74. See Case C-460/06, *Paquay*, ECLI:EU:C:2007:601, for equivalence between different Union rights.

authority and those involving the enforcement of an act of an EU institution must be treated equally.[267]

6. Conclusions

We have argued that Member State equality and the prohibition of discrimination based on nationality are different from traditional, fundamental, equality rights. Member State equality is a concept familiar from public international law but there is little to indicate that it was introduced into EU law against that background. The prohibition of discrimination based on nationality hardly has parallels in public international law and is best seen as an idiosyncratic principle of EU law more or less *ab initio*. It is, with effective judicial protection, the most axiological of the structural principles discussed here.

Member State equality would seem to protect the interests of the Member States but has had weak normative effects until now. Quite unexpectedly, it has rather been invoked to protect the Union's interest in the uniform application of its law through supremacy. This can be explained by early case law that has mentioned Member State equality together with solidarity to argue against (national) unilateralism.

The prohibition of discrimination based on nationality protects individuals similar to a fundamental right but has equally been relied on to rationalise supremacy. Recall also its interrelation with autonomy for ensuring the uniform interpretation and application of EU law. The prohibition of discrimination based on nationality does therefore not only enshrine a substantive principle such as fundamental rights but has a much broader, more systemic function in EU law. It could be called a fundamental right of European integration.

Both principles have in common that their roots lie in the meta-principle of equality, which, at least in theory, requires that comparability is considered when assessing the existence of discrimination in respect of unequal treatment. Politically, this is a sensitive matter when dealings with Member States are concerned.

5. National (Constitutional) Identity

1. Introduction

Of all the principles discussed in this chapter, including national identity is certainly the least obvious choice. It is not in the list of essential characteristics of EU law developed by the ECJ. It is also not mentioned in the literature when

[267] See M Klamert and B Schima, 'Commentary on Article 19 TEU' in Kellerbauer, Klamert and Tomkin (eds), *Commentary*, para 44 with further references.

general or structural principles of EU law are discussed, as shown in chapter two. However, it has been termed the 'principle of national (constitutional) identity' in the literature.[268] Indeed, it would appear that considering national constitutional identity as being a 'principle' is without alternative because of its location amongst other key principles in Article 4 TEU and because it has been applied in a wide range of EU law contexts.[269]

It is rather the question of whether it should be seen as a *structural* principle on a par with supremacy or autonomy. While we have discussed the identity of the European Union and of EU law, especially under the principle of autonomy, national identity is about the Member States' identities. This could prompt and has indeed raised expectations that Article 4(2) TEU might be an antagonist to provisions such as loyalty that have a 'federal' bend. As we will see, the European courts have so far blunted such potential of Article 4(2) TEU.

Nonetheless, we would suggest that national (constitutional) identity should also be seen as a structural principle of EU law. It may be an outlier but its interrelations with other structural principles discussed below show that the structure of the European Union and of EU law is not one-dimensionally geared at EU 'sovereignty' but must be counterbalanced with the sovereignty of the Member States.[270] And this sovereignty is, at least as far as primary law is concerned, channelled through national identity.

As we most other principles discussed in this book, the literature on national identity is abundant and it is not the aim here to engage with all of it.

2. Origins

Article 6(3) of the Treaty of Amsterdam and Article F(1) of the Treaty of Maastricht provided that the Union respects the national identities of its Member States but did not further elaborate on this.

Contrary to most other structural principles, where it is more or less clear that they are not derived from or inspired by national law, the opposite is the case with national identity, which cannot have roots in international law. The notion of 'constitutional identity' first appeared in a decision by the French Conseil constitutionnel, where it served as a conflict resolution mechanism in favour of national interests.[271] Nonetheless, the Court, in developing this concept, did not seem to

[268] See K Lenaerts and JA Gutiérrez-Fons, 'A Constitutional Perspective' in R Schütze and T Tridimas (eds), *Oxford Principles of European Union Law: The European Union Legal Order: Volume I* (Oxford, Oxford University Press, 2018) 103, 140.

[269] See Lenaerts and Gutiérrez-Fons, 'A Constitutional Perspective' (n 268) 140.

[270] Compare also J Larik, 'Pars Pro Toto: The Member States' Obligations of Sincere Cooperation, Solidarity and Unity' in Cremona (ed), *Structural Principles* 175, 191.

[271] See B de Witte, 'Direct Effect, Primacy and the Nature of the Legal Order' in Craig and de Búrca (eds), *The Evolution of EU Law*, 2nd edn, 323, 355.

follow the 'method' laid down in Article 6(3) TEU seeking input from concepts existing in the constitutional law of the Member States.

In the case law of the European courts, national identity in the sense it is understood today, seems to have first been mentioned in the *Groener* judgment of 1989, where the Court held that 'the policy followed by Irish governments for many years has been designed not only to maintain but also to promote the use of Irish as a means of expressing national identity and culture'.[272]

3. Locations

According to Article 4(2) TEU, the Union must respect the national identities of the Member States that are 'inherent in their fundamental structures, political and constitutional, inclusive of regional and local self-government'.[273] The third indent of the preamble to the CFR states that the Union 'contributes to the preservation and to the development of these common values while respecting the diversity of the cultures and traditions of the peoples of Europe as well as the national identities of the Member States and the organisation of their public authorities at national, regional and local levels'.

Article 4(2) TEU also includes a requirement that the Union respect 'essential State functions' of the Member States, which comprise 'ensuring the territorial integrity of the State, maintaining law and order and safeguarding national security', which appears to be distinct from national identity.[274] The last sentence of Article 4(2) TEU declares national security as the sole responsibility of each Member State.

4. Applications

National identity is an elusive concept in EU law beyond the protection of long-standing and uncontroversial interests of Member States about language matters and national federal structures as shown below.[275] It has been said that the principle of national (constitutional) identity would oblige the European Union to protect the 'integrity' of Member States, meaning that the European Union (under current primary law) may not transform the Member States into the component states of a federation.[276] It is unclear what this means exactly, not least because conceptions of federations famously differ.[277] It would seem to call on the ECJ

[272] Case C-379/87, *Groener*, ECLI:EU:C:1989:599, para 18.
[273] The provision replaces Article I-5(1) of the failed Constitutional Treaty in this respect.
[274] See the discussion in G Martinico, 'Taming National Identity: A Systematic Understanding of Article 4.2 TEU' (2021) 27 *European Public Law* 447, 457–59.
[275] See also R Bruggeman and J Larik, 'The Elusive Contours of Constitutional Identity: Taricco as a Missed Opportunity' (2020) 35 *Utrecht Journal of International and European Law* 20.
[276] See Lenaerts and Gutiérrez-Fons, 'A Constitutional Perspective' (n 268) 140.
[277] See Klamert, 'Commentary on Article 1 TEU' (n 108) para 11.

especially to respect certain boundaries in its law-developing function but it is not clear where these boundaries should lie.

We have mentioned that the ECJ has in some cases referred to 'principles of a national constitutional structure' of Member States, which could not affect the primacy of EU law.[278] The legal systems of the Member States do comprise such structural principles.[279] Under Austrian law, they are called *Baugesetze*, as mentioned in the Introduction. However, these principles as defined under national law would not seem to necessarily correspond to what the ECJ accepts as elements of national identity under Article 4(2) TEU. While the 'status of the State as a Republic' is a Baugesetz under Austrian constitutional law, restrictions on nobility on issue in *Sayn-Wittgenstein*, albeit connected, do not really qualify as such.[280]

National identity does not have direct effect because it concerns the relationship between the Union and the Member States, not individuals. In theory, it could be applied as a standard of review for Union law measures. However, as far as can be seen, this has never been brought up in a case before the European courts and even if such a claim were made, it seems very unlikely that the Court would accept such a function of that part of Article 4(2) TEU. This can be deduced from case law, according to which Article 4(2) TEU does not oblige the European Union to give priority to national interests over Union interests.[281]

By contrast, national identity has been applied in case law as a guide for the interpretation of Union law. Thus, the Court has interpreted EU law as to not oppose the devolution of powers to regional authorities.[282] The ECJ has considered the autonomous status of regions when interpreting ex Article 87(1) EC (now Article 107(1) TFEU).[283] Also, the concept of a 'region' in the context of cohesion policy has been interpreted in light of Article 4(2) TEU.[284]

Under the fundamental freedoms, the Court has recognised national constitutional law as an element of national identity, which must be taken into

[278] Case 11/70, *Internationale Handelsgesellschaft*, ECLI:EU:C:1970:114, para 3; Case 97/87, *Dow Chemical Ibérica*, ECLI:EU:C:1989:380, para 38.

[279] See S Schill and C Krenn, 'Artikel 4 EUV' in Grabitz, Hilf and Nettesheim (eds), *EU-Kommentar*, para 18; and R Streinz, 'Art 4 EUV' in R Streinz (ed), *EUV/AEUV*, 3rd edn (Munich, Beck, 2018) paras 21 and 23.

[280] See Case C-208/09, *Sayn-Wittgenstein*, ECLI:EU:C:2010:806, para 92. See K Stöger, 'Art 4 EUV' in T Jaeger and K Stöger (eds), *Kommentar zu EUV und AEUV* (Vienna, Manz, 2024) paras 34–35. Compare I Kaczorowska-Ireland, 'What is the European Union required to respect under Article 4(2) TEU?: The uniqueness approach' (2019) 25 *European Public Law* 57.

[281] See the discussion in M Claes, 'Negotiating Constitutional Identity or Whose Identity is it Anyway?' in M Claes et al (eds), *Constitutional Conversations in Europe: Actors, Topics and Procedures* (Cambridge, Intersentia, 2012) 205, 226–27.

[282] Joined Cases 21 to 24/72, *International Fruit*, ECLI:EU:C:1972:115, para 4; Case C-428/07, *Horvath*, ECLI:EU:C:2009:47, para 49. See E Cloots, 'The European Court of Justice and Member State Federalism: Balancing or Categorisation?' in E Cloots, G de Baere and S Scottiaux (eds), *Federalism in the European Union* (Oxford, Hart Publishing, 2012) 322, 344.

[283] See Case C-88/03, *Portugal v Commission (Azores)*, ECLI:EU:C:2006:511, paras 54–68; Joined Cases C-428–434/06, *UGT-Rioja*, ECLI:EU:C:2008:488. See D Fromage, 'National Constitutional Identity and Its Regional Dimension Post-Lisbon as Part of a General Trend Towards Multilevel Governance Within the EU' (2021) 27 *European Public Law* 497.

[284] Case T-529/13, *Balázs-Árpád Izsák*, ECLI:EU:T:2016:282.

consideration 'when a balance is struck between legitimate interests and the right of free movement of persons recognised under European Union law'.[285] It has been argued that Article 4(2) TEU could be understood as permitting domestic constitutional courts to invoke, under certain limited circumstances, constitutional limits to the primacy of EU law, thereby 'reconciling' national identity with supremacy.[286] However, arguably, in its case law on the fundamental freedoms, the Court did not balance supremacy with national identity as if they were competing principles because there was no question that Union law in the form of the fundamental freedoms takes precedence over national law. The 'only' relevant question was how primary or secondary law must be interpreted taking into account certain fundamentals of the national constitutional order. It has also been argued that national identity should be seen as an absolute standard.[287]

5. Interrelations

5.1. National Identity and Conferral

Article 4(2) TEU has been referred to by the ECJ when stating that EU law would not require Member States to adopt a particular constitutional model governing the relationships and interaction between the various branches of the State, in particular as regards the definition and delimitation of their competences.[288]

In the literature, Article 4(2) TEU has been linked to the exercise of competences, arguing that the provision 'could be used to interpret existing derogations broadly within EU law or even potentially to recognise national identity as an independent derogation or as a basis for setting aside EU measures as invalid'.[289] The possibility to set aside EU measures based on Article 4(2) TEU could be seen 'as limiting the scope of the EU's competence or at least the exercise thereof in light of the principles of subsidiarity and proportionality'.[290]

[285] *Sayn-Wittgenstein* (n 280) para 83. See Opinion of AG Poiares Maduro in Case C-213/07, *Michaniki*, ECLI:EU:C:2008:544, para 33. See also Case C-391/20, *Cilevičs and Others*, ECLI:EU:C:2022:638, para 83. Compare N Nic Shuibhne, 'Primary Laws: Judging Free Movement Restrictions after Lisbon' in P Koutrakos, N Nic Shuibhne and P Syrpis (eds), *Exceptions from EU Free Movement Law: Derogation, Justification and Proportionality* (Oxford, Hart Publishing, 2016) 297, 312–17.

[286] See A von Bogdandy and S Schill, 'Overcoming absolute primacy: Respect for national identity under the Lisbon Treaty' (2011) 48 *CML Rev* 1417. This is denied by E Cloots, *National Identity in EU Law* (Oxford, Oxford University Press, 2015) 181–82, and by M Claes, 'Primacy of EU Law in European and National Law' in A Arnull and D Chalmers (eds), *The Oxford Handbook of European Union Law* (Oxford, Oxford University Press, 2015) 178, 205.

[287] See T Weber, *Bundesstaatliche Identitäten und ihre Achtung im Unionsrecht* (Baden-Baden, Nomos, 2022) 132–35.

[288] *RS (Effet des arrêts d'une cour constitutionnelle)* (n 257) para 43.

[289] See M Dobbs, 'Sovereignty, Article 4(2) TEU and the Respect of National Identities: Swinging the Balance of Power in Favour of the Member States?' (2014) 33 *Yearbook of European Law* 298, 300.

[290] See Dobbs, 'Sovereignty' (n 289) 301.

Similarly, AG Kokott has argued that national identity 'also has a vertical dimension, that is to say the Treaties confer on it a role in the delimitation of competences between the European Union and the Member States'.[291] This would be apparent in the title of Article I-5 of the Constitutional Treaty, on which the current Article 4 TEU is based, which was worded 'Relations between the Union and the Member States' and would be supported by the other two paragraphs in the current version of Article 4 TEU.[292]

Indeed, the national identities clause is embedded not only in a paragraph containing the principle of Member State equality as discussed above, but is also grouped with Article 4(1) TEU emphasising that 'competences not conferred upon the Union in the Treaties remain with the Member States'. As mentioned, Article 4(2) TEU also states that national security 'remains the sole responsibility of each Member State'. This has been called a 'negative competence' provision owed to fears of the Member States that the European Union would arrogate competence in the area of internal security in the context of combating terrorism.[293] Arguably, this must be read in context with Articles 69 and 72 TFEU, among others, conferring competence in these matters, albeit with particular emphasis on the principle of subsidiarity and the competences of the Member States. This national security clause has been of limited relevance in case law so far.[294]

Based on this systematic interpretation, AG Kokott has argued that 'the Court may carry out only a limited review of the measures adopted by a Member State for the purposes of safeguarding its national identity', thus reducing the intensity of the review carried out by the Court.[295] According to AG Kokott, this should mean that fundamental political and constitutional structures specific to each Member State would eliminate a review of the proportionality of such national measures.[296] This is an interesting approach although it has not been picked up by the Court in that case.[297] It would only operationalise national identity if a proportionality test is applicable, which however is the case in quite many constellations.[298] It would thus make qualified concerns regarding national identity a sort of 'super'-public interest justifying Member State measures especially vis-a-vis EU law prohibitions such as the fundamental freedoms and free movement rights under Union citizenship.

However, it would not, notably, mean that any exercise of Union competence would need to be checked against national identity. It especially would not affect

[291] Opinion of AG Kokott in Case C-490/20, *Pancharevo*, ECLI:EU:C:2021:296, para 83.

[292] Opinion of AG Kokott in *Pancharevo* (n 291) paras 84–85.

[293] See W Kahl, 'Art 4 EUV' in C Calliess and M Ruffert (eds), *EUV/AEUV*, 6th edn (Munich, Beck, 2022) para 45.

[294] See also de Witte, 'Exclusive Member State Competences' (n 165) 71–72. See also Joined Cases C-511/18, C-512/18 & C-520/18, *La Quadrature du Net*, ECLI:EU:C:2020:791, para 135.

[295] Opinion of AG Kokott in *Pancharevo* (n 291) para 90. See also Opinion of AG Poiares Maduro in Case C-135/08, *Rottmann*, ECLI:EU:C:2009:588, points 24 and 25.

[296] Opinion of AG Kokott *Pancharevo* (n 291) paras 90, 107.

[297] Case C-490/20, *Pancharevo*, ECLI:EU:C:2021:1008.

[298] See Klamert, 'Commentary on Article 5 TEU' (n 171) para 38.

if the Union has a certain competence. From a systematic perspective, this makes sense because there is (only) one part of Article 4(2) TEU that explicitly reads to that effect, viz the national security clause and the curtailing effects even with this clause are uncertain.[299]

5.2. National Identity and Loyalty

In the literature, the identity clause has been linked to the loyalty principle in Article 4(3) TEU discussed below.[300] It has been argued that Article 4 TEU should be read systematically and the interventionist effects of the duty of loyalty could be counterbalanced by the antagonistic national identity clause in Article 4(2) TEU. There is certainly a point in emphasising the need to see Article 4 TEU in its entirety and such a point is made in the following when we discuss the relation between national identity and supremacy. The effect of Article 4(3) TEU is primarily centripetal in the sense of furthering integration, whereas Article 4(2) TEU is primarily centrifugal.[301]

It has to be noted however that there is little to be found in case law suggesting that the Court sees a close relation between national identity and loyalty. Loyalty has been given especially strong effects in external relations and the enforcement of EU law by national authorities, as will be explained in detail later. Especially in these two areas, however, national identity would not seem to be easily operationalised. Because of its supervisory system for data protection, Germany had claimed that the organisation and working of national legal systems should be respected when implementing Union law.[302] The Court held that Member States cannot justify the failure to apply a requirement of secondary Union law on grounds that it has well-established national arrangements and that the requirement at issue would impose a system foreign to its legal order.[303]

5.3. National Identity and Supremacy

The ECJ has consistently denied precedence of EU law over national law including national constitutional law, national fundamental rights, and 'principles of a national constitutional structure'.[304] Thus, Article 4(2) TEU does not provide an exception from the supremacy of EU law and cannot exempt national authorities

[299] See Klamert, 'Commentary on Article 4 TEU' (n 123) para 23. See also M Klamert and S Bucher, 'Investment Screening in der EU' (2021) 8 *European Journal of Business Law* 335 on FDI screening in that light.

[300] See B Guastaferro, 'Sincere cooperation and respect for national identities' in Schütze and Tridimas (eds), *Oxford Principles of European Union Law* 350, 379–82.

[301] See also Kahl, 'Art 4 EUV' (n 293) para 105.

[302] See Case C-518/07, *Commission v Germany*, ECLI:EU:C:2010:125.

[303] See *Commission v Germany* (n 302) paras 53–54.

[304] *Internationale Handelsgesellschaft* (n 278) para 3. See also *Dow Chemical Ibérica* (n 278) para 38.

from the obligation to apply EU law.[305] In the judgment by the ECJ imposing record fines on Hungary for defying previous Court judgments on the asylum acquis, the Hungarian Constitutional Court was reported to have issued a Decision (No 32/2021, XII.20) in which it had held, among others, that 'the protection of Hungary's inalienable right to determine its territorial integrity, its population, its form of government and its State structure formed part of its constitutional identity'.[306] The Court did not even bother to address that argument in the merits of that judgment.

It has been argued that the national identity clause in Article 4(2) TEU should be read in conjunction with the part of Article 4(2) TEU requiring respect for the equality of Member States as well as with the principle of loyalty in Article 4(3) TEU.[307] Indeed, both provisions have been invoked as foundations for the supremacy of EU law by the Court as discussed later and thus constitute strong antagonistic elements to the centrifugal thrust of the national identities clause. In *RS*, the Grand Chamber of the Court held concerning national identity in Article 4(2) TEU:

> By contrast, that provision has neither the object nor the effect of authorising a constitutional court of a Member State, in disregard of the obligations under, in particular, Article 4(2) and (3) and the second subparagraph of Article 19(1) TEU, which are binding upon it, to disapply a rule of EU law, on the ground that that rule undermines the national identity of the Member State concerned as defined by the national constitutional court.[308]

National (constitutional) identity could, in theory, be considered a *differentia specifica*, ie, a factor determining why one Member State would, on a fundamental level, be different from the other Member States, thereby countering the claim that it would need to be treated equally with the other Member States. However, while this might affect the strength of the argument for supremacy based on Member State equality, the other rationales for supremacy discussed later in this chapter remain valid.[309]

The Full Court has also stressed that, whilst they have separate national identities, inherent in their fundamental structures, political and constitutional, which the European Union respects, the Member States 'adhere to a concept of 'the rule of law' which they share, as a value common to their own constitutional traditions, and which they have undertaken to respect at all times'.[310] This adds Article 2 TEU

[305] See Joined Cases C-58–59/13, *Torresi*, ECLI:EU:C:2014:2088, paras 53–8; Case C-393/10, *O'Brien*, ECLI:EU:C:2012:110, para 49; Case C-317/18, *Correia Moreira*, ECLI:EU:C:2019:499, paras 61–63.

[306] *Commission v Hungary* (n 252) para 22.

[307] See Martinico, 'Taming National Identity' (n 274) 447. See also, arguing for a narrow reading, B de Witte, 'Article 4(2) TEU as a Protection of the Institutional Diversity of the Member States' (2021) 27 *European Public Law* 559.

[308] See *RS (Effet des arrêts d'une cour constitutionnelle)* (n 257) para 70.

[309] Compare also Weber, *Bundesstaatliche Identitäten* (n 287) 112–13 for further rebuttals against this argument.

[310] Case C-156/21, *Hungary v Parliament and Council (Conditionality mechanism)*, ECLI:EU:C:2022:97, para 129, repeated in Case C-204/21, *Commission v Poland (Independence and private life of judges)*,

to the equation, further diminishing the effect of that part of Article 4(2) TEU through systematic interpretation.[311]

6. Conclusions

The principle of national (constitutional) identity in Article 4(2) TEU is an outlier among the principles discussed in this book because it is exclusively inspired by national constitutional law. However, this does not mean that it has been developed through evaluative comparison as the principles under Article 6 TEU. So far, its contours have remained largely elusive.

Compared with other structural principles, national identity has limited normative functions until now, which may be justified by a systematic reading of Article 4 TEU, which overall clearly is integrationist. It has so far neither applied as a standard of legality for Union law nor can it be balanced with other structural principles, such as with those having an 'integrationist' effect like supremacy or effectiveness. While the latter characteristic makes national identity normatively similar to most other principles discussed in this book, the former means that the solitary structural principle that unequivocally protects *Member State* interests is also one of the weakest.

Nonetheless, theoretically, it provides at least some counterweight in favour of national sovereignty in the face of the centripetal force of all the other principles discussed in this book. This will also be illustrated when we discuss its role in external relations law and in the CFSP in particular.

6. The Principle of Loyalty

1. Introduction

Loyalty is one of the most difficult principles of Union law.[312] Together with the principle of effectiveness, itself derived from Article 4(3) TEU as will be shown later, it runs like a common thread through all aspects of Union law, above all where its application and effect depend on action by the Member States.[313] Loyalty, again together with effectiveness, has been qualified as being inherent in the Union

ECLI:EU:C:2023:442, para 73. Compare LD Spieker, 'Framing and Managing Constitutional Identity Conflicts: How to Stabilize the Modus Vivendi between the Court of Justice and National Constitutional Courts' (2020) 57 *CML Rev* 361, 392.

[311] See, now, Case C-808/21, *Commission v Czech Republic,* ECLI:EU:C:2024:962, para 158. Compare Spieker, 'Framing and Managing Constitutional Identity Conflicts' (n 310) 392.

[312] See Klamert, *The Principle of Loyalty in EU Law* (n 188) 4 ff.

[313] Compare Kahl, 'Art 4 EUV' (n 293) para 92, who speaks of 'sub-principles' in connection with the manifestations of loyalty.

legal order as discussed later. This makes it a central element in the network of structural principles in EU law discussed in this book. Interrelations with loyalty have been and will be discussed with all other principles included in this book, such as with autonomy earlier and with solidarity later in this chapter.

I have elsewhere distinguished the constitutional functions of loyalty as furthering the 'constitutionalisation' of EU law, the prevention of conflicts between EU measures and national measures, requiring cooperation and coordination both between the European Union and the Member States and between the Member States themselves, and as safeguarding the compliance of Member States with their obligations under Union law.[314] In the following, we will, as with all other principles analysed in this book, focus on selected aspects and can therefore not discuss loyalty comprehensively.

As we will see, while some functions of loyalty have been developed more recently or are still not fully clarified, it has played a pivotal role in case law from the very beginning of European integration. Its role with regard to the foundations of the principle of supremacy has only recently been revisited in case law and the literature. It is also the only principle discussed in this book that has been inspired by *both* national constitutional law and public international law. Similar to conferral discussed earlier, EU law has introduced a novel, distinct term for a concept that has, at least in parts, already existed.

2. Origins

2.1. National Constitutional Law

One source of inspiration for loyalty in the European Union was the German constitutional law principle of federal fidelity (*Bundestreue*), as I have also explained elsewhere.[315]

The German Federal Constitutional Court (BVerfG) has held that it would be per the federal principle that all entities in the federation are bound by a mutual constitutional duty to be loyal and to cooperate.[316] It is submitted that *Bundestreue* has more to do with the allocation of competences within a federation than is the case with good faith in international law discussed below. In a federal state with competing competences of the federal and the state level such as Germany, a principle such as *Bundestreue* manages the potential conflicts ensuing from such a constitutional set-up.[317]

[314] Klamert, 'Commentary on Article 4 TEU' (n 123) para 60 ff.

[315] Klamert, *The Principle of Loyalty in EU Law* (n 188) 9.

[316] BVerfG, 2 BvH 2/52, *Wohnungsbauförderung*, BVerfGE 1, 299. See also G de Baere and T Roes, 'EU Loyalty as Good Faith' (2015) 64 *ICLQ* 829, 859.

[317] See also, for Austrian constitutional law, VfGH, *Wiener Behindertengesetz*, VfSlg 8831/1980, and VfGH, *Niederösterreichisches Jagdgesetz*, VfSlg 10.292/1984, on the duty of consideration (*Berücksichtigungspflicht*) for dealing with contradictory yet validly enacted provisions by the federal

2.2. Public International Law

Another source of inspiration for loyalty is the related principles of good faith and *pacta sunt servanda* in public international law.

Good faith has been called perhaps the most important general principle underpinning many international legal rules.[318] Article 2(2) of the UN Charter states that:

> All Members, in order to ensure to all of them the rights and benefits resulting from membership, shall fulfill in good faith the obligations assumed by them in accordance with the present Charter.

In the *Nuclear Tests* case, the ICJ stated:

> One of the basic principles governing the creation and performance of legal obligations, whatever their source, is the principle of good faith. Trust and confidence are inherent in international co-operation, in particular in an age when this co-operation in many fields is becoming increasingly essential. Just as the very rule of pacta sunt servanda in the law of treaties is based on good faith, so also is the binding character of an international obligation assumed by unilateral declaration. Thus interested States may take cognizance of unilateral declarations and place confidence in them, and are entitled to require that the obligation thus created be respected.[319]

However, while good faith would constitute 'an indispensable part of the rules of international law generally', it has been noted that other Opinions by the ICJ have shown that it would not in itself be a source of obligations and could only relate to the fulfilment of existing obligations.[320]

The principle of *pacta sunt servanda* is a related but distinct principle of international treaty law.[321] According to Article 26 of the Vienna Convention on the Law of Treaties, every treaty in force 'is binding upon the parties to it and must be performed by them in good faith'. This principle can be generalised to the effect that when a state enters into an agreement or joins an international organisation, not only may it not act against its interests, but it must actively support its functioning.[322] This has implications for the way Treaties are interpreted, as will be discussed later in the section on effectiveness.[323] It also has implications for

state and the provinces, respectively. Compare also B de Witte, 'The Role of Institutional Principles in the Judicial Development of the European Union Legal Order' in F Snyder (ed), *The Europeanisation of Law: The Legal Effects of European Integration on General Institutional Principles of EU law* (Oxford, Hart Publishing, 2000) 83, 86 with further references also to Belgian constitutional law.

318 M Shaw, *International Law*, 9th edn (Cambridge, Cambridge University Press, 2021) 87 with further references.

319 ICJ Advisory Opinion, *Nuclear Tests (Austl v Fr)* (1974) ICJ Reports 253, para 46.

320 See Shaw, *International Law* (n 318) 88 with references from Opinions by the ICJ. Compare, however, R Kolb, *Good Faith in International Law* (Oxford, Hart Publishing, 2017) 29–31.

321 See Kolb, *Good Faith in International Law* (n 320) 33–34.

322 Compare, in the context of the EU, V Constantinesco, 'L'article CEE de la bonne foi à la loyauté communautaire' in F Capotorti et al (eds), *Du Droit International au Droit de l'Intégration: Liber Amicorum Pierre Pescatore* (Baden-Baden, Nomos, 1987) 97, 108–09.

323 See Article 31 of the Vienna Convention on the Law of Treaties.

the application of treaty law, with *pacta sunt servanda* prohibiting frustrating the objective of a treaty before its ratification.[324] Also, the rule of law has been understood to include the principle *pacta sunt servanda* as a general duty of states to comply with international obligations.[325]

2.3. EU Law

2.3.1. Introduction

The principle of loyalty has been part of (written) primary law since the beginning of the EU (formerly the EEC). Article 5 EEC provided:

> Member States shall take all general or particular measures which are appropriate for ensuring the carrying out of the obligations arising out of this Treaty or resulting from the acts of the institutions of the Community. They shall facilitate the achievement of the Community's aims. They shall abstain from any measures likely to jeopardise the attainment of the objectives of this Treaty.

Article 5 EEC was inspired by Article 86 ECSC, whose first and second paragraphs provided:

> Member States undertake to take all appropriate measures, whether general or particular, to ensure fulfilment of the obligations resulting from decisions and recommendations of the institutions of the Community and to facilitate the performance of the Community's tasks.
>
> Member States undertake to refrain from any measures incompatible with the common market referred to in Articles 1 and 4.

Article 5 EEC thus had nearly identical wording to today's Article 4(3) TEU, except for the 'reverse vertical' duty of cooperation incumbent on Union institutions now provided in the first sentence as discussed below. The abstention obligation under Article 86 ECSC, by contrast, was still limited to the common market, in line with the generally more limited objectives of that Community.

2.3.2. The Early Case Law

Some observations can be made about the role of loyalty in the early case law of the ECJ. It seems loyalty (or more precisely the first and second paragraphs of Article 86 ECSC) played hardly any role in case law on the ECSC, with the notable exception of the *Humblet* case, discussed below. It took some years before what

[324] See Article 18 of the Vienna Convention on the Law of Treaties. See A Aust, 'Pacta Sunt Servanda' in *Max Planck Encyclopedia of Public International Law* (Oxford, Oxford University Press, 2013) paras 5 and 8. On Article 18 VCLT in the context of EU law, see also M Klamert, 'Legal Certainty and Customary International Law: Opel Austria' in G Butler and R Wessel (eds), *EU External Relations Law: The Cases in Context* (Oxford, Hart Publishing, 2022) 367.

[325] Compare T Bingham, *The Rule of Law* (London, Allen Lane, 2010) 110 et seq. See P Gragl, 'Rechtstaatlichkeit' in M Klamert (ed), *Europarecht. Jahrbuch 22* (NWV, BWV, 2022) 37, 66.

was then Article 5 EEC was applied, but when that time came, the succession of cases was quite remarkable. As with all other principles discussed in this book, the ECJ never made the connection with either national constitutional law or public international law.[326]

In the *Humblet* case of 1960, Article 86 ECSC was central for the Court holding the following:

> In fact if the Court rules in a judgment that a legislative or administrative measure adopted by the authorities of a Member State is contrary to Community law, that Member State is obliged, by virtue of Article 86 of the ECSC Treaty, to rescind the measure in question and to make reparation for any unlawful consequences which may have ensued. This obligation is evident from the Treaty and from the Protocol which have the force of law in the Member States following their ratification and which take precedence over national law. Consequently if in the present dispute the Court were to rule that the tax assessment in question was unlawful, it would necessarily follow that the Belgian government would be obliged to adopt the requisite measures to cancel it and to reimburse to the applicant any amounts which were wrongfully collected.[327]

The duty to rescind or nullify national law contravening EU law has also been introduced in EU law and is at the crossroads of loyalty and supremacy, as shown later. *Humblet* has also been cited in *Francovich* of 1990 for introducing state liability, another principle that has been based on loyalty as shown later as well.

It is noteworthy that of the first 10 cases Article 5 EEC was applied by the ECJ, five cases were landmark judgments. *Costa* of 1964 was only the second case in which Article 5 EEC was invoked. Joined Cases 6 & 11/69, *Commission v France*, prohibiting unilateral Member States measures invoking both loyalty and solidarity, discussed later in the context of the principle of solidarity, came in fourth place. This was followed by *ERTA* in 1971, discussed below and above in the context of conferral.

Two other cases decided in 1971 were *Deutsche Grammophon* and *International Fruit*. In the former, the ECJ held:

> According to the second paragraph of Article 5 of the Treaty, Member States 'shall abstain from any measure which could jeopardize the attainment of the objective of this Treaty'. This provision lays down a general duty for the Member States, the actual tenor of which depends in each individual case on the provisions of the Treaty or on the rules derived from its general scheme.[328]

Deutsche Grammophon led to claims that Article 5 EEC and its successor provisions could not provide a basis for obligations incumbent on the Member States because of their abstract nature and the discretion it grants to the Member States.[329] This view has probably been influenced by the fact that good faith under international

[326] Also noted by de Witte, 'The Role of Institutional Principles' (n 317) 86–87.
[327] Case C-6/60-IMM, *Humblet*, ECLI:EU:C:1960:48, 569.
[328] Case 78/70, *Deutsche Gramophon*, ECLI:EU:C:1971:59, para 5.
[329] For references to the literature, see Klamert, *The Principle of Loyalty in EU Law* (n 188) 32.

law lacks such capacity, as explained above. As shown below, this view cannot be sustained today with loyalty providing for a range of self-standing obligations mainly of the Member States.[330]

International Fruit of 1971 concerned the indirect enforcement of EU law by the Member States and is a precursor of the *Rewe*-line of case law that is discussed under the principle of effectiveness later.[331] Although the Member States would be obliged under Article 5 EEC to take all appropriate measures, whether general or particular, to ensure fulfilment of the obligations arising out of the Treaty, 'it is for them to determine which institutions within the national system shall be empowered to adopt the said measures'.[332]

An example of the many important judgments based on loyalty that have come later is the case law on obligations for the Member States to take account of soft law acts of the Union.[333] While loyalty was not mentioned in *Grimaldi* of 1989, its relevance has been clarified by follow-up case law.[334] There is also a parallel with ECSC case law from 1985 based on Article 86 ECSC. In *Gerlach*, the Court held:

> Article 74 of the ECSC Treaty authorizes the Commission to make recommendations to the governments if 'it is found that countries not members of the Community or undertakings situated in such countries are engaging in dumping'. Under Article 86 of the ECSC Treaty the Member States are under a duty to take all appropriate measures to ensure fulfilment of the obligations resulting from recommendations of the Commission. It follows that the Commission is empowered to make binding recommendations designed to combat dumping by non-member countries.[335]

3. Locations

3.1. *Primary Law*

As already mentioned above, loyalty is included in Article 4 TEU together with other distinct principles of EU law such as the principle of conferral in paragraph 1, the principle of the equality of Member States in paragraph 2, and the national identity clause also in paragraph 2.

Article 4(3) TEU contains the 'principle of sincere cooperation' comprising three separate indents or subparagraphs. Under the first indent, the Union and the

[330] Compare, however, de Baere and Roes, 'EU Loyalty as Good Faith' (n 316) 871, who claim that loyalty would not create new obligations, but would only clarify the full scope of existing obligations and would thus not be conceptionally different from good faith in international law.

[331] Joined Cases 51 to 54/71, *International Fruit Company*, ECLI:EU:C:1971:128.

[332] *International Fruit Company* (n 331) para 2.

[333] Case C-322/88, *Grimaldi*, ECLI:EU:C:1989:646. See the Opinion of AG Wahl in Case C-526/14, *Kotnik*, ECLI:EU:C:2016:102, para 38.

[334] Case C-69/13, *Mediaset*, ECLI:EU:C:2014:71, para 31.

[335] Case 239/84, *Gerlach*, ECLI:EU:C:1985:443, para 12.

Member States are required, in full mutual respect, to assist each other in carrying out tasks which flow from the Treaties.[336]

Furthermore, the Member States must take appropriate measures, general or particular, to ensure the fulfilment of the obligations arising out of the Treaties or resulting from the acts of the institutions of the Union.

According to the third subparagraph of Article 4(3) TEU, the Member States must facilitate the achievement of the Union's tasks and refrain from any measure that could jeopardise the attainment of the Union's objectives. According to recent case law, the negative obligation set out in Article 4(3) TEU would require 'a certain level of seriousness' limiting the scope of that obligation to situations of a particularly serious nature.[337]

Loyalty also applies to the relations between Union institutions under the principle of institutional balance, which is now explicitly provided in Article 13 TEU and which has already been discussed in the context of conferral.

Article 4(3) TEU and loyalty are probably unique in EU primary law regarding the number of Treaty provisions that have or can be considered their specifications.[338] Article 24(3) TEU requires the Member States to 'support the Union's external and security policy actively and unreservedly in a spirit of loyalty and mutual solidarity and shall comply with the Union's action in this area'. We will discuss this manifestation of loyalty in chapter four.

3.2. Unwritten, Inherent Principle

Loyalty is one of the principles the Court has qualified as 'inherent' in the Union legal order,[339] respectively a principle 'underlying' what is today Article 4(3) TEU.[340] Also the 'reverse vertical' duty of cooperation of the Union institutions was found to apply at a time when this was not provided explicitly in Article 4(3) TEU.[341] Thus, there arguably would be a principle of loyalty applying in Union law if Article 4(3) TEU did not exist.[342]

Different from solidarity, where the Court has come to a similar conclusion in recent case law as discussed later, the Court never makes a systematic argument invoking all the expressions of loyalty in the Treaties mentioned above as proof that there should exist an underlying unwritten principle. The most likely explanation recalls that loyalty in EU law has been inspired by similar principles in public international law and national constitutional law, as discussed above. Hence, one

[336] Case C-514/19, *Union des industries de la protection des plantes*, ECLI:EU:C:2020:803, para 49.

[337] Case C-15/22, *Finanzamt G (Projets d'aide au développement)*, ECLI:EU:C:2023:636, para 63.

[338] See Klamert, 'Commentary on Article 4 TEU' (n 123) paras 33–35.

[339] Joined Cases C-46/93 & C-48/93, *Brasserie du Pêcheur*, ECLI:EU:C:1996:79, para 39.

[340] Case C-404/97, *Commission v Portugal*, ECLI:EU:C:2000:345, para 40.

[341] Case C-2/88 Imm, *Zwartveld*, ECLI:EU:C:1990:440. See also de Witte, 'The Role of Institutional Principles' (n 317) 88.

[342] See P Pescatore, 'Das Zusammenwirken der Gemeinschaftsrechtsordnung mit den nationalen Rechtsordnungen' (1970) *Europarecht* 307, 322.

could make the argument that, because *pacta sunt servanda* is (also) an unwritten customary principle in public international law and because loyalty is derived from it, loyalty would also be such an unwritten principle.

4. Applications

Loyalty is of general application because Member States are bound by it in all areas covered by Union law,[343] irrespective of the kind of competence the Union has in a certain matter. Member States are even subject to obligations under Article 4(3) TEU if they act in the exercise of their own competences.[344] The 'trigger' for the applicability of Article 4(3) TEU can be not more than a 'Union interest'.[345] In that sense, loyalty is a very powerful structural principle.

The ECJ has repeatedly assumed that Article 4(3) TEU is superseded by another provision as *lex specialis*.[346] However, while in infringement judgments against Member States, only an infringement of the regulation concerned itself has been found and the Court has expressly rejected the need to rely on Article 4(3) TEU,[347] in the case of Union directives, the Court has regularly relied on Article 288 TFEU in conjunction with Article 4(3) TEU.[348]

Loyalty has the orthodox role of a general principle in EU law by furthering the development of EU law through gap-filling.[349] Moreover, it can be shown that loyalty has been applied in conjunction with other treaty rules to produce effects that could otherwise not be achieved by these (other) rules alone, thereby extending either their scope or their effect.[350]

Loyalty can, albeit rarely, provide guidance for the interpretation of secondary law.[351] It may, under certain circumstances, impose procedural obligations on the Commission when drafting a legal act, in particular to the extent that it may be obliged to take note of and examine the submissions of a Member State against this legal act.[352] This could be understood as opening a role for a legality review based on loyalty.[353] However, it has until now never been applied for reviewing the legality of an act of Union law.

[343] See Case C-518/11, *UPC Nederland*, ECLI:EU:C:2013:709, para 59.
[344] See Klamert, 'Commentary on Article 4 TEU' (n 123) para 31.
[345] See Klamert, 'Commentary on Article 4 TEU' (n 123) paras 68–70.
[346] Joined Cases C-332/92, C-333/92 & C-335/92, *Eurico Italia*, ECLI:EU:C:1994:79, para 22; Case C-459/03, *Commission v Ireland (MOX Plant)* (n 123) para 169 ff.
[347] Case C-84/04, *Commission v Portugal*, ECLI:EU:C:2006:640, para 40.
[348] See Schill and Krenn, 'Artikel 4 EUV' (n 279) para 74.
[349] See Klamert, *The Principle of Loyalty in EU Law* (n 188) 63–83.
[350] I have referred to this as 'amplification'. See Klamert, *The Principle of Loyalty in EU Law* (n 188) 275–80 with further references.
[351] See Case C-38/14, *Gobierno en Gipuzkoa*, ECLI:EU:C:2015:260, para 25; Case C-176/15, *Guy Riskin Timmermans*, ECLI:EU:C:2016:488; Case C-116/11, *Bank Handlowy*, ECLI:EU:C:2012:739.
[352] Case C-677/18, *Amoena*, ECLI:EU:C:2019:1142, para 56.
[353] Compare also Joined Cases C-36/97 & C-37/97, *Kellinghusen*, ECLI:EU:C:1998:499, para 30 et seq.

Elsewhere, I have argued that the duty of (sincere or loyal) cooperation is a subcategory of a more general principle of loyalty that is relevant for more technical, procedural matters of the relation between the European Union and the Member States and has been the basis of obligations for the Member States.[354] This has been especially relevant in the EU's law of external relations and will be discussed in chapter four. However, also in cases outside external relations, Member States were found in breach of loyalty, such as for failing to seek to clarify a Commission request in an infringement proceeding,[355] or in connection with the duty to transpose Union directives.[356] Recently, the Court held that under Article 4(3) TEU, a Member State is bound by a duty of sincere cooperation throughout the State aid procedure requiring Member States to provide the Commission with all relevant information requested by it.[357] In this context (reverse vertical) obligations have also been imposed on the Union institutions, but they are still much less numerous.[358]

Thus, despite its general and imprecise wording and irrespective of secondary law concretisations, Article 4(3) TEU can establish autonomous obligations for the Union and the Member States.[359] The ECJ in these cases does not weigh up the legal interests at stake, as is characteristic of a review such as under fundamental rights or the fundamental freedoms and there is no real balancing of the interests of the Commission in compliance with EU law and whatever interests the Member States bring forward in these cases.[360] Such a 'rule-like' application would not conform with the classic distinction between principles and rules, which we do not find useful as discussed in chapter one, and we will see that something similar can be assumed with supremacy discussed later.

The fact that obligations for the Member States, their national courts and authorities can arise from Article 4(3) TEU does not necessarily mean that it can be invoked directly by private individuals. In *Hurd*, relying on what is now Article 4(3) TEU, the Court found that although Member States were not allowed to tax the salaries of teachers in the European schools if the burden resulting from the levying of national taxes falls on the Community budget, this obligation did not have direct effect.[361] In a similar vein, Article 4(3) TEU does not oblige

[354] Klamert, *The Principle of Loyalty in EU Law* (n 188) 33. In the same vein, E Neframi, 'The Duty of Loyalty: Rethinking its Scope Through its Application in the Field of EU External Relations' (2010) 47 *CML Rev* 323, 325; Delgado Casteleiro, 'Loyalty in External Relations Law' (n 127) 385.

[355] Case C-82/03, *Commission v Italy*, ECLI:EU:C:2004:433; Case C-22/20, *Commission v Sweden*, ECLI:EU:C:2021:669.

[356] Case C-29/14, *Commission v Poland*, ECLI:EU:C:2015:379, paras 32–33; Case C-456/03, *Commission v Italy*, ECLI:EU:C:2005:388, paras 26–27.

[357] Case C-555/22 P, *UK v Commission*, ECLI:EU:C:2024:763, para 99; Joined Cases C-451/21 P & C-454/21 P, *Luxembourg and Others v Commission*, ECLI:EU:C:2023:948, para 122.

[358] See Klamert, 'Commentary on Article 4 TEU' (n 123) paras 47, 54–58.

[359] See Schill and Krenn, 'Artikel 4 EUV' (n 279) para 61.

[360] See, eg, *Commission v Sweden (PFOS)* (n 190).

[361] Case 44/84, *Hurd*, ECLI:EU:C:1986:2, para 59. See also Case 9/73, *Schlüter*, ECLI:EU:C:1973:110, para 39.

Member States to bring an action for annulment or for failure to act against one of their citizens.[362]

In *Finanzamt G*, the Court held concerning the second subparagraph of Article 4(3) TEU that it would be clear from the wording of that (positive) obligation imposed on the Member States that it 'does not by itself confer individual rights, but that it exists only in conjunction with a specific obligation on the part of the Member States pursuant to the Treaties or to an act of the EU institutions, such as that relating to the rules on competence'.[363] The same would apply to the obligations set out in Article 208(1) and Article 210(1) TFEU requiring Member States and the European Union to cooperate and consult each other under the development policy.[364] The precise arrangements for such cooperation would depend on a range of parameters exclusively for the Member States and the European Union to define, for which reason the Member States and the Union would be able to rely on those obligations, but they cannot be raised by individuals as against a Member State or the European Union.[365]

5. Interrelations

5.1. Loyalty and Mutual Trust

It has been argued that mutual trust would be an evolution of the horizontal dimension of sincere cooperation with the ultimate aim of guaranteeing the effectiveness of EU criminal law.[366] Indeed, we have discussed the role of effectiveness with conferral in the area of criminal law earlier.

As mentioned, in Opinion 2/13, the Full Court found that the common and shared values in Article 2 TEU would 'imply and justify the existence of mutual trust between the Member States that those values will be recognised and, therefore, that the law of the EU that implements them will be respected'.[367] The Court concluded that the draft accession agreement to the ECHR would be liable adversely to affect the specific characteristics and the autonomy of EU law in so far it 'does not avert the risk that the principle of Member States' mutual trust under EU law may be undermined'.[368] This would seem to suggest that a principle of mutual trust came out of thin air, which is not quite the case.

[362] Case C-511/03, *Ten Kate Holding Musselkanaal and others*, ECLI:EU:C:2005:625, para 28. See also Case C-341/95, *Betatti*, ECLI:EU:C:1998:353, para 77. See Schill and Krenn, 'Artikel 4 EUV' (n 279) para 61; de Witte, 'The Role of Institutional Principles' (n 317) 98.

[363] *Finanzamt G (Projets d'aide au développement)* (n 337) para 59.

[364] *Finanzamt G (Projets d'aide au développement)* (n 337) paras 60–61.

[365] *Finanzamt G (Projets d'aide au développement)* (n 337) paras 60–61.

[366] See C Saenz Perez, 'Mutual trust as a driver of integration: which way forward?' in Ziegler, Neuvonen and Moreno-Lax (eds), *Research Handbook* 530, 534.

[367] *ECHR II* (n 62) para 168.

[368] *ECHR II* (n 62) para 258.

Already in the *Altun* judgment six years before Opinion 2/13, the Grand Chamber of the Court, in the much more mundane context of social security and the E 101 certificate, held that 'the principle of sincere cooperation also implies that of mutual trust'.[369] Member State authorities were required to consider themselves bound by the E 101 certificate and not subject workers from other Member States to their own social security system.[370]

Even when it has not been called as such, the principle of mutual recognition in the internal market, especially in the areas of free movement of goods as well as the freedom to provide services, must also be seen as predicated by mutual trust. In the context of the freedom to provide services, it was expressly qualified by the Court of Justice as an expression of Article 4(3) TEU.[371]

5.2. Loyalty and Supremacy

There are several levels on which the principle of loyalty interrelates with the principle of supremacy, which will be discussed in detail in the next chapter.

As already mentioned above in the context of equality, in *Costa/ENEL* the Court held that the 'executive force of Community law cannot vary from one State to another in deference to subsequent domestic laws, without jeopardizing the attainment of the objectives of the Treaty set out in Article 5(2) [now Article 4(3) TEU] and giving rise to the discrimination prohibited by Article 7 [now Article 18 TFEU]'.[372] In 2014, I argued that the abstention obligation provided in what is now Article 4(3) TEU constituted (and still constitutes) the only treaty-based justification why national law must yield to Union law.[373] I have also discussed why loyalty has not been mentioned in any subsequent judgment on supremacy until that year.[374] Only very recently, in the context of the rule of law crisis in the European Union, has the Court again resorted to loyalty, among other considerations. In *Commission v Hungary*, the Court held that compliance with the obligations following from the principle of primacy 'is necessary in particular in order to ensure respect for the equality of Member States before the Treaties

369 Case C-359/16, *Altun*, ECLI:EU:C:2018:63, para 40.

370 *Altun* (n 369) paras 38–39.

371 Case C-340/89, *Vlassopoulou*, ECLI:EU:C:1991:193, para 14; Case C-31/00, *Dreessen*, ECLI:EU:C:2002:35, para 30. See M Möstl, 'Preconditions and Limits of Mutual Recognition' (2010) 47 *CML Rev* 405; C Janssens, *The Principle of Mutual Recognition in EU Law* (Oxford, Oxford University Press, 2013) 199.

372 *Costa/ENEL* (n 21) 594.

373 Klamert, *The Principle of Loyalty in EU Law* (n 188) 72.

374 Klamert, *The Principle of Loyalty in EU Law* (n 188) 72: 'It is as if once loyalty had served its purpose of rationalising a quite audacious interpretation of the Treaties, it quickly was put back into the "closet" again'. The argument based on loyalty was not repeated in subsequent case law on supremacy, such as *Simmenthal*, where the Court referred to Union law's 'effectiveness'. See Case 106/77, *Simmenthal II*, ECLI:EU:C:1978:49, paras 18, 20, 22 and 23.

and constitutes an expression of the principle of sincere cooperation set out in Article 4(3) TEU'.[375]

Interestingly, the Court has referred to loyalty in two cases related to the *Simmenthal II* line of judgments on the disapplication effect of primacy, although *Simmenthal II* itself did not rely on loyalty but on effectiveness, discussed later.[376]

There is also a close connection between the effects of the principle of loyalty and the effects of primacy. It follows from Article 4(3) TEU that national authorities are obliged 'to take all appropriate measures to ensure the validity and effectiveness of Union law and to remedy the unlawful consequences of any breach of Union law'.[377] According to the case law of the ECJ, the Member States must adapt national law to the requirements of Union law, irrespective of whether the latter has direct effect.[378] In *Inter-Environnement Wallonie and Terre wallonne*, the Court relied on both *Humblet* and *Francovich*, holding that 'under the principle of cooperation in good faith laid down in Article 4(3) TEU, Member States are required to nullify the unlawful consequences of a breach of European Union law'.[379] This could be seen as flowing from Article 4(3) TEU or could just as well be ascribed to the effects of primacy. In the context of supremacy and not loyalty, the Court found that the consequences of a conflict with EU law must be neutralised 'without having to request or await the prior repeal of those articles by way of legislation or any other constitutional procedure'.[380]

Similarly, Article 4(3) TEU is the basis of case law of the ECJ, according to which administrative authorities are generally obliged to withdraw final (legally binding) administrative decisions if the consequences of an infringement of Union law can thereby be eliminated.[381] In *Ciola*, an administrative act was declared inapplicable as being in breach of the freedom to provide services without imposing these conditions.[382] This case law can also been seen in the context of supremacy in the sense that it could be conceived as an exception to it.[383]

[375] *Commission v Hungary* (n 252) para 122. See also *Commission v Poland (Independence and private life of judges* (n 310) para 77.

[376] *Simmenthal II* (n 374). See Case C-409/06, *Winner Wetten*, ECLI:EU:C:2010:503, para 55; Case C-308/19, *Whiteland Import Export*, ECLI:EU:C:2021:47, para 31.

[377] *Euro Box Promotion* (n 257) para 173; Case C-231/06, *Jonkman*, ECLI:EU:C:2007:373, para 37; Case C-201/02, *Wells*, ECLI:EU:C:2004:12, para 64.

[378] Case C-120/88, *Commission v Italy*, ECLI:EU:C:1991:74, para 10; Case C-160/99, *Commission v France*, ECLI:EU:C:2000:410, para 22.

[379] Case C-41/11, *Inter-Environnement Wallonie and Terre wallonne*, ECLI:EU:C:2012:103, para 43. See also Case C-379/15, *Association France Nature*, ECLI:EU:C:2016:603, para 31; Case C-597/17, *Belgisch Syndicaat van Chiropraxie and Others*, ECLI:EU:C:2019:544, para 54.

[380] Case C-105/14, *Taricco*, ECLI:EU:C:2015:555, para 49; Joined Cases C-387/02, C-391/02 & C-403/02, *Berlusconi*, ECLI:EU:C:2005:270, para 72. See also Case C-73/23, *Chaudfontaine Loisirs*, ECLI:EU:C:2024:734; Case C-741/22, *Casino de Spa and Others*, ECLI:EU:C:2024:732, para 51 ff.

[381] Case C-453/00, *Kühne & Heitz*, ECLI:EU:C:2004:17, para 28; Joined Cases C-392/04 & C-422/04, *i-21 Germany*, ECLI:EU:C:2006:586, para 72; Case C-2/06, *Kempter*, ECLI:EU:C:2008:78, para 34 ff.

[382] Case C-224/97, *Ciola*, ECLI:EU:C:1999:212, para 34.

[383] See Klamert, 'Commentary on Article 1 TEU' (n 108) para 37.

6. Conclusions

Loyalty is one of the few structural principles that have their origins not (only) in public international law, but also in (federal) constitutional law. I have explained elsewhere that some of the obligations arising from Article 4(3) TEU in EU law are indeed similar or even identical to those arising from federal fidelity, *pacta sunt servanda* respectively the principle of good faith.[384] In general, however, both with its interpretation and with its application, the duties that can be associated with loyalty in EU law are much stronger, much more elaborated, and also much more 'invasive' concerning Member State sovereignty. It has been argued that the reason for this divergence is that loyalty in EU law commits all actors, thus Member States and EU institutions, to a 'higher' purpose of ensuring the functioning of the EU legal order.[385]

It has been submitted, similarly, that the strictures of the principle of good faith as a general concept applying in all areas of law would increase with the level of integration of the legal order to which it is applied.[386] Again, the EU's broadly understood common interest discussed already with autonomy and conferral earlier seems important here. While such interest can be assumed with all members of an international organisation, it arguably is stronger the more tasks are conferred on the organisation and the more robust its law-making capacities are. This explains the role of loyalty both with expanding the rules on competence through implied powers and by complementing them through duties managing their often blurry borders.

Loyalty has become highly instrumental in a succession of cases in the 1960s mainly to fill gaps in the Treaties regarding the effective implementation and in general the effective application of EU law. While it has not been applied as a standard of legality of Union law, it has developed to generate self-standing obligations mainly for the Member States. This capacity makes loyalty a showcase that the 'orthodox' distinction between principles and rules does not apply to Union law unless one would want to categorically distinguish a *principle* of loyalty from a *duty* of sincere cooperation. We consider the latter as encompassed by the former, which makes for a parallel to supremacy where we will also submit that a structural *principle* of supremacy comprises a more technical *duty* of primacy/disapplication. We have discussed the connection between loyalty and supremacy above and will return to it in the section on supremacy later.

[384] See Klamert, *The Principle of Loyalty in EU Law* (n 188) 41 ff; M Klamert, 'Loyalty and Solidarity as General Principles' in Ziegler, Neuvonen and Moreno-Lax, *Research Handbook* 118, 119 with references to case law. See also Guastaferro, 'Sincere cooperation and respect for national identities' (n 300) 350.

[385] Eckes, *EU Powers Under External Pressure* (n 77) 46 and 72.

[386] See de Baere and Roes, 'EU Loyalty as Good Faith' (n 316) 874.

7. The Principle of Solidarity

1. Introduction

Solidarity is yet another structural principle of EU law that is very challenging to describe and analyse.[387] Recently, it has been called a federal principle of EU law.[388] It has been distinguished between 'legal and institutional solidarity or systemic solidarity' that would have been 'the cement of EU integration from the outset', 'political and strategic solidarity', and the EU budget as an expression of solidarity between the Member States.[389] We will, in the following, by contrast, distinguish between (positive and negative) Member State solidarity on the one hand and solidarity concerning other actors and relationships in EU law on the other hand, with a focus on the former variety.[390]

Since the beginning of European integration, solidarity has always been about equality in EU law as will be shown, but its structural dimension has been 'dormant' until quite recently. Only recently, the Court has again relied on solidarity to make the point for compliance of the Member States with EU law, also in the context of supremacy. The long-time not-so-structural role of solidarity is surprising in view of the early case law as well as the prominent political use of the notion in the Schuman Declaration cited below. It is less surprising if we consider that a normative, compliance-related role of solidarity does not seem to have parallels in either national or international law, as discussed in the following.

Even though it is never mentioned as a structural or systemic principle in the literature discussed in chapter two and even though one would hardly know about its systemic relevance when consulting standard textbooks about EU law as mentioned in the Introduction, (Member State) solidarity thus is, without doubt, a structural principle of EU law. Especially since the Treaty of Lisbon, Member State solidarity is mentioned in many places in the TEU, the TFEU and also the Charter. More recently, the Court has repeatedly alluded to a 'general principle of solidarity'.

[387] See, eg, the contributions in A Biondi, E Dagilytė and E Küçük (eds), *Solidarity in EU Law: Legal Principle in the Making* (Cheltenham, Elgar Publishing, 2018); Klamert, 'Loyalty and Solidarity as General Principles' (n 384) 125.

[388] See K Lenaerts and S Adam, 'La solidarité, valeur sociale commune aux États membres et principe fédératif de l' Union européenne' (2021) 58 *Cahiers de droit européen* 307.

[389] See K Lenaerts and S Adam, 'Sink or Swim Together: Solidarity between the Member States as a Foundational Principle of the European Union' in C Barnard, A Łazowski, and D Sarmiento (eds), *Pursuit of Legal Harmony in a Turbulent Europe: Essays in Honour of Eleanor Sharpston* (Oxford, Hart Publishing, 2024) 41.

[390] See Klamert, 'Commentary on Article 4 TEU' (n 123) paras 10–11.

2. Origins

2.1. National Constitutional Law

In nation states, solidarity of course is a storied political concept, which is not what interests us here. In federal systems, more pertinently, there will normally be rules and mechanisms based on solidarity between the federations' entities, especially in financial terms.

Thus, the federal principle (*bundesstaatliches Prinzip*) has been deemed to include aspects such as concerning the safeguarding of the budgetary balance between the German federal state and the provinces (*Länder*) or duties of financial support among the *Länder*.[391] While loyalty has (also) been inspired by (German) federal fidelity as discussed above, the same arguably cannot be said of solidarity. What exists in German law is referred to below as positive (Member State) solidarity and has only been introduced to EU primary law in more recent times.

2.2. Public International Law

Solidarity in public international law can be associated with matters as diverse as non-reciprocal financial and in-kind assistance, and mutual military assistance.[392] It has also been argued that the principle of solidarity has helped structure the WTO regime, especially through the most-favoured-nation principle already mentioned earlier under equality.[393] For the protection of human rights, the concept of solidarity would be particularly relevant in the areas of humanitarian assistance and for the responsibility to protect.[394]

It has been claimed that solidarity would be a 'structural principle' of international law, serving the achievement of common objectives through common actions of states, the achievement of common objectives through differentiated obligations of states and actions to benefit particular states.[395] However, the prevailing view in the literature seems to deny a normative, legally binding role under international law.[396]

[391] See Klamert, *The Principle of Loyalty in EU Law* (n 188) 56 with further references to case law of the German Federal Constitutional Court.

[392] See Klamert, 'Loyalty and Solidarity as General Principles' (n 384) 120; K Gorobets, 'Solidarity as a Practical Reason: Grounding the Authority of International Law' (2022) 69 *Netherlands International Law Review* 3, 9–10, each with further references.

[393] See R Wolfrum, 'Solidarity' in D Shelton (ed), *The Oxford Handbook of International Human Rights Law* (Oxford, Oxford University Press, 2013) 401, mentioning that altruistic solidarity would only be dominant in so far as developing countries are concerned.

[394] See Wolfrum, 'Solidarity' (n 393).

[395] See R Wolfrum, 'Solidarity Amongst States: An Emerging Structural Principle of International Law' (2009) 49 *Indian Journal of International Law* 8, 9. See also R MacDonald, 'Solidarity in the practice and discourse of public international law' (1996) 8 *Pace International Law Review* 259.

[396] See Gorobets, 'Solidarity as a Practical Reason' (n 392) 10–11 with further references, concluding (at 23) that solidarity 'is amongst those ideas that ground international law's authority by legitimising its rules, procedures, and institutions', but would not be a legal principle.

2.3. EU Law

2.3.1. Introduction

The Schuman Declaration of 9 May 1950 recognised that 'Europe will not be made all at once, or according to a single plan. It will be built through concrete achievements which first create a de facto solidarity'. The third recital to the ECSC Treaty referred to solidarity in a very similar manner by 'recognising that Europe can be built only through practical achievements which will first of all create real solidarity, and through the establishment of common bases for economic development'.

Notably, the EEC Treaty did not contain any reference to solidarity.[397]

2.3.2. The Early Case Law on Solidarity between Member States

Solidarity was, memorably, referred to in connection with unilateral acts by Member States. In this constellation, the beneficiaries of obligations of solidarity incumbent on a certain Member State were the other Member States.

The first such pronunciation in case law occurred in 1969 regarding a preferential rediscount rate for export credits granted by France in violation of EEC and ECSC secondary law.[398] Powers of authorisation or intervention of the Community institutions conferred by the Treaties 'would be otiose if the Member States were free, on the pretext that their action related only to monetary policy, unilaterally to derogate from their obligations under the provisions of the Treaty and without being subject to control by the institutions'.[399] The Court continued:

> The solidarity which is at the basis of these obligations as of the whole of the Community system in accordance with the undertaking provided for in Article 5 of the Treaty, is continued for the benefit of the States in the procedure for mutual assistance provided for in Article 108 where a Member State is seriously threatened with difficulties as regards its balance of payments.
>
> The exercise of reserved powers cannot therefore permit the unilateral adoption of measures prohibited by the Treaty.[400]

In 1973, the Court held the following in the infringement case *Premiums for Slaughtering Cows* against Italy:

> In permitting Member States to profit from the advantages of the Community, the Treaty imposes on them also the obligation to respect its rules. For a State unilaterally to break, according to its own conception of national interest, the equilibrium between advantages and obligations flowing from its adherence to the Community brings into

[397] See, however, Article 86 ECSC: 'To the extent of their competence, the member States will take all appropriate measures to assure the international payments arising out of trade in coal and steel within the common market; they will lend assistance to each other to facilitate such payments'.

[398] Joined Cases 6/69 & 11/69, *Commission v France*, ECLI:EU:C:1969:68.

[399] Joined Cases 6/69 & 11/69, *Commission v France* (n 398) para 15.

[400] Joined Cases 6/69 & 11/69, *Commission v France* (n 398) paras 16–17.

> question the equality of Member States before Community law and creates discriminations at the expense of their nationals, and above all of the nationals of the State itself which places itself outside the Community rules.
>
> This failure in the duty of solidarity accepted by Member States by the fact of their adherence to the Community strikes at the fundamental basis of the Community legal order. It appears therefore that, in deliberately refusing to give effect on its territory to one of the systems provided for by Regulations Nos 1975/69 and 2195/69, the Italian Republic has failed in a conspicuous manner to fulfil the obligations which it has assumed by virtue of its adherence to the European Economic Community.[401]

This was followed up by another infringement case against the United Kingdom, again concerning compliance with Community regulations. The Court referred to the case just quoted and affirmed that 'it cannot therefore be accepted that a Member State should apply in an incomplete or selective manner provisions of a Community regulation so as to render abortive certain aspects of Community legislation which it has opposed or which it considers contrary to its national interests'.[402] The Court continued:

> In particular, as regards the putting into effect of a general rule intended to eliminate certain abuses to which workers are subject and which in addition involve a threat to road safety, a Member State which omits to take, within the requisite period and simultaneously with the other Member States, the measures which it ought to take, undermines Community solidarity by imposing, in particular as regards intra-Community transport, on the other Member States the necessity of remedying the effects of its own omissions, while at the same time taking an undue advantage to the detriment of its partners.[403]

I have called this 'negative Member State solidarity' elsewhere.[404] This case (law) has since then only been revisited (and referred to) by the Court after the Treaty of Lisbon in the course of the rule of law-crisis:

> By unilaterally upsetting the balance between the advantages and obligations arising from its membership of the European Union, a Member State calls into question observance of the principle of equality of the Member States before EU law. That failure in the duty of solidarity accepted by the Member States by the fact of their accession to the European Union strikes at the very root of the EU legal order.[405]

2.3.3. The Case Law on Solidarity between Undertakings

There is a steady line of case law, especially under the ECSC Treaty, which referred to solidarity in the context of undertakings and producers. In this constellation,

[401] *Premiums for slaughtering cows* (n 211) paras 24–25.

[402] Case C-128/78, *Commission v United Kingdom (Tachographs)*, ECLI:EU:C:1979:32, para 9.

[403] *Tachographs* (n 402) para 9.

[404] See Klamert, 'Loyalty and Solidarity as General Principles' (n 384) 125–26. Compare also M Kotzur, 'Solidarity as a legal concept' in A Grimmel and S My Giang (eds), *Solidarity in the European Union: A fundamental value in crisis* (New York, Springer, 2017) 37, 40.

[405] See *Commission v Hungary* (n 252) para 117.

undertakings in one Member State owed solidarity to undertakings in other Member States.

The Court explained in 1983, in the context of steel quotas, that

> it is in fact impossible to entertain the concept of necessity in relation to the quota system provided for by Article 58 of the ECSC Treaty, which is based on solidarity between all Community steel undertakings in the face of the crisis and seeks an equitable distribution of the sacrifices arising from unavoidable economic circumstances.[406]

Similarly, the Court held that

> the Council was justified in dividing the [sugar] quotas between the individual undertakings on the basis of their actual production … such a distribution of the burden is … consistent with the principle of solidarity between producers, since production is a legitimate criterion for assessing the economic strength of producers and the benefits which they derive from the system.[407]

For a very long time, it was only in this case law that the Court spoke regularly of a 'principle of solidarity' (between undertakings). Interestingly, this form of solidarity has recently also been 'constitutionalised' and been seen as an expression of the consequences of EU integration as such and of the required solidarity between the Member States.[408] This is a fair observation but arguably only with hindsight. When reading these judgments at face value, they would seem to be concerned with market integration and the fair allocation of quotas, not with unilateralism.

2.3.4. The Case Law on Solidarity with Union Citizens

In cases such as *Grzelczyk*, the Court invoked 'a certain degree of financial solidarity between nationals of a host Member State and nationals of other Member States' to require Member State X to give a student from Member State Y access to all benefits due in Member State X.[409] In *Bidar*, the Court added that a Member State can require 'a certain degree of integration' with the host Member State before it showed financial solidarity, however, it could not impose additional conditions that made it impossible for Union citizens from other Member States who satisfied those residence requirements to obtain student loans.[410]

The Court has also held that it would be legitimate for a Member State to protect the 'special relationship of solidarity and good faith between it and its nationals and also the reciprocity of rights and duties, which form the bedrock of the bond of nationality'.[411]

[406] Case 263/82, *Klöckner-Werke*, ECLI:EU:C:1983:373, para 17.

[407] Case 250/84, *Eridania zuccherifici nazionali*, ECLI:EU:C:1986:22, para 20. See also Opinion of AG Sharpston in Joined Cases C-715/17, *Commission v Poland*, C-718/17, *Commission v Hungary*, and C-719/17, *Commission v Czech Republic*, ECLI:EU:C:2019:917, para 249.

[408] See Lenaerts and Adams, 'Sink or Swim Together' (n 389) 43.

[409] Case C-184/99, *Grzelczyk*, ECLI:EU:C:2001:458, para 44.

[410] Case C-209/03, *Bidar*, ECLI:EU:C:2005:169, paras 56–63.

[411] Joined Cases C-684/22 to C-686/22, *Stadt Duisburg (Loss of German nationality)*, ECLI:EU:C:2024:345, para 37.

2.4. *Interim Conclusions*

For our discussion in this book, it is noteworthy that all three constellations above are closely connected with different forms of discrimination: inequality between Member States but also 'discriminations at the expense of their nationals, and above all of the nationals of the State itself which places itself outside the Community rules', discrimination between Union companies in the second strand discussed above, and discrimination between Union citizens in the latter line of case law. All this case law, it bears emphasising, was handed down without solidarity at that time being mentioned in primary law.

It is also worth noting that, while 'negative Member State solidarity' was developed very early, there was nothing in early case law on what can be called 'positive Member State solidarity', thus on obligations for Member States to support one another in kind or financially. This side of solidarity has only been added by treaty revision, now accounting for most of the mentions of solidarity in primary law. We will focus on (positive and negative) Member State solidarity in the following.

3. Locations

3.1. *Primary Law*

According to Article 2 TEU, solidarity is one of the values that are 'common to the Member States in a society in which pluralism, non-discrimination, tolerance, justice, solidarity and equality between women and men prevail'. Article 3(3) TEU lists solidarity among Member States in the context of the promotion of economic, social and territorial cohesion as an objective of the European Union. Thus, in contrast to for instance loyalty, solidarity is both a value of the European Union under Article 2 TEU and an objective of the EU under Article 3 TEU, discussed in chapter two.

Article 24(2) and (3) TEU, on the common foreign and security policy, refers to 'mutual political solidarity' among Member States.[412] These CFSP provisions will be discussed in chapter four. Article 42(2) TEU on mutual defence mimics the mutual defence obligation under Article 5 of the NATO Treaty.

Article 67 TFEU on the area of freedom, security and justice calls on the Union to 'frame a common policy on asylum, immigration and external border control, based on solidarity between Member States'. Article 80 TFEU says that the policies of the Union in this field shall be 'governed by the principle of solidarity and fair sharing of responsibility, including its financial implications, between the Member States'. Article 80 TFEU is the only place where the Treaties mention a 'principle' of solidarity. Besides Article 42(2) TEU, it is also the only area of EU law, where solidarity appears in a form that recalls international (refugee) law.

[412] Case C-848/19 P, *Germany v Poland (OPAL)*, ECLI:EU:C:2021:598, para 39.

In Article 122(1) TFEU, a mandate is given to the Council to decide, 'in a spirit of solidarity between Member States', upon measures addressing severe difficulties in the supply of certain products, notably in the area of energy. This legal basis has been used extensively to combat especially the COVID pandemic with solidarity-infused measures.[413] Before that, it had already been applied in response to the debt crisis.[414]

Article 194 TFEU states that Union policy on energy shall aim to attain certain objectives such as ensuring the security of energy supply in the Union and promoting energy efficiency and energy saving and the development of new and renewable forms of energy 'in a spirit of solidarity between Member States'. The 'solidarity clause' of Article 222 in Part V of the TFEU, on the external action of the Union, mandates that '[t]he Union and its Member States shall act jointly in a spirit of solidarity if a Member State is the object of a terrorist attack or the victim of a natural or man-made disaster'.

Solidarity is the heading of Title IV of the Charter of Fundamental Rights, which includes provisions on 'social rights' such as labour rights and protections for individuals on health care and consumer matters. Most of these are worded in a way that dilutes their effectiveness.[415]

Besides these explicit mentions of solidarity in the Treaties, other provisions can also be seen against its backdrop such as Article 136(3) TFEU on financial assistance to other Member States, Articles 174–78 TFEU on cohesion policy, Articles 208–11 TFEU on development policy, and Article 214 TFEU on humanitarian aid.[416] The Union budget and Article 322(1)(a) TFEU as the legal basis for the rule of law conditionality mechanism[417] has been qualified by the Full Court as 'one of the principal instruments for giving practical effect, in the Union's policies and activities, to the principle of solidarity, mentioned in Article 2 TEU'.[418]

[413] See, among others, Council Regulation (EU) 2020/672 of 19 May 2020 on the establishment of a European instrument for temporary support to mitigate unemployment risks in an emergency (SURE) following the COVID-19 outbreak [2020] OJ L159/1; Council Regulation (EU) 2020/2094 of 14 December 2020 establishing a European Union Recovery Instrument to support the recovery in the aftermath of the COVID-19 crisis [2020] OJ L433/23.

[414] See M Klamert, 'Solidarität in der Wirtschafts- und Währungsunion' in P-C Müller-Graff, A Hatje, U Hufeld and C Ohler (eds), *Enzyklopädie Europarecht, Band 9, Europäische Wirtschafts- und Währungsunion* (Baden-Baden, Nomos, 2021) with further references.

[415] See Case C-176/12, *Association de médiation sociale*, ECLI:EU:C:2014:2, on Article 27 of the Charter. See T Lock, 'Introduction to Title IV Solidarity (CFR)' in Kellerbauer, Klamert and Tomkin (eds), *Commentary*, para 2.

[416] See Klamert, 'Commentary on Article 4 TEU' (n 123) para 13 with further references.

[417] Regulation (EU, Euratom) 2020/2092 of the European Parliament and of the Council of 16 December 2020 on a general regime of conditionality for the protection of the Union budget [2020] OJ L433I/1/1.

[418] *Poland v Parliament and Council (Conditionality mechanism)* (n 227) para 147; *Hungary v Parliament and Council (Conditionality mechanism)* (n 210) para 129. See Case C-409/05, *Commission v Greece*, ECLI:EU:C:2009:782, para 55; Case C-38/06, *Commission v Portugal*, ECLI:EU:C:2010:108, para 67. See also, now, *Commission v Malta* (n 253) para 93, on Union citizenship.

3.2. Unwritten Principle

In recent case law, the Court seems to argue for the existence of an (unwritten) principle of solidarity generally applicable in Union law. In *Commission v Hungary*, it held that 'it should be recalled that the principle of solidarity is one of the fundamental principles of EU law and is one of the values common to the Member States on which the European Union is founded, pursuant to Article 2 TEU'.[419] In other recent cases, the Court speaks of 'the principle of solidarity, mentioned in Article 2 TEU'.[420]

The spirit of solidarity between Member States, mentioned in Article 194 TFEU, would constitute 'a specific expression, in the field of energy, of the principle of solidarity, which is itself one of the fundamental principles of EU law'.[421] The Court recalled all the references to solidarity in the Treaties as well as its case law from the 1970s mentioned above, from which it would follow that 'the principle of solidarity underpins the entire legal system of the European Union'.[422] The principle of solidarity would entail rights and obligations 'both for the European Union and for the Member States, the European Union having an obligation of solidarity towards the Member States and the Member States having the same obligation between themselves and with regard to the common interest of the European Union'.[423]

Recall that the Court did not argue the same way with loyalty, which is also an unwritten principle of EU law. With loyalty, the Court has never made a comparable systematic argument. I have suggested above that the reason might be that loyalty, different from solidarity, harks back to customary international law.

It is not quite clear whether this unwritten principle of solidarity encompasses all the expressions of solidarity in the (early) case law we have discussed above. Because the Court refers to mentions of solidarity in the Treaties and these concern exclusively solidarity between Member States, it seems likely that it only refers to an unwritten principle of solidarity between Member States, not between companies or with individuals.

4. Applications

For a long time, it could be said that the 'normative premises of solidarity have remained weak'.[424] However, solidarity has always guided the interpretation of

[419] *Commission v Hungary* (n 252) para 116.

[420] *Poland v Parliament and Council (Conditionality mechanism)* para 147; *Hungary v Parliament and Council (Conditionality mechanism)* (n 310) para 129.

[421] *Germany v Poland (OPAL)* (n 412) para 38.

[422] *Germany v Poland (OPAL)* (n 412) paras 39–41.

[423] *Germany v Poland (OPAL)* (n 412) paras 43 and 46.

[424] See E Küçük, 'Solidarity in EU Law – An Elusive Political Statement or a Legal Principle with Substance?' (2016) 23 *Maastricht Journal* 965.

secondary law in those fields where it was mentioned in the Treaties. This was the case with secondary law based on Article 67 TFEU, Article 122 TFEU and Article 80 TFEU.[425]

The Court has also recently relied on solidarity to justify imposing a particularly severe financial penalty on a Member State.[426] The Court held that Hungary's conduct would have the effect of transferring to the other Member States its responsibility, including financial responsibility, for ensuring the reception of applicants for international protection in the European Union, among others.[427] Such conduct 'seriously undermines the principle of solidarity and fair sharing of responsibility, including its financial implications, between the Member States, which governs, in accordance with Article 80 TFEU, the common policy on asylum, subsidiary protection and temporary protection and the common immigration policy'.[428]

The strongest normative force has been accorded to solidarity under Article 194 TFEU in the *OPAL* case already mentioned above. In an annulment proceeding on the conditions for access to the Baltic Sea Pipeline Connector, the Court held that acts adopted by the EU institutions, including by the Commission under the EU's energy policy, must be interpreted, and their legality assessed, in the light of the principle of energy solidarity, even if there is no express reference to that principle in the secondary legislation applicable.[429] Solidarity would form 'the basis of all of the objectives of the European Union's energy policy, serving as the thread that brings them together and gives them coherence'.[430]

It is yet unclear if solidarity, including under Article 194 TFEU, could also be applied in infringement cases against Member States. This distinguishes solidarity from loyalty, where the Court regularly finds infringements of the 'duty of sincere cooperation', as explained above. However, at least under Article 194 TFEU, such an application does not seem implausible. It is also still unclear whether solidarity, especially under Article 194 TFEU, could be given direct effect (beyond indirect effects as a standard of legality such as discussed with autonomy and conferral). Against such direct effect argues that solidarity in the provisions and case law discussed above primarily protects Member States and not the rights of individuals.

Similar to national identity, solidarity has allowed Member States to justify measures that would otherwise be deemed restrictive under the fundamental

[425] See Opinion of AG Mengozzi in Case C-638/16 PPU *X*, ECLI:EU:C:2017:93, para 174; Opinion of AG Mengozzi in Case C-226/16, *Eni*, ECLI:EU:C:2017:616, para 37 on Regulation (EU) No 994/2010 concerning measures to safeguard security of gas supply [2010] OJ L295/1; Joined Cases C-643/15 & C-647/15, *Slovak Republic and Hungary v Council (Relocation quotas)*, ECLI:EU:C:2017:631, paras 252 and 291; Joined Cases C-715/17, *Commission v Poland*, C-718/17, *Commission v Hungary*, and C-719/17, *Commission v Czech Republic*, ECLI:EU:C:2020:257, paras 80 and 181 on asylum measures.

[426] *Commission v Hungary* (n 252).

[427] *Commission v Hungary* (n 252) para 114.

[428] *Commission v Hungary* (n 252) para 115.

[429] *Germany v Poland (OPAL)* (n 412) paras 43 and 46.

[430] *Germany v Poland (OPAL)* (n 412) para 43.

freedoms,[431] respectively would fall under the prohibition of Article 102 TFEU.[432] This has insulated Member State measures meant to give expression to solidarity with their citizens. While we would not consider this a form of balancing comparable to how general principles under Article 6 TEU operate, in the *OPAL* case, the Commission was faulted for not examining the impact that the decision at issue could have on the gas market of the Member States liable to be affected.[433] The Court held that the principle of energy solidarity would require that the EU institutions, including the Commission, 'conduct an analysis of the interests involved in the light of that principle, taking into account the interests both of the Member States and of the European Union as a whole'.[434] This would imply that energy solidarity, but also perhaps solidarity more broadly, requires a weighing of the interests of the actors concerned.

5. Interrelations

5.1. Solidarity and Equality

As mentioned above, the early case law on solidarity was all about different forms of discrimination.

On the one hand, this is evident in the *Premiums for Slaughtering Cows* judgment of 1973 already discussed earlier. I have suggested elsewhere that the principle of solidarity is connected with the equality of Member States under Article 4(2) TEU.[435] The argument would be that for Member States to accept the disadvantages that come with adhering to Union law is acceptable because they share in the benefits that come with membership. If one of these two elements is lopsided, the basis for solidarity/compliance would be undermined. That means that it would be detrimental to solidarity if Member States were not to be treated equally as regards the advantages such as funds as well as the disadvantages such as being targeted with infringements. It thus makes perfect sense to frame the budget in terms of solidarity as well as to rely on Article 322(1)(a) TFEU as the legal basis for the rule of law conditionality mechanism, as mentioned above. This mechanism, as is well known, aims at making sure that Member States do not receive money out of the EU budget if they do not follow commonly agreed values and the rules concretising them.

In the same 1973 judgment, the Court also made a connection between solidarity and 'discriminations at the expense of their nationals, and above all of the nationals of the State itself which places itself outside the Community rules'.[436]

[431] Case C-192/05, *Tas-Hagen*, ECLI:EU:C:2006:676, para 35. See also M Ross, 'Solidarity: A New Constitutional, paradigm for the EU?' in M Ross and Y Borgmann-Prebil (eds), *Promoting Solidarity in the European Union* (Oxford, Oxford University Press, 2010) 23.

[432] Case C-437/09, *AG2R Prévoyance*, ECLI:EU:C:2011:112.

[433] *Germany v Poland (OPAL)* (n 412) para 51.

[434] *Germany v Poland (OPAL)* (n 412) para 53.

[435] See Klamert, 'Solidarität in der Wirtschafts- und Währungsunion' (n 414) para 38.

[436] *Premiums for Slaughtering Cows* (n 211) paras 24–25.

As I will explain in the next section, this statement is perfectly aligned with *Costa*, where the Court also linked compliance with Union law (through supremacy) with the prohibition of discrimination based on nationality. Interestingly, this element of the *Premiums for Slaughtering Cows* judgment has not been further mentioned in this context as far as can be seen.

5.2. *Solidarity and Loyalty*

A connection between solidarity and loyalty has often been emphasised in the literature.[437] As mentioned, according to the case law of the ECJ, the principle of solidarity is 'consistent with the principle of loyalty' respectively is 'closely linked to the principle of loyal cooperation'.[438] I have argued elsewhere that loyalty and solidarity today are complementary, integrative forces in EU law, but still differ in terms of both their effect and their function.[439] While Member State solidarity as discussed above has become the dominant manifestation of solidarity in EU law, the most important developments regarding loyalty have occurred in the (vertical) relationship between the Member States and the European Union. It therefore does not do justice to the principle of solidarity to consider it a mere 'sub-category' of the principle of loyalty or vice versa. This can also not be inferred from the words 'consistent with' or 'closely linked' cited above, it is submitted.

Where loyalty and solidarity overlap in EU law is in the obligation to comply with Union law, even if this is disadvantageous to Member State interests.[440] The reason for this can be seen in the prevalence of the 'common interest of the European Union and the policies pursued by it', to quote the ECJ in the *OPAL* case. Article 351(3) TFEU on the obligations of Member States concerning their 'old' agreements with third states is a good illustration of this. This provision requires Member States to 'take into account the fact that the advantages accorded under the Treaties by each Member State form an integral part of the establishment of the Union and are thereby inseparably linked with the creation of common institutions, the conferring of powers upon them and the granting of the same advantages by all the other Member States'. While Article 351 TFEU is commonly considered a manifestation of Article 4(3) TEU, there clearly is an element of solidarity present as well.

6. Conclusions

Solidarity is no less multifaceted than autonomy or loyalty. While it has been and remains important in many ways in EU law, its focus has changed over the years as

[437] See, eg, F Casolari, 'Loyalty after Lisbon: An Expectation Gap to Be Filled?' in LS Rossi and F Casolari (eds), *The Principle of Equality in EU Law* (New York, Springer, 2017) 93.

[438] Joined Cases 6/69 & 11/69, *Commission v France* (n 398) para 16; *Germany v Poland (OPAL)* (n 412) para 41.

[439] See Klamert, 'Loyalty and Solidarity as General Principles' (n 384) 128 ff.

[440] See also Küçük, 'Solidarity in EU Law' (n 424) 965.

we have shown. The Member State-centric manifestations of solidarity in early case law have only been revisited recently and are now also very visible in primary law.

While a principle of solidarity exists in public international law, the prevailing view does not assign it a normative function. This is different in EU law, which is illustrated by the specific principle of energy solidarity that has recently been applied forcefully in case law. Many questions regarding the broader normative role of solidarity in EU law, however, remain unresolved. The *OPAL* case would seem to suggest that solidarity might involve a weighing of interests, different from other structural principles.

It is noteworthy how strong the interrelations of Member State solidarity are with both loyalty and the two forms of equality discussed in this book, one protecting the equal status of Member States on the one hand and the other protecting individuals against discrimination based on nationality on the other hand. As such, there is also a close connection between (negative) Member State solidarity and supremacy, discussed next.

8. The Principles of Supremacy/Primacy and Direct Effect

1. Introduction

Supremacy or primacy of EU law is often seen as an idiosyncratic principle of EU law, as perhaps the most characteristic of all such principles. As with most other principles in this book, this impression is misleading, as the concept of supremacy in public international law discussed below will show. In a normative sense, supremacy is as hard to analyse as autonomy, as will be shown.[441]

While supremacy, without doubt, is a structural principle of EU law within the remit of this book, this is not so obvious with direct effect. The direct effect of many provisions of Union law can be seen as a (mere, technical) modality of the domestic effect of Union law norms and must often first be established for a certain provision.[442] It is also a feature of the principles under Article 6(3) TEU and is generally concerned with rights granted by Union law, which would seem to link it to axiological principles.

At the same time, the direct effect 'of a whole series of provisions' has been mentioned by the ECJ, together with supremacy, as an essential characteristic of

[441] See, however, D Chalmers et al, *European Union Law: Text and Materials*, 5th edn (Cambridge, Cambridge University Press, 2024) 194: 'The primacy of EU law is the most straightforward of all doctrines'.

[442] It is therefore sometimes also referred to as (mere) doctrine or theory. See J Bengoetxea, 'Is Direct Effect a General Principle of European Law?' in U Bernitz and J Nergelius (eds), *General Principles of European Community Law* (The Hague, Kluwer, 2000) 6. See also P Pescatore, 'The Doctrine of "Direct Effect": An Infant Disease of Community Law' (2015) 40 *EL Rev* 135 (reprint).

the Union legal order.[443] The literature also commonly qualifies it as a structural/systemic principle as discussed in chapter two. Moreover, in *Popławski II*, the Court clarified that primacy cannot have the effect of 'undermining the essential distinction between provisions of EU law which have direct effect and those which do not and, consequently, of creating a single set of rules for the application of all of the provisions of EU law by the national courts'.[444] This means that supremacy and direct effect are even more closely connected than previously thought: only directly effective provisions of Union law can set aside national law under the principle of primacy.[445] Thus, there may be direct effect without supremacy but there cannot be supremacy without direct effect.

We will therefore deal with both supremacy and direct effect in the following with a focus on the former. Different from other sections, we will discuss the location of the principle of supremacy only at a later stage. As with the other principles, note that this is not the place to fully explore all the pertinent case law. In particular, supremacy has been further developed by the Court in recent years and the literature has taken a renewed interest in its operation.[446]

2. Origins

2.1. National Constitutional Law

In (German) federal constitutional law, federal law derogates state law rendering the latter invalid in case of a conflict (*Bundesrecht bricht Landesrecht*).[447] At the beginning of European integration, the German literature sought to apply this federal concept to EU (then EEC) law.[448] However, it soon became clear that this was not the right analogy. It has been noted that even a superficial survey would show that the relationship between federal and state law may be regulated differently from Germany, and a federal state would therefore not necessarily have a specific priority rule.[449]

[443] *EEA I* (n 43) para 21; *Unified Patents Court* (n 67) para 65; *Popławski II* (n 67) para 52.

[444] *Popławski II* (n 67) para 60. See also Case C-205/20, *Bezirkshauptmannschaft Hartberg-Fürstenfeld*, ECLI:EU:C:2022:168, para 37.

[445] See D Miasik and M Szwarc, 'Primacy and Direct Effect – Still Together: Popławski II' (2021) 58 *CML Rev* 571. Compare K Lenaerts and T Corthaut, 'Of Birds and Hedges: The Role of Primacy in Invoking Norms of EU Law' (2006) 31 *EL Rev* 289. See J Kokott, 'Zur unmittelbaren Wirkung des Unionsrechts (Aufgaben der Kriterien von Van Gend & Loos)' (2023) 148 *Archiv des öffentlichen Rechts* 496, on how much the understanding of direct effect has changed since *Van Gend*.

[446] See, eg, M Dougan, 'The Primacy of Union Law over Incompatible National Measures: Beyond Disapplication and Towards a Remedy of Nullity?' (2022) 59 *CML Rev* 1301.

[447] See Article 31 German Basic Law. See also the 'Supremacy Clause' in Article VI, Clause 2 of the US Constitution. Compare also BVerfG, 2BvE 2/08 et al, *Lisbon Treaty*, ECLI:DE:BVerfG:2009:es20090630.2bve000208, para 335.

[448] See especially E Grabitz, *Gemeinschaftsrecht bricht nationales Recht* (Hamburg, Appel, 1966).

[449] See M Nettesheim, 'Artikel 1 AEUV' in Grabitz, Hilf and Nettesheim (eds), *EU-Kommentar*, para 71; L Kirchmair, *Rethinking the Relationship between International, EU and National Law: Consent-Based Monism* (Cambridge, Cambridge University Press, 2024) 230–31.

Different from loyalty, which was written into the EEC Treaty and was moulded (also) against the background of federal fidelity, as discussed earlier, there thus is no indication that the principle of supremacy has been introduced (by the ECJ) with federal law in mind.[450]

2.2. Public International Law

The principle of supremacy has been considered 'one of the great principles of international law, informing the whole system and applying to every branch of it'.[451] According to Article 27 of the Vienna Convention on the Law of Treaties, a party to a Treaty 'may not invoke the provisions of its internal law as justification for its failure to perform a treaty'.[452] Supremacy would thus be at the heart of both the law of treaties and the law of international responsibility and be 'key to the international rule of law, which, if anything, requires that states exercise their powers in accordance with international law, not domestic law'.[453] As such, supremacy in international law is related to *pacta sunt servanda* and the duty of compliance with international contract law derived from it discussed earlier in the context of loyalty.

The Venice Commission of the Council of Europe has stated the following under the subtitle 'Legality (supremacy of the law)':

> The importance of the principle of legality was underlined by Dicey. It first implies that the law must be followed … Law should, within the bounds of possibility, be enforced.
>
> The term 'law', as used in this chapter, refers primarily to national legislation and common law. However, the development of international law as well as the importance given by international organisations to the respect of the rule of law lead to addressing the issue at international level as well: the principle pacta sunt servanda is the way in which international law expresses the principle of legality.[454]

In international law, 'the principle of supremacy does not, out of its own force, make international law supreme in the domestic legal order, at least not in the same manner as European law has relatively successfully claimed supremacy over, and forced itself into, domestic law'.[455] Thus, under international law, states are barred from invoking domestic law to justify the non-performance of an international obligation only at the international level, such as before international

[450] Compare also C Rauchegger, 'Four functions of the principle of primacy in post-Lisbon case law' in Ziegler, Neuvonen and Moreno-Lax (eds), *Research Handbook* 157, 159.

[451] See G Fitzmaurice, 'The General Principles of International law Considered from the Standpoint of the Rule of Law' (1957) 92 *Recueil des cours* (II) 85.

[452] See also Articles 3 and 32 of the Articles on the Responsibility of States for Internationally Wrongful Acts.

[453] See A Nollkaemper, 'Rethinking the Supremacy of International Law' (2010) 65 *Zeitschrift fur Offentliches Recht* (ZoR): *Journal of Public Law* 65, 66–67.

[454] European Commission for Democracy through Law (Venice Commission), Report on the Rule of Law, Study No 512/2009, CDL-AD(2011)003rev, paras 42–43.

[455] See Nollkaemper, 'Rethinking the Supremacy of International Law' (n 453) 68.

courts and tribunals. At the domestic level, by contrast, the supremacy of international law does not automatically apply, except in monist states such as the Netherlands.[456]

Similarly, while there is the concept of directly effective (self-executing) international law, traditionally national authorities decide on whether a norm of international law has such effect in domestic law.[457] Moreover, under international law it has been suggested that the concepts of supremacy and direct effect should be separated.[458]

2.3. The Early Case Law of the European Courts

The *Humblet* case of 1960 under the ECSC, discussed earlier in the context of loyalty, can be seen as an early case on EU law supremacy in general and its *Simmenthal*-line in particular.[459] *Humblet* was concerned with the question of whether a Belgian tax law violated the privileges and immunities of civil servants of the ECSC. The Court clarified that it had *no* jurisdiction to annul legislative or administrative measures of one of the Member States and made the following argument to this end:

> Thus, if the High Authority believes that a State has failed to fulfil an obligation under the Treaty by adopting or maintaining in force provisions contrary to the Treaty, it may not itself annul or repeal those provisions but, in accordance with Article 88 of the Treaty, it may merely record such a failure and subsequently institute proceedings as set out in the Treaty to prevail upon the State in question itself to rescind the measures which it had adopted. The same applies to the Court of Justice. Under the terms of Article 31 of the Treaty it has responsibility for ensuring that Community law is observed and by Article 16 of the Protocol has jurisdiction to rule on any dispute relating to the interpretation or application of the Protocol but it may not, on its own authority, annul or repeal the national laws of a Member State or administrative measures adopted by the authorities of that State.
>
> This statement of the limits of the jurisdiction of the Court may further be supported by an argument stemming from the Treaties of Rome, in particular from Article 171 of the EEC Treaty and Article 143 of the EAEC Treaty which merely attach declaratory effect to the decisions of the Court in cases of failure to comply with the Treaties, albeit obliging the Member States to take the necessary measures to comply with the judgment. The Court finds that there is no foundation to the argument of the applicant that the protection of the privileges and immunities conferred by the Protocol would be ineffective

[456] See Nollkaemper, 'Rethinking the Supremacy of International Law' (n 453) 68.

[457] See de Witte, 'Direct Effect, Primacy and the Nature of the Legal Order' (n 271) 323; S Weatherill, 'From Myth to Reality: The EU's "New Legal Order" and the Place of General Principles Within It' in S Vogenauer and S Weatherill (eds), *General Principles of Law: European and Comparative Perspectives* (Oxford, Hart Publishing, 2017) 21, 29–30. Compare also, critically, A Somek, 'Is Legality a Principle of EU Law?' in Vogenauer and Weatherill (eds), *General Principles of Law* 53, 66–67.

[458] Compare A Nollkaemper, *National Courts and the International Rule of Law* (Oxford, Oxford University Press, 2012) 120.

[459] See already de Witte, 'Retour à "Costa"' (n 263) 426.

> and the judgment of the Court of Justice reduced to a mere opinion if it were unable to annul illegal measures adopted by national authorities and order the Member States to make reparation for the resultant damage.[460]

Interestingly, in *Humblet*, the argument that rights stemming from EU law would *not* be protected in a sufficiently effective way by infringement proceedings was refuted by the Court. It is also noteworthy that neither *Humblet* nor *Costa* below dealt with state responsibility, as would be expected under international law as mentioned above.[461] However, years later in *Francovich*, *Humblet* has been relied on to introduce the principle of state liability, discussed later under effectiveness.

In *Van Gend*, decided in February 1963, the ECJ found that a provision of primary law may be directly effective if it contains a clear and unconditional prohibition and is not qualified by any reservation on the part of Member States, which would make its implementation conditional upon a positive Member State measure.[462] The Court relied on the 'spirit, the general scheme and the wording' of the Treaty provisions concerned. The Court further underlined that the functioning of the common market was of direct concern to the people in the Member States and that the preamble of the EEC referred not only to governments but also to peoples. For these reasons, the EEC was held to be 'more than an agreement which merely creates mutual obligations between the contracting states'. Moreover, the preliminary reference procedure would confirm that subjects of EU law were not only Member States but also their nationals. Different from *Humblet*, the Court held that remedies against violations of EU law would be ineffective by only relying on the vigilance of the Commission and of the Member States under what are now Articles 258 and 267 TFEU.[463]

We have already discussed the *Dairy Products* case of 1964 in the context of (external substantive) autonomy, where the Court also mentioned 'a new legal order' and implicitly disavowed the international law principle of retaliation/reciprocity.[464] This was later, in *Mutton and Lamb* of 1978, reframed in terms of a repudiation of unilateralism, as also discussed earlier.[465]

In *Costa*, also discussed in the context of autonomy earlier, the parties had still argued in the 'language' of public international law, relying on the principle of *lex posterior derogat legi priori*. The Court, instead, repeated *Van Gend*'s *sui generis* argument about the specific nature of obligations under (then) Community law and 'the terms and the spirit of the Treaty', the systematic argument that 'wherever the Treaty grants the States the right to act unilaterally, it does this by clear and

[460] Case 6/60-IMM, *Humblet* (n 153) 568.

[461] Also noted by de Witte, 'Retour à "Costa"' (n 263) 432.

[462] *Van Gend & Loos* (n 21).

[463] This was not the prevailing view among Member States. See Somek, 'Is Legality a Principle of EU Law?' (n 457) 62 with further references.

[464] Joined Cases 90–91/63, *Commission v Belgium and Luxemburg (Dairy Products)* (n 39) 626. See also Phelan, 'The Revolutionary Doctrines of European Law' (n 39) 938–40; Phelan, *Great Judgments of the European Court of Justice* (n 39) 84–122.

[465] *Commission v France (Mutton and Lamb)* (n 40) para 9. While no reference was given in this paragraph, *Hedley Lomas* (n 40) para 20, shows that *Dairy Products* was the authority for this case.

precise provisions', and that the existence of regulations under (now) Article 288 TFEU would otherwise be 'meaningless'.[466] The Court held, moreover, that [t]he executive force of Community law cannot vary from one State to another in deference to subsequent domestic laws, without jeopardizing the attainment of the objectives of the Treaty set out in Article 5(2) [now Article 4(3) TEU] and giving rise to the discrimination prohibited by Article 7 [now Article 18 TFEU]'.[467]

2.4. *Interim Conclusions*

It is submitted that the Court, as with autonomy and conferral, painstakingly avoided any 'external' considerations in introducing both supremacy and direct effect to EU law, the rationale put forward being one purely built on European Union law (then Community law). However, we have seen that the thinking and language underlying the early case law had an international law (not federal law) subtext. This also aligns with the reliance in *Costa* on what is now Article 4(3) TEU, which was inspired by *pacta sunt servanda*, which is concerned with compliance with treaty obligations as we have discussed earlier.

The arguments in *Costa* have been categorised as 'contractarian' (ie, the Member States have given away their sovereignty by agreeing to membership), 'functional'/'pragmatic' (the aims of the Treaties and integration require it, thus essentially *effet utile*), and 'analytical' (the instrument of the regulation would be negated otherwise).[468] We will return to the strength and topicality of these arguments below.

3. Applications

3.1. *Introduction*

Supremacy does not apply as a standard of legality of Union law. It also does not apply as such a standard with regard to national law, at least not in the way this is usually understood. A measure of national law cannot normally be found to violate the 'principle of primacy'.[469] Thus, the application of supremacy can hardly be discussed in the same terms as with general principles under Article 6 TEU, but also not in the same terms as with conferral, (energy) solidarity, or possibly also autonomy.

[466] *Costa/ENEL* (n 21).
[467] *Costa/ENEL* (n 21).
[468] See P Craig and G de Búrca, *EU Law: Text, Cases, and Materials*, 7th edn (Oxford, Oxford University Press, 2021) 305. Compare also J Wouters, 'National Constitutions and the European Union' (2000) 27 *Legal Issues of Economic Integration* 25, 64–65, who, pointing to Case 44/79, *Hauer*, ECLI:EU:C:1979:290, discussed below, speaks of the 'practical concern' that the status of Community rules would differ from Member State to Member State, of which non-discrimination based on nationality would only be a further concretisation.
[469] See, however, *Commission v Poland (Independence and private life of judges)*, ECLI:EU:C:2021:593 (Order of the Vice-President of the Court) para 184.

Supremacy is not applied for the interpretation of either Union or national law, at least not in a technical sense.[470] Moreover, as with conferral and autonomy, one could only speak of a very 'indirect' direct effect through infringement or preliminary ruling procedures. Thus, it is not at all straightforward to understand how supremacy applies compared with other (structural) principles.

It is often noted that primacy would be a (mere) 'technicality' or 'functionality'.[471] If this were true, primacy would operate like a rule not like a principle in the orthodox understanding of that term as discussed in chapter one. While our (wide) definition of principles as fundamental structural decisions would accommodate that, we will suggest in the following to distinguish a broader, more structural 'principle of supremacy' from a more technical 'principle of primacy' as part of the former.[472] This distinction between principle and duty (of disapplication) arguably is similar to the principle of loyalty, which we have understood earlier to comprise a more 'rule-like' duty of sincere cooperation.

Note that we will refer to 'supremacy' on the one hand because it is an established notion in international but also national federal law as shown above, and to 'primacy' on the other hand because it is used in case law for the duty of disapplication as shown below. It has been explained above that the term 'supremacy', when considering its international law as opposed to a (federal) constitutional background, does not allude to claims of hierarchy in terms of validity.[473] Concerns that the notion of supremacy would send the 'wrong' signals conceptionally therefore seem unwarranted.

3.2. *Supremacy as Gatekeeper and Equaliser*

According to the Court, the principle of the primacy of EU law 'establishes the pre-eminence of EU law over the law of the Member States', requiring all Member State bodies to give full effect to the various EU provisions, and that the law of the Member States 'may not undermine the effect accorded to those various provisions in the territory of those States'.[474] The 'primacy and uniform application of EU

[470] See also de Witte, 'The Role of Institutional Principles' (n 317) 89: 'very peculiar "principles"', 100: 'pseudo-principles', concerning primacy and direct effect.

[471] See Claes, 'Primacy of EU Law in European and National Law' (n 286) 178. See, similarly, R Schütze, *European Constitutional Law*, 2nd edn (Cambridge, Cambridge University Press, 2016) 117–118; H Hofmann, 'Conflicts and Integration: Revisiting *Costa v ENEL* and *Simmenthal II*' in MP Maduro and L Azoulai (eds), *The Past and Future of EU Law: The Classics of EU Law Revisited on the 50th Anniversary of the Rome Treaty* (Oxford, Hart Publishing, 2010) 60.

[472] Compare T Tuominen, 'Reconceptualizing the Primacy–Supremacy Debate in EU Law' (2020) 47 *Legal Issues of Economic Integration* 245, for another distinction between primacy and supremacy.

[473] For a different perspective, compare M Avbelj, 'Supremacy or Primacy of EU Law – (Why) Does it Matter?' (2011) 17 *European Law Journal* 744. Compare also Claes, 'Primacy of EU Law in European and National Law' (n 286) 182, who rejects the term supremacy in the context of EU law because it would allude to supremacy in the federal (German) mould. See, critically, Kirchmair, *Rethinking the Relationship* (n 449) 230–31.

[474] *Popławski II* (n 67) paras 53–54, referring to Case C-399/11, *Melloni*, ECLI:EU:C:2013:107, para 59, and Case C-378/17, *An Garda Síochána*, ECLI:EU:C:2018:979, point 39.

law would be undermined if national courts had the power to give provisions of national law primacy in relation to EU law contravened by those provisions, even temporarily'.[475]

Case law thus emphasises the application of primacy as a (conflict) rule requiring the disapplication, the setting aside of national law when it conflicts with Union law. However, this case law also refers to a broader objective of systemic uniformity that is served by supremacy.

It has been argued that the principle of primacy would be more than a conflict rule but that it would additionally 'mark the boundaries of the applicability of national fundamental rights within the scope of EU law', 'justify a particular feature of the preliminary reference procedure of Article 267 TFEU', and be an essential characteristic of EU law that is part of the very identity of the European Union.[476] It has, moreover, in this context been distinguished between 'first category' conflicts about the very authority of Union law and 'second category' disputes 'concerning the practical consequences of a finding of incompatibility between Union and national law, focused on finding an appropriate balance between the demands of primacy and the needs of legal certainty'.[477]

Indeed, we will discuss in chapter six that supremacy is, together with equality, the key to the pervasive requirement of uniformity in EU law, which has both institutional and substantive implications. As we will see below, it is founded both on the need to ensure the equality of individuals as well as the equality between Member States in the European Union. The term 'supremacy' in this vein would refer to a principle that ensures legal unity and uniformity in the relation of EU law with the laws of the Member States.

In this sense, supremacy is also a gatekeeper, structuring and synchronising the relations between the European Union and the Member States. It is thus similar to autonomy, which we earlier qualified as a gatekeeper with respect to international law. As suggested for autonomy, supremacy could therefore also be seen as a 'hinge principle' establishing an obligation to take EU law into account (for the Member States).

3.3. *Primacy as Conflict Rule*

The distinction suggested between supremacy and primacy, it is submitted, can also elucidate whether supremacy can be balanced with other legal principles. This is a different question from whether there are exceptions to supremacy under *EU* law such as Article 351 TFEU on 'old' Member State agreements.[478]

[475] *Chaudfontaine Loisirs* (n 380) para 61; Case C-355/22, *Osteopathie Van Hauwermeiren*, ECLI:EU:C:2023:737, para 31; *Casino de Spa and Others* (n 380) para 51 ff.

[476] See Rauchegger, 'Four functions' (n 45) 157.

[477] See M Dougan, 'Primacy and the remedy of disapplication' (2019) 56 *CML Rev* 1459, 1478.

[478] See the references in A Arena, 'The Twin Doctrines of Primacy and Pre-emption' in Schütze and Tridimas (eds), *Oxford Principles of European Union* Law 300, 312; Klamert, 'Commentary on Article 1 TEU' (n 108) para 27.

In 2009, it was argued that the CJEU would deliberately not characterise primacy as a principle in order not to suggest that it could be weighed with countervailing principles such as national identity.[479] This changed in 2010 with *Winner Wetten*, it seems, and since then the Court regularly speaks of a 'principle of primacy'.[480] We would guess that it now feels safer for the Court to refer to primacy as a principle because the 'threat' of a countervailing, weighing application of national identity has in the meantime been defused, as discussed earlier.

Recently the Court has handed down judgments where it seems to balance supremacy with competing interests recognised by EU law. Thus in *Inter-Environnement Wallonie and Terre wallonne*, the Court allowed exceptionally and provisionally the maintenance of certain effects of an annulled national measure in light of the Treaties' environment objectives.[481] In *Inter-Environnement Wallonie and Bond Beter Leefmilieu Vlaanderen*, it stressed that only the Court itself may, 'for overriding considerations of legal certainty, allow temporary suspension of the ousting effect of a rule of EU law with respect to national law that is contrary thereto'.[482] This arguably goes back to the *Winner Wetten* case, where the ECJ laid the ground by making an analogy with case law on the maintenance of the effects of Union measures which have been annulled or declared invalid.[483]

It is submitted that the Court would not qualify that Union law has (structural) supremacy over national law. What is qualified is primacy, thus the need to set aside national law in a 'second category' dispute as mentioned above. While primacy can be weighed with other considerations under EU law such as legal certainty, supremacy is, such as most other structural principles discussed in this book, *not* open to a balancing with competing principles or interests.

4. Interrelations and Rationale

4.1. Introduction

In 2014, I showed that for many years, the Court has invoked *Costa* as an authority without repeating the judicial foundation of this judgment itself. I proffered

[479] See A von Bogdandy, 'Grundprinzipien des Unionsrechts – eine verfassungstheoretische und -dogmatische Skizze' (2009) *Europarecht* 749, 760.

[480] *Winner Wetten* (n 376). Also noted by Rauchegger, 'Four functions' (n 450) 158.

[481] *Inter-Environnement Wallonie and Terre wallonne* (n 379) paras 58–63. Confirmed in *Association France Nature* (n 379) paras 28–43.

[482] Case C-411/17, *Inter-Environnement Wallonie and Bond Beter Leefmilieu Vlaanderen*, ECLI:EU:C:2019:622, paras 172–82, on account of overriding considerations relating to the security of the electricity supply of the Member States concerned. See also *Chaudfontaine Loisirs* (n 380) para 60; *Osteopathie Van Hauwermeiren* (n 475) para 30. See, by contrast, Case C-817/19, *Ligue des droits humains*, ECLI:EU:C:2022:491, paras 292–98.

[483] *Winner Wetten* (n 376) paras 61–69. See the discussion by Dougan, 'Primacy and the remedy of disapplication' (n 477) 1491–96.

that one reason for this might be that the way the Court rationalised supremacy in *Costa* was multilayered and to continue arguing based on the rationale in *Costa* may have exposed the delicate structure the principle of supremacy has been built on methodologically.[484] Only in the judgments in *Euro Box Promotion* and in *RS*, facing increasing resistance from national constitutional courts in Romania and Poland especially, did the Court set out to reaffirm the authority of the principle of supremacy. It thereby repeated the reasoning in *Costa*, but crucially added several arguments whose relevance for justifying supremacy had not been obvious before, to put it carefully.

The arguments offered by the Court connect supremacy with several other principles of EU law besides what is now Article 4(3) TEU discussed earlier. In the case of supremacy, its interrelations can thus tell us something about its underlying rationale and also where it may be located in the Treaties. This is different from other structural principles such as loyalty and solidarity discussed above.

4.2. The Updated Rationale for Supremacy

Supremacy can be rationalised either from a Union law perspective or from a national constitutional law perspective.[485] In the following, we will discuss only the former.[486]

As mentioned, in *Euro Box Promotion* and in *RS* the Grand Chamber of the Court repeated the argument based on Article 18 TFEU that had not been made in this form since *Costa*.[487] In *RS*, it referred to Article 19(1) TEU, which would require ensuring the full application of EU law in all Member States, for which again compliance with supremacy would be essential.[488] In *Euro Box Promotion*, the Court also held as follows:

> It must be added that Article 4(2) TEU provides that the Union is to respect the equality of Member States before the Treaties. The Union can respect such equality only if the Member States are unable, under the principle of the primacy of EU law, to rely on, as against the EU legal order, a unilateral measure, whatever its nature.[489]

In *RS*, this was slightly re-phrased arguing that compliance with supremacy would also be necessary 'in order to ensure respect for the equality of Member States

[484] See Klamert, *The Principle of Loyalty in EU Law* (n 188) 73.

[485] See, eg, M Klamert, 'Editorial: Vorrang, Schranken und Österreich' (2021) *European Journal of Business Law* 1057.

[486] For a critical discussion of the German perspective, compare M Ruffert, 'Art 1 AEUV' in Calliess and Ruffert (eds), *EUV/AEUV*, paras 6–7 and 16–17.

[487] *Euro Box Promotion* (n 257) para 246; *RS (Effet des arrêts d'une cour constitutionnelle)* (n 257) para 48. See LD Spieker, 'Werte, Vorrang, Identität: Der Dreiklang europäischer Justizkonflikte vor dem EuGH' (2022) 33 *European Journal of Business Law* 305.

[488] *RS (Effet des arrêts d'une cour constitutionnelle)* (n 257) para 54.

[489] *Euro Box Promotion* (n 257) para 249; *RS (Effet des arrêts d'une cour constitutionnelle)* (n 257) para 55.

before the Treaties, which precludes the possibility of relying on, as against the EU legal order, a unilateral measure, whatever its nature'.[490]

The Court in *RS* added that, following the entry into force of the Lisbon Treaty, it has consistently confirmed that the primacy of EU law 'would require all Member State bodies to give full effect to the various EU provisions, and the law of the Member States may not undermine the effect accorded to those various provisions in the territory of those States'.[491] It would follow that, 'by virtue of the principle of the primacy of EU law, a Member State's reliance on rules of national law, even of a constitutional order, cannot be allowed to undermine the unity and effectiveness of EU law'.[492]

Euro Box Promotion and *RS* were preceded, in 2021, by a press release following the German Constitutional Court's *Weiss*/PSPP/*Ultra vires*-decision[493] where it was stated that authorities of the Member States including national courts were required to ensure that EU law takes full effect, which would be the only way of ensuring the equality of Member States in the Union they created.[494] In the same vein, it has been argued that Article 4(2) TEU would underpin the supremacy of EU law by requiring the equality of Member States 'before the law'.[495]

The fact that the Court has gone to great lengths to rationalise supremacy arguably shows that the need to resolve conflicts between (directly effective) Union law and national law is not sufficient to make the case for supremacy.[496] It is submitted that this fact only explains why there must be *some* sort of conflict resolution mechanism in EU law, but not why this must necessarily be supremacy. Recall that the EEC Treaty had foreseen the infringement procedure for that purpose, thus the 'Masters of the Treaties' had apparently not deemed a mechanism such as supremacy necessary to resolve conflicts within the European Union.

In the following, it will be shown that not all of these new rationales are equally convincing. This also pertains to arguments based on effectiveness, whose connection with supremacy will be discussed later in this chapter.

[490] *Euro Box Promotion* (n 257) para 249.

[491] *RS (Effet des arrêts d'une cour constitutionnelle)* (n 257) para 50; *Euro Box Promotion* (n 257) para 250.

[492] *RS (Effet des arrêts d'une cour constitutionnelle)* (n 257) para 51.

[493] See Case C-493/17, *Weiss*, ECLI:EU:C:2018:1000, and *Public Sector Asset Purchase Programme (PSPP)* (n 258). See on this, eg, J Basedow et al, 'European Integration – Quo Vadis? A critical commentary on the ECB judgment of the German Federal Constitutional Court of 5 May 2020' (2021) 19 *ICON* 1.

[494] ECJ Press Release 58/20 of 8 May 2020, available at: curia.europa.eu/jcms/upload/docs/application/pdf/2020-05/cp200058en.pdf. See, critically, J Lindeboom, 'Is the Primacy of EU Law Based on the Equality of the Member States?' (2020) 21 *German Law Journal* 1032.

[495] See K Lenaerts, 'No Member State is More Equal than Others' (*Verfassungsblog* 8 October 2020): 'It would mean in essence "that all provisions of EU law are to have the same meaning and to be applied in the same fashion throughout the EU"'. See also F Fabbrini, 'After the OMT Case: The Supremacy of EU Law as the Guarantee of the Equality of the Member States' (2015) 16 *German Law Journal* 1003.

[496] See also C Krenn, 'Warum Unionsrecht Vorrang hat: Zur aktualisierten Begründung des Vorrangprinzips in den Urteilen Euro Box Promotion und R.S.' (2024) *Europarecht*, Special Issue No 1, 59.

4.3. *Supremacy and the Equality of Union Citizens*

According to the rationale in *Costa* that was resurrected in *Eurobox* and *RS*, Member States must abstain from 'unilateral acts' conflicting with Union law, since this would risk subjecting nationals of the Member States to divergent and therefore discriminatory treatment. In other words, the Court found that the denial of supremacy by a Member State would jeopardise the attainment of the objectives of the Treaty and give rise to discrimination based on nationality. I have mentioned above that a very similar finding has been based on the principles of Member State equality and solidarity when the Court in *Premiums for Slaughtering Cows* held that the adoption of unilateral Member State measures 'creates discriminations at the expense of their nationals, and above all of the nationals of the State itself which places itself outside the Community rules'.[497]

It is submitted that the reference to Article 18 TFEU by the Court makes perfect sense if we understand the prohibition of discrimination based on nationality as also including a comparison between the situation of a person subject to Union law in one Member State with the situation of a person subject to Union law in (an)other Member State(s).[498] This pertains to a Union directive on workers' rights that is not applied by a Member State as much as to rules on the set-up of a Member State's judicial system. While the latter are directly addressed only to the Member State, the functioning or malfunctioning of national courts also affects the rights of individuals coming under their jurisdiction. Even failing to follow ECB decisions ultimately touches the interests of natural and legal persons in the respective Member State.

While this might not be explicitly covered by Article 18 TFEU, this provision can be seen as expressing the objective or principle that equality must also be upheld in this constellation. 'Equality before Union law' would then be a Treaty objective as referred to in Article 4(3) TEU, thereby activating the only basis in the Treaties for obliging Member States to either abstain from doing something or to actively do something to this end.[499] In this sense, equal treatment in the light of Union law between persons subject to the laws of different Member States would be the objective that is jeopardised if Member States fail to abstain from applying national law over Union law.

This reading can also be seen against the view that *Costa* and also *Van Gend* would have been animated by the logic of improving the protection of the individual.[500]

[497] *Premiums for slaughtering cows* (n 211) paras 24–25.

[498] See M Klamert, 'Rationalizing Supremacy: Supremacy, effectiveness, and two standards of equality in EU law' (*Verfassungsblog*, 18 October 2021); LD Spieker, 'The Conflict over the Polish Disciplinary Regime for Judges – An Acid Test for Judicial Independence, Union Values and the Primacy of EU Law: Commission v Poland' (2022) 59 *CML Rev* 777, 808–09. See, however, the objections by de Witte, 'Retour à "Costa"' (n 263) 441.

[499] See Klamert, *The Principle of Loyalty in EU Law* (n 188) 72.

[500] Compare Weatherill, 'From Myth to Reality' (n 457) 36.

4.4. Supremacy and the Equality of Member States

The problem with rationalising supremacy by relying on Article 4(2) TEU is that it imposes an obligation on the Union and not on the Member States, as already mentioned. The argument makes more sense when framing it in a way suggested in the literature:

> If a Member State law could unilaterally take precedence over EU law then that would lead to discrimination in the application of EU law as between the Member States, and would mean also that a state was taking the benefits of EU law without accepting all the burdens.[501]

This 'egalitarian' reading of supremacy emphasises that Member States would have an unfair advantage *vis-a-vis* the other Member States without supremacy.

Again, this argument has already been made in the context of the principle of solidarity, when the Court held that unilateral Member State action 'brings into question the equality of Member States before Community law' (besides causing discrimination of citizens).[502] It would be 'unfair' *vis-a-vis* the other Member States if one Member State fails to respect common(ly agreed) rules.[503]

On the one hand, this 'egalitarian' argument focusing on the Member States reinforces the argument that a denial of supremacy causes discrimination towards individuals. If one Member State does not comply with the same rules as other Member States, the persons residing in that Member State are also subject to different rules. The equality of Member States before Union law thus entails the equality before Union law of the individuals on their territory.[504]

On the other hand, this argument complements the argument based on Article 18 TFEU by rationalising those few situations where the rights of Union citizens to be subjected to the same rules in the European Union are not in the foreground. This, for instance, concerns a case such as *Commission v Hungary*, where the Grand Chamber of the Court found that a deliberate evasion by a Member State of the application of a common policy as a whole would represent a significant threat to the principle of equality of the Member States, among others.[505] The Court held furthermore that compliance with the obligations following from the principle of primacy 'is necessary in particular in order to ensure respect for the equality of Member States before the Treaties'.[506] In that case, at stake above all was the repudi-

[501] See Craig and de Búrca, *EU Law* (n 468) 305. See also the Opinion by AG Maduro in *Michaniki* (n 285) para 33, in connection with Article 4(2) TEU: 'Furthermore, it could lead to discrimination between Member States based on the contents of their respective national constitutions'.

[502] *Premiums for slaughtering cows* (n 211) paras 24–25.

[503] See Klamert, 'Loyalty and Solidarity as General Principles' (n 384) 130.

[504] See also F Meyer, 'The Rule of Law in the Enforcement of EU Law: Shortcomings and Future Standards' Jean Monnet Network on EU Law Enforcement Working Paper Series 2023: 'In securing the same standards across the union, Art. 4, para 2 and the principle of effectiveness also guard again discrimination of EU citizens. Their equal treatment would be threatened if subjected to diverging implementations of EU law by different Member States'.

[505] *Commission v Hungary* (n 252) para 120.

[506] *Commission v Hungary* (n 252) para 122. See also *Commission v Poland (Independence and private life of judges)* (n 310) para 77.

ation of the authority of EU law by Hungary as such, not the failure to apply specific EU rules. The point was that the infringement in that case was of a deliberate and systematic nature. In such cases, it really is the unfairness of the behaviour vis-a-vis all other Member States that takes front and centre.

4.5. *Supremacy and Loyalty*

In *Commission v Hungary*, the Court held that compliance with the obligations following from the principle of primacy 'constitutes an expression of the principle of sincere cooperation set out in Article 4(3) TEU'.[507]

Indeed, as mentioned earlier, the abstention obligation provided in what is now Article 4(3) TEU constituted (and still constitutes) the only treaty-based justification why national law would have to yield to Union law in case of a conflict.[508] Loyalty and the duty of abstention provided in Article 4(3) TEU thus adds the operative element to the more aspirational foundations for supremacy mentioned above.

This, arguably, is confirmed by the *Winner Wetten* case law, where the Court held:

> It is also settled case-law that any national court, hearing a case within its jurisdiction, has, as an organ of a Member State, the obligation pursuant to the principle of cooperation set out in Article 10 EC, fully to apply the directly applicable law of the Union and to protect the rights which the latter confers upon individuals, disapplying any provision of national law which may be to the contrary, whether the latter is prior to or subsequent to the rule of law of the Union (see to that effect, in particular, Simmenthal, paragraphs 16 and 21, and Factortame, paragraph 19).[509]

As far as can be seen, this has only been referred to again in 2021, first in a lesser known case, and then with the updated rationale in *RS* in early 2022.[510] It is noteworthy that *Simmenthal* had not relied on what was then Article 10 EC but on the principle of effectiveness, discussed later.[511]

5. Locations

As is well known, supremacy is not mentioned in primary EU law, despite an attempt to include it with the failed Constitutional Treaty.[512] That such an express guarantee specifying the precedence of the application of EU law is miss-

[507] *Commission v Hungary* (n 252) para 122.
[508] See Klamert, *The Principle of Loyalty in EU Law* (n 188) 72.
[509] See *Winner Wetten* (n 376) para 55.
[510] *Whiteland Import Export* (n 376) para 31; *RS (Effet des arrêts d'une cour constitutionnelle)* (n 257) para 55.
[511] *Simmenthal II* (n 374). Also Case C-213/89, *Factortame*, ECLI:EU:C:1990:257, para 19, did not make this explicit connection between loyalty and disapplication.
[512] See Claes, 'Primacy of EU Law in European and National Law' (n 286) 200–01.

ing from the EU Treaties was emphasised by the German Federal Constitutional Court in June 2021.[513] It might be no coincidence that in *Euro Box Promotion* of December 2021 and again in *RS*, the Court made the point that supremacy was confirmed by treaty changes since *Costa* as well as by Declaration No 17 concerning primacy,[514] annexed to the Final Act of the Intergovernmental Conference which adopted the Treaty of Lisbon.[515] It was the first time, as far as can be seen, that such an argument was put forward by the Court.

Earlier, in May 2020, as mentioned, the German Constitutional Court had declared Union law *ultra vires* and thus challenged the supremacy of EU law.[516] It may thus also be no coincidence that, in August 2020, the President of the Court of Justice, writing in a personal capacity, argued that primacy would be provided in Article 4(2) TEU per the equality of Member States.[517]

We have seen above that there are indeed provisions in the Treaties that could provide a treaty-based foundation for supremacy. What we have called primacy, thus the duty of disapplication, could be located in Article 4(3) TEU. The broader principle of supremacy could be seen as being anchored in Article 4(2) in conjunction with Article 18 TFEU as well as in Article 19(1) TEU for reasons that will be explained in the following section. In chapter five, we will further discuss the 'piling'-technique the Court has used for anchoring supremacy more firmly in primary law.

6. Conclusions

Supremacy is the only principle discussed in this book that is commonly seen as a rule, viz a conflict rule. This would not be surprising considering that supremacy in international law is also 'only' a conflict rule. However, the Court has always rationalised supremacy very differently from how it is normally done in international law, linking it to the autonomy of EU law and the principle of equality, among others.

We have therefore suggested distinguishing a more technical function of supremacy, which can be referred to as primacy, from the more structural, systematic function of a principle of supremacy in EU law. Normatively, we have argued that the recent recognition of balancing particularly with legal certainty only affects the application of the primacy of Union law, thus the consequence of disapplication, not the broader claim to supremacy.

[513] BVerfG, 2 BvR 2216/20 & 2 BvR 2217/20, *Einheitliches Patentgericht*, ECLI:DE:BVerfG:2021:rs20210623.2bvr221620, para 76.

[514] [2012] OJ C 326, 346: 'In accordance with well settled case law of the Court of Justice of the European Union, the Treaties and the law adopted by the Union on the basis of the Treaties have primacy over the law of Member States, under the conditions laid down by [that] case law'.

[515] *RS (Effet des arrêts d'une cour constitutionnelle)* (n 257) para 49.

[516] *Public Sector Asset Purchase Programme (PSPP)* (n 258).

[517] See Lenaerts, 'No Member State is More Equal than Others' (n 495).

While primacy operates in a decidedly more centralised manner in EU law compared with international law, it is submitted that the broader functions of EU law supremacy set it even further apart from orthodox supremacy. We will discuss the role of supremacy with unity and uniformity in chapter six.

The rationales for this specific, unional principle of supremacy have evolved recently, in an approach by the Court that we will describe as 'piling'. In chapter five, we have argued that the prohibition of discrimination based on nationality is the strongest argument underpinning supremacy. Member State equality has been suggested as playing a role in cases on compliance that are not of concern for the position of individuals vis-a-vis Union law.

9. The Principles of Effectiveness and Effective Judicial Protection

1. Introduction

After the discussions of structural principles so far in this chapter, it will come as no surprise that effectiveness is also a particularly multifaceted legal principle in Union law.[518] It has been noted that there is no general agreement on a single meaning and scope.[519] The reason might be that it is conceptually difficult to grasp and that it manifests itself in several specific ways that are easier to explore by themselves, such as *effet utile* or direct effect already discussed earlier. It must be cautioned, as with other principles in this book, that we cannot comprehensively deal with effectiveness in EU law for lack of space. Effectiveness has its specific functions in external relations law, which will be explored in chapter four.

The title of this chapter mentions effective judicial protection for a reason. It is quite obvious that the effective judicial protection of an individual's rights under EU law is 'a general principle of EU law stemming from the constitutional traditions common to the Member States, enshrined in Articles 6 and 13 of the Convention for the Protection of Human Rights and Fundamental Freedoms, signed in Rome on 4 November 1950, and now reaffirmed in Article 47 of the Charter'.[520] It would thus seem 'merely' another fundamental right, which is not within the remit of this book, as explained in chapter two.

[518] See M Ross, 'Effectiveness in the European Union Legal Order(s): Beyond Supremacy to Constitutional Proportionality?' (2006) 31 *EL Rev* 476; M Accetto and S Zleptning, 'The Principle of Effectiveness: Rethinking its Role in Community Law' (2005) 11 *EPL* 375; S Demkova and H Hofmann, 'General principles of procedural justice' in Ziegler, Neuvonen and Moreno-Lax (eds), *Research Handbook* 209; M Eliantonio and E Muir, 'The principle of effectiveness: under strain?' (2019) 12 *Review of European Administrative Law* 255.

[519] See E Mendez-Pinedo, 'The principle of effectiveness of EU law: a difficult concept in legal scholarship' (2021) 11 *Juridical Tribune* 5, 25.

[520] *Commission v Hungary* (n 252) para 109.

However, it is submitted that the principle of effective judicial protection should be qualified differently from the fundamental rights it serves to protect.[521] As we will show below, in contrast to other fundamental rights, it is part of a network of structural principles that all have a similar purpose in EU law. It is also the only fundamental right which has been deemed an 'expression of a constitutional guarantee in a community based on the rule of law'.[522] Last but not least, it is indissolubly intertwined with a more general principle of effectiveness, as will be shown below. It should therefore be seen as a structural principle within the meaning proposed in this book.

2. Origins

2.1. Legal Theory and Public International Law

It has been observed that the effectiveness of a legal order is a (necessary) condition of its validity.[523] More lyrically, effectiveness has been referred to as the very soul of legal rules.[524] In a similar vein, it has been seen as 'an indispensable capacity, or an inherent element, of an international legal rule'.[525] According to the common law principle *magis est ut res valeat quam pereat*, a thing may rather have an effect than be destroyed.[526] This entails an interpretation seeking the *effet utile* of a provision of law by interpreting it so that it has 'any' effect, ie, in order not to be pointless or useless.[527]

As discussed earlier in the context of conferral, while treaties constituting international organisations define and limit their competences, international organisations can exercise the powers laid down in the constituent Treaty 'to their full extent, in so far as the Statute does not impose restrictions'.[528] In the *Iron Rhine* Arbitral Award, it was stated that:

> The Tribunal further observes that there exist other well-established principles relevant to the process of interpretation. Of particular importance is the principle of effectiveness: *ut res magis valeat quam pereat*. The relevance of effectiveness is in relation to the

[521] See, eg, P Gragl, 'Die strukturierende Wirkung der Unionsgrundrechte: Dreidimensionalität und Föderalisierung' (2024) *Europarecht*, Special Issue No 1, 89.

[522] *Kadi* (n 94) para 316.

[523] See H Kelsen, *Introduction to the Problems of Legal Theory* (Oxford, Clarendon Press, 1992) 61. See, critically, A Jakab, *European Constitutional Language* (Cambridge, Cambridge University Press, 2016).

[524] See Pescatore, 'The Doctrine of "Direct Effect"' (n 442) 155.

[525] See GA Serghides, 'The Principle of Effectiveness in the European Convention on Human Rights, in Particular its Relationship to the other Convention Principles' (2017) 30 *Hague Yearbook of International Law / Annuaire de La Haye de droit international* 1. See also D Rietiker and S Steller, 'The Principle of Effectiveness: And its Overarching Role in the Interpretation and Application of the ECHR' (*Völkerrechtsblog*, 10 October 2022).

[526] See Jakab, *European Constitutional Language* (n 523) 35.

[527] See M Klamert, *EU-Recht*, 3rd edn (Vienna, Manz, 2021) para 1153.

[528] ICJ Advisory Opinion, *Legality of the Use by a State of Nuclear Weapons in Armed Conflict* (n 18) para 25 (78–79).

object and purpose of a treaty; at the same time this does not entitle a Tribunal to revise a treaty.[529]

This would reflect an *effet utile* approach entailing that there may be 'necessary corollaries' to the powers conferred and that these need to be interpreted to 'guarantee their fullest effect'.[530] This kind of reasoning can also justify the recognition of 'implied powers' out of 'functional necessity'.[531]

It has been argued that interpretations that seek to maximise the autonomy of an international organisation so that it fulfils its mandate to the widest extent are limited under international law.[532] However, in the *Iron Rhine* Arbitral Award, it has been noted that the 'doctrine of restrictive interpretation never had a hierarchical supremacy, but was a technique to ensure a proper balance of the distribution of rights within a treaty system'. Instead, the object and purpose of a treaty, taken together with the intentions of the parties, would be the prevailing elements for interpretation, and 'too rigorous an application of the principle of restrictive interpretation might be inconsistent with the primary purpose of the treaty'.[533]

The European Court of Human Rights has interpreted the right to life guaranteed by Article 2 of the European Convention on Human Rights in conjunction with a Contracting Party's general duty under Article 1 to 'secure to everyone within [its] jurisdiction the rights and freedoms defined in [the] Convention', finding that the object and purpose of the Convention as an instrument for the protection of individual human beings 'require that its provisions be interpreted and applied so as to make its safeguards practical and effective'.[534]

Notably, with regard to an international judicial organ with specific and exclusive jurisdiction such as the WTO Appellate Body, it has moreover been argued that it would have a particular responsibility to safeguard the Treaty provisions' useful effect and ensure their 'continued relevance for the (distant) future'.[535]

While the discussions and references above are concerned with the interpretation of legal rules, it has also been noted that international law would be the only legal order 'largely deprived of self-sufficiency', referring 'to internal law and to the organs of the States a great share of the duties of implementation and enforcement'.[536]

[529] Arbitration Award, *Iron Rhine ('Ijzeren Rijn') Railway*, 24 May 2005, Reports of International Arbitral Awards, Vol XXVII, 35–125, para 49.

[530] See Engström, *Constructing the Powers of International Institutions* (n 145) 34. See also H Krieger, *Das Effektivitätsprinzip im Völkerrecht* (Berlin, Duncker & Humblot, 2000).

[531] See Moreno-Lax and Ziegler, 'Autonomy of the EU Legal Order' (n 6) 239.

[532] See Moreno-Lax and Ziegler, 'Autonomy of the EU Legal Order' (n 6) 243.

[533] *Iron Rhine* (n 529) para 53.

[534] ECtHR, App no 8351/17, *Romeo Castaño v Belgium*, ECLI:CE:ECHR:2019:0709JUD000835117, para 234.

[535] See I van Damme, 'Treaty Interpretation by the WTO Appellate Body' (2010) 21 *European Journal of International Law* 605, 616, 644.

[536] See R Kolb, *Theory of International Law* (Oxford, Hart Publishing, 2016) 179.

2.2. *EU Law*

2.2.1. The Case Law on *Effet Utile*

Effet utile has come to epitomise the preference of the Court for an (objective) purposive approach to the construction of the Treaties and of secondary law.[537] In view of the prominence of *effet utile*, it is striking how rarely this precise term has appeared in the case law of the Court.

In *Grad* of 1970, the Court justified extending the direct effect (respectively applicability) of regulations to decisions under what is now Article 288 TFEU.[538] In doing so, the Court held:

> It would be incompatible with the binding effect attributed to decisions by Article 189 to exclude in principle the possibility that persons affected may invoke the obligation imposed by a decision. Particularly in cases where, for example, the Community authorities by means of a decision have imposed an obligation on a Member State or all the Member States to act in a certain way, the effectiveness ('l'effet utile') of such a measure would be weakened if the nationals of that State could not invoke it in the courts and the national courts could not take it into consideration as part of Community law.[539]

Only very recently, in *Tecno 37*, the Court seems to have again referred explicitly to *effet utile* for justifying why the scope of the Services Directive 2006/123 must be deemed broader than the Treaty provisions it is meant to concretise:

> In order to achieve a genuine internal market in services, the approach adopted by the EU legislature in Directive 2006/123 is based, as set out in recital 7 thereof, on a general legal framework composed of a mix of various measures designed to ensure a high degree of legal integration within the European Union. Consequently, to ensure that the *effet utile* of the specific legal framework that the EU legislature intended to establish in adopting Directive 2006/123 is not undermined, it must be accepted that the scope of that directive may extend, in certain cases, beyond what is strictly laid down in the provisions of the FEU Treaty relating to freedom of establishment and the free movement of services.[540]

This does not mean, of course, that the Court has not applied this method more often. It only did so by referring to the 'practical effect' or 'useful effect' of a provision of Union law or that a provision should not be devoid of any effect, or a similar formulation.[541] In the *Fédéchar* judgment of 1956, the ECJ had already held that 'it is possible … to apply a rule of interpretation, according to which the rules laid down by … a law presuppose the rules without which that … law would have no

[537] See S Seyr, *Der effet utile in der Rechtsprechung des Europäischen Gerichtshofs* (Duncker & Humblot, 2008).

[538] Case 9/70, *Grad*, ECLI:EU:C:1970:78.

[539] *Grad* (n 538) para 5. See also Case 20/70, *Lesage*, ECLI:EU:C:1970:84, para 5; Case 23/70, *Haselhorst*, ECLI:EU:C:1970:85, para 5.

[540] Case C-242/23, *Tecno*37*, ECLI:EU:C:2024:831, para 60.

[541] See, eg, Case 41/74, *Van Duyn*, ECLI:EU:C:1974:133, para 12.

meaning or could not be reasonably or usefully applied'.[542] This was the basis for implied powers, as discussed earlier.

While all this case law embodies an effectiveness logic, it can be shown that there are in fact two very distinct forms of effectiveness at play here. Effectiveness in a narrow sense aims at ensuring some/any effect of a certain Union law provision. This might even be the prevailing use of effectiveness as an interpretation technique by the Court. This is also fully in line with an interpretation according to the principle *magis est ut res valeat quam pereat* as discussed above.

However, such a conventional approach must be distinguished from effectiveness/*effet utile* in a broader sense, where an interpretation does not only seek to ensure any useful effect but rather seeks to realise a very strong or even the fullest effect of a provision of Union law.[543] The *Grad* and *Tecno 37* cases cited above illustrate this approach. It is through this second variant of *effet utile* that the Court has sidestepped 'the presumptive rule of interpretation typical in international law, that treaties must be interpreted in a manner that minimizes encroachment on state sovereignty'.[544] It is this 'integrationist' form of *effet utile* that is hard to keep apart from certain 'law-developing' applications of effectiveness discussed below. It is submitted that under international law, such an approach could only be justified by ensuring the necessary degree of continuity in the development of an international organisation and the treaty or treaties on which it is based, as mentioned above.[545]

2.2.2. The Early Case Law on Effective Judicial Protection

In case law starting with *Rewe* in 1976, the Court invoked the principle of sincere cooperation in what is now Article 4(3) TEU and found that national courts were required to ensure the legal protection, 'which citizens derive from the direct effect of the provisions of Community law'.[546] It would be for the domestic legal system of each Member State 'to designate the courts having jurisdiction and to determine the procedural conditions with respect to such protection'.[547] The European Union thereby regonised a (procedural and institutional) 'autonomy' (in this case) of the Member States, allowing them to choose which 'specific national bodies' should be competent in the Member States, as well as how those bodies should be entrusted with the powers to implement Union law.[548]

[542] *Fédéchar* (n 26) 299.

[543] See M Potacs, 'Effet utile als Auslegungsgrundsatz' (2009) *Europarecht* 465.

[544] See Weiler, 'The Transformation of Europe' (n 141) 2416.

[545] See de Baere and Roes, 'EU Loyalty as Good Faith' (n 316) 873; G Conway, *The Limits of Legal Reasoning and the European Court of Justice* (Cambridge, Cambridge University Press, 2012) 141.

[546] Case 33/76, *Rewe*, ECLI:EU:C:1976:188, para 5; Case C-664/15, *Protect*, ECLI:EU:C:2017:987, para 35. See Klamert, 'Commentary on Article 4 TEU' (n 123) para 76.

[547] Case C-231/96, *Edis*, ECLI:EU:C:1998:401, para 34; Case C-470/04, *Almelo*, ECLI:EU:C:2006:525, para 59; *Wells* (n 377) para 67.

[548] *International Fruit Company* (n 331) para 3; Joined Cases C-231/00, C-303/00 & C-451/00, *AIMA*, ECLI:EU:C:2004:178, para 57.

However, in *Rewe*, the Court also held, among others, that this deference to the Member States 'would be different only if the conditions and time-limits made it impossible in practice to exercise the rights which the national courts are obliged to protect'.[549] This was later, for the first time in *Edis* in 1998, paraphrased in the following terms:

> In such circumstances, as pointed out in paragraph 19 of this judgment, it is for the domestic legal system of each Member State to designate the courts and tribunals having jurisdiction and to lay down the detailed procedural rules governing actions for safeguarding rights which individuals derive from Community law, provided, first, that such rules are not less favourable than those governing similar domestic actions (principle of equivalence) and, second, that they do not render virtually impossible or excessively difficult the exercise of rights conferred by Community law (principle of effectiveness).[550]

In *UPA*, the ECJ held that individuals 'are … entitled to effective judicial protection of the rights they derive from the Community legal order, and the right to such protection is one of the general principles of law stemming from the constitutional traditions common to the Member States'.[551] It concluded that it would be for the Member States 'to establish a system of legal remedies and procedures which ensure respect for the right to effective judicial protection'.[552]

This form of effectiveness is also referred to as *Rewe*-effectiveness.[553] It is concerned with the effectiveness of concrete rights derived from Union law and relies on national authorities to this end.[554] Arguably, its main purpose is to require Member States to adapt national rules where necessary. It is coupled with effective judicial protection that is a fundamental right and thus operates at the individual rather than at the Member State level.[555]

2.2.3. The Early Case Law on the Effective Application of EU Law

Recall that in *Van Gend* the Court held that remedies against violations of EU law would be ineffective by relying only on the vigilance of the Commission and of the Member States under what are now Articles 258 and 267 TFEU. In *Van Gend*, the Court also relied on the 'spirit, the general scheme and the wording' of the Treaty objectives and its preamble. This 'functional'/'pragmatic' argument was repeated by the Court in *Costa/ENEL*, as already mentioned earlier.

549 *Rewe* (n 546) para 5.
550 *Edis* (n 547).
551 Case C-50/00 P, *UPA*, ECLI:EU:C:2002:462, para 39.
552 *UPA* (n 551) para 41.
553 See S Prechal and R Widdershoven, 'Redefining the Relationship between 'Rewe-effectiveness and Effective Judicial Protection' (2011) 4 *Review of European Administrative Law* 31.
554 See Prechal and Widdershoven, 'Redefining the Relationship' (n 553) 39–50 with references.
555 See Prechal and Widdershoven, 'Redefining the Relationship' (n 553) 39.

As is well known, *Simmenthal II* has established the main effect of primacy, which is the setting aside of national law.[556] It is noteworthy, and I have already pointed this out earlier, in *Simmenthal* the Court did not repeat any of the arguments justifying supremacy it made in *Costa*,[557] but referred to Union law's effectiveness instead:

> Indeed any recognition that national legislative measures which encroach upon the field within which the Community exercises its legislative power or which are otherwise incompatible with the provisions of Community law had any legal effect would amount to a corresponding denial of the effectiveness of obligations undertaken unconditionally and irrevocably by Member States pursuant to the Treaty and would thus imperil the very foundations of the Community.[558]

Note that the requirement of effectiveness in this paragraph related to what was then Community law as such, not to one specific Treaty provision. This was different in the following paragraphs, where the Court referred to the effectiveness of what is now Article 267 TFEU:

> The same conclusion emerges from the structure of Article 177 of the Treaty which provides that any court or tribunal of a Member State is entitled to make a reference to the Court whenever it considers that a preliminary ruling on a question of interpretation or validity relating to Community law is necessary to enable it to give judgment.
>
> The effectiveness of that provision would be impaired if the national court were prevented from forthwith applying Community law in accordance with the decision or the case-law of the Court.[559]

The Court concluded in *Simmenthal* by holding that

> any provision of a national legal system and any legislative, administrative or judicial practice which might impair the effectiveness of Community law by withholding from the national court having jurisdiction to apply such law the power to do everything necessary at the moment of its application to set aside national legislative provisions which might prevent Community rules from having full force and effect are incompatible with those requirements which are the very essence of Community law.[560]

This would also be the case 'if such an impediment to the full effectiveness of Community law were only temporary'.[561]

Factortame built on *Simmenthal* in holding that

> the full effectiveness of Community law would be just as much impaired if a rule of national law could prevent a court seised of a dispute governed by Community law from

[556] *Simmenthal II* (n 374).
[557] *Costa/ENEL* (n 21).
[558] *Simmenthal II* (n 374) para 18.
[559] *Simmenthal II* (n 374) paras 19–20.
[560] *Simmenthal II* (n 374) para 22. See also Case 54/81, *Fromme*, ECLI:EU:C:1982:142, para 6.
[561] *Simmenthal II* (n 374) para 23. See also *Winner Wetten* (n 376) para 57.

> granting interim relief to ensure the full effectiveness of the judgment to be given on the existence of the rights claimed under Community law.[562]

Also in this case the Court followed this finding up with an argument based on the former Article 177 EEC (now Article 267 TFEU),

> whose effectiveness would be impaired if a national court, having stayed proceedings pending the reply by the Court of Justice to the question referred to it for a preliminary ruling, were not able to grant interim relief until it delivered its judgment following the reply given by the Court of Justice.[563]

Arguably, the argument made in *Simmenthal* and *Factortame* was of a much more categorical nature compared with the *Rewe* case law. The *Rewe* case law does not make a general claim to the functioning of the EU law legal order. It is focused on individuals, their rights and their needs to enforce these rights, which are (in theory) balanced with the interests of Member States in their national procedural and institutional autonomy. By contrast, the view of the *Simmenthal* case law is firmly set on (what is now) Union law and the 'needs' of the Union legal order in relation to national law.

However, clearly, both strands of case law are closely connected with direct effect. This is obvious from the wording of the *Rewe* case law quoted above, but also from the fact that supremacy/disapplication is only pertinent with directly effective provisions of Union law, as discussed in the chapter on supremacy.

2.3. Interim Conclusions

If we look at the sequence of the case law as discussed above, it is arguably confirmed that the origins of the principle of effectiveness lie in the interpretative techniques of the Court 'which, even at an early stage, favoured a liberal construction of Treaty provisions so as to ensure their *effet utile*'.[564] From the integrationist form of *effet utile* and against the backdrop of Article 4(3) TEU and its precursors starting with the EEC Treaty, it is not surprising that effectiveness has acquired such a strong legal status in EU law, as further discussed below.

While the right to effective judicial protection is focused on judicial protection in a *rule of law* way, *Rewe* and *Simmenthal* effectiveness are mainly motivated by ensuring the effective application of EU law.[565] It has been noted that these two objectives could come into conflict,[566] as also illustrated by the *Deutsche Umwelthilfe* case discussed below.

[562] *Factortame* (n 511) para 21. See also *Melloni* (n 474) para 59.

[563] *Factortame* (n 511) para 22; *Winner Wetten* (n 376) para 56.

[564] See W Burley and A-M Matti, 'Europe Before the Court: A Political Theory of Legal Integration' (1993) 47 *International Organization* 41, 72–73.

[565] See Prechal and Widdershoven, 'Redefining the Relationship' (n 553) 39–50 with references.

[566] See Saenz Perez, 'Mutual trust as a driver of integration' (n 366) 535; Meyer, 'The Rule of Law in the Enforcement of EU Law' (n 504).

3. Locations

3.1. Primary Law

As shown above, *Rewe*-effectiveness has been based on what is now Article 4(3) TEU. Indeed, the second indent of Article 4(3) TEU, according to which 'Member States must take appropriate measures, general or particular, to ensure fulfilment of the obligations arising out of the treaties or resulting from the acts of the institutions of the Union', seems a suitable basis for this obligation. However, the generally worded Article 4(3) TEU can hardly be considered the location of all the prescriptions the Court has introduced under the title 'principle of effectiveness' in the *Rewe* line of case law. There thus still exists no provision in the Treaties that could be seen as a location for this form of effectiveness. It is also doubtful which legal basis would allow the Union to pass general prescriptions for national (procedural) law.[567]

The second subparagraph of Article 19(1) TEU requires Member States to 'provide remedies sufficient to ensure effective legal protection in the fields covered by Union law'. This codifies the *UPA* case law discussed above. The close relationship between loyalty and effective judicial protection has led to the argument that this part of Article 19(1) TEU would better have been included in Article 4(3) TEU.[568] The second subparagraph of Article 19(1) TEU also corresponds to the right enshrined in Article 47 CFR, according to which everyone whose rights and freedoms guaranteed by the law of the Union are violated has the right to an effective remedy before a tribunal.[569]

Concerning a possible location in the Treaties for the *Simmenthal* case law, we have already earlier in the section on supremacy discussed the role of Article 4(3) TEU in providing a basis for the duty of disapplication. In more recent case law discussed below, the second sentence of the first paragraph of Article 19 TEU, according to which the CJEU 'shall ensure that in the interpretation and application of the Treaties the law is observed' has been invoked in that sense.

3.2. Unwritten, Inherent Principle

Effectiveness is, together with loyalty as discussed earlier, one of the principles the Court has qualified as being 'inherent' in the Union legal order.[570] The Court has also held the principle of state liability and the obligation to interpret national law

[567] See Klamert, *The Principle of Loyalty in EU Law* (n 188) 60, and Guastaferro, 'Sincere cooperation and respect for national identities' (n 300) 350.

[568] See A Arnull, 'The Principle of Effective Judicial Protection in EU Law: An Unruly Horse?' (2011) 36 *EL Rev* 51, 53.

[569] See Case C-73/16, *Puškár*, ECLI:EU:C:2017:725, paras 57–58; Case C-896/19, *Repubblika*, ECLI:EU:C:2021:311, para 45.

[570] *Brasserie du Pêcheur* (n 339) para 39. See also Case C-455/14 P, *EUPM in Bosnia and Herzegovina*, ECLI:EU:C:2016:569; Case C-362/14, *Schrems*, ECLI:EU:C:2015:650, para 95.

in conformity with EU law to be inherent to EU law or intrinsic to the system of treaties, both of which are connected with effectiveness.[571]

Would this mean that, as with loyalty, there would be a principle of effectiveness applying in Union law even if Article 4(3) TEU and probably also Article 19(1) TEU did not exist? As with loyalty, such a categorical statement is not self-explanatory. Different from solidarity, where the Court has come to a similar conclusion in recent case law as discussed earlier, the Court has never made a systematic argument invoking all the expressions of effectiveness in the Treaties. The most likely explanation arguably recalls, similar to loyalty, that in international law effectiveness has been seen as an inherent element of an international legal rule.

However, two objections to such an argument could be made. First, as discussed, the integrationist form of *effet utile* is quite different from the prevailing methods of interpretation in international law. Secondly, in public international law, it would seem unthinkable to apply considerations of effectiveness to questions of the application of international law within domestic law such as in *Simmenthal*.

4. Applications

4.1. *Effective Judicial Protection*

The principle of effective judicial protection applies as the fundamental right that it is, as shown above. This means that it can also serve as a standard for the interpretation of Union law, including Treaty provisions. Thus, in a case on restrictive measures taken with regard to Venezuela, the Court has interpreted Article 263(4) TFEU in the light of the principles of effective judicial review and the rule of law, finding that a third state should have standing to bring proceedings as a 'legal person' within the meaning of that provision.[572]

Effective judicial protection, being (also) a fundamental right, is also open to balancing. *Deutsche Umwelthilfe*, an environmental NGO, had applied for an injunction to be enforced by ordering the coercive detention of a minister of the German province of Bavaria or, failing that, of its Minister-President. The referring court wanted to know whether EU law, in particular Article 47(1) CFR, must be interpreted as meaning that, in circumstances in which a national authority persistently refuses to comply with a judicial decision enjoining it to perform a clear, precise and unconditional obligation flowing from EU law, EU law empowers or

[571] See, eg, Case C-300/04, *Eman und Sevinger*, ECLI:EU:C:2006:545, para 69; Case C-42/11, *João Pedro Lopes Da Silva Jorge*, ECLI:EU:C:2012:517, para 54; Joined Cases C-6/90 & C-9/90, *Francovich*, ECLI:EU:C:1991:428, para 36; Joined Cases C-397/01 & C-403/01, *Pfeiffer*, ECLI:EU:C:2004:584, para 114; *Popławski II* (n 67) para 55.

[572] Case C-872/19 P, *Venezuela v Council*, ECLI:EU:C:2021:507, paras 48–50. See Gragl, 'Rechtstaatlichkeit' (n 325) 59–60.

even obliges the national court having jurisdiction to order the coercive detention of office holders involved in the exercise of official authority. The Court referred to its earlier case law according to which final binding decisions of national courts must not remain ineffective.[573]

After restating its case law on the obligation to interpret national law in conformity with EU law and on the *Simmenthal*-obligation to set aside national law, it continued:

> Nevertheless, that case-law of the Court cannot be understood as meaning that the principle of effectiveness of EU law and observance of the right, guaranteed by the first paragraph of Article 47 of the Charter, to effective judicial protection oblige the national court to disapply a provision of national law or not to follow the only interpretation of that provision which seems to it to accord with the national constitution if, in so doing, it infringes another fundamental right guaranteed by EU law.
>
> Indeed, and as is apparent from Article 52(1) of the Charter, the right to effective judicial protection is not an absolute right and may be restricted, in particular in order to protect the rights and freedoms of others. A coercive measure such as coercive detention entails a limitation on the right to liberty, guaranteed by Article 6 of the Charter.[574]

The Court concluded that without a law empowering a court to deprive a person of his or her liberty that meets certain conditions, thus solely based on the principle of effectiveness and the right to effective judicial protection, a national court cannot order coercive detention.[575]

4.2. Rewe-*Effectiveness and* Simmenthal-*Effectiveness*

Matters are less clear with the other forms of effectiveness discussed here.

It is unclear whether *Rewe*-effectiveness has been overlaid by a broader principle of effective judicial protection as now provided in Article 19(1) TEU.[576] However, that (*Rewe*-) effectiveness and effective judicial protection are two different, yet connected matters in EU law, is also suggested by the *Commission v Hungary* case quoted above, where the Court speaks of ensuring 'the effectiveness of the principle of effective judicial protection' (*sic*).[577]

[573] Case C-752/18, *Deutsche Umwelthilfe*, ECLI:EU: C:2019:1114, paras 35–37, referring to ECtHR, App no 18357/91, *Hornsby v Greece*, ECLI:CE:ECHR:1997:0319JUD001835791, paras 41 and 45. See also European Commission for Democracy through Law (Venice Commission), Report on the Rule of Law, Study No 512 / 2009, CDL-AD(2011)003rev, para 58: 'Finally, judicial decisions must be effectively implemented'.

[574] *Deutsche Umwelthilfe* (n 573) paras 43–44.

[575] *Deutsche Umwelthilfe* (n 573) paras 46–49.

[576] See, among others, A Arnull, 'Remedies Before National Courts' in Schütze and Tridimas (eds), *Oxford Principles of European Union Law* 1011, 1023–25; A Wallerman Ghavanini, 'Remedies for Non-Material Damages: Striking Out in a New Direction? Braathens' (2022) 59 *CML Rev* 151; X Groussot and J Lindholm, 'General principles: taking rights seriously and waving the rule-of-law stick in the European Union' in Ziegler, Neuvonen and Moreno-Lax (eds), *Research Handbook* 308, 319.

[577] *Commission v Hungary* (n 252) para 109.

A distinction is also made between *Rewe*-effectiveness and a general principle of effectiveness that has played a role in constitutionalising EU law.[578] It is this latter form of effectiveness that interests us here. In several cases (the principle of) effectiveness is the (solitary) basis for some other fundamental principles and obligations of EU law. However, as with supremacy discussed later, it often is unclear whether a certain obligation exists for Union law to be effective or whether Union law is effective because of that obligation.

In *Francovich*, which has introduced the principle of state liability and which is discussed in more detail further below, the Court relied on *Simmenthal* and *Factortame* and held as follows:

> The full effectiveness of Community rules would be impaired and the protection of the rights which they grant would be weakened if individuals were unable to obtain redress when their rights are infringed by a breach of Community law for which a Member State can be held responsible.[579]

State liability as introduced in *Francovich* was only later concretised.[580] Thus, at the time of *Francovich*, effectiveness rationalised another principle of a similarly opaque nature. We will return to this technique in chapter five.

In *Adeneler*, the Court held as follows:

> The requirement for national law to be interpreted in conformity with Community law is inherent in the system of the Treaty, since it permits national courts, for the matters within their jurisdiction, to ensure the full effectiveness of Community law when they determine the disputes before them.[581]

National courts would be required 'to do whatever lies within their jurisdiction, taking the whole body of domestic law into consideration and applying the interpretative methods recognised by domestic law, to ensure that the directive in question is fully effective and achieving an outcome consistent with the objective pursued by it'.[582]

It is difficult to compare the application of effectiveness in such cases with the applications of other principles discussed in this book. Effectiveness does not apply as a standard of legality, it also does not have direct effect in the orthodox meaning. It can also not be claimed that effectiveness operates as a guide for the interpretation of Union law in any usual form. The Court has applied effectiveness

[578] See Klamert, 'Commentary on Article 1 TEU' (n 108) para 40. See also Episcopo, 'The Vicissitudes of Life at the Coalface' (n 264) 290–91. See Opinion of AG Kokott in Case C-75/08, *Mellor*, ECLI:EU:C:2009:32, para 28, arguing that the principle of effective legal protection is a specific expression of the principle of effectiveness. Compare also the Opinion of AG Léger in Case C-453/00, *Kühne & Heitz*, ECLI:EU:C:2003:350, para 47.

[579] *Francovich* (n 571) para 33.

[580] See R Nazzini, 'Potency and Act of the Principle of Effectiveness: The Development of Competition Law Remedies and Procedures in Community Law' in C Barnard and O Odudu (eds), *The Outer Limits of European Union Law* (Oxford, Hart Publishing, 2009) 401, 416.

[581] See, eg, Case C-212/04, *Adeneler*, ECLI:EU:C:2006:443, para 109.

[582] See, eg, *Adeneler* (n 581) para 111.

rather to fill perceived gaps in Union law.[583] Effectiveness has been called a 'versatile door-opener that empowers the ECJ to dictate results or procedures in lieu of specific legislation or specific legislative competences'.[584] There is indeed a 'disingenuousness to the appeal of effectiveness as a rationale for development – who, after all, would advocate rules, methods or systems that proclaimed themselves to be ineffective?'[585]

The form of effectiveness applied in cases such as *Simmenthal*, *Factortame*, *Francovich* and *Adeneler*, which should be distinguished from the other forms of effectiveness and which builds on an integrationist variant of *effet utile*, arguably has no other function than to justify the judicial development of Union law.

5. Interrelations

5.1. Effectiveness and Autonomy

We have discussed earlier that, according to the ECJ, autonomy resides in the fact that the Union possesses a constitutional framework that is unique to it.[586] Such reasoning might seem to make autonomy from a means to an end 'into an end in itself'.[587] However, it is submitted, the *Simmenthal*-strand of case law can only be explained under the premise that effectiveness in and of Union law is entirely detached from any understanding of effectiveness in international law.

Thus, autonomy, even in its most general and apodictic form as advocated by the Court serves a purpose: It justifies why Union law can be developed relying on its effectiveness without any regard for limits such reasoning might meet elsewhere. In other words, the European Union is unique, therefore it is autonomous, and the effectiveness of its law is only determined by itself. Without autonomy, there could perhaps be *effet utile*, but already its more integrationist manifestations would be questionable and, it is submitted, there could certainly not be a principle of effectiveness such as that invoked in cases such as *Simmenthal*, *Factortame* and *Francovich*.

5.2. Effectiveness and Loyalty

As mentioned, in case law such as *Rewe*, effectiveness has emerged from what is now Article 4(3) TEU as a means to ensure that rights provided in Union law take full effect in national law. One way to ensure this is through an interpretation of

[583] See Klamert, *The Principle of Loyalty in EU Law* (n 188) 261–62.
[584] See Meyer, 'The Rule of Law in the Enforcement of EU Law' (n 504).
[585] See Ross, 'Beyond Supremacy to Constitutional Proportionality?' (n 518) 481.
[586] *CETA* (n 53) para 110.
[587] See Moreno-Lax, 'The Axiological Emancipation of a (Non-)Principle' (n 55) 61.

national law in the light of Union law, which is an obligation that was also based on what is now Article 4(3) TEU. National courts are thus required

> so far as possible, to interpret and apply national procedural rules governing the exercise of rights of action in a way that enables natural and legal persons to challenge before the courts the legality of any decision or other national measure relative to the application to them of a Community act of general application, by pleading the invalidity of such an act.[588]

We have already discussed earlier how conferral is connected with effectiveness when it comes to the case law empowering the Union to pass measures regarding sanctions in connection with ensuring the full effect of Union directives. Thus, in Case C-176/03, effectiveness provided the basis for establishing competence for the approximation of criminal laws and regulations of the Member States, which was later codified in Article 83 TFEU.

The connection of this case law with loyalty is illustrated by the first cases on the requirement of sanctions for ensuring the effectiveness of Union law. In *Amsterdam Bulb* of 1977, the Court noted that national provisions would not provide for sanctions in respect of infringements of certain prohibitions by individuals predicated by Union rules. It continued:

> Although Article 5 of the EEC Treaty places Member States under a duty to take all appropriate measures, whether general or particular, to ensure fulfilment of the obligations resulting from action taken by the institutions of the Community, it allows the various Member States to choose the measures which they consider appropriate, including sanctions which may even be criminal in nature.[589]

In *Commission v Greece* of 1989, the Court held as follows:

> It should be observed that where Community legislation does not specifically provide any penalty for an infringement or refers for that purpose to national laws, regulations and administrative provisions, Article 5 of the Treaty requires the Member States to take all measures necessary to guarantee the application and effectiveness of Community law.
>
> For that purpose, whilst the choice of penalties remains within their discretion, they must ensure in particular that infringements of Community law are penalized under conditions, both procedural and substantive, which are analogous to those applicable to infringements of national law of a similar nature and importance and which, in any event, make the penalty effective, proportionate and dissuasive.[590]

In the *Zwartveld* Order of 1990, which is best known for establishing a 'reverse vertical' duty of cooperation of the Union institutions as discussed earlier, the Court found that the principle of sincere cooperation requires the Member States

[588] *UPA* (n 551) para 42; Case C-362/06 P, *Sahlstedt*, ECLI:EU:C:2009:243, para 43.
[589] Case 50/76, *Amsterdam Bulb*, ECLI:EU:C:1977:13, para 32.
[590] Case 68/88, *Commission v Greece*, ECLI:EU:C:1989:339, paras 23 and 24.

'to take all the measures necessary to guarantee the application and effectiveness of Community law, if necessary by instituting criminal proceedings'.[591]

In Case C-176/03, the Commission, while admitting that there was no precedent for recognising Union competence in this area at that time, relied on 'the duty of loyal cooperation and the principles of effectiveness and equivalence' and the *Amsterdam Bulb* and *Zwartveld* cases.[592] The Court in its judgment establishing such competence did not mention loyalty but relied on effectiveness, as discussed.

The case law on sanctions thus shows how the Court invoked (a principle of) effectiveness to establish competence for Union sanction measures and invoked loyalty to determine what national sanction measures should look like, namely effective and dissuasive among others. While the former case law can be considered to be in the law-developing mould of *Francovich*, it is submitted that the latter can be seen as a variation of *Rewe*-effectiveness.

5.3. *Effectiveness and Supremacy*

It cannot be disputed that there is a close link between effectiveness and supremacy. Both principles are concerned with the full application of Union law in the legal orders of the Member States. I have already argued elsewhere that effectiveness is a necessary complement to direct effect and supremacy.[593] Effectiveness adds the concrete prescriptions that derive from supremacy, be it disapplication as in *Simmenthal* or ensuring that individuals can secure their Union rights in the national legal order as in *Rewe*.[594]

It is a different matter to claim that effectiveness is the foundation, the rationale of supremacy (and direct effect).[595] The following observation has been made in this respect:

> The process of constitutionalization in the jurisprudence of the Court of Justice can be explained entirely in terms of the apparently quite orthodox legal philosophy adopted by the Court. The principle of effectiveness – enshrined in the basic maxim of pacta sunt servanda – which is at the root of the doctrine of direct effect, coupled with the principle of uniformity derived from procedural elements (e.g. article 177) and substantive elements (e.g. article 5) in the Treaty, lead by an inevitable logic to supremacy and pre-emption.[596]

[591] *Zwartveld* (n 341) para 17.

[592] Case C-176/03, *Commission v Council* (n 197) para 20.

[593] See Klamert, *The Principle of Loyalty in EU Law* (n 188) 261–66.

[594] Compare P Nebbia, 'The Double Life of Effectiveness' (2007/08) 10 *Cambridge Yearbook of European Legal Studies* 287.

[595] See Weiler, 'The Transformation of Europe' (n 141) 2415–16: 'One possible rationale underlying the Court's jurisprudence in both direct effect and supremacy has been its attempt to maximize the efficiency by which the Community performs the tasks entrusted to it by the Treaty'. See also Klamert, *The Principle of Loyalty in EU Law* (n 188) 69.

[596] See M Cappelletti, M Seccombe and JHH Weiler, 'Integration Through Law: Europe and the American Federal Experience. A General Introduction' in M Cappelletti, M Seccombe and J Weiler

It is not surprising that uniformity is also mentioned here. In *Hauer* of 1979, the Court held that the

> introduction of special criteria for assessment stemming from the legislation or constitutional law of a particular Member State would, by damaging the substantive unity and efficacy of Community law, lead inevitably to the destruction of the unity of the Common Market and the jeopardizing of the cohesion of the Community.[597]

We will revisit the uniformity theme in the final chapter of this book.

As mentioned, the press release following the German Constitutional Court's *Weiss*/PSPP/*ultra vires* decision stated that Member States were required to ensure that EU law takes full effect, which would be the only way of ensuring the equality of Member States.[598] This seems to claim that EU law must be effective and must therefore take precedence over national law.

Rationalising supremacy with the need for Union law to be effective or to have *effet utile* may seem intuitive but it is submitted that it is not very compelling at a second look.[599] First, this reasoning confuses cause and effect: does EU law have precedence to be effective or is it effective because of its supremacy? Secondly, if we rely on *effet utile*, it should be noted that it would have to be its 'integrationist' variant discussed above. Union law would not be devoid of any effect without supremacy. Other instruments might be less effective but that would not render Union law meaningless.[600] This will also be illustrated with the principle of state liability discussed below which was also based on effectiveness.

It makes more sense to link Article 19(1) TEU with supremacy, as the Court has done in recent case law.[601] In *RS*, the Court, referring to *Simmenthal* among others, held as follows:

> As regards the obligations deriving from Article 19 TEU, it should be noted that that provision, which gives concrete expression to the value of the rule of law affirmed in Article 2 TEU, entrusts the responsibility for ensuring the full application of EU law in all Member States and judicial protection of the rights of individuals under that law to national courts and tribunals and to the Court of Justice …
>
> As has been recalled in paragraph 39 above, compliance with that obligation to apply in full any provision of EU law with direct effect must be regarded as essential in

(eds), *Integration Through Law: Europe and the American Federal Experience*, Vol I (Berlin, de Gruyter, 1986) 3, 30.

[597] *Hauer* (n 468) para 14. See also *Melloni* (n 474) para 60; Case C-206/13, *Siragusa*, ECLI:EU:C:2014:126, para 32; and the Opinion of AG Kokott in Case C-550/07 P, *Akzo Nobel*, ECLI:EU:C:2010:229, para 168.

[598] See *Public Sector Asset Purchase Programme (PSPP)* (n 258).

[599] Compare de Witte, 'Direct Effect, Primacy, and the Nature of the Legal Order' (n 271) 329, finding all arguments not particularly convincing by themselves and settling for the *effet utile*-argument as most apposite.

[600] See Klamert, 'Supremacy, the Uniformity of EU Law, and the Principle of Equality' (n 243) 82. See already de Witte, 'Retour à "Costa"' (n 263) 441–42.

[601] *Commission v Poland (Independence of the Supreme Court)* (n 179) para 47; *Euro Box Promotion* (n 257) para 217; *RS (Effet des arrêts d'une cour constitutionnelle)* (n 257) para 54.

order to ensure the full application of EU law in all Member States, as is required by Article 19(1) TEU.[602]

Any national rule or practice which might impair the effectiveness of EU law by withholding from the national court having jurisdiction to exercise 'the power to do everything necessary at the moment of its application to disregard a national provision or practice which might prevent directly effective EU rules from having full force and effect would be incompatible with the requirements which are the very essence of EU law'.[603] In *RS*, this was held to be the case when national courts are barred from assessing for themselves whether national provisions are compatible with EU law if the national constitutional court has already held that those provisions would be consistent with national constitutional law.[604]

This in a way takes the effectiveness theme full circle. As discussed, Article 19(1) TEU is meant to codify the *UPA* case law, which is in the *Rewe* line of case law. Both are concerned with effectuating individual rights derived from Union law within national law. Effectiveness here is no end in itself: it serves a purpose, which is to secure Union rights that are directly effective. Indeed, these directly effective rights would not be directly effective without supremacy preventing Member States from denying their validity at will. This is consistent with the recent clarification in case law that supremacy exclusively applies to directly effective provisions of Union law.

6. Conclusions

Effectiveness has become such a pervasive principle in EU law that it is sometimes hard to see 'the wood for the trees'. One cannot underestimate the importance of a particular understanding of effectiveness, based on a particular understanding of autonomy, for the development of EU law.

We have explained that it can be distinguished between different manifestations of effectiveness: one that is a classic fundamental right that has been tailored to the specifics of the European Union; one that is a method of interpretation familiar from legal theory and international law; and one that is essentially a justification for judicial developments of EU law.

It has been shown that *effet utile* is a method of interpretation that has a more conventional and a very integrationist application in EU law. The latter is closely related to what we have called the *Simmenthal*-effectiveness and as such bears little resemblance to methods of interpretation in international law. We have argued that

[602] *RS (Effet des arrêts d'une cour constitutionnelle)* (n 257) paras 39, 54, and also paras 62 and 63. *Commission v Poland (Independence of the Supreme Court)* (n 179) para 47; *Euro Box Promotion* (n 257) para 217.

[603] *RS (Effet des arrêts d'une cour constitutionnelle)* (n 257) para 63, referring to *Simmenthal II* (n 374) para 22.

[604] Article 19(1) TEU was read in conjunction with Articles 2 and 4(2) and (3) TEU, with Article 267 TFEU and with the principle of the primacy of EU law.

autonomy is a central factor to be considered in this. Loyalty is also intertwined with effectiveness in manifold and sometimes unclear ways. Loyalty and effectiveness have in common that both have been deemed to be inherent in EU law. While it is true that effectiveness is a characteristic of (all) legal rules and loyalty obliges Member States to ensure this effectiveness, case law such as *Simmenthal* or *Francovich* cannot fully be rationalised on this basis, as we will further discuss in chapter five.

10. Conclusions

We have shown that most structural principles have their roots in public international law. This should not be surprising because, at least in the beginning, the EEC was a creature of international law. What *is* surprising is that, in its case law, the Court has never bothered to acknowledge that principles such as autonomy, conferral, loyalty, or effectiveness have a storied background in international law. Instead, case law has created and maintained the impression that these principles would be specific to the European Union and to EU law. The Court has largely avoided mentioning the term 'autonomy' in its early case law because, arguably, it would not have helped its claim that the European Union was something entirely different from both national and international law.

This, perhaps counterintuitively, leaves the prohibition of discrimination on grounds of nationality as the single structural principle of EU law that has been idiosyncratic from the beginning. It is the only principle that cannot and therefore does not exist in domestic laws and that also does not in this form exist in international law. Because it is also similar to fundamental rights under Article 6 TEU by empowering individuals, we have called it a fundamental right of European integration.

Other structural principles can also be seen as specific to the European Union and EU law, but because of the way they have been developed in case law. It has been shown that principles such as supremacy, loyalty, solidarity and effectiveness have been transformed to serve similar, strongly integrationist purposes. Comparative law or generally non-unional sources of legal knowledge have hardly played a role in this process, unlike with the principles under Article 6(3) TEU.

The Otherness that structural principles represent as explained in chapter one aligns with what we have called the gatekeeper function of autonomy and supremacy. They are 'hinge' principles regulating the permeability of EU law vis-a-vis both national and international law, thus deciding about the normative and substantive 'openness' of EU law.

It is a characteristic of structural principles that they do not (directly) protect the interests of individuals, different from fundamental rights. They either protect the interests of the Member States such as with (the limits of) conferral, reverse vertical loyalty, national identity, Member State equality, and positive Member

State solidarity; or they safeguard the interests of the European Union, its law and its institutions, such as with autonomy, all other forms of loyalty, negative Member State solidarity, supremacy, and effectiveness. Only effective judicial protection, which is also a fundamental right and, as mentioned, non-discrimination based on nationality, protect individuals, while also having 'structural' roles such as by underpinning autonomy and supremacy.

When taking stock of all structural principles, there clearly is an integrationist bias. The limits to conferral are few and lack of competence does not in any event prevent the application of EU law; loyalty obligations for the Union institutions are marginal compared with those imposed on Member States, and national identity has been weak normatively. In that context, it is also telling that even Member State equality has been 'repurposed' by the Court for rationalising supremacy.

It is submitted that the different thrust of structural principles compared with Article 6 TEU principles explains why they do not have direct effect in national law in the traditional sense. While this has only been ruled out explicitly for Article 4(3) TEU, the same would seem to apply to all other structural principles, again with the exceptions of Article 19(1) TEU and Article 18 TFEU.

Whether structural principles protect the interests of the Member States or rather those of the European Union would also seem to determine how they have been applied as standards of interpretation and legality. Conferral has been applied against EU law measures, mainly as a standard of legality. Member State solidarity has been relied on to interpret EU secondary law and as a standard of legality for Union law measures (in the case of energy solidarity). Loyalty has been used as a standard for the interpretation of secondary law and the ECJ has indicated that (reverse vertical) loyalty could also be a standard for the legality of EU law acts. In most cases, however, Article 4(3) TEU has been applied as a grounds for infringement against acts by the Member States.[605] The principle of autonomy is, in a rather opaque manner, applied against both Union acts and Member State measures, but always for the protection of Union interests.[606] Thus, it could be said that structural principles in that sense operate like conventional general principles as being part of the law that should guide the judicial review of all EU actions.[607] Exceptions are national identity and Member State equality, which have (so far) not been allowed as a standard of review for Union measures. For the sake of completeness, it must be added that effectiveness, supremacy (and direct effect) do not operate in that manner at all.

It has also been shown that different from fundamental rights, structural principles normally cannot be balanced or weighed when they operate as standards of

[605] In external relations especially, it is also applied in conflicts between Union institutions as discussed in ch 4.

[606] See *ECHR II* (n 62), on the one hand and *Achmea* (n 65), on the other.

[607] See P Craig, 'General principles of law: treaty, historical, and normative foundations' in Ziegler, Neuvonen and Moreno-Lax (eds), *Research Handbook* 25, 38.

legality. Most structural principles thus apply in a binary, absolute manner. This is true for loyalty and also conferral in cases where a Union measure is based on no or the wrong legal basis. It is true for the principle of autonomy if it is applied to review the legality of Union or Member State measures. We have also argued that supremacy as such cannot be weighed with other principles. This would only be the case for primacy, thus the duty of disapplication. An exception seems to be (energy) solidarity, which requires the taking into account of Member State interests according to more recent case law.

A distinction between ('relational') structural principles that govern relations between actors in the European Union (mentioned is loyalty) and 'systemic' structural principles that affect the entire system of Union law, for which autonomy is given as an example, could not be confirmed when looking at EU law overall.[608] We have shown that loyalty or conferral is no less systemic than autonomy. We will discuss in the following chapter whether this finding might indeed be somewhat different when looking only at external relations law.

This chapter has shown that all structural principles are connected. This is illustrated by a (thin) line in the figure below. Some structural principles are a foundation for or shape other principles, which is illustrated with a (thick) arrow. The dashed lines illustrate relations that have been discussed in the literature but which we do not find convincing as discussed earlier. All this clearly shows that there indeed is a network of structural principles in EU law.

Figure 1 The Network of Structural Principles

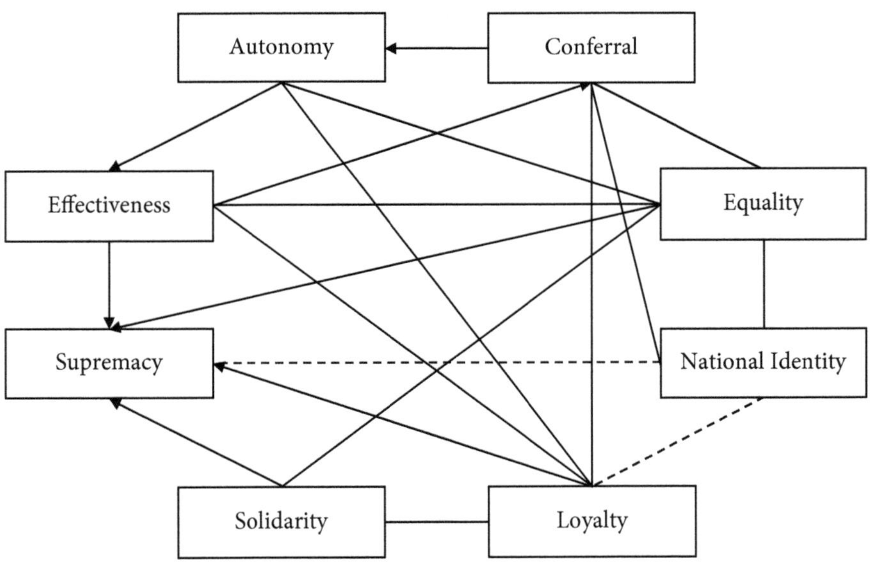

[608] Compare Cremona, 'Structural Principles of External Relations Law' in Cremona (ed), *Structural Principles* 3.

IV

Structural Principles in External Relations

1. Introduction

We have so far only touched upon the application of the principles discussed in this book in external relations law. The principle of autonomy has been discussed against this background because it originated in the external sphere. With other principles, we have so far not focused on their respective roles there. While external relations law has been and continues to be a somewhat specialised discipline, we would fully subscribe to the remark that 'any meaningful study of the Union constitutional order should include the external relations dimension'.[1] We only do this now, towards the end of this book, because we can now build upon the discussions in the previous chapters, and also because some issues explored in the following require some introduction, which would have made the previous chapters quite unreadable.

It has been shown that some of the Union's external actions influence the understanding of certain structural principles of EU law (so-called 'Outside-in'-effect).[2] By contrast, in the following, we will discuss whether and how structural principles play a distinct role when applied in the context of external relations. It has been noted that there is a presumption that general principles under Article 6 TEU would be applicable in all areas of EU law unless expressed otherwise in the Treaties.[3] Even if that were also the case with structural principles, it would not necessarily mean that these principles might not operate differently when applied externally than when applied internally.

We will, in the following, distinguish between the Common Foreign and Security Policy (CFSP) and other areas of external relations, because such distinction is also made in the Treaties, even though the entire external action of the European Union is now subject to the same objectives and values, as

[1] See A Rosas, 'EU external relations law: Time for a reality check?' (2020) 27 *Maastricht Journal* 277.

[2] See C Eckes, *EU Powers Under External Pressure: How the EU's External Actions Alter its Internal Structures* (Oxford, Oxford University Press, 2019).

[3] See P Craig, 'General principles of law: treaty, historical, and normative foundations' in KS Ziegler, PJ Neuvonen, and V Moreno-Lax (eds), *Research Handbook on General Principles in EU Law: Constructing Legal Orders in Europe* (Cheltenham, Edward Elgar, 2022) 25, 30.

is explained below. Outside the CFSP we will focus on policy areas (common commercial policy, development cooperation and cooperation with non-developing countries, humanitarian aid, sanctions, and association) and the specific role of structural principles therein. However, we will also touch upon the role of structural principles in the external sphere more broadly, ie, with the external dimension of policy areas outside Part V of the Treaty on the Functioning of the European Union (TFEU), including with external competence per se.

2. The Common Foreign and Security Policy

1. Introduction

Since the Treaty of Lisbon, the CFSP no longer contains specific objectives because these have been integrated into the general list of Union external action objectives in Article 21 of the Treaty on European Union (TEU). However, despite this and other factors of convergence between the CFSP and other external action, Article 24(1) TEU states that the CFSP has retained its specificity being 'subject to specific rules and procedures'.[4] This 'fragmentation' has already been established in primary law for a long time.[5]

Article 23 TEU is the bridge between the CFSP and the rest of the Union's external action, providing that the same principles, objectives and general provisions apply to the CFSP as to all other areas of Union external action.[6] This is meant to instil consistency and coherence across the Union's external action.[7] In addition, the requirement for consistency laid down in Article 7 TFEU requires the Union institutions to ensure that all its activities are coherent, making this a general obligation requiring consistency also between external actions of the Union and its other actions and policies.[8]

It has also been clarified that Article 6 TEU principles, thus especially the Union's fundamental rights, apply fully within the external action of the Union. Thus, it has been opined that a combined reading of Article 3(5) TEU, Articles 21 and 23 TEU and Article 205 TFEU would mean that 'human rights and their

[4] See T Ramopolous and L Havas, 'Commentary on Article 24 TEU' in M Kellerbauer, M Klamert and J Tomkin (eds), *The EU Treaties and the Charter of Fundamental Rights: A Commentary*, 2nd edn (Oxford, Oxford University Press, 2024) para 1.

[5] See A von Bogdandy, 'Grundprinzipien des Unionsrechts – eine verfassungstheoretische und -dogmatische Skizze' (2009) *Europarecht* 749, 764–67.

[6] 'The Union's action on the international scene, pursuant to this Chapter, shall be guided by the principles, shall pursue the objectives of, and be conducted in accordance with, the general provisions laid down in Chapter 1'. See also Article 205 TFEU.

[7] See Ramopolous and Havas, 'Commentary on Article 24 TEU' (n 4) para 2.

[8] 'The Union shall ensure consistency between its policies and activities, taking all of its objectives into account and in accordance with the principle of conferral of powers'.

protection are among the principles and essential values of the European Union which must guide its action on the international scene'.[9] For the same reasons, the Court held that compliance with the principles of the rule of law and human rights, as well as respect for human dignity, 'is required of all actions of the European Union, including those in the area of the CFSP, as is clear from the provisions, read together'.[10]

All this, it is submitted, does not answer the question of whether the principles discussed in this book apply within the CFSP and if yes, in what way. As explained in chapter two, there is a link between the values in Article 2 TEU and the principles coming under Article 6 TEU such as fundamental rights. Article 2 TEU is integrated into external action and the TEU because it is referenced in Article 21 TEU. There is no such (clear) link between structural principles and the CFSP. Article 24(1) TEU, as mentioned, states that the CFSP is 'subject to specific rules and procedures'. Thus, the question discussed in the following is whether the CFSP is also subject to specific structural principles.

2. Does CFSP-Specificity Concern Structural Principles?

Article 23(1) TEU mentioned above only applies within the field of external action and can thus not provide a bridge between non-CFSP areas and the CFSP when it comes to structural principles.[11] The wording in Article 24(1) TEU discussed above according to which the CFSP is 'subject to specific rules and procedures' would seem to refer to the different instruments available in the CFSP and the absence of the legislative procedures. However, it has been pointed out that it does not mention 'principles' which would confirm that there is no CFSP specificity as regards such principles.[12]

Indicative of an application of structural principles in the external action of the European Union including its CFSP as a matter of principle is also Article 21(1) TEU, according to which the Union's 'action on the international scene shall be guided by the principles which have inspired its own creation, development and enlargement, and which it seeks to advance in the wider world'. Besides democracy, the rule of law, the universality and indivisibility of human rights and fundamental freedoms, and respect for human dignity, Article 21(1) TEU also mentions the

[9] See the Opinion of AG Wathelet in Case C-104/16 P, *Council v Front Polisario ('Fisheries Agreement')*, ECLI:EU:C:2016:677, para 254.

[10] Case C-263/14, *Parliament v Council (Tanzania Pirates Agreement)*, ECLI:EU:C:2016:435, para 47.

[11] For a different perspective, see C Hillion, 'A Powerless Court? The European Court of Justice and the Common Foreign and Security Policy' in M Cremona and A Thies (eds), *The European Court of Justice and External Relations Law* (Oxford, Hart Publishing, 2014) 47, 69; RA Wessel, 'General Principles in EU Common Foreign and Security Policy' in Ziegler, Neuvonen and Moreno-Lax (eds), *Research Handbook* 607, 609 f.

[12] See Hillion, 'A Powerless Court?' (n 11) 69; Ramopolous and Havas, 'Commentary on Article 24 TEU' (n 4) para 26.

(structural) principles of equality and solidarity.[13] Moreover, Article 7 TFEU refers to all areas and states that consistency must be 'in accordance with the principle of conferral of powers'.

These arguments remain rather theoretical if the Court of Justice of the European Union (CJEU) were not competent to apply structural principles within the CFSP. Article 24(1) TEU states, among others, that the Court of Justice shall not have jurisdiction with respect to 'these [i.e. the CFSP] provisions, except for its jurisdiction to monitor compliance with Article 40 of this Treaty and to review the legality of certain decisions as provided for by the second paragraph of Article 275 of the Treaty on the Functioning of the European Union'.

There are two anchors in the Treaties for the Court to also exercise its jurisdiction in CFSP matters. The first, more obvious one is Article 40 TEU, the non-affection clause discussed below. The second, somewhat less expected is Article 218 TFEU, the procedure for concluding agreements also within the CFSP. While the Court has been cautious to apply Article 40 TEU, it has been more forthcoming concerning Article 218 TFEU, as explained below.

We will now look at the different principles in more depth. We will show in the following that while all structural principles do apply in the CFSP, they do so in more or less distinct versions. In other words, structural principles apply in the CFSP but the way they apply is determined by the specific character of the CFSP.

3. Autonomy

3.1. Autonomy and Jurisdiction Over the CFSP

We have noted in chapter three that with autonomy there can be no debate about whether it applies in the CFSP because it protects the (entire) Union legal order and is thus a principle that is attached to the EU legal order as such. As also explained in chapter three, external institutional autonomy had first been applied in the context of the European Economic Area (EEA).[14] Shortly afterwards it was invoked for the first time in connection with accession to the European Convention on Human Rights (ECHR) in Opinion 2/94.[15] At that time, the question of who would have jurisdiction over CFSP measures had not presented itself. It did, however, on occasion of the second Opinion on accession to the ECHR in 2013.[16] Article 6(2) TEU in the meantime expressly obliged the European Union to accede to the ECHR.

In Opinion 2/13, as is well known, the European Court of Justice (ECJ) held the draft accession agreement of 2013 to be incompatible with the Treaties.[17] Among

[13] This is also emphasised by Wessel, 'General Principles in EU Common Foreign and Security Policy' (n 11) 610.

[14] Opinion 1/91, *EEA I*, ECLI:EU:C:1991:49.

[15] Opinion 2/94, *ECHR I*, ECLI:EU:C:1996:140.

[16] Opinion 2/13, *ECHR II*, ECLI:EU:C:2014:2454.

[17] *ECHR II* (n 16). See, critically, among others, RA Wessel and A Łazowski, 'When Caveats Turn into Locks: Opinion 2/13 on Accession of the European Union to the ECHR' (2015) 16 *German Law*

others, the ECJ criticised the fact that the draft agreement did not exclude a review of CFSP measures by the European Court of Human Rights (ECtHR) even though the ECJ's own jurisdiction is curtailed in this regard, as explained above.

This has motivated the Court to interpret the scope of its jurisdiction for the CFSP broadly so as 'to defend the autonomy of the EU legal order', as it has been submitted.[18] In a line of cases, the Court chipped away at the limitations to its jurisdiction as they would appear to exist under a broad reading of the final sentence of the second subparagraph of Article 24(1) TEU and the first paragraph of Article 275 TFEU. As derogations from the rule of general jurisdiction in Article 19 TEU, they would have to be interpreted narrowly.[19]

In the *EUPM* case concerning CFSP decisions taken by the Head of the mission in Bosnia and Herzegovina established based on Article 28 TEU and Article 43(2) TEU, the Court held as follows:

> In that regard, it must be noted that, as is apparent from both Article 2 TEU, which is included in the common provisions of the EU Treaty, and Article 21 TEU, concerning the European Union's external action, to which Article 23 TEU, relating to the CFSP, refers, the European Union is founded, in particular, on the values of equality and the rule of law (see, to that effect, in particular, judgment of 27 February 2007 in *Segi and Others* v *Council*, C-355/04 P, EU:C:2007:116, paragraph 51, and Opinion 2/13 of 18 December 2014, EU:C:2014:2454, paragraphs 168 and 169). The very existence of effective judicial review designed to ensure compliance with provisions of EU law is inherent in the existence of the rule of law.[20]

In *KS and KD*, on an action for damages in relation to the EU's Rule of Law Mission in Kosovo, the ECJ found that its jurisdiction may be 'based on the fact that the acts and omissions at issue are not directly related to the political or strategic choices made by the institutions, bodies, offices and agencies of the Union in the context of the CFSP, and in particular the CSDP'.[21] The precedents the Court relied on for this finding had not been clear about laying down such a categorical distinction between judiciable and non-judiciable CFSP measures.[22]

In *Rosneft*, which did not concern a CFSP measure, the Court did not rely on the bridging clause of Article 23 TEU to bring the values of the European Union including the rule of law into the equation, but instead took the route via the

Journal 179; E Spaventa, 'A Very Fearful Court? The Protection of Fundamental Rights in the European Union after Opinion 2/13' (2015) 22 *Maastricht Journal* 35. However, see also D Halberstam, '"It's the Autonomy, Stupid!" A Modest Defense of Opinion 2/13 on EU Accession to the ECHR, and the Way Forward' (2015) 16 *German Law Journal* 105.

[18] See T Ramopolous and L Havas, 'Commentary on Article 23 TEU' in Kellerbauer, Klamert and Tomkin (eds), *Commentary*, para 3.

[19] Case C-658/11, *Parliament v Council (Mauritius Agreement)*, ECLI:EU:C:2014:2025, para 69; Case C-439/13 P, *Elitaliana v Eulex Kosovo*, ECLI:EU:C:2015:753, para 41.

[20] Case C-455/14 P, *EUPM in Bosnia and Herzegovina*, ECLI:EU:C:2016:569, para 41; Case C-134/19 P, *Bank Refah Kargaran v Council*, ECLI:EU:C:2020:793, para 35.

[21] See Joined Cases C-29/22 P & C-44/22 P, *KS and KD*, ECLI:EU:C:2024:725, para 116.

[22] Compare *Elitaliana v Eulex Kosovo* (n 19) para 49; *EUPM in Bosnia and Herzegovina* (n 20) para 55; and Case C-14/19 P, *SatCen v KF*, ECLI:EU:C:2020:492, para 66. Compare G Butler, *Constitutional Law of the EU's Common Foreign and Security Policy* (Oxford, Hart Publishing, 2021) 202–12.

preliminary reference procedure. A strict interpretation of Article 24(1) TEU and Article 275 TFEU would 'be contrary to the objectives of that provision and to the principle of effective judicial protection'.[23]

Thus, while external institutional autonomy concerning the CFSP was also defensive as far as it concerned Opinion 2/13, it had a quite peculiar consequence because it led to an *expansion* of the jurisdiction of the CJEU in this area. This has not happened with case law such as *Achmea* or *CETA* discussed later.

3.2. Autonomy and the Prerogatives of (Other) Union Institutions in the CFSP

We discussed the *Pringle* case earlier in chapter three, which concerned the allocation of tasks to the Commission and the ECB under the ESM-Treaty. Referring to Opinions 1/00 and 1/09, among others, the Court in this case held that Member States could entrust tasks to the institutions in areas not falling under the exclusive competence of the Union if those tasks 'do not alter the essential character of the powers conferred on those institutions by the EU and FEU Treaties'.[24]

More than in other areas of EU law, Union institutions have been assigned specific powers reflecting the constitutional set-up of the CFSP, including particular roles for the High Representative.[25] It has been argued that the principle of institutional balance in Article 13(2) TEU, while formally only applying to the Union institutions listed in Article 13(1) TEU, would limit the freedom of Member States to ignore or change these tasks assigned to the institutions including the High Representative.[26] The High Representiative is not an institution of the Union under Article 13(2) TEU but has been equated with the 'bodies, offices and agencies of the Union' for the purpose of applying the second paragraph of Article 40 of the Statute of the Court of Justice of the European Union.[27]

Because the mandates for the Council, the European Council and the High Representative in the CFSP are so broad as discussed in the following, it could be argued that it would be difficult to see how the essential character of their powers could be altered. However, the converse argument could be made as well. The powers are so broad that there is more chance that they are affected by the Member States.

[23] Case C-72/15, *Rosneft*, ECLI:EU:C:2017:236, para 75.

[24] Case C-370/12, *Pringle*, ECLI:EU:C:2012:756, para 158.

[25] See Article 27(2) TEU on the High Representative who 'shall represent the Union for matters relating to the common foreign and security policy'. See also Articles 22(2), 24(1) TEU and 218(3) TFEU. The European External Actions Service is also not listed in Article 13(1) TEU.

[26] See Wessel, 'General Principles in EU Common Foreign and Security Policy' (n 11) 614, mentioning the conclusion of the 2016 'EU–Turkey Statement', which was not based on Article 218 TFEU.

[27] See the Order of the President of the Court in Case C-551/21, *Commission v Council (Fisheries Partnership Agreement)*, ECLI:EU:C:2022:163.

4. Conferral

4.1. Introduction

Article 5(1) TEU provides that '[t]he limits of Union competences are governed by the principle of conferral'. Article 2(4) TFEU speaks of the CFSP as a Union competence, which already suggests that conferral also applies to the CFSP.[28] Recently, in *KS and KD*, the Grand Chamber of the ECJ clarified that 'the principles of conferral and of institutional balance also apply in the area of the CFSP'.[29] Otherwise, the Court explained, the Treaty provisions limiting its jurisdiction in the CFSP 'would be deprived of their effectiveness in part and the principles of conferral and of institutional balance infringed'.[30] This has in this constellation been a 'defensive' statement, providing the basis for the Court to deny its jurisdiction in the case at hand.

This, however, does not mean that both conferral and institutional balance operate in the CFSP in the same way as the operate in other areas of EU law, including in external action outside the CFSP.

4.2. Competences

According to Article 24(1) TEU, the Union's CFSP competence 'shall cover all areas of foreign policy and all questions relating to the Union's security, including the progressive framing of a common defence policy that might lead to a common defence'. While the CFSP is a competence of the Union as provided by Article 2(4) TFEU, its specificity prevents its strict categorisation among the general types of Union competence.[31] It is argued that the CFSP should be considered a special type of Union competence between coordinated shared competence (Article 5 TFEU) and supportive competence (Article 6 TFEU).[32]

Not only is the nature of CFSP competence ambiguous but so is its scope. According to Article 24(1) TEU, it covers all of the Union's foreign policy and security, 'including the progressive framing of a common defence policy that might lead to a common defence'.[33] In annulment cases initiated by the Commission against decisions by the Council on concluding international agreements, the issue was

[28] See E Chiti, 'Enforcement of and Compliance with Structural Principles' in M Cremona (ed), *Structural Principles in EU External Relations Law* (Oxford, Oxford University Press, 2018) 47, 53.

[29] *KS and KD* (n 21) para 72. See also Case C-24/20, *Commission v Council (Accession to the Geneva Act)*, ECLI:EU:C:2022:911, para 83.

[30] *KS and KD* (n 21) para 73.

[31] See Ramopolous and Havas, 'Commentary on Article 24 TEU' (n 4) para 3.

[32] See Ramopolous and Havas, 'Commentary on Article 24 TEU' (n 4) para 4. See also F Erlbacher and T Ramopolous, 'Commentary on Article 215 TFEU' in Kellerbauer, Klamert and Tomkin (eds), *Commentary*, para 10.

[33] See Case C-130/10, *Parliament v Council (Restrictive Measures against Bin Laden and Others)*, ECLI:EU:C:2012:472, para 62.

which parts of the respective agreements fall under CFSP competence.[34] However, even in these cases, the ECJ has not abstractly defined CFSP competences.[35]

The determination of what falls under the CFSP has become more difficult now that the Treaties only contain a common set of Union external action objectives.[36] It has been suggested that Article 24(1) TEU is better understood as reflecting an open-ended mandate for coordination and cooperation between Member States and the Union within the institutional framework of the European Union, rather than as a clear delineation of the powers conferred on the European Union.[37] By this understanding, competences would not be conferred to achieve a specific objective such as the creation of an internal market or an area of freedom, security and justice but would relate to the creation of a CFSP of the Union and its Member States as a 'cohesive force in international relations', as it is put in Article 24(3) TEU.[38] Different from all other fields of EU law, the focus in the CFSP arguably is to establish and secure the 'actorness' of the European Union in the international sphere.[39]

It has been argued that 'the CFSP attribution in Article 24(1) TEU is so broad that an application of the doctrine of implied powers implying all the competences needed for an effective CFSP would lead to an extensive grant of external action competences going far beyond what the Treaty permits'.[40] Implied powers indeed do not seem to exist in the CFSP, making for another distinction compared with non-CFSP areas. However, the reason for that, it is submitted, is not that these powers would be too extensive but that the Union's powers in the CFSP are so broad by express conferral that they are not needed.[41]

Article 29 TEU provides that the Council 'shall define the approach of the Union to a particular matter of geographical or thematic nature'. The General Court has confirmed a broad reading of this, covering 'not only acts programmatic in nature or mere declarations of intent, but also, in particular, decisions providing for measures capable of directly affecting the legal position of individuals may be adopted on the basis of Article 29 TEU'.[42] The competence under Article 29 TEU thus is broad, and it is also disputed as can be seen by

[34] Case C-244/17, *Commission v Council (Agreement with Kazakhstan)*, ECLI:EU:C:2018:662, para 42; Case C-180/20, *Commission v Council (Agreement with Armenia)*, ECLI:EU:C:2021:658, paras 42, 44, 46–48.

[35] See L-J Wagner, 'Competence in Common Foreign and Security Policy' in S Garben and L Gormley (eds), *The Oxford Encylopedia of EU Law* (Oxford, Oxford University Press, 2024).

[36] See Ramopolous and Havas, 'Commentary on Article 24 TEU' (n 4) paras 8–9. See also Opinion of AG Pitruzzella in *Commission v Council (Agreement with Armenia)*, ECLI:EU:C:2021:495, para 37.

[37] See Wagner, 'Competence in Common Foreign and Security Policy' (n 35).

[38] See Wagner, 'Competence in Common Foreign and Security Policy' (n 35). Similar also M Cremona, 'Structural Principles of External Relations Law' in Cremona (ed), *Structural Principles* 3, 5.

[39] See A Thies, 'The Search for Effectiveness and the Need for Loyalty in EU External Action' in Cremona (ed), *Structural Principles* 263, 265.

[40] See G de Baere, 'Subsidiarity as a Structural Principle Governing the Use of EU External Competences' in Cremona (ed), *Structural Principles* 93, 103.

[41] Similar Wessel, 'General Principles in EU Common Foreign and Security Policy' (n 11) 617.

[42] Case C-220/14 P, *Ezz and Others*, ECLI:EU:C:2015:147, para 42.

the example of restrictive measures. These are commonly passed as decisions based on Article 29 TFEU, which then need to be implemented with a measure under Article 215(1) TFEU or can be implemented with smart sanctions under Article 215(2) TFEU. The Court held that the CFSP decisions and the Article 215 TFEU regulations must not be substantively identical and that travel bans imposed on natural persons are likely to be included in CFSP decisions, without necessarily being included in regulations based on Article 215 TFEU.[43] Also, arms embargoes were previously only regulated in the CFSP sanctions decisions, not in the regulations under Article 215 TFEU. However, the ECJ has now established that arms embargoes must also be implemented through a regulation under Article 215 TFEU.[44] Thus, both the restriction of travel of individuals and of the trade in arms fall under the CFSP, but, in the case of the former, perhaps not under the TFEU. This illustrates that the CFSP competence is broader than the non-CFSP competence, even in matters that would intuitively seem to fall under the TFEU.

Unanimity in the European Council and the Council grants veto rights for Member States in the CFSP.[45] In addition, Article 31(1) subparagraph 2 TEU provides for the possibility of a qualified abstention which dispenses a Member State from having to implement a CFSP measure, as also discussed later. Article 31(2) subparagraph 2 TEU moreover allows to abstain from a vote and seek a common solution in those exceptional cases, where the Council could act by a qualified majority, but a Member State 'declares that for vital and stated reasons of national policy, it intends to oppose the adoption of a decision'. It must also be noted that, for most substantive policy decisions, the Council relies on less formal instruments, such as strategies, action plans, statements or Memoranda of Understanding, all of which do not involve voting.[46] Thus, in CFSP matters the Union is generally not perceived as a competitor to the Member States and their ability to conduct and shape their own foreign and security policy.[47]

4.3. Subsidiarity and Proportionality

According to Article 5(3) TEU, in areas that do not fall within its exclusive competence, the Union can act only if and in so far as the objectives of the proposed action cannot be sufficiently achieved by the Member States but can rather be better achieved at Union level. Subsidiarity has not been a very effective

[43] *Bank Refah Kargaran* (n 20) para 41.

[44] Case C-351/22, *Neves 77 Solutions*, ECLI:EU:C:2024:723, para 56 ff.

[45] This has caused problems with restrictive measures. See Erlbacher and Ramopolous, 'Commentary on Article 215 TFEU' (n 32) para 8 with further references.

[46] See Wessel, 'General Principles in EU Common Foreign and Security Policy' (n 11) 615.

[47] See M Cremona, 'Defining competence in EU external relations: Lessons from the Treaty reform process' in A Dashwood and S Maresceau (eds), *Law and Practice of EU external Relations: Salient Features of a Changing Landscape* (Cambridge, Cambridge University Press, 2008) 34, 65 ff; Butler, *Constitutional Law* (n 22) 48.

shield against centralisation at the EU level and the ensuing loss of national sovereignty.[48]

It has been argued that subsidiarity does not apply in the CFSP,[49] or that this would be unclear.[50] However, considering that conferral unequivocally applies to the CFSP, as explained above, it would be odd if subsidiarity would not apply there. Moreover, CFSP is not an exclusive competence as shown above and Article 5 TEU applies as a matter of principle to all other EU measures.[51] Member States indeed require no protection against a loss of sovereignty in the CFSP because of unanimity in the Council.[52] However, this is a political argument, not a legal justification for not applying subsidiarity.

In any case, the bigger issue lies with the control of subsidiarity. According to Article 5(3) second sentence TEU, the institutions of the Union are required to apply the principle of subsidiarity as laid down in Protocol No 2 on the application of the principles of subsidiarity and proportionality. This Protocol essentially only applies to (draft) legislative acts, which CFSP measures are not. Thus, the requirements of especially Article 5 of Protocol No 2 on providing justifications with regard to the principles of subsidiarity (and proportionality) and on providing a detailed statement making it possible to appraise compliance with the principles of subsidiarity (and proportionality) do not apply.

4.4. *Institutional Balance*

The principle of institutional balance provided in Article 13(2) TEU is concretised by a CFSP-specific non-affection clause in Article 40 TEU.[53] Article 40 TEU provides:

> The implementation of the common foreign and security policy shall not affect the application of the procedures and the extent of the powers of the institutions laid down by the Treaties for the exercise of the Union competences referred to in Articles 3 to 6 of the Treaty on the Functioning of the European Union.
>
> Similarly, the implementation of the policies listed in those Articles shall not affect the application of the procedures and the extent of the powers of the institutions laid down by the Treaties for the exercise of the Union competences under this Chapter.

[48] See, eg, Klamert, 'Commentary on Article 5 TEU' in Kellerbauer, Klamert and Tomkin (eds), *Commentary*, para 24.

[49] See Eckes, *EU Powers Under External Pressure* (n 2)89.

[50] See de Baere, 'Subsidiarity as a Structural Principle' (n 40) 114.

[51] See also de Baere, 'Subsidiarity as a Structural Principle' (n 40) 107–08; Wessel, 'General Principles in EU Common Foreign and Security Policy' (n 11) 617; Klamert, 'Commentary on Article 5 TEU' (n 48) para 23.

[52] See also de Baere, 'Subsidiarity as a Structural Principle' (n 40) 107. Critical Wessel, 'General Principles in EU Common Foreign and Security Policy' (n 11) 607.

[53] See I Govaere, 'To Give or to Grab: The Principle of Full, Crippled and Split Conferral of Powers Post-Lisbon' in Cremona (ed), *Structural Principles* 71, 79 who sees Article 40 TEU as the best reflection of the principle of conferral. See further C Hillion, 'Conferral, Cooperation and Balance in the Institutional Framework of EU External Action' in Cremona (ed), *Structural Principles* 117, 142 ff.

Different from ex Article 47 TEU, Article 40 TEU is a double-edged non-affection clause.[54] This means that, while the CFSP has been integrated into the other fields of external action of the European Union through common objectives, the institutional divisions have become more pronounced.[55] It would violate Article 40 TEU if measures where taken outside the CFSP, which should be dealt with under the CFSP with its special rules and procedures. While the areas outside the CFSP have been largely streamlined under the ordinary legislative procedure, the CFSP is still characterised by unanimity and by a diminished role of the European Parliament, which is an obstacle to the adoption of measures combining CFSP and non-CFSP legal bases.[56]

Also, the Member States have been very clear that they would not want that to change. Declaration 14 attached to the Lisbon Treaty states 'that the provisions covering the Common Foreign and Security Policy do not give new powers to the Commission to initiate decisions nor do they increase the role of the European Parliament'.

The only outlier in terms of special procedures are international agreements of the European Union, which are concluded under the rules of Article 218 TFEU in all fields of EU law.[57] In cases concerning international agreements concluded with, respectively, Kazakhstan and Armenia as well as concerning the withdrawal agreement with the United Kingdom, the Court has confirmed that the centre of gravity test (also known as the theory of absorption) is also applicable when competences involve the CFSP.[58] Decisions on international agreements of the European Union can thus (exceptionally) be based on both CFSP and TFEU competences.[59] In the *Mauritius Agreement* case, the ECJ relied on the principle of symmetry between internal and external procedures to guarantee the observance

[54] See Ramopolous and Havas, 'Commentary on Article 24 TEU' (n 4) para 4 ff.

[55] See P Van Elsuwege, 'The potential for inter-institutional conflicts before the Court of Justice: Impact of the Lisbon Treaty' in Cremona and Thies (eds), *The European Court of Justice and External Relations Law* 115, 115 ff; Wessel, 'General Principles in EU Common Foreign and Security Policy' (n 11) 613.

[56] See M Klamert, 'Conflicts of Legal Basis: No Legality and No Basis but a Bright Future under the Lisbon Treaty?' (2010) 35 *EL Rev* 497; R Wessel, 'Legality in EU Common Foreign and Security Policy: The Choice of the Appropriate Legal Basis' in C Kilpatrick and J Scott (eds), *Contemporary Challenges to EU Legality* (Oxford, Oxford University Press, 2021) 71, 89 ff. See Case C-28/12, *Commission v Council (Voting Arrangements)*, ECLI:EU:C:2015:282, para 52. Compare also Opinion of AG Pitruzzella in *Commission v Council (Agreement with Armenia)* (n 36) para 37.

[57] However, some specifics apply there as well. See J Wouters et al, *The Law of EU External Relations: Cases, Materials, and Commentary on the EU as an International Legal Actor*, 3rd edn (Oxford, Oxford University Press, 2021) 365.

[58] *Commission v Council (Agreement with Kazakhstan)* (n 34) para 42; *Commission v Council (Agreement with Armenia)* (n 34) para 44; Case C-479/21 PPU, *Governor of Cloverhill Prison*, ECLI:EU:C:2021:929. See F Naert, 'The Use of the CFSP Legal Basis for EU International Agreements in Combination with Other Legal Bases' in J Czuczai and F Naert (eds), *The EU as a Global Actor: Bridging Legal Theory and Practice. Liber Amicorum in Honour of Ricardo Gosalbo Bono* (Leiden, Brill, 2017) 394, 407; Wagner, 'Competence in Common Foreign and Security Policy' (n 35).

[59] See Wessel, 'General Principles in EU Common Foreign and Security Policy' (n 11) 614.

of institutional balance and the principle of legal certainty.[60] In particular, the legal bases of Article 217 TFEU for association agreements and Article 209 TFEU for development cooperation agreements would not require the addition of a CFSP legal basis.[61] It is submitted that this might have to do with the special nature of these two legal bases as 'umbrella' competences, as discussed later.[62]

5. Member State Equality, National Identity, Supremacy, and Direct Effect

Article 21(1) TEU requires Union action on the international scene to be guided by, among others, the principle of equality. It is not clear whether this refers to the equality of Member States stipulated in Article 4(2) TEU or to individual-centred equality as in Article 18 TFEU. It is more likely that the latter is meant here because the CFSP is the least supranational of all areas and thus not geared towards individuals. This is irrespective of the smart sanctions under Article 215(2) TFEU that are based on CFSP decisions.

It is submitted that the equality of Member States is more pronounced in the CFSP compared with other areas of EU law. This is because of unanimity and the other safeguards to the sovereignty of Member States contained in Article 31 TEU discussed above. There is hardly any risk that the sensibilities of Member States will be disturbed such as was the case with legislative measures, against which outvoted Member States have (unsuccessfully) tried to invoke Member State equality as discussed in chapter three.

The deference to national interests is confirmed by Declaration No 13 attached to the Treaty of Lisbon, which states that the provisions of the CFSP 'do not affect the responsibilities of the member States, as they currently exist, for the formulation and conduct of their foreign policy nor of their national representation in third countries and international organizations'. This can be seen in the context of the national identity clause in Article 4(2) TEU discussed in chapter three.[63] The last sentence of Article 4(2) TEU also retains 'national security' as the sole responsibility of each Member State, which links closely to the security the CFSP carries in its name.

CFSP measures are not directly effective and the Court has clarified that only directly effective provisions of Union law can take precedence over national law, as discussed in chapter three. Thus, primacy would not seem to apply in the CFSP and it seems unlikely that the Court would assign a CFSP act primacy, had it the

[60] *Parliament v Council (Mauritius Agreement)* (n 19) paras 55–56 and 60.

[61] See *Governor of Cloverhill Prison* (n 58) paras 62–66 and the case law cited.

[62] Compare also Ramopolous and Havas, 'Commentary on Article 24 TEU' (n 4) para 16.

[63] See J Larik, 'Pars Pro Toto: The Member States' Obligations of Sincere Cooperation, Solidarity and Unity' in Cremona (ed), *Structural Principles* 175, 187, 191; Wessel, 'General Principles in EU Common Foreign and Security Policy' (n 11) 615.

cognition to do so.[64] This is despite the application of Member State equality in the CFSP, which has been considered one rationale for supremacy by the ECJ. The only opening for supremacy in the CFSP might (again) be international agreements with a CFSP basis, which arguably could include directly effective provisions in theory and which could possibly be cognisable by the Court under Article 218 TFEU.

However, CFSP measures must as a rule be implemented by the Member States under Article 29 second sentence TEU, or, in the case of country sanctions, by the Union under Article 215(1) TFEU.[65] Thus, unless a Member State has lodged a constructive abstention under Article 31(1) subparagraph 2 TEU as mentioned above which dispenses from this duty to implement, Member States must comply with CFSP measures arguably not much differently from how they have to comply with (non-directly effective) Union measures outside the CFSP.

6. Loyalty and Solidarity

6.1. Introduction

Solidarity is mentioned very often in the CFSP part of the TEU. Article 21(1) TEU requires Union action on the international scene to be guided, among others, by the principle of solidarity. Article 24(2) TEU obliges the Union to 'conduct, define and implement a common foreign and security policy, based on the development of mutual political solidarity among Member States, the identification of questions of general interest and the achievement of an ever-increasing degree of convergence of Member States' actions'. Article 24(3) TEU adds that Member States 'shall support the Union's external and security policy actively and unreservedly in a spirit of loyalty and mutual solidarity and shall comply with the Union's action in this area'. Article 31(1) TEU provides that an abstaining Member State shall refrain from any action likely to conflict with or impede Union action based on the decision concerned and the other Member States shall respect its position, in a 'spirit of mutual solidarity'. Article 32 TEU contains a broad obligation to consult in all CFSP matters and demands that 'Member States shall show mutual solidarity'.

6.2. The OPAL *Case*

In the *OPAL* case on the principle of energy solidarity under Article 194 TFEU, the Court made general statements on solidarity, declaring among others that the principle of solidarity is 'one of the fundamental principles of EU law' as already discussed in chapter three.[66] This case, as explained, did not concern the CFSP or

[64] See K Lenaerts and P Van Nuffel, *European Union Law*, 3rd edn (London, Sweet & Maxwell, 2011) 754. Compare Butler, *Constitutional Law* (n 22) 181–84.

[65] Smart sanctions can be implemented by the Union under Article 215(2) TFEU.

[66] Case C-848/19 P, *Germany v Poland (OPAL)*, ECLI:EU:C:2021:598, para 39.

external relations, for that matter. However, the Court referred to both Article 21 and 24 TEU in making its arguments on the importance of solidarity:

> In accordance with Article 21(1) TEU, solidarity is also one of the principles governing the European Union's external action and, under Article 24(2) and (3) TEU, it is among the provisions relating to the common foreign and security policy as 'mutual political solidarity' among Member States.[67]

The Court also stressed that the principle of solidarity is closely linked to the principle of sincere cooperation in Article 4(3) TEU. That principle would not only oblige the Member States to take all the measures necessary to guarantee the application and effectiveness of EU law 'but also imposes on the EU institutions mutual duties to cooperate in good faith with the Member States'.[68]

In the *OPAL* case, the Commission was faulted for not examining the impact that the decision at issue could have on the gas market of the Member States liable to be affected.[69] The principle of energy solidarity would require that the EU institutions, including the Commission, 'conduct an analysis of the interests involved in the light of that principle, taking into account the interests both of the Member States and of the European Union as a whole'.[70]

This is not far removed from Article 32(1) TEU, which reads:

> Member States shall consult one another within the European Council and the Council on any matter of foreign and security policy of general interest in order to determine a common approach. Before undertaking any action on the international scene or entering into any commitment which could affect the Union's interests, each Member State shall consult the others within the European Council or the Council. Member States shall ensure, through the convergence of their actions, that the Union is able to assert its interests and values on the international scene. Member States shall show mutual solidarity.

While this has correctly been described as a reinforcement of the information and consultation principle, it has also been noted that the only effective 'sanction' for a violation of this obligation would be peer-pressure.[71] Thus, the pledge to solidarity in Article 32 TEU when acting on the international political scene is, by its wording and context, not legally binding.[72] Assuming the Court is competent via Article 218 TFEU, Member States could therefore not complain that the Council when concluding an international agreement had failed to take account of the interests of affected Member States. This might only be different if the agreement related to energy policy because in that case Article 194 TFEU

[67] *Germany v Poland (OPAL)* (n 66) para 39.

[68] *Germany v Poland (OPAL)* (n 66) para 41. See also Case C-514/19, *Union des industries de la protection des plantes*, ECLI:EU:C:2020:803, para 49.

[69] *Germany v Poland (OPAL)* (n 66) para 51.

[70] *Germany v Poland (OPAL)* (n 66) para 53.

[71] See G de Baere, *Constitutional Principles of EU External Relations* (Oxford, Oxford University Press, 2008) 263–64.

[72] Compare Ramopolous and Havas, 'Commentary on Article 24 TEU' (n 4) para 25.

arguably would be applicable in the same way as in the *OPAL* case (in conjunction with Article 218 TFEU).

6.3. *Loyalty*

It is noteworthy that the term 'loyalty' is mentioned in the CFSP, whereas (the English version of) Article 4(3) TEU uses 'sincere cooperation'. More importantly, the CFSP part of the Treaty is much more explicit in requiring mutual coordination and information, between the Member States but also with the EU institutions. Several provisions in the CFSP part, such as Articles 32, 34 and 35 TEU, require the Member States to coordinate between themselves and with the EU institutions and to keep each other informed. It has also been noted that Article 24(3) TEU quoted above introduces 'a CFSP-specific duty of loyalty' inspired by Article 4(3) TEU.[73]

Indeed, those (technical) duties of (mutual) sincere cooperation that apply under Article 4(3) TEU in the non-CFSP areas of EU law would also seem to apply in the CFSP.[74] The CFSP lacks the enforcement instruments available to the Commission in all other areas of EU law to ensure compliance by Member States and also by EU institutions.[75] This makes the CFSP particularly dependent on ensuring coherence and avoiding conflicts through 'softer' means, ie, through coordination and information obligations.[76]

However, this does not necessarily mean that all other duties the Court has derived from what is now Article 4(3) TEU equally apply within the CFSP. In the *Pupino* case, also discussed in chapter five, the Court relied on first pillar Article 10 EC to justify an obligation of consistent interpretation for framework decisions under the former third pillar.[77] In *Pupino*, the Court argued that it would be difficult for the Union to carry out its task effectively if the principle of loyal cooperation were not also binding in the area of police and judicial cooperation in criminal matters.[78] The difference between the former third pillar and the CFSP is that framework decisions (which *Pupino* was about) were always normatively much closer to the former first pillar than CFSP measures, witness of which is

[73] See Ramopolous and Havas, 'Commentary on Article 24 TEU' (n 4) para 23.

[74] See Case 230/81, *Luxembourg v Parliament*, ECLI:EU:C:1983:32, para 37 on ex-Article 10 EC. For the breadth of these duties see, eg, M Klamert, 'Commentary on Article 4 TEU' in Kellerbauer, Klamert and Tomkin (eds), *Commentary*, paras 71–79.

[75] See, in this regard, Opinion of AG Wahl in Case C-455/14 P, *EUPM in Bosnia and Herzegovina*, ECLI:EU:C:2016:212, para 39.

[76] See Ramopolous and Havas, 'Commentary on Article 24 TEU' (n 4) para 2: 'Constant cooperation and coordination at all levels from policy design to implementation, is thus required to ensure consistence and effectiveness of action'.

[77] Case C-105/03, *Pupino*, ECLI:EU:C:2005:386, para 42. See P van Elsuwege and H Merket, 'The Role of the Court of Justice in Ensuring the Unity of the EU's External Representation' in S Blockmans and RA Wessel (eds), *Principles and Practices of EU External Representation* (CLEER Working Paper 5, 2012) 37, 69; Ramopolous and Havas, 'Commentary on Article 24 TEU' (n 4) para 26.

[78] *Pupino* (n 77) para 39.

the fact that they are now passed as 'normal' directives. It seems unlikely that a similar obligation of consistent interpretation would apply in the CFSP or would be needed at all.

It has also been submitted that abstention duties imposed on the Member States in cases such as *PFOS* based on Article 4(3) TEU in external relations and discussed later could be transferred to the CFSP given the wording of Article 32 TEU, which links coordination and information duties to the emergence of a 'common approach' defined by the European Council or the Council.[79] Indeed, it does not seem inconceivable that such duties of abstention would apply when the common approach pertains to the conclusion of a CFSP agreement based on Article 37 TEU and concluded under the procedure of Article 218 TFEU. While the Court has derived abstention duties in cases such as *PFOS* from Article 4(3) TEU, it arguably could derive them just as well directly from Article 218 TFEU, which is a concretisation of Article 4(3) TEU.[80]

7. Effectiveness and Unity

As mentioned, Article 24(3) TEU refers to the obligation of the Member States to 'refrain from any action which is contrary to the interests of the Union or likely to impair its effectiveness as a cohesive force in international relations'. Indeed, as discussed in chapter three, the principle of effectiveness can be considered a separate principle with its own rationale applying to the whole of external relations law.[81] It has been argued that it should therefore also be taken into account in the CFSP context, whenever CFSP instruments are being adopted or implemented.[82]

Effectiveness is another good example of how structural principles apply distinctly in the CFSP and external relations more generally. In internal Union law, the principle of effectiveness has a lot to do with ensuring full compliance with EU law by and in the Member States, as shown earlier. As such, it is central to the indirect enforcement of EU law through the Member States, imposing itself on national administrative laws, among others. Externally, effectiveness is also very important, witness of which is the wording of Article 24(3) TEU quoted above, but it is mainly associated with the requirement of unity in the international representation of the Union.[83] It is about the 'actorness' of the European Union.[84] It thus is less about the effectiveness of specific EU rules but about the effectiveness of the

[79] See Case C-246/07, *Commission v Sweden (PFOS)*, ECLI:EU:C:2010:203. See C Hillion and RA Wessel, 'Restraining External Competences of EU Member States under CFSP' in M Cremona and B de Witte (eds), *EU Foreign Relations Law: Constitutional Fundamentals* (Oxford, Oxford University Press, 2006) 79, 91–96.

[80] See Larik, 'Pars Pro Toto' (n 63) 188.

[81] Compare Thies, 'The Search for Effectiveness' (n 39) 263.

[82] See Wessel, 'General Principles in EU Common Foreign and Security Policy' (n 11) 612.

[83] See Eckes, *EU Powers Under External Pressure* (n 2) 78.

[84] See Thies, 'The Search for Effectiveness' (n 39) 265, 280.

European Union as an organisation. We will discuss this further in the following section because the unity of international representation has played a bigger role in external relations outside the CFSP.

Similar with internal EU law, effectiveness is closely connected with loyalty. Sincere cooperation, coordination and mutual information are the preconditions, in theory as well as in practice, for enabling the European Union to have an impact in the international sphere.[85] This impact is alluded to with the wording that the European Union should be a 'force' in international relations. I have used the notion of 'cohesion' elsewhere to describe the manifold duties based on loyalty connecting EU law with national law.[86] Here, in the CFSP, it would seem to mean that there should be cohesion between the European Union and the Union in order to achieve the objectives of external relations. The high-flying objectives as stated in Articles 3 and 21 TEU, arguably, cannot be attained without a coordinated and unified performance of the European Union and its Member States.

3. Structural Principles in Other Areas of External Relations

1. Introduction

The EU's external relations are subject to a set of specific principles and objectives in Article 21 TEU and Article 205 TFEU. According to Article 21(1) TEU, the Union's action on the international scene 'shall be guided by the principles which have inspired its own creation, development and enlargement, and which it seeks to advance in the wider world'.[87] The objectives of the Union's external action are laid down in Article 21(2) TEU, but also in policy-area specific clauses such as in Article 206 TFEU (common commercial policy), Article 208(1) TFEU (development cooperation), and Article 214(1) TFEU (humanitarian aid).[88]

In the *Memorandum of Understanding* case, the Court held that the decision on the signing of an EU agreement 'requires an assessment to be made, in compliance with … the principles and objectives of the Union's external action laid down in Article 21(1) and (2) TEU'.[89] Also in Article 3(5) TEU, as

[85] See van Elsuwege and Merket, 'The Role of the Court of Justice' (n 77) 43 on the frequent struggles between the EU and its Member States on representation issues.

[86] See M Klamert, *The Principle of Loyalty in EU Law* (Oxford, Oxford University Press, 2014) ch II.

[87] These are democracy, the rule of law, the universality and indivisibility of human rights and fundamental freedoms, respect for human dignity, the principles of equality and solidarity, and respect for the principles of the United Nations Charter and international law.

[88] See F Erlbacher and T Ramopolous, 'Commentary on Article 205 TFEU' in Kellerbauer, Klamert and Tomkin (eds), *Commentary*, para 3.

[89] Case C-660/13, *Council v Commission (Memorandum of Understanding)*, ECLI:EU:C:2016:616, paras 38–40.

mentioned in chapter two, there are specific objectives for the European Union to pursue in its 'relations with the wider world'. We will see that this background and context have implications for how the law of external relations operates on a structural level.

Another important factor for the discussion in the following is the fact that international agreements are much more prevalent in the areas of external relations than in other areas of EU law. This prevalence of international agreements as an instrument for the European Union is a reflection of the fact that external relations concern the interaction of the European Union with third states and international organisations. Such interaction would often mean that the European Union becomes a party to an international organisation. This, however, depends on whether such membership is allowed by the latter's constituent Treaty, such as by providing a so-called Regional (Economic) Integration Organisation (R(E)IO) clause. In the absence of such a clause, the European Union is precluded from acting directly in its forum as a member and must therefore rely on its Member States to act on its behalf.[90]

2. Autonomy

As mentioned in chapter three, EU case law in recent years has focused on so-called external autonomy. It was thus in the external sphere that autonomy has been elaborated on and where it had the biggest impact, especially since Opinion 2/13, already discussed above in the context of the CFSP. In chapter five, we will briefly return to this case law when we analyse the way the Court argues relying on structural principles.

In *Achmea*, the Court has confirmed that investor–state dispute settlement (ISDS) clauses in intra-EU bilateral investment Treaties (BITs) are precluded by the principle of the autonomy of the Union legal order, among others.[91] This had real-life implications as the relevant offers for arbitration in the existing large number of intra-EU BITs have become inapplicable as of the date on which both parties had become Member States.[92] It also has yet unresolved consequences for the participation of the European Union and the Member States in the Energy

[90] See also P van Elsuwege, 'The Duty of Sincere Cooperation and its Implications for Autonomous Member State Action in the Field of External Relations' in M Varju (ed), *Between Compliance and Particularism: Member State Interests and European Union Law* (New York, Springer, 2019) 283. See the Opinion of AG Szpunar in Case C-161/20, *Commission v Council*, ECLI:EU:C:2021:957, paras 57–63.

[91] Case C-284/16, *Achmea*, ECLI:EU:C:2018:158. See, generally, M Klamert, 'Commentary on Article 1 TEU' in Kellerbauer, Klamert and Tomkin (eds), *Commentary*, paras 24–26.

[92] See F Erlbacher and TM Rusche, 'Commentary on Article 207 TFEU' in Kellerbauer, Klamert and Tomkin (eds), *Commentary*, para 66. See also S Hindelang, 'Conceptualisation and Application of the Principle of Autonomy of EU Law: The CJEU's Judgment in Achmea Put into Perspective' (2019) 44 *EL Rev* 383.

Charter Treaty (ECT), whose Article 26 ECT was deemed not to be allowed to contain an offer of arbitration between Member States.[93]

On the other hand, the Court has confirmed in Opinion 1/17 that in agreements concluded by the European Union (and the Member States) with third countries such as the Comprehensive Economic Trade Agreement (CETA) between the European Union, its Member States and Canada, it is possible to establish an investment court, provided that the latter does not apply EU law as a matter of law (but merely as a matter of fact), and the substantive provisions on investment protection offer sufficient safeguards to protect the autonomy of the EU legal order and the principle of democracy.[94]

As will also be discussed below, the Court has emphasised that there is a fundamental difference between the relations between Member States and between Member States and third states because only the former would be 'specifically' characterised by the principle of mutual trust.[95] The underlying rationale of *Achmea* has often been seen, negatively, in a defensive application of external institutional autonomy as explained in chapter three. By contrast, it could also, positively, be seen as predicated on the principle of mutual trust Member State courts, which are the keystones of the preliminary reference procedure under Article 267 TFEU, which has always been fiercely protected in the case law of the Court, as explained in chapter three with autonomy and in chapter six with the unity and uniformity of EU law.

3. Conferral

3.1. Introduction

The Court has clarified that the principle of conferred powers 'must be respected in both the internal action and the international action of the Community'.[96] While this is also true for the CFSP, as shown above, the other areas of external relations are not distinguished by specific rules and procedures and an unclear nature of competence. Thus, one would assume that conferral would work the same internally and externally in areas such as the common commercial policy (Article 207 TFEU), association (Article 217 TFEU), or sanctions (Article 215 TFEU). As we will explore in the following, this is not the case, even though the differences tend to be smaller compared with the differences regarding the CFSP discussed earlier.

[93] Case C-741/19, *Komstroy*, ECLI:EU:C:2021:655, paras 41–66. See also Case C-109/20, *PL Holdings*, ECLI:EU:C:2021:875, para 44, on ad hoc arbitration agreements with identical content. See, on this, A Dashwood, 'Article 26 ECT and intra-EU disputes – the case against an expansive reading of Achmea' (2021) 46 *EL Rev* 415; B Bohme, 'The Future of the Energy Charter Treaty after Moldova v. Komstroy' (2022) 59 *CML Rev* 853.

[94] See Article 8.31 CETA on the law applied in dispute settlement. See Opinion 1/17, *CETA*, ECLI:EU:C:2019:341, paras 120–60. See Erlbacher and Rusche, 'Commentary on Article 207 TFEU' (n 92) para 67.

[95] Case C-202/24, *Alchaster*, ECLI:EU:C:2024:649, para 61.

[96] *ECHR I* (n 15) paras 24–25.

Recall also that, as discussed in chapter three, implied powers are much more relevant in external relations law.

The following is not concerned with the differences between internal and external competence generally, as these differences apply to all areas of EU law.[97]

3.2. Competences

It seems fair to say that competences in the areas of external relations are generally broader and especially dynamic when compared with the competences in other areas of EU law. This is to some degree a reflection of the objectives of external relations as mentioned above, which embed the respective policy areas in international law and international political developments.

Thus, the scope of the common commercial policy has been described as 'dynamic' allowing the European Union to conduct an effective policy which is determined to a large extent by a constantly evolving international commercial environment, in particular but not only in the context of, the WTO.[98] The competence under Article 207(1) TFEU is also very broad, covering all measures specifically relating to international trade in that they are essentially intended to promote, facilitate, or govern trade and have direct and immediate effects on trade.[99] Moreover, it can be noted that Member States have less leeway under Article 114 TFEU, the most important competence outside external relations, compared with its 'mirror' competence in Article 207 TFEU.[100] Only under Article 114 TFEU there is a mechanism for retaining conflicting national measures or introducing new national measures deviating from Union measures in paragraphs 4 and 5, while there is no such flexibility built into Article 207 TFEU.

Other legal bases in external relations have also been qualified as being so broad that they allow measures that would normally require a combination of distinct legal bases.

The legal basis for development policy under Article 209 TFEU has been deemed broad in the sense that it must be possible for measures required to concern a variety of specific areas.[101] It can therefore be called an 'umbrella' legal

[97] I have dicussed these differences in Klamert, *The Principle of Loyalty in EU Law* (n 86) 147 ff. Compare also E Neframi 'The Dynamic of the EU Objectives in the Analysis of the External Competence' in E Neframi and M Gatti (eds), *Constitutional Issues of EU External Relations Law* (Baden-Baden, Nomos, 2018) 63.

[98] See, the View of AG Sharpston in Opinion 2/15, *Singapore FTA*, ECLI:EU:C:2016:992, para 99 et seq. See Erlbacher and Rusche, 'Commentary on Article 207 TFEU' (n 92) para 9.

[99] Case C-414/11, *Daiichi Sankyo*, ECLI:EU:C:2013:520, paras 51–52 and Case C-137/12, *Commission v Council*, ECLI:EU:C:2013:675, paras 57–58; Case C-389/15, *Commission v Council (Lisbon Agreement)*, ECLI:EU:C:2017:798, para 51.

[100] See also Eckes, *EU Powers Under External Pressure* (n 2) 125–26.

[101] See M Cremona, 'The principle of conferral and express and implied external competences' in Neframi and Gatti (eds), *Constitutional Issues* 29, 48–50.

basis.[102] The same applies to Article 212 TFEU on cooperation with third countries other than developing countries, which allows the Union to cover basically all policy areas as long as the thrust of the measure does not lie in any of the specific sectoral policies but in an overarching objective of economic, financial and technical cooperation with the third country concerned.[103]

Association under Article 217 TFEU can equally extend to any area of Union competence, be they exclusive, shared, or parallel, and does not necessarily depend on the previous exercise of all these policies within the Union.[104] Thus, association agreements can cover a variety of issues, such as trade, the approximation of rules, and cooperation in matters such as asylum, judicial cooperation, transport, environmental protection and the protection of workers, all based on Article 217 TFEU, which also makes Article 217 TFEU an 'umbrella legal basis'.[105]

Moreover, Article 215 TFEU on restrictive measures is a special case in that it grants the Union a comprehensive authorisation to adopt sanction measures covering a seemingly unlimited material scope.[106] Thus, the ECJ held in *Kadi* as follows on ex Article 301 TEC, the precursor of Article 215 TFEU:

> That interpretation of Article 301 EC threatens to reduce the ambit and, therefore, the practical effect of that provision, for, having regard to its actual wording, the subject of that provision is the adoption of potentially very diverse measures affecting economic relations with third countries which, therefore, by necessary inference, must not be limited to spheres falling within other material powers of the Community such as those in the domain of the common commercial policy or of the free movement of capital.
>
> Moreover, that interpretation finds no support in the wording of Article 301 EC, which confers a material competence on the Community the scope of which is, in theory, autonomous in relation to that of other Community competences.[107]

This broad scope is also explained by the role of Article 215 TFEU as a link to the respective CFSP decisions, which are required as a basis for measures under Article 215 TFEU. The scope of the CFSP legal bases, as explained, is very broad and this also applies to restrictive measures,[108] so the same must apply to Article 215 TFEU for it to fulfil its constitutional function.

[102] See F Erlbacher, 'Commentary on Article 212 TFEU' in Kellerbauer, Klamert and Tomkin (eds), *Commentary*, para 3.

[103] See M Klamert, 'Commentary on Article 209 TFEU' in Kellerbauer, Klamert and Tomkin (eds), *Commentary*, para 9, on among others the Partnership agreement between the Union and Canada concluded based on Article 37 TEU for CFSP and Article 212 TFEU for all other matters covered.

[104] F Erlbacher, 'Commentary on Article 217 TFEU' in Kellerbauer, Klamert and Tomkin (eds), *Commentary*, para 4.

[105] See Erlbacher, 'Commentary on Article 217 TFEU' (n 104) para 4. See also *Governor of Cloverhill Prison* (n 58) paras 58–69.

[106] See generally, the sanctions regime against Russia, including eg, media sanctions. See Case T-12/22, *RT France*, ECLI:EU:T:2022:483. See M Klamert, 'Art 215 AEUV' in T Jaeger and K Stöger (eds), *Kommentar zu EUV und AEUV* (Vienna, Manz, 2025).

[107] Joined Cases C-402/05 P & C-415/05 P, *Kadi*, ECLI:EU:C:2008:461, paras 177–78 on Article 301 TEC.

[108] *Rosneft* (n 23) paras 88–89.

3.3. Subsidiarity

Subsidiarity review is curtailed in external relations for two distinct reasons, one relating to the nature of competences in the areas of external relations, and the other relating to the use of the instrument of international agreements dominant in these areas.

According to Article 5(3) TEU, in areas which do not fall within its exclusive competence, the Union

> shall act only if and in so far as the objectives of the proposed action cannot be sufficiently achieved by the Member States, either at central level or at regional and local level, but can rather, by reason of the scale or effects of the proposed action, be better achieved at Union level.

Thus, because Article 5(3) TEU speaks very generally of 'proposed action', subsidiarity applies as a matter of principle.

In matters of exclusive competence, Member States are either not allowed or not able to take the measures foreseen by the Treaties.[109] This applies both to exclusive competence in the areas listed under Article 3(1) TFEU, as well as to exclusive competence to enter into international agreements under the conditions provided by Article 3(2) TFEU. Arguably the most important areas mentioned in Article 3(1) TFEU pertain to external relations (customs union, common commercial policy). None of the areas listed in Article 4(2) TFEU on shared competences, by contrast, relate to such areas. Thus, a comparably larger part of external relations is powered by exclusive competences than is the case with the other areas of EU law. This means, conversely, that Article 5(3) TEU simply does not apply to important areas of external relations.[110]

According to Article 5(3) second sentence TEU, the institutions of the Union are required to apply the principle of subsidiarity as laid down in Protocol No 2 on the application of the principles of subsidiarity and proportionality. However, the Protocol essentially only applies to (draft) legislative acts, which do not include international agreements concluded under Article 218 TFEU.[111] Thus, as already the case with the CFSP discussed above, the requirements of especially Article 5 of Protocol No 2 on providing justification with regard to the principles of subsidiarity (and proportionality) and on providing a detailed statement making it possible to appraise compliance with the principles of subsidiarity (and proportionality) do not apply.

It has been argued that there is a strong presumption of both necessity and added value where the EU measure has the aim of resolving problems with a

[109] See M Klamert, 'Commentary on Article 3 TEU' in Kellerbauer, Klamert and Tomkin (eds), *Commentary*, paras 1 and 4.

[110] See also Eckes, *EU Powers Under External Pressure* (n 2) 89.

[111] Compare also I Bosse-Platière, 'L'application du principe de subsidiarité dans le cadre de l'action extérieure de l'Union européenne' in Neframi and Gatti (eds), *Constitutional Issues* 111, 134–36.

cross-border dimension.[112] With the environment, it has been argued that the subsidiarity principle should be relatively easily satisfied even in cases where the cross-border dimension is limited.[113] While this has been argued in the context of the internal market, it is of course also and particularly true with international agreements.

Recently, with some cases on mixed agreements, the constitutional limitations curtailing the discretion of the Council in exercising shared external competences in such context have been the issue.[114] The question arose whether structural principles such as subsidiarity or conferral could serve as such limitations, and if so, how these principles would operate in this context.[115]

4. Member State Equality and Mutual Trust

According to the Court, there is a fundamental difference between the relations between Member States and between Member States and third states. Only the relations between Member States would be 'specifically' characterised by the principle of mutual trust.[116] However, it cannot be ruled out that an international agreement may establish a similarly high level of confidence between the Member States and certain third countries, such as Norway as regards the European arrest warrant.[117]

Because mutual trust is connected with Member State equality, it is thus not surprising that in Opinion 1/17, among others, the Court clarified that the EU law principle of equal treatment does not apply to relations between the Union and non-Member States and that Article 18(1) TFEU does not apply to cases where there is a possible difference in treatment between nationals of Member States and nationals of non-Member States.[118] Article 18 TFEU also does not apply between different categories of third-country nationals.[119] That difference in treatment

[112] Opinion of AG Kokott in Case C-358/14, *Poland v Parliament and Council*, ECLI:EU:C:2015:848, paras 162–64.

[113] See S Garben, 'Commentary on Article 191 TFEU' in Kellerbauer, Klamert and Tomkin (eds), *Commentary*, para 5 and the examples given there.

[114] Case C-600/14, *Germany v Council (COTIF I)*, ECLI:EU:C:2017:935; Case C-620/16, *Commission v Germany (COTIF II)*, ECLI:EU:C:2019:256; Joined Cases C-626/15 & C-659/16, *Commission v Council (MPA Antarctic)*, ECLI:EU:C:2018:925.

[115] See de Baere, 'Subsidiarity as a Structural Principle' (n 40) 93; I Bosse-Platière and M Cremona, 'Facultative Mixity in the Light of the Principle of Subsidiarity' in M Chamon and I Govare (eds), *EU External Relations Post-Lisbon: The Law and Practice of Facultative Mixity* (Oxford, Hart Publishing, 2020) 48; L Prete, 'The Constitutional Limits to the Choice of Mixity after EUSFTA, COTIF I, MPA Antarctic and COTIF II: Towards a More Constructive Discourse?' (2020) 45 *EL Rev* 113.

[116] *Alchaster* (n 95) para 61.

[117] *Alchaster* (n 95) paras 65–67. See also Case C-71/21, *Sofiyska gradska prokuratura (Successive arrest warrants)*, ECLI:EU:C:2023:668.

[118] *CETA* (n 94) paras 81, 169. See also Joined Cases C-22/08 & C-23/08, *Vatsouras and Koupatantze*, ECLI:EU:C:2009:344, para 52.

[119] Case C-930/19, *X v Belgian State*, ECLI:EU:C:2021:657, paras 51–52; Case C-105/89, *Buhari Haji*, ECLI:EU:C:1990:402; Case C-291/09, *Guarnieri*, ECLI:EU:C:2011:217.

would be justified by the objective of contributing to free and fair trade, within the meaning of Article 3(5) TEU, and by the objective of integrating all countries into the world economy, as laid down in Article 21(2)(e) TEU.[120] The competence of the Union to conclude, under Article 207 TFEU, agreements concerning direct investments with non-Member States and, under Article 4(1) and (2)(a) TFEU, agreements concerning investments other than direct investments with such states, 'would be meaningless' if the EU law principle of equal treatment were to prohibit the Union from entering into specific commitments concerning investments deriving from non-Member States.[121]

This would only be different with the *meta*-principle of equality provided in Article 20 CFR ('everyone is equal before the law') because it would not contain any express limitation on its scope and would therefore apply to all situations governed by EU law.[122] Likewise this, however, would not 'oblige the Union to accord, in its external relations, equal treatment to different non-Member States', but only requires to examine whether an international agreement establishes a difference in treatment, within the Union itself, of persons of a non-Member State and persons of Member States.[123]

This distinction in treatment is also reflected in the context of restrictions on capital movements, which according to the Court may be justified by a Member State for movements to or from non-member countries where that reason would not constitute a valid justification for a restriction on capital movements between Member States.[124]

5. Direct Effect and (Individual-Centred) Equality

EU law as a rule integrates international agreements concluded by the European Union fully, thus granting their provisions direct effect, if they contain a clear and precise obligation and are not subject to a condition to be applicable, while considering the overall object and purpose of the respective agreement ('two-stage test').[125] On that basis, the Court has rejected direct effect of rules of most multilateral agreements such as the General Agreement on Tariffs and Trade (GATT), the World Trade Organization (WTO) and the Agreement on Trade-Related Aspects of Intellectual Property Rights (TRIPS) agreements, the UN Convention on the Law of the Sea, the Kyoto Protocol, and (certain provisions of) the Aarhus

[120] *CETA* (n 94) para 84.
[121] *CETA* (n 94) para 84.
[122] *CETA* (n 94) para 171.
[123] *CETA* (n 94) paras 173–74.
[124] Case C-446/04, *Test Claimants in the FII Group Litigation*, ECLI:EU:C:2006:774, para 171.
[125] See Joined Cases 21 to 24/72, *International Fruit*, ECLI:EU:C:1972:115, para 20; Case 12/86, *Demirel*, ECLI:EU:C:1987:400, para 14. See on this generally, M Mendez, *The Legal Effects of EU Agreements* (Oxford, Oxford University Press, 2013).

Convention.[126] This can be seen against the background of these agreements often providing for dispute settlement mechanisms other than the ECJ.[127] Recently, the Member States (not the ECJ) have excluded the direct effect for a number of trade related agreements with third states that contain WTO-like provisions ('WTO plus', 'WTO minus' agreements).[128] By contrast, direct effect has been affirmed by the Court for provisions of most bilateral cooperation agreements concluded by the Union with third countries as well as acts taken by bodies established by such agreements.[129] This means that investors from WTO-member states cannot challenge EU law before the CJEU by relying on the WTO agreements as a standard of review.

Direct effect has been defined as 'the obligation of a court or another authority to apply the relevant provision of Community law, either as a norm which governs the case or as a standard for legal review'.[130] While this stresses the justiciability aspect, direct effect also has a 'subjective' side in that it enables individuals to invoke a provision before national authorities.[131] This subjective perspective makes denying direct effect with some agreements but not with others harder to justify. Wherever direct effect is excluded, it entails that persons subject to such agreements both in the European Union and in third states are treated differently from the persons subject to other EU agreements.[132] This practice has therefore also been criticised as 'anti-citizen clauses' and as 'intergovernmental "disempowerment" of EU citizens'.[133] It seems doubtful whether the EU legislator could do the same with a Union directive, viz including in the text of the directive or its recitals that it is not meant to have direct effect.[134]

[126] See Case C-307/99, *OGT Fruchthandelsgesellschaft*, ECLI:EU:C:2001:228, para 25, where the Court pointed out that the provisions of the TRIPS are 'not such as to create rights on which individuals may rely directly before the courts by virtue of Community law'. See, among others, S Griller, 'Judicial enforceability of WTO law in the European Union: Annotation to Case C-149/96, Portugal v. Council' (2000) 3 *Journal of International Economic Law* 441; J Klabbers, 'Straddling the Fence: The EU and International Law' in A Arnull and D Chalmers (eds), *The Oxford Handbook of European Union Law* (Oxford, Oxford University Press, 2015) 52, 64–65.

[127] See Case C-149/96, *Portugal v Council*, ECLI:EU:C:1999:574. See A Semertzi, 'The Preclusion of Direct Effect in the Recently Concluded EU Free Trade Agreements' (2014) 51 *CML Rev* 1125, 1126–27.

[128] See, eg, Article 30.6. of the Comprehensive Economic and Trade Agreement with Canada. See Semertzi, 'The Preclusion of Direct Effect' (n 127) 1125.

[129] See F Erlbacher, 'Commentary on Article 216 TFEU' in Kellerbauer, Klamert and Tomkin (eds), *Commentary*, para 12 with references.

[130] See S Prechal, 'Direct Effect, Indirect Effect, Supremacy and the Evolving Constitution of the European Union' in C Barnard (ed), *The Fundamentals of EU Law Revisited: Assessing the Impact of the Constitutional Debate* (Oxford, Oxford University Press, 2007) 35, 37–38.

[131] See P Pescatore, 'The Docrine of "Direct Effect": An Infant Disease of Community Law' (2015) 40 *EL Rev* 135 (reprint).

[132] See F Casolari, 'The Acknowledgment of the Direct Effect of EU International Agreements: Does Legal Equality Still Matter?' in LS Rossi and F Casolari (eds), *The Principle of Equality in EU Law* (New York, Springer, 2017) 83, 85.

[133] See E-U Petersmann, 'CETA, TTIP, and TiSA: New Trends in International Economic Law' in S Griller, W Obwexer and E Vranes (eds), *Mega-Regional Trade Agreements: CETA, TTIP, and TiSA* (Oxford, Oxford University Press, 2017) 17, 38.

[134] See generally P Syrpis, 'Theorising the Relationship' in P Syrpis (ed), *The Judiciary, the Legislature and the EU Internal Market* (Cambridge, Cambridge University Press, 2012) 3.

Another argument can be made in this respect.[135] In *Van Gend*, as discussed, the Court went to great lengths to argue how the functioning of the (then) common market was of direct concern to the people in the Member States, that the preamble of the EEC not only referred to governments but also to peoples, and that subjects of EU law were not only Member States but also their nationals.[136] Thus, the Court co-opted the citizens for the enforcement of EU law to ensure that remedies against violations of EU law are not ineffective, which would be the case by only relying on the vigilance of the Commission and of the Member States under what are now Articles 258 and 267 TFEU. International agreements concluded by the Union equally serve the fulfilment of Union goals, such as the expansion of the internal market in the case of free trade agreements. If a person is seen as a guardian of the legal system of the Union concerning (internal) EU law and is thus, for example, entitled to rely on provisions of a directive that are not implemented in time, this responsibility should also be seen as extending to international agreements.

6. Supremacy, National (Constitutional) Identity, and Loyalty

Coordination obligations compensate for the lack of formal pre-emption in two external relations policies, viz development cooperation under Articles 208–11 TFEU and humanitarian aid under Article 214 TFEU.[137] Thus, Article 210 TFEU contains a specification of the principle of loyalty in Article 4(3) TEU, requiring coordination among the Member States as well as in relationship with the Union. Article 214(6) TFEU provides that the Commission may take any useful initiative to promote coordination between actions of the Union and those of the Member States, to enhance the efficiency and complementarity of Union and national humanitarian aid measures.

It has been pointed out that supremacy does not have the same force externally as it does in the relations between Member States.[138] In case of a direct conflict between Union law and national law, supremacy requires national authorities to set aside such national laws and regulations. This does not apply in the same manner when a Member State concludes an international agreement. A directive or regulation is not capable of directly disapplying a Member State Treaty concluded with a third state under public international law. Thus, substantive unity cannot be ensured to the same extent as in cases where no third countries are involved, as

[135] See, for the following, R Arnold and M Klamert, 'Außenhandelsrecht, K I. Grundlagen' in M Dauses and M Ludwigs (eds), *Handbuch des EU Wirtschaftsrechts* (Munich, Beck, 2020) para 78.

[136] Case 26/62, *Van Gend & Loos*, ECLI:EU:C:1963:1.

[137] See Klamert, 'Commentary on Article 4 TEU' (n 74) para 18.

[138] See Eckes, *EU Powers Under External Pressure* (n 2) 74–76; Klamert, *The Principle of Loyalty in EU Law* (n 86) 105.

the primacy of Union law cannot be invoked against them.[139] The safeguarding of Union interests in such a case depends entirely on the obligation incumbent on the Member State concerned to renegotiate or denounce their international obligations.[140]

The principle of loyalty compensates for this external 'weakness' of supremacy by being more stringently applied and interpreted in the external sphere than in the internal context, making its effects in curtailing the actions of Member States more pronounced.[141] Based on Article 4(3) TEU, the Court has imposed duties of abstention on the Member States because Commission proposals submitted to the Council can represent the point of departure for 'concerted Community action' in the *Sea fisheries* case law (under exclusive competence),[142] because a Council mandate to the Commission to negotiate an EU agreement can mark the start of a concerted Union action at international level in the *Inland waterway* cases (under shared competence),[143] and because a 'concerted common strategy' adopted by the Council can bar Member States from unilaterally making proposals in a committee set up under a (mixed) multilateral agreement in the *PFOS* case (under shared competence).[144] In particular in the context of mixed agreements, duties of cooperation have often translated into procedural constraints on Member State action at the external level.[145]

It has been argued that, while exceptions that are claimed based on national constitutional identity under Article 4(2) TEU would, in theory, be limited to extreme cases, Member States could fall back on this line of defence if the scope of loyalty obligations continues to expand further.[146]

[139] Therefore, Article 351 TFEU on 'old' Member State agreements can be seen as an exception to primacy. See Klamert, 'Commentary on Article 1 TEU' (n 91) para 37.

[140] See also J Temple Lang, 'The ERTA Judgment and the Court's Case-law on Competence and Conflict' (1986) 6 *Yearbook of European Law* 183, 197, 200. On the relation between loyalty and solidarity, see M Klamert, 'Loyalty and Solidarity as General Principles of EU Law' in Ziegler, Neuvonen and Moreno-Lax (eds), *Research Handbook* 118.

[141] See also Eckes, *EU Powers Under External Pressure* (n 2) 11, 74.

[142] Case 804/79, *Commission v UK (Sea fisheries)*, ECLI:EU:C:1981:93, para 28; Joined Cases 47/83 & 48/83, *Pluimveeslachterij*, ECLI:EU:C:1984:131, paras 22 et seq. See also the analogue Case 325/85, *Ireland v Commission*, ECLI:EU:C:1987:546, para 15; Case 326/85, *Netherlands v Commission*, ECLI:EU:C:1987:547, para 21; Case 332/85, *Germany v Commission*, ECLI:EU:C:1987:549, para 20. In respect of whether this case law empowers or even obliges the Member States to act unilaterally as 'trustees of the common interest' in an area of exclusive competence, see M Klamert, 'Commentary on Article 2 TFEU' in Kellerbauer, Klamert, and Tomkin (eds), *Commentary*, para 8.

[143] Case C-266/03, *Commission v Luxembourg (Inland Waterway)*, ECLI:EU:C:2005:341, paras 60–74; Case C-433/03, *Commission v Germany (Inland Waterway)*, ECLI:EU:C:2005:462, para 72.

[144] *Commission v Sweden (PFOS)* (n 79) paras 93–103. See also A Delgado Casteleiro and J Larik, 'The Duty to Remain Silent: Limitless Loyalty in EU External Relations?' (2011) 36 *EL Rev* 524.

[145] See M Cremona, 'Defending the Community Interest: The Duties of Cooperation and Compliance' in Cremona and de Witte (eds), *EU Foreign Relations Law* 125, 126. See also E Neframi, 'The Duty of Loyalty: Rethinking its Scope Through its Application in the Field of EU External Relations' (2010) 47 *CML Rev* 323, 325–31.

[146] See Larik, 'Pars Pro Toto' (n 63) 188, 193.

7. Effectiveness and Unity

Loyalty has shown to be difficult to disentangle conceptionally from effectiveness (see chapter three) and the same can be said concerning external relations law. However, there is an obvious yet crucial difference between their roles internally and externally: internally, loyalty and effectiveness are mainly concerned with the relation between the European Union and EU law on the one side and national law and national authorities on the other. Externally, loyalty and effectiveness mainly govern the relation of the European Union and its Member States with third states and other international actors. The expression of this internally has been supremacy and disapplication, effective judicial protection, and generally the effective application of EU law in the Member States. Externally, the main manifestation of loyalty and effectiveness is the requirement of unity in the international representation of the Union.[147]

While Article 24(3) TEU on the Member States' obligation to be 'a cohesive force in international relations' technically only applies within the CFSP, the underlying rationale would seem to be the same in all external relations. Thus, it has been argued that structural principles would 'promote a smooth articulation of the EU's system of external relations and its effective presentation of an international identity'.[148]

The Court referred to such unity in Opinion 2/91, where it held that the duty of cooperation must not only apply in mixed agreements under the Euratom Treaty but also in the EEC context 'since it results from the requirement of unity in the international representation of the Community'.[149] Especially in a number of judgments involving mixed agreements such as the *PFOS* case, the Court made a connection between duties of cooperation and the requirement of unity, in the following words:

> Where it is apparent that the subject-matter of an agreement or convention falls partly within the competence of the Community and partly within that of its Member States, it is essential to ensure close cooperation between the Member States and the Community institutions, both in the process of negotiation and conclusion and in the fulfilment of the commitments entered into. That obligation to cooperate flows from the requirement of unity in the international representation of the Community.[150]

[147] As will be explained later, this should not be confused with uniformity.

[148] See Cremona, 'Structural Principles of External Relations Law' (n 38) 5, 12.

[149] Opinion 2/91, *ILO Convention 170*, ECLI:EU:C:1993:106, para 36, referring to Ruling 1/78, *Convention on Nuclear Protection*, ECLI:EU:C:1979:224, points 34–36. See A Södersten, 'The Birth of the Principle of Close Cooperation, Declaration of Competences, and the Ruling Procedure: Ruling 1/78 (Convention on Nuclear Protection)' in G Butler and RA Wessel (eds), *EU External Relations Law. The Cases in Context* (Oxford, Hart Publishing, 2022) 111.

[150] *Commission v Sweden (PFOS)* (n 79) para 73. Identical wording in Opinion 1/94, *WTO*, ECLI:EU:C:1994:384, para 108; Case C-25/94, *FAO*, ECLI:EU:C:1996:114, para 48. Similar wording in Opinion 1/08, *Accession to GATS*, ECLI:EU:C:2009:739, para 136; Opinion 2/00, *Cartagena Protocol*, ECLI:EU:C:2001:664, para 18. But see Case C-45/07, *Commission* v *Greece (IMO)*, ECLI:EU:C:2009:81, where this argument was not applied.

The *PFOS* case and also the *OIV* case have involved struggles between the European Union and certain Member States in bodies set up under (mixed) international agreements under the Stockholm Convention on Persistent Organic Pollutants in the first case and the International Organisation of Vine and Wine in the latter.[151]

The *COTIF II* case concerned compliance on the part of a Member State with a (binding) decision under Article 218(9) TFEU on a common EU position in a body set up under an international agreement.[152] The Commission had brought infringement proceedings against Germany claiming that Germany had failed to comply with Decision 2014/699[153] by expressing a separate point of view from the position adopted by the European Union, as defined in that decision, and by voting against that position in the Revision Committee of the Organisation for International Carriage by Rail (OTIF).[154] The Court held that complying with such a decision would be 'a specific expression of the requirement of unity in representation of the European Union, arising from the obligation of sincere cooperation'.[155] By doubting the EU's ability to express a position and represent its Member States on the international stage and by distancing itself from the EU's position in a session of the Revision Committee, Germany was found to have 'harmed the effectiveness of the international action of the European Union, as well as the latter's credibility and reputation on the international stage'. The breach was not only the failure to respect Decision 2014/699 itself but also the violation of the duty of sincere cooperation in Article 4(3) TEU.

I have suggested elsewhere that one way to understand the relationship between loyalty and unity relies on the interests of the Union when it acts in pursuance of treaty objectives.[156] Unity vis-a-vis third states and when acting within international organisations is in the interests of the Union because letting internal conflicts play out openly undermines the trust of third parties in the European Union as a capable and autonomous external actor and could ultimately lead to a preference for dealing with the Member States rather than the Union.[157] In that sense, it has been argued that effectiveness would be a central underlying concern when EU loyalty is invoked to orchestrate external actions, bringing together a multitude of international actors and bridging the mismatch between internal competences and

[151] Case C-399/12, *Germany v Council (OIV)*, ECLI:EU:C:2014:2258. See A Thies, 'Shared Competence and the EU Member States' Obligations to Refrain from Unilateral External Action: PFOS and Beyond' in J Diez-Hochleitner et al (eds), *Recent Trends in the Case Law of the Court of Justice of the European Union (2008–2011)* (Madrid, La Ley, 2012) 703, 721.

[152] *Commission v Germany (COTIF II)* (n 114).

[153] Council Decision of 24 June 2014 establishing the position to be adopted on behalf of the European Union at the 25th session of the OTIF Revision Committee as regards certain amendments to the Convention concerning International Carriage by Rail (COTIF) and to the Appendices thereto [2014] OJ L293/26.

[154] At that time, an action for annulment was pending against parts of the Decision, which eventually was rejected. See *Germany v Council (COTIF I)* (n 114).

[155] *Commission v Germany (COTIF II)* (n 114) para 94.

[156] See Klamert, *The Principle of Loyalty in EU Law* (n 86) 190.

[157] See Eckes, *EU Powers Under External Pressure* (n 2) 78.

international rules.[158] The requirement of unity can thus be seen as a cypher for the interests of the Union in coherence in the management of external relations in general and mixed agreements in particular.[159] This would explain why the Court has never made recourse to it in its own right, but always in combination with the duty of cooperation.[160] It would also explain why the unity *topos* did not appear in the *MOX Plant* case, which primarily concerned the protection of the prerogatives of the ECJ and where the Court invoked ex Article 10 EC and 'an obligation of close cooperation'.[161]

4. Conclusions

External relations law is characterised by certain specificities. In general, objectives are much broader in scope and application than with other areas of EU law. International agreements are a much more important legal instrument. Because the field is by definition outward looking, the interests of third states and the rules set up by international organisations matter more. The CFSP is governed by 'specific rules and procedures' concerning voting in the Council, the role of the High Representative, and the jurisdiction of the Court, among others.

All this does not affect whether structural principles apply in this area, but it has an impact on *how* they apply there.

Different from its thrust in other areas, autonomy has been shown not only to shield EU law from other courts and tribunals but also to underpin an expansion of the jurisdiction of the CJEU in matters of the CFSP.

Conferral applies in the CFSP but it looks quite different from any other area of EU law. Competences are of unclear nature, without clear boundaries, and exceedingly functional. This has been illustrated by the example of the sanctions regime, among others. Subsidiarity, while applicable in theory, is not applied in practice and would be difficult to control. Institutional balance is specifically protected under Article 40 TEU, exacerbating the institutional and procedural divisions retained by the Treaty of Lisbon. Also, conferral in other areas of external relations

[158] See Eckes, *EU Powers Under External Pressure* (n 2) 78. See also van Elsuwege and Merket, 'The Role of the Court of Justice' (n 77) 37.

[159] See the link between close cooperation and the coherence and consistency of Union actions and representation in *Commission v Luxembourg (Inland Waterway)* (n 143) para 60. See, for a more narrow perspective on unity as opposed to consistency and coherence, C Hillion, 'Mixity and Coherence in EU External Relations: The Significance of the Duty of Cooperation' in C Hillion and P Koutrakos (eds), *Mixed Agreements Revisited – The EU and its Member States in the World* (Oxford, Hart Publishing, 2010) 87, 114–15.

[160] See Larik, 'Pars Pro Toto' (n 63) 183. See also Opinion of AG Poiares Maduro in *Commission v Sweden (PFOS)*, ECLI:EU:C:2009:589, para 37: '[t]he unity of international representation of the Community and its Member States does not have an independent value; it is merely an expression of the duty of loyal cooperation'.

[161] Case C-459/03, *Commission v Ireland (MOX Plant)*, ECLI:EU:C:2006:345, para 175. See Hillion, 'Mixity and Coherence in EU External Relations' (n 159) 92.

is characterised by a great dynamism such as with the common commercial policy and respectively untypically broad 'umbrella' competences such as for development cooperation and association.

Concerning equality and mutual trust, there is a fundamental difference between the relations between Member States and between Member States and third states. Moreover, direct effect is regularly excluded with international agreements, which arguably could not be done in 'internal' matters.

Since principles that in other areas of EU law ensure unity and uniformity, such as supremacy and the conferral of the jurisdiction of the Court, are less effective or curtailed, the relational side of principles such as loyalty and solidarity is more in focus.[162] They are also important in these areas because the European Union is mandated to be a 'cohesive force' in its relations with the outside world. This makes the EU's 'actorness' a dominant factor in the CFSP, but also in external relations more generally. Thus, loyalty especially has been relied on by the Court prominently and forcefully in the external field in recent years, manifesting itself as a specific requirement of ensuring the unity of international representation of the European Union.

One unifying factor is Article 218 TFEU as the procedural basis for concluding international agreements, also within the CFSP. This allows for some inroads for the jurisdiction of the Court concerning issues of institutional balance, conflicts of legal bases and duties of sincere cooperation when these agreements involve CFSP matters.

[162] Compare also Cremona, 'Structural Principles of External Relations Law' (n 38) 3.

V

Reasoning with Structural Principles

1. Introduction

It has been noted that the Union legal order is a 'legal order based on a framework treaty', 'a mere skeleton of rules'.[1] While there are no general methodical rules on how the gaps in the EU legal order can be filled, principles have always been used for the development of EU law.[2] We have discussed in chapter two how this has been done with those general principles that are now covered by Article 6 of the Treaty on European Union (TEU), which provides for a certain comparative method. We have seen in chapter three, by contrast, that the Court has not relied on any methodology or coherent approach for introducing structural principles.

We will show in the following that, while there is no real methodology in the traditional sense at play, the European Court of Justice (ECJ) employs certain ways of reasoning that could be considered specific to structural principles. This concerns both the introduction of structural principles as well as the reasoning used in applying them. It will be shown that many of the approaches discussed in the following are variations of self-referential reasoning. I will refer to them as (simple) circularity, autopoieses and snowballing.[3] Before that, we will briefly recapitulate why certain approaches are not suitable as an explanation for developments in the present context.

While the following may seem very critical of the Court, it is not being ignored that the Court has a mandate to develop EU law and thus also to develop EU law by introducing and developing structural principles. It is also, in my view, legitimate to treat EU law as a constitutional legal order, which means that there can be and arguably should be overarching, fundamental principles that underpin and inform it. What is done in the following is primarily to lay bare some of the processes that have occurred deliberately or unintentionally to that end.

[1] Opinion of AG Mazák in Case C-411/05, *Palacios de la Villa*, ECLI:EU:C:2007:604, para 85. See also S Weatherill and S Vogenauer, 'Introduction' in S Weatherill and S Vogenauer (eds), *General Principles of Law: European and Comparative Perspectives* (Oxford, Hart Publishing, 2017) 1.

[2] See T Tridimas, *General Principles of EU Law*, 2nd edn (Oxford, Oxford University Press, 2006) 17–18.

[3] The following builds in parts on M Klamert, *The Principle of Loyalty in EU Law* (Oxford, Oxford University Press, 2014) ch 13, and M Klamert, 'The Autonomy of the EU (and of EU Law): Through the Kaleidoscope' (2017) 42 *EL Rev* 815.

2. How the Court Argues with Structural Principles

1. Introduction

I have discussed elsewhere how difficult it is to transplant the civil law methodology on closing gaps by analogy to EU law, mainly because this would require showing that the legislature had not foreseen a certain situation that needs to be addressed by case law.[4] Often, there is no gap in EU law in that sense because the treaty-makers intended for the EU legal order to be incomplete in a certain respect.[5] An analogy then cannot be justified merely because a certain situation is not covered, even if it would be convenient if it were.[6]

With the principles discussed in this book, we can also not speak of a *non-liquet* situation, such as was the issue in *Algera* discussed in chapter three. This case concerned the question of whether orders by the Common Assembly of the European Coal and Steel Community declaring that certain employees are brought within the ambit of the Staff Regulations could be withdrawn only with their consent. The Court held as follows:

> The possibility of withdrawing such measures is a problem of administrative law, which is familiar in the case-law and learned writing of all the countries of the Community, but for the solution of which the Treaty does not contain any rules. Unless the Court is to deny justice it is therefore obliged to solve the problem by reference to the rules acknowledged by the legislation, the learned writing and the case-law of the member countries.[7]

This is not comparable to the constellation that gave rise to state liability, autonomy, or supremacy, as discussed in the following. These principles do not exist because otherwise there could not have been a decision by the Court, but because there would be a less desirable, less 'integrationist' outcome.[8]

2. 'Autonomous' Reasoning

One persistent feature of the way the Court has established and applied structural principles is that any analogies or parallels to international law in particular have been omitted, as has been shown in chapter three. This concerns the principle of autonomy, which is an established legal principle under international law. This

[4] See Klamert, *The Principle of Loyalty in EU Law* (n 3) 258–60.

[5] See K Langenbucher, 'Argument by Analogy in European Law' (1998) 57 *Cambridge Law Journal* 481, 482 with illustrations from German law.

[6] See T Hartley, *Constitutional Problems of the EU* (Oxford, Hart Publishing, 1999) 44–45.

[7] Joined Cases 7/56 & 3/57 to 7/57, *Algera*, ECLI:EU:C:1957:7, para 55. Compare this with the Opinion of AG Lagrange in Case 10/55, *Mirossevich v High Authority*, ECLI:EU:C:1956:9, 346, 348.

[8] See also G Conway, *The Limits of Legal Reasoning and the European Court of Justice* (Cambridge, Cambridge University Press, 2012) 169.

concerns the principle of conferral, which pertains (in other names) to all international organisations. This concerns the principles of loyalty and effectiveness and their international law 'relatives' of good faith and *pacta sunt servanda*. It also concerns supremacy and direct effect, which are among the most important principles in international law.

With all these structural principles, case law has created the impression that they were something genuinely and uniquely European. And it is certainly true; these principles have indeed taken shapes that cannot be compared with how they apply in international law. This is testimony to the uniqueness of the European Union as an international organisation. All these principles have been adopted and transformed to 'fit' the European Union and Union law.

However, it must be noted that by camouflaging the origins of these principles by not engaging with the established international law discourse and often also with its terminology, the transparency and more generally the rationality of the reasoning of the Court regarding these principles was not helped. It might have made it more difficult for the literature to assess these principles. Autonomy also shows that it was not only international law that was not referenced but even ECSC law, where a certain form of autonomy existed years before *Van Gend* and *Costa*.

Thus, it would seem that the ECJ has developed some structural principles in the understanding that they are themselves 'autonomous' concepts, whose contours are defined by the ECJ alone, without requiring recourse to meanings held in national or international law. It can be noted that the Court has not only developed a principle or concept of autonomy of EU law but has also employed an 'autonomous' reasoning for introducing and developing this principle as well as other structural principles. As already argued earlier with the principle of autonomy, this might have been intentional. Situating principles such as autonomy or conferral in an international law background might have complicated the narrative that the European Union is *sui generis* and would therefore not need to follow orthodoxy.

3. Forms of Self-Referential Reasoning with Structural Principles

3.1. Introduction

It has been argued as follows in the literature:

> Negatively, autonomy seeks to define what EU law is not, i.e. it is not ordinary international law. Positively, autonomy seeks to define what EU law is, i.e. a legal order that has the capacity to operate as a self-referential system of norms that is both coherent and complete.[9]

[9] See K Lenaerts, JA Gutiérrez-Fons and S Adam, 'Exploring the Autonomy of the European Union Legal Order' (2021) 81 *Zeitschrift für ausländisches öffentliches Recht und Völkerrecht* 47, 51.

This frames self-reference as something positive because it would ensure the coherence and self-sufficiency of EU law.[10] As will be discussed in chapter six, coherence relates to the concept of legal unity which is an objective for all legal orders. Interpreting and developing legal terms used in one area of EU law by reference to analogue terms used in another area of EU law is therefore good practice and is called systemic interpretation. It is also not to be criticised that gaps in EU law are closed by reference to legal principles already existing within EU law. So, indeed, self-referential reasoning is nothing negative per se.

However, this arguably is not exactly what has happened with the structural principles discussed in this book. In the following, I will try to describe some cases involving structural principles where self-referential reasoning has been taken to another level.

3.2. *Circularity*

In *Pupino*, the Court exported an obligation incumbent on Member States concerning directives in the former first pillar to framework decisions under the former third pillar.[11] The obligation to interpret national law in the light of directives had been based on loyalty and on Article 288 of the Treaty on the Functioning of the European Union (TFEU).[12] The Court argued in *Pupino* that it would be 'difficult for the Union to carry out its task effectively if the principle of loyal cooperation were not also binding in the area of police and judicial cooperation in criminal matters'.[13] This means that loyalty was extended to the former third pillar because otherwise the tasks of the Union under this pillar could not be carried out effectively.

Arguably, there was no real reason to invoke effectiveness in this case. Effectiveness is based on loyalty, as shown earlier, so it could simply have been argued that loyalty applies in the former third pillar (as has later been confirmed by the Treaty of Lisbon). As I have already argued elsewhere:

> Effectiveness in *Pupino* provided a strong and nearly irrefutable rationale, which could be presented as being distinct from both loyalty and indirect effect. With this, criticism that such a strong principle of Union law as loyalty simply was exported to another pillar could be avoided.[14]

[10] See also HP Hestermeyer, 'European Union Law, Autonomy of' in *Max Planck Encyclopedia of Public International Law* (Oxford, Oxford University Press, 2025) para 1: 'Autonomy of EU law refers to EU law constituting a self-referential legal system without normative gaps'.

[11] Case C-105/03, *Pupino*, ECLI:EU:C:2005:386. See M Ross, 'Effectiveness in the European Union Legal Order(s): Beyond Supremacy to Constitutional Proportionality?' (2006) 31 *EL Rev* 476, 483 for the 'export'-metaphor. This 'inter-pillar' transfer of loyalty is validated by the Lisbon Treaty, which applies the former Community loyalty provision to the entire Union law regime.

[12] See also M Klamert, 'Judicial Implementation of Directives and Anticipatory Indirect Effect: Connecting the Dots' (2006) 43 *CML Rev* 1251.

[13] *Pupino* (n 11) para 39.

[14] Klamert, *The Principle of Loyalty in EU Law* (n 3) 273.

The reasoning of the Court in *Pupino* thus was highly self-referential, even circular to use a more negative connotation.

Another example in this respect is the line of arguments the Court has employed in a central case on the principle of autonomy. In Opinion 1/17 on the conclusion of *CETA*, the Court makes the following argument on the autonomy of the EU legal order a multilateral investment tribunal must not have adverse effects on:

> That autonomy, which exists with respect both to the law of the Member States and to international law, stems from the essential characteristics of the European Union and its law. EU law is characterised by the fact that it stems from an independent source of law, namely the Treaties, by its primacy over the laws of the Member States, and by the direct effect of a whole series of provisions that are applicable to their nationals and to the Member States themselves. …
>
> That autonomy accordingly resides in the fact that the Union possesses a constitutional framework that is unique to it.[15]

As we have discussed earlier, some essential characteristics of EU law, such as supremacy and conferral, are also structural principles and have been shaped against the background of the uniqueness of the European Union. In other words, the constitutional framework of the European Union is unique because the European Union itself is deemed unique. In Opinion 1/17, this uniqueness is then invoked to define the principle of autonomy that has been introduced to safeguard these very essential characteristics in the first place. It has been noted that the principle of autonomy of the EU law order would thus be fashioned in the name of the autonomy of the EU legal order, thus showing a circularity exemplary of a systemic understanding of the law.[16]

This recalls an observation that has already been made regarding supremacy and *Costa*. It has been noted that there would be a double logic underlying that judgment: on the one hand, a logic deriving supremacy from the special nature of EU law; on the other hand, the exact converse logic justifying the *sui generis* nature of EU law by its need to have primacy in the Member States.[17]

3.3. Autopoiesis

With state liability, this circularity arguably has been taken one step further. In *Pupino*, two seemingly distinct principles were applied to justify why an obligation imposed on Member States should be applied broadly. By contrast, with state

[15] Opinion 1/17, *CETA*, ECLI:EU:C:2019:341, paras 109–10.

[16] See J van de Beeten, 'On Metaphor and Meaning: The Autonomy of EU Legal Order Through the Lens of Project and System' (2023) 8 *European Papers* 1441, 1455, pointing to P Kahn, *Origins of Order: Project and System in the American Legal Imagination* (New Haven, CT, Yale University Press, 2019), according to whom in a system 'the whole operates as a principle of order at every moment'.

[17] See B de Witte, 'Retour à "Costa" – La primauté du droit communautaire à la lumière du droit international' (1984) *Revue trimestrielle de droit européen* 425, 445.

liability, two seemingly distinct principles were applied to create another seemingly distinct principle. I have called this form of reasoning 'autopoietic'.[18]

Recall that, in *Francovich*, the Court grounded state liability in the *Simmenthal* form of effectiveness, which emphasises the need to ensure the effectiveness of Union law as such. Paragraphs 32–34 of the *Francovich* judgment are only concerned with this form of effectiveness.[19] All these arguments based on effectiveness would entail, according to the Court, 'that the principle whereby a State must be liable for loss and damage caused to individuals as a result of breaches of Community law for which the State can be held responsible is inherent in the system of the Treaty'.[20] Ex Article 5 EEC was also mentioned as a 'further basis' for state liability.[21]

In *Brasserie du Pêcheur*, the Court rephrased this line of reasoning in the following manner:

> In order to determine those conditions, account should first be taken of the principles inherent in the Community legal order which form the basis for State liability, namely, first, the full effectiveness of Community rules and the effective protection of the rights which they confer and, second, the obligation to cooperate imposed on Member States by Article 5 of the Treaty.[22]

It could be argued that the Court here, by sleight of hand, has moulded three self-standing principles of Union law out of one: loyalty gave birth to effectiveness, and effectiveness gave birth to state liability.[23] This means that EU law may not possess the power to assign itself new competences, thus there is no *Kompetenz-Kompetenz*, but it can produce new fundamental/essential/constitutional/structural principles.

As is clear from the example of state liability, this capacity has a lot to do with a certain concept of effectiveness and, by implication, loyalty. Effectiveness in *Francovich* acquired an independent function that no longer seemed to require a reference to the Treaty as an authority. In *Francovich* and *Brasserie du Pêcheur*, the Court unmoored both principles from the Treaty text, lifting the reasoning to a 'fundamental level of *systemic* debate'.[24] It has also been noted that relying on effectiveness in such a manner has 'a self-legitimating aspect, since the seemingly

[18] See Klamert, *The Principle of Loyalty in EU Law* (n 3) 268.

[19] Joined Cases C-6/90 & C-9/90, *Francovich*, ECLI:EU:C:1991:428: 'the provisions of Community law in areas within their jurisdiction must ensure that those rules take full effect'; 'The full effectiveness of Community rules'; 'the full effectiveness of Community rules is subject to prior action on the part of the State'.

[20] *Francovich* (n 19) para 35.

[21] *Francovich* (n 19) para 36.

[22] Joined Cases C-46/93 & C-48/93, *Brasserie du Pêcheur*, ECLI:EU:C:1996:79, para 39. See also Case C-752/18, *Deutsche Umwelthilfe*, ECLI:EU: C:2019:1114, para 54.

[23] See Klamert, 'The Autonomy of the EU (and of EU Law)' (n 3) 815, for an explanation of this shift in reasoning.

[24] See M Lasser, *Judicial Deliberations: A Comparative Analysis of Judicial Transparency and Legitimacy* (Oxford, Oxford University Press, 2009) 210–11.

stable and entrenched nature of effectiveness can compensate or camouflage the novelty of the development which it is invoked to justify'.[25]

However the key here is, as explained earlier in the section on effectiveness, that the Court has not only detached effectiveness and loyalty from the Treaty texts but has also unmoored the normativity of the EU legal order itself by deeming it 'unique' under autonomy, as we have just mentioned.[26] To paraphrase what has been said in the context of national law, autonomy is the stepstone on which to construe a 'self-determined legal order'; it is the 'fundamental rule which autopoietically establishes the normativity of a domestic legal order'.[27] Only this has allowed employing effectiveness in ways that would be unthinkable in other legal orders.

It is submitted that a similar argumentative loop could be seen recently with supremacy. The obligation to interpret national law in accordance with Union directives (indirect effect) respectively with EU law as such was initially based on loyalty and effectiveness, similar to state liability.[28] As discussed in chapter three, loyalty and effectiveness are also rationales that have been invoked to justify the principle of supremacy.[29] According to the Court in *Popławski II*, primacy would now provide the foundation of both the obligation to interpret national law in light of Union law and of state liability.[30] Thus, supremacy was invoked to rationalise obligations (indirect effect, state liability) that were rationalised earlier with the same arguments that have been used to support supremacy (loyalty and effectiveness).

3.4. *Snowballing*

Autonomy has been invoked in EU law at least since *Van Gend en Loos*, as shown earlier. Over the years, in case law spanning from *Kadi* and Opinion 2/13 to Opinion 1/17 and *Rosneft*, it has been applied in a range of different contexts and for different purposes, as also examined earlier. Arguably, the Court has signalled continuity in its case law, while at the same time adapting the original principle to new situations and making different uses of it.[31] This has caused quite some confusion in the literature.[32]

[25] See Ross, 'Beyond Supremacy to Constitutional Proportionality?' (n 11) 481.

[26] *CETA* (n 15) para 110.

[27] See E Cannizzaro, 'Nine Theses on Autonomy: Making Sense of a Controversial Doctrine' (2023) 8 *European Papers* 1317, 1323.

[28] *Francovich* (n 19) para 36; Joined Cases C-397/01 & C-403/01, *Pfeiffer*, ECLI:EU:C:2004:584, para 114; Case C-573/17, *Popławski II*, ECLI:EU:C:2019:530, para 55.

[29] Case C-430/21, *RS (Effet des arrêts d'une cour constitutionnelle)*, ECLI:EU:C:2022:99, para 55.

[30] *Popławski II* (n 28) paras 53–57, on Framework Decisions.

[31] See Klamert, 'The Autonomy of the EU (and of EU Law)' (n 3) 815.

[32] See M-L Öberg, 'Autonomy of the EU Legal Order: A Concept in Need of Revision?' (2020) 26 *European Public Law* 705; P Koutrakos, 'More on autonomy – Opinion 1/17 (CETA)' (2019) 44 *EL Rev* 293, 294: 'autonomy means different things in different contexts'.

With Opinion 2/13, it has been noted that the Court would have 'moved the goalposts and, without expressly admitting it, extended the meaning of the autonomy of EU law'.[33] Specifically concerning autonomy and investment arbitration, it has been noted that the Court has shown a tendency to expanding and merging existing criteria and requirements as well as adding new ones, creating 'an all-encompassing argumentative amalgam'.[34]

This 'method' has been called 'snowballing' and it made it difficult to predict whether and why a certain arrangement adversely affected the autonomy of the EU legal order.[35] At the same time, autonomy has been called 'a functional rather than a formal' concept by the President of the ECJ, suggesting that avoiding such clear definitions might have been intentional.[36]

4. Piling

We have discussed how the Court introduced supremacy in *Costa* and has then 'updated' its rationale in recent years. It has done so by adding arguments to the original rationale in *Costa*, which had essentially relied on what are now Article 4(3) TEU and Article 18 TFEU. In recent case law, it is submitted that two new treaty-based arguments stand out. First, reference was made to Article 19(1) TEU, which would require to ensure the full application of EU law in all Member States.[37] Secondly, compliance with supremacy would also be necessary to ensure respect for the equality of Member States before the Treaties under Article 4(2) TEU.[38] We have discussed both aspects earlier. Arguably, the Court thought that it needed to restate and reinforce the foundation for supremacy, which was under pressure from Poland and Hungary in particular in the context of the rule of law, but also from the German Constitutional Court through its *PSPP* judgment.[39]

It is suggested that the approach taken here could be called 'piling', in a twofold sense. On the one hand, it would express that the Court has literally piled several arguments upon each other, summing up everything it had previously held that

[33] See T Lock, 'The future of the European Union's accession to the European Convention on Human Rights after Opinion 2/13: is it still possible and is it still desirable?' (2015) 11 *European Constitutional Law Review* 239, 243.

[34] See S Mayr, *EU Law and International Law – An Uneasy Relationship? The Case of Investor-State Arbitration* (forthcoming). See also JW van Rossem, 'Pushing Limits: The Principle of Autonomy in the External Relations Case Law of the European Court of Justice' in M Andenas et al (eds), *EU External Action in International Economic Law* (The Hague, Springer, 2020) 35, 46, 50 ff.

[35] See Mayr, *EU Law and International Law* (n 34): 'In brief: autonomy is whatever the Court says it is. This makes it an effective tool, but also unpredictable'.

[36] See Lenaerts, Gutiérrez-Fons and Adam, 'Exploring the Autonomy' (n 9) 47. See also P Koutrakos, 'What is the principle of autonomy really about?' (2018) 43 *EL Rev* 1, 1, describing autonomy as a 'seductively ill-defined principle'.

[37] See *RS (Effet des arrêts d'une cour constitutionnelle)* (n 29) para 54.

[38] See Joined Cases C-357/19 et al, *Euro Box Promotion*, ECLI:EU:C:2021:1034, para 249.

[39] BVerfG, BvR 859/15 et al, *Public Sector Asset Purchase Programme (PSPP)*, ECLI:DE:BVerfG:2020:rs20200505.2bvr085915.

could be useful for rationalising supremacy. On the other hand, the term 'piling' is also used in the construction sector. There it refers to the process of 'inserting structural piles into the ground with the purpose of giving buildings foundational support'. Piling in this sense would generally be required 'when a traditional, shallower foundation doesn't provide enough support to bear the load of a structure'.[40] One might say that the Court inserted metaphorical legal piles to prop up the foundation of the principle of supremacy, for which the original foundations did not provide sufficient support in the face of the backlash from some Member States. Notably, this reasoning is less self-referential than the approaches discussed above. The Court seems to make an effort to ground its arguments more firmly in the Treaties.

We could also see the whole subject of this book as an example of piling. Indeed, as it has been noted, relying on structural principles makes EU law more 'stable', and more 'resilient'.[41] Contestation of the authority of EU law is more difficult when that authority is grounded on several structural 'piles' and when it can additionally be shown that the origins of principles date back to the beginnings of European integration. Thus, recently, as we have discussed in chapter three, the principle of solidarity that has been invoked against unilateralism in the *Premiums for Slaughtering Cows* case of the early 1970s, and has seemingly been forgotten afterwards, has been 'resurrected'. Solidarity has the undeniable benefit of framing the EU's authority in more positive terms than with supremacy/primacy because who could be against more solidarity? It also adds another angle why EU law should be respected, by emphasising 'Commonness' in the sense of common interests, shared burdens and joint obligations that come along with EU membership.

Not all such attempts in case law have been equally convincing. Even though early case law has also mentioned Member State equality in the context of unilateral measures by Member States, equating this concept with what is provided in Article 4(2) TEU would seem to ignore that this provision has a different, more 'sovereignist' background. Re-purposing Article 4(2) TEU by the Court for rationalising supremacy, as discussed in chapter three, runs the risk of undermining one of the already very few structural principles in EU law that are 'Member State-centric'.

3. Conclusions

If structural principles are as important in EU law as we have argued for them to be, it is equally important that we understand how they are established and applied. We have suggested that autonomy has not only been relevant for the safeguarding

[40] See: hertstools.co.uk/what-is-piling/.

[41] L Azoulai, 'Structural Principles in EU Law: Internal and External' in M Cremona (ed), *Structural Principles in EU External Relations Law* (Oxford, Oxford University Press, 2018) 31, 33.

of EU law as it stands, but also for introducing and developing structural principles, thus for the shaping of EU law.

Every legal order is to some extent self-referential, and EU law is no (and should not be an) exception. However, it has been argued, attention should be paid when this self-reference reaches levels that must be considered unorthodox and/or intransparent. We are not saying that decisions such as *Francovich* or Opinion 1/17 are legally defective, but that it is too often unclear what exactly has happened in terms of their rationality. The strength of the network we have shown to exist (chapter three) also depends on the strength of its individual threads. Thus, the standards of reasoning with structural principles should be particularly high in our view, especially when the network-weaving shall serve integrationist, centripetal purposes such as with supremacy.

In the following chapter, we will look at some concepts that are pervasive in EU law but that cannot very well be fitted into the discussion in the previous chapters and therefore merit a separate assessment.

VI

Meta-Principles and Grand Narratives

1. Introduction

In chapter two, we have shown that when we look only at primary law, there does not appear to be a certain hierarchy among the principles discussed in this book. It has, however, been claimed that principles discussed in this book would have an overarching relevance in EU law: that they would be more important than others, being somehow on a higher level than other principles.[1]

The rule of law is a value mentioned in Article 2 of the Treaty on European Union (TEU), as discussed in chapter two, but has in the last years acquired importance in case law that so far exceeds other values. We will therefore explore whether the rule of law should also be considered a structural principle of EU law in its own right.

In chapter two, we have discussed the different conceptions of legal unity that are used in the context of EU law, such as with differentiated integration. In the following, we will show that different, quite specific concepts of unity and uniformity have been invoked in case law again and again. It will be argued that, while unity and uniformity do not qualify as legal principles in the strict sense, they could be seen as 'grand narratives' in and about EU law and its interrelation with national law. While this runs the risk of oversimplification, this perspective can serve as 'a broad, overarching story or metanarrative' that attempts to explain essential elements of EU law.[2]

2. Is there a Hierarchy among Structural Principles?

1. Introduction

The prohibition of discrimination on grounds of nationality has been deemed 'the single most important principle of Community law', 'the leitmotiv'.[3] Citizenship

[1] With fundamental rights, it can be argued that the principle of human dignity underlies and structures all other rights. See P Gragl, 'Die strukturierende Wirkung der Unionsgrundrechte: Dreidimensionalität und Föderalisierung' (2024) *Europarecht*, Special Issue No 1, 89.

[2] See: philonotes.com/2022/11/what-is-grand-narrative.

[3] Opinion of AG Jacobs in Joined Cases C-92/92 & C-326/92, *Phil Collins*, ECLI:EU:C:1993:276, paras 9 and 11.

and non-discrimination have been considered 'meta-principles that shape the application of the more detailed Treaty articles in this area'.[4] In a case of 2019, the following was stated by the Advocate General:

> If it were possible to condense the entire body of EU law into a few commandments, the prohibition of discrimination, in particular discrimination based on nationality, would probably be one of the first.[5]

Ex Article 10 EC (now Article 4(3) TEU) on the duty of sincere cooperation has been called 'the most important and most dynamic single Article in the E.C. Treaty'.[6] It has been argued that a meta-principle of effectiveness underlies and informs most of the EU's general principles, including the principle of sincere cooperation.[7] Primacy and direct effect have been called 'meta-norms'.[8] Solidarity has been considered a 'founding meta-principle of European integration', governing 'the lawfulness, interpretation, and operationalization of the entire body of EU law'.[9] Autonomy has been called the 'most foundational element of the Court's reasoning, ensuring the coherence of its decision-making, its predictability and consistent development of legal principles'.[10]

2. The Picture Emerging So Far

As we have seen in chapter three, all principles discussed are very much intertwined with each other, often even interdependent. Intuitively, there would not seem to be a ranked order between them, as in general, as also mentioned in chapter two, there is no clear order in the way they are presented in the Treaties if they are mentioned there in the first place. It has been noted that the nature of structural principles would not be hierarchic as they would accommodate each other and a principle may be given more weight in one case than in another.[11]

[4] See P Craig, 'The ECJ and ultra vires action: A conceptual analysis' (2011) 48 *CML Rev* 395, 415. For a qualification of 'the ever-closer-Union' principle as a meta-principle of the EU legal order as a whole, which leads to interpretative ambiguities being resolved in favour of European integration, see G Beck, *The Legal Reasoning of the Court of Justice of the EU* (Oxford, Hart Publishing, 2013) 319.

[5] Opinion of AG Wahl in Case C-591/17, *Austria v Germany*, ECLI:EU:C:2019:99, paras 2–3.

[6] See J Temple Lang, 'The Duties of Cooperation of National Authorities and Courts under Article 10 EC: Two More Reflections' (2001) 26 *EL Rev* 84, 85.

[7] See M Ortino, 'A Reading of the EU Constitutional Legal System through the Meta-Principle of Effectiveness' (2016) 52 *Cahiers de droit européen* 91.

[8] See B de Witte, 'The Role of Institutional Principles in the Judicial Development of the European Union Legal Order' in F Snyder (ed), *The Europeanisation of Law: The Legal Effects of European Integration on General Institutional Principles of EU Law* (Oxford, Hart Publishing, 2000) 83, 89.

[9] See V Moreno-Lax, 'Solidarity's Reach: Meaning, Dimensions, and Implications for EU (External) Asylum Policy' (2017) 24 *Maastricht Journal* 740. See also M Ross, 'Solidarity: A New Constitutional, paradigm for the EU?' in M Ross and Y Borgmann-Prebil (eds), *Promoting Solidarity in the European Union* (Oxford, Oxford University Press, 2010) 23.

[10] See D Kukovec, 'Autonomy: The Central Idea of the Reasoning of the Court of Justice' (2023) 8 *European Papers* 1403.

[11] See M Cremona, 'Structural Principles of External Relations Law' in M Cremona (ed), *Structural Principles in EU External Relations Law* (Oxford, Oxford University Press, 2018) 3, 14.

It is submitted that some structural principles are considered more important than others because they are found to be more 'systemic' in the sense of being mentioned more often in primary law, such as solidarity, or having more provisions as their specifications, such as with loyalty and its many *leges speciales*. This would not seem a useful guideline because principles such as primacy or autonomy are not explicitly mentioned in primary law at all.

Autonomy might be considered more important because it describes and explains the European Union and EU law better than other principles capturing or claiming to capture in a single term the nature of the European Union and of EU law, as discussed in chapter three. Thus, it could be argued that, as a descriptor, autonomy is unparalleled among the structural principles. We have also shown in chapters three and five that autonomy is pivotal in shaping the understanding not only of the nature of EU law in general but also, more specifically, of other structural principles.[12] It has been noted that, because autonomy protects these core elements of EU law and requires that they remain unaltered, it would be more 'extreme', more 'existential' than other structural principles.[13] It is certainly true that autonomy has a very broad scope. However, autonomy is at the same time to a lesser or a less clear extent normative and is therefore often dependent on other principles, such as loyalty/sincere cooperation, or provisions such as Article 344 of the Treaty on the Functioning of the European Union (TFEU) for its application. As explained in chapter three, it is also contingent on conferral because conferral ultimately determines what autonomy serves to protect.

Equality is a meta-principle of EU law in the sense that it manifests itself in a variety of permutations and *leges specialis*. This, however, does not appear to assign it a higher rank compared with other principles. Recall, as discussed in chapter three, that some international agreements concluded by the European Union are denied direct effect, and as a consequence individuals subject to these agreements are treated differently from persons subject to other EU agreements where direct effect is not excluded. Moreover, since direct effect is the precondition of supremacy, as also explained in chapter three, this at the same time undermines the principle of supremacy. If equality really were a superior principle in EU law, would this not render this practice illegal? At the same time, we have shown that the prohibition of discrimination based on nationality is an idiosyncratic principle of EU law pervading many areas of EU law and that it also plays a central role for what we have called 'internal substantive autonomy' in chapter three.

I have made the claim for the importance of loyalty elsewhere and it certainly explains certain developments and characteristics of EU law especially well.

[12] Compare JWC Van Rossem, 'The Autonomy of EU Law: More is Less?' in R Wessel and S Blockmans (eds), *Between Autonomy and Dependence: The EU Legal Order under the Influence of International Organisations* (The Hague, Springer, 2013) 13, 14, who argues that forming the premise upon which other structural principles are built does not place autonomy in the same league as these principles.

[13] See N Nic Shuibhne, 'What is the autonomy of EU law, and why does that matter?' (2019) 88 *Nordic Journal of International Law* 9.

However, we have shown in chapter three that it is so closely connected with other structural principles such as conferral and effectiveness in particular that it cannot be considered in isolation. The same applies to solidarity, it is submitted. It has been argued that without Member State solidarity connecting other structural principles they 'would probably be doomed to fail'.[14] Politically, that may be true. Normatively, however, Member State solidarity by itself has been weak and, since very early case law, it has been closely related to equality and loyalty.

Also when we look at supremacy and national constitutional identity, there is no evidence of supremacy being the higher principle. The discussion in chapter three has shown that national constitutional identity so far could not provide for an exemption to supremacy. Nonetheless, it arguably would be difficult to assume therefore that national identity would be subordinated to supremacy as a legal principle. We have seen that the Court has been careful not to directly juxtapose these two principles when applying them.

3. Is Conferral the Most Important Principle?

It is submitted that conferral stands out among the structural principles discussed in this book for a specific reason. It is the structural principle that can most easily be undermined by other structural principles, especially when we consider that conferral also includes the competence of the Court. The reason is that, of all the principles discussed in this book, it is the only one that is conferring powers on the EU (institutions) and setting limits to these powers at the same time. Conferral is equally concerned with what the European Union and its institutions are allowed to do and with what they are *not* allowed to do. By contrast, principles such as loyalty, solidarity, supremacy and effectiveness focus on what the Europen Union can do and on what the *Member States* are not allowed to do. Thus, among all structural principles, conferral is most likely to be 'challenged' and respectively undermined by other, more 'integrationist' principles.

It arguably is for this reason that case law has been clearest in finding that the principle of conferral cannot be qualified by other principles. In the *UPA* case, discussed in chapter three, the Court found that the principle of effective judicial protection (now in subparagraph 2 of Article 19(1) TEU) cannot override the limitations built into Article 263 TFEU on non-privileged applicants.[15] Moreover, the Court noted that while under Article 13(2) TEU the institutions are to practise mutual sincere cooperation, such cooperation must be exercised

[14] See K Lenaerts and S Adam, 'Sink or Swim Together: Solidarity between the Member States as a Foundational Principle of the European Union' in C Barnard, A Łazowski and D Sarmiento (eds), *Pursuit of Legal Harmony in a Turbulent Europe: Essays in Honour of Eleanor Sharpston* (Oxford, Hart Publishing, 2024) 41, 44.

[15] Case C-50/00 P, *UPA*, ECLI:EU:C:2002:462, para 44. See also Case C-263/02 P, *Jégo-Quéré*, ECLI:EU:C:2004:210, para 36.

within the limits of the powers conferred by the Treaties on each institution.[16] This was found in response to a claim by the European Parliament that its involvement was reduced to an advisory role because a directive had falsely been enacted based on a Euratom legal basis instead of a TFEU legal basis. The 'obligation resulting from Article 13(2) TEU is therefore not such as to change those powers', and respectively 'the powers that Parliament and the Council derive from Articles 30 EA and 31 EA cannot be limited or extended, respectively, under the principle of sincere cooperation'.[17] In other words, sincere cooperation does not go so far as to modify the competences conferred by the Treaties on each institution and cannot undermine one EU institution's capacity to exercise its powers to the benefit of another institution.[18]

At the same time, as already mentioned in chapter three, in a case on restrictive measures taken with regard to Venezuela, the Court has interpreted Article 263(4) TFEU in the light of the principles of effective judicial review and the rule of law, finding that a third state should have standing to bring proceedings as a 'legal person' within the meaning of that provision, where the other conditions laid down therein are satisfied.[19] The General Court, by contrast, had conceded that Article 263 TFEU must be interpreted in the light of the right to effective judicial protection, but had held that 'that right cannot have the effect of setting aside those conditions, which are expressly laid down in the TFEU'.[20]

Even with conferral, hence, the picture that emerges is not unequivocal. Recall also, as already explained in chapter three, that the 'power' of conferral (pun intended) has its limits as lack of conferred competence does not insulate from the prohibition of discrimination based on nationality under Article 18 TFEU.

3. Is Rule of Law a Structural Meta-Principle of EU Law?

A lot has been written about the rule of law in previous years and it is not my intention to fully engage with this rich discussion. The rule of law is a value according to Article 2 TEU. However, it has also been referred to as a principle in case law. The second subparagraph of Article 19(1) TEU would require the existence of a tribunal 'previously established by law', which would reflect, inter alia, the 'principle of

[16] Case C-48/14, *Parliament v Council*, ECLI:EU:C:2015:91, paras 57–58. See also Case C-73/14, *ITLOS*, ECLI:EU:C:2015:663, para 84. See RA Wessel, 'General Principles in EU Common Foreign and Security Policy' in KS Ziegler, PJ Neuvonen and V Moreno-Lax (eds), *Research Handbook on General Principles in EU Law: Constructing Legal Orders in Europe* (Cheltenham, Edward Elgar, 2022) 607, 616 with respect to the CFSP.

[17] *Parliament v Council* (n 16) paras 59, 62.

[18] Case C-5/16, *Poland v Parliament and Council*, ECLI:EU:C:2018:483, para 90.

[19] Case C-872/19 P, *Venezuela v Council*, ECLI:EU:C:2021:507, paras 48–50. See P Gragl, 'Rechtstaatlichkeit' in M Klamert (ed), *Europarecht. Jahrbuch 22* (NWV, BWV 2022) 37, 59–60.

[20] Case T-65/18, *Venezuela v Council*, ECLI:EU:T:2019:649. See also Case T-600/15, *PAN Europe*, ECLI:EU:T:2016:601, para 50.

the rule of law'.[21] Thus, with the rule of law, we do not necessarily need to discuss the normative quality of Article 2 TEU to qualify the rule of law (also) as a principle applicable in EU law.

In the literature, it has been called 'a meta principle [that] dictates certain principles rather than being simply channelled and expressed through them'.[22] In an external relations context, the rule of law has been discussed as being a structural principle.[23] Also, judicial protection has been called the meta-norm in the EU judicial architecture.[24]

As discussed in chapter two, there are overlaps between the rule of law and several general principles falling under Article 6 TEU. The Commission has stated that the rule of law would be 'stemming from the common constitutional traditions of all the Member States of the EU',[25] as is the case with Article 6 TEU principles but not with (most) structural principles. Recall that, in *Kadi*, the Court saw the review of Union measures implementing UN Security Council resolutions in the light of fundamental rights in the context of the rule of law.[26] It has referred to *Les Verts*, where the Court has emphasised that the European Union is 'based on the rule of law'.[27] In cases such as *EUPM* and *Bank Refah Kargaran*, discussed in chapter four, the Court invoked Article 2 TEU to stress that 'the European Union is founded, in particular, on the values of equality and the rule of law' and that the 'very existence of effective judicial review designed to ensure compliance with provisions of EU law is inherent in the existence of the rule of law'.[28]

Thus, the principle of effective protection as enshrined in the second subparagraph of Article 19(1) TEU is undoubtedly at the core of the rule of law, also within the European Union. We could stop here and conclude that because we have qualified effective judicial protection (also) as a structural principle as explained in chapter three, the principle of the rule of law is structural as well.

However, the rule of law arguably is a more complex concept and there are further aspects to be considered.[29] The European Commission has suggested that

[21] See, eg, the Grand Chamber in Case C-554/21, *Hann-Invest*, ECLI:EU:C:2024:594, para 55.

[22] See L Pech and J Gorgan (Reconnect), *Meaning and Scope of the EU Rule of Law*, available at: reconnect-europe.eu/wp-content/uploads/2020/05/D7.2-1.pdf, 18.

[23] See I Vianello, 'The Rule of Law as a Relational Principle Structuring the Union's Action Towards its External Partners' in Cremona (ed), *Structural Principles* 225.

[24] See V Roeben, 'Judicial Protection as the Meta-norm in the EU Judicial Architecture' (2020) 12 *Hague Journal on the Rule of Law* 29.

[25] Communication from the Commission to the European Parliament and the Council, A new EU Framework to strengthen the Rule of Law, COM/2014/0158 final, 2.

[26] See Joined Cases C-402/05 P & C-415/05 P, *Kadi*, ECLI:EU:C:2008:461, para 316.

[27] Case 294/83, *Les Verts*, ECLI:EU:C:1986:166, para 23; Case C-2/88 Imm, *Zwartveld*, ECLI:EU:C:1990:440, para 16; Case C-229/05 P, *Oçalan*, ECLI:EU:C:2007:32, para 109; *Kadi* (n 26) para 281.

[28] Case C-455/14 P, *EUPM in Bosnia and Herzegovina*, ECLI:EU:C:2016:569, para 41; Case C-134/19 P, *Bank Refah Kargaran v Council*, ECLI:EU:C:2020:793, para 35. See also Case C-355/04 P, *Segi*, ECLI:EU:C:2007:116, para 51; Opinion 2/13, *ECHR II*, ECLI:EU:C:2014:2454, paras 168 and 169.

[29] Compare M Klamert and D Kochenov, 'Commentary on Article 2 TEU' in M Kellerbauer, M Klamert and J Tomkin (eds), *The EU Treaties and the Charter of Fundamental Rights: A Commentary*, 2nd edn (Oxford, Oxford University Press, 2024) paras 24–29.

adherence to the rule of law would be 'a prerequisite for upholding all rights and *obligations* deriving from the Treaties and from international law'.[30] Similarly, overall compliance by Member States with Union law obligations has been mentioned in this context.[31] According to a report from the Council of Europe, the EU concept of the rule of law would encompass several meanings, including formal notions such as the supremacy of law, but also substantive notions such as respect for fundamental rights and notions specific to EU law, such as fair application of the law and the effective enjoyment of Union law rights.[32] Thus, it is not only the second subparagraph of Article 19(1) TEU that is relevant for the rule of law, but also the first subparagraph, according to which the Court of Justice of the European Union shall ensure that in the interpretation and application of the Treaties 'the law' is observed, and which has now been invoked by the Court in relation to the principle of supremacy as shown in chapter three.[33]

If we consider the rule of law to be more generally concerned with (also systemic) compliance with EU law, the principles of solidarity and loyalty can also be seen in this context.[34] It has also been noted that effectiveness would be 'inextricably linked to the rule of law and the very nature of EU governance through law' and would constitute 'a conditio sine qua non for the functioning of the rule of law and the unity of EU law'.[35] The preliminary ruling procedure provided for in Article 19(3)(b) TEU and Article 267 TFEU would be the keystone of the judicial system within the European Union and be essential to preserving the rule of law.[36] This connects the rule of law also with the uniform application and interpretation of EU law and again with supremacy as discussed below.

Moreover, it has been argued that it can be seen as pertaining to the rule of law if EU law were not applied to all Member States indiscriminately.[37] In a case brought by Poland claiming privileged standing for challenging a measure adopted based on its Accession Treaty, the Court referred to *Kadi* and held that the European Union is 'a union based on the rule of law, its institutions being subject to review of the conformity of their acts, inter alia, with the Treaty and the general principles of law'.[38] The Court continued:

[30] COM/2014/0158 final, 4 (emphasis added).

[31] See Editorial Comments, 'The Rule of Law in the Union, the Rule of Union Law and the Rule of Law by the Union: Three interrelated problems' (2016) 53 *CML Rev* 597.

[32] European Commission for Democracy through Law (Venice Commission), Report on the Rule of Law, Study No 512/2009, CDL-AD(2011)003rev, para 28.

[33] Compare also I Pernice, 'The Autonomy of the EU Legal Order – Fifty Years After Van Gend' in A Tizzano, J Kokott and S Prechal (eds), *50ème Anniversaire de l'arrêt/50th anniversary of the judgment in Van Gend en Loos, 1963–2013* (Luxembourg, Office des publications de l'Union européenne, 2013) 55, 69.

[34] Compare also S Schill and C Krenn, 'Artikel 4 EUV' in E Grabitz, M Hilf and M Nettesheim (eds), *EU-Kommentar* (Munich, Beck, 2023) para 63.

[35] See F Meyer, 'The Rule of Law in the Enforcement of EU Law: Shortcomings and future standards' Jean Monnet Network on EU Law Enforcement Working Paper Series 2023.

[36] *ECHR II* (n 28) para 176; Case C-351/22, *Neves 77 Solutions*, ECLI:EU:C:2024:723, para 52.

[37] See Klamert and Kochenov, 'Commentary on Article 2 TEU' (n 29) para 26.

[38] Case C-336/09 P, *Poland v Commission*, ECLI:EU:C:2012:386, para 36.

> Those principles are the very foundation of that union and compliance with them means, as is now provided for expressly in Article 4(2) EU, that the new Member States are to be treated on the basis of equality with the old Member States.[39]

This seems to imply that respecting the equality of Member States is required because of the rule of law, among others. It has also, in this context, been argued that mutual trust would be closely related to the rule of law in the European Union.[40]

Hence, the rule of law is connected to several structural principles discussed in this book. It could thus indeed be considered a structural meta-principle of EU law, comprising the protection of individual rights, the safeguarding of Member State rights, and ensuring the uniform application and interpretation of EU law. The Court has so far not applied the rule of law in such a broad manner. It also would not seem to be necessary to do so, because there is nothing to be gained from superseding the structural principles mentioned above by one 'super-principle' of the rule of law. This is true especially when the rule of law is already as politically contested a concept as is currently the case in the European Union.

4. Unity and Uniformity: Grand Narratives about EU Law

1. Introduction

I have argued elsewhere that, while unity, integrity and uniformity are relevant for the functioning of any legal order, they are paramount when two (or more) legal orders interact and overlap as is the case with EU law and the legal regimes of the Member States.[41] Recall that it has been argued in the context of international law that the preservation of unity 'in a legal order … is the function of the overarching principles that sustain its normative edifice and keep it together'.[42] However, it has been noted that in international law, the 'constitutional function of interpretation is but weakly developed'.[43] General principles of EU law have been said to create a 'common constitutional space'.[44] Moreover, structural principles would rationalise

[39] *Poland v Commission* (n 38) para 37.

[40] See K Lenaerts, 'La vie après l'avis: Exploring the Principle of Mutual (Yet Not Blind) Trust' (2017) 54 *CML Rev* 805, 808.

[41] See M Klamert, 'Einheit und Fragmentierung im Unionsrecht' (2019) *Europarecht* Special Issue No 2, 133.

[42] See G Abi-Saab, 'Fragmentation or Unification: Some Concluding Remarks' (1999) 31 *New York University Journal of International Law and Policy* 919, 926.

[43] R Kolb, *Theory of International Law* (Oxford, Hart Publishing, 2016) 160.

[44] See JA Gutiérrez-Fons and K Lenaerts, 'The constitutional allocation of powers and general principles of EU law' (2010) 47 *CML Rev* 1629.

'a highly valuable but essentially unstable project'.[45] The potential of general principles to create coherence in the EU law order has also been mentioned.[46]

In the following, we will start by discussing the difference between the concepts of uniformity and unity in relation to EU law by example of the internal market. We will then show that practically all structural principles discussed in this book partake in fostering legal unity. Thus, all principles, in one way or another, relate to the uniform application of EU law. The only exception is the principle of national constitutional identity, which however is firmly embedded in Article 4 TEU that otherwise contains several unity-enhancing provisions, as discussed below.

2. Is it Unity or is it Uniformity?

2.1. Positive Integration in the Internal (and 'External') Market[47]

Different concepts especially of unity have been proposed in the context of the internal market.

It would concern the question of whether only the 'whole' or also parts of the (rules governing the) internal market can be extended to third countries.[48] The unity of the internal market has been understood by some as the substance of the common and complete order of the internal market.[49]

More to the point, the Court has referred to the internal market as an 'economically integrated entity with a single market, based on common rules between its members'.[50] Harmonisation under the common agricultural policy must be exercised 'from the perspective of the unity of the market to the exclusion of any unilateral measures by the Member States'.[51] Directives would aim to prevent damage to the unity of the internal market resulting from unilateral measures by

[45] L Azoulai, 'Structural Principles in EU Law: Internal and External' in Cremona (ed), *Structural Principles* 33.

[46] See PJ Neuvonen and KS Ziegler, 'General principles in the EU legal order: Past, present and future directions' in Ziegler, Neuvonen and Moreno-Lax (eds), *Research Handbook* 7, 23, pointing to the 'inter-legality' approach.

[47] This part is based on M Klamert, 'Supremacy, the Uniformity of EU Law, and the Principle of Equality' (2022) *Austrian Law Journal* 82.

[48] See N Nic Shuibhne, 'The Integrity of the EU Internal Market: Connecting Purpose and Context for Brexit – and Beyond' in F Amtenbrink et al (eds), *The Internal Market and the Future of European Integration: Essays in Honour of Laurence W Gormley* (Cambridge, Cambridge University Press, 2019) 549, 555–57. See also P van Elsuwege, 'Exporting the Internal Market Beyond the EU's Borders: Between Political Ambition and Legal Reality' in F Amtenbrink et al (eds), *The Internal Market and the Future of European Integration: Essays in Honour of Laurence W Gormley* (Cambridge, Cambridge University Press, 2019) 637, 645–46. See also, on this, M-L Öberg, *The Boundaries of the EU Internal Market* (Cambridge, Cambridge University Press, 2020) 32–36.

[49] See R Barents, *The Autonomy of Community Law* (The Hague, Kluwer Law International, 2004) 208; Öberg, *The Boundaries of the EU Internal Market* (n 48) 92–93.

[50] Case C-351/08, *Grimme*, ECLI:EU:C:2009:697, para 27, in the context of the refusal of Switzerland to accede to the EEA.

[51] Joined Cases 80/77 & 81/77, *Commissionaires Réunis and Ramel*, ECLI:EU:C:1978:87, paras 35–36.

Member States.[52] Also in the *Hauer* case, further discussed below, the Court has referred to 'the unity of the Common Market'.[53]

It means that harmonisation measures by the Union specifically do not permit deviations caused by national law of any level unless this is explicitly allowed by the Treaty or by the Union act itself.[54] In this sense, the unity of the market means the uniform application of internal market rules in all Member States. Thus, (re) regulation[55] through harmonisation is very much about the 'uniformity' of EU law in the sense discussed further below.

One can, however, only speak of uniformity with full or maximum harmonisation barring any stricter Member State measures ('gold-plating'). While full harmonisation contributes to the unity of the internal market, minimum harmonising and the stricter standards adopted by Member States within their framework perpetuate or introduce heterogenic rules and thus undermine this unity, as I have argued elsewhere.[56]

The unifying effect of full harmonisation is also extended to the area of fundamental rights. In *Melloni*, the Spanish Constitutional Court had asked the European Court of Justice (ECJ) whether Article 53 of the Charter of Fundamental Rights (CFR) would allow a national constitutional provision to depart from the framework decision on the European arrest warrant.[57] According to Article 53 CFR, nothing in the Charter shall be interpreted as restricting or adversely affecting human rights and fundamental freedoms as recognised, among others, by the Member State constitutions. The Court, after referring to *Simmenthal* and *Winner Wetten*, both discussed in chapter three, replied as follows:

> It is true that Article 53 of the Charter confirms that, where an EU legal act calls for national implementing measures, national authorities and courts remain free to apply national standards of protection of fundamental rights, provided that the level of protection provided for by the Charter, as interpreted by the Court, and the primacy, unity and effectiveness of EU law are not thereby compromised.[58]

This, however, would be the case with Article 4a(1) of Framework Decision 2002/584 because it exhaustively regulates when a Member State may refuse to execute a European arrest warrant.[59] By adding considerations of 'primacy, unity and

[52] Case C-377/98, *Netherlands v Parliament and Council*, ECLI:EU:C:2001:523. See also Case C-359/92, *Germany v Council*, ECLI:EU:C:1994:306, para 37.

[53] Case 44/79, *Hauer*, ECLI:EU:C:1979:290, para 14.

[54] See the derogations in Article 114(4) TFEU. See also Case 14/68, *Walt Wilhelm*, ECLI:EU:C:1969:4, on Article 103(2)(e) TFEU (ex Article 87(2)(e) EEC).

[55] See S Weatherill, *The Internal Market as a Legal Concept* (Oxford, Oxford University Press, 2017) 151–56.

[56] See M Klamert, 'What We Talk About When We Talk About Harmonisation' (2015) 17 *Cambridge Yearbooks of European Legal Studies* 360. See also Meyer, 'The Rule of Law in the Enforcement of EU Law' (n 35).

[57] Case C-399/11, *Melloni*, ECLI:EU:C:2013:107.

[58] *Melloni* (n 57) para 60.

[59] *Melloni* (n 57) para 61.

effectiveness' to the reading of Article 53 CFR, the Court thus cut off any attempts to interpret that provision as allowing exceptions to (fully harmonising) Union law.[60]

Notably, within the framework of the common commercial policy under Article 207 TFEU, thus in the external dimension of the internal market, there is full harmonisation because the only measures foreseen are regulations. The uniformity that is thus inherent in the common commercial policy has been stressed in the literature.[61] The ECJ also appears to have established a link between exclusive Union competence and the unity of the internal market in some external relations cases.[62]

2.2. Negative Integration in the Internal Market

In the context of the competition rules, the Court has sometimes referred to the unity of the internal market in economic terms in the sense that the uniformity of trade conditions would ensure a level playing field for all operators on the market.[63]

In the context of the prohibitions governing the internal market, Articles 34 et seq TFEU have been deemed by the Court to ensure the unity of the (now) internal market.[64] In a case in 1981, where Italy had claimed that before pursuing an action for violation of the free movement of goods, the Commission should have proposed harmonisation, the Court held:

> That argument must be rejected. The fundamental principle of a unified market and its corollary, the free movement of goods, may not under any circumstances be made subject to the condition that there should first be an approximation of national laws for if that condition had to be fulfilled the principle would be reduced to a mere cipher. Moreover, it is apparent that the purposes of Articles 30 and 100 are different. The purpose of Article 30 is, save for certain specific exceptions, to abolish in the immediate future all quantitative restrictions on the imports of goods and all measures having an equivalent effect, whereas the general purpose of Article 100 is, by approximating the laws, regulations and administrative provisions of the Member States, to enable obstacles of whatever kind arising from disparities between them to be reduced. The elimination of quantitative restrictions and measures having an equivalent effect, which is unreservedly affirmed in Article 3 (a) of the Treaty and carried into effect by Article 30, may not therefore be made dependent on measures which, although capable of promoting the free movement of goods, cannot

[60] See J Bering Liisberg, 'Does the EU Charter of Fundamental Rights Threaten the Supremacy of Community Law?' (2001) 38 *CML Rev* 1171, 1181; C Krenn, 'Autonomy and Effectiveness as Common Concerns: A Path to ECHR Accession After Opinion 2/13' (2015) 16 *German Law Journal* 147, 157–58.

[61] See Cremona, 'Structural Principles of External Relations Law' in Cremona (ed), *Structural Principles* 3.

[62] Opinion 1/94, *WTO*, ECLI:EU:C:1994:384, para XIV; See also Case 22/70, *Commission v Council (ERTA)*, ECLI:EU:C:1971:32, para 31.

[63] See *Walt Wilhelm* (n 54) para 5.

[64] Case 51/75, *EMI*, ECLI:EU:C:1976:85, para 11.

> be considered to be a necessary condition for the application of that fundamental principle.[65]

Similarly, in cases such as *France v Commission* of 1988, the Court made the following statement regarding what is now the exception in Article 106 TFEU to the prohibitions in Articles 101 and 102 TFEU:

> In allowing derogations to be made from the general rules of the Treaty on certain conditions, that provision seeks to reconcile the Member States' interest in using certain undertakings, in particular in the public sector, as an instrument of economic or fiscal policy with the Community's interest in ensuring compliance with the rules on competition and the preservation of the unity of the Common Market.[66]

The unity that is referred to here, it is submitted, is not the same as with harmonisation discussed above. It does not mean unity because common rules have been enacted and Member States must respect those rules and not deviate from them. Unity with negative integration arguably has a more economic connotation in that the free movement and the competition rules provide for a level playing field in a unified market.

Prohibitions of discrimination and restrictions under the fundamental freedoms and prohibitions with cartels and the abuse of a dominant position under the competition rules do not establish uniform rules for all market actors. They 'only' prevent Member States (with the fundamental freedoms) and undertakings (with the competition rules) from applying certain harmful national rules and enterpreneural practices. As regards the Member States, they do not prevent 'unilateral measures' and they do not ensure that rules and regulations do not diverge between Member States.[67]

2.3. *Where Unity and Uniformity Converge*

The discussion above shows that Union law might not always require that the laws of and in all Member States are the same. Thus, there is no substantive (material) uniformity in the sense that the *national* rules within the scope of EU law must be uniform at all times. This is not the case with the prohibitions governing the internal market, and it is also not true for minimum harmonisation measures.

What EU law requires, however, is substantive (material) uniformity in the sense that the same *EU* rules must apply in all Member States. Legal unity requires, on the one hand, that Union law is applied uniformly in all Member States and, on the other hand, that the uniform interpretation of Union law in all Member States

[65] Case 193/80, *Commission v Italy*, ECLI:EU:C:1981:298, para 17.

[66] Case C-202/88, *France v Commission*, ECLI:EU:C:1991:120, para 12. See also Case C-660/15, *Viasat Broadcasting*, ECLI:EU:C:2017:178, para 31; Case C-159/94, *Commission v France*, ECLI:EU:C:1997:501, para 55.

[67] Compare M Klamert, *Services Liberalization in the EU and WTO: Concepts, Standards and Regulatory Approaches* (Cambridge, Cambridge University Press, 2014) 283.

is ensured.[68] It is this form of uniformity in the combined application of Union and Member State legal systems that manifests legal unity.[69]

In *Hauer*, on the effects of Union regulations in national law, the Court speaks of the 'substantive unity' of (then) Community law.

> The establishment of special assessment criteria dependent on the legislation or constitutional system of a particular Member State would undermine the substantive unity and effectiveness of Community law and would therefore inevitably result in the destruction of the unity of the common market and jeopardise the cohesion of the Community.[70]

The BVerfG has also acknowledged in its *Lisbon* judgment that 'no effects jeopardising integration should result from the unity of the Community legal order being called into question by different decisions on applicability by the courts of the Member States'.[71]

This does not ignore that these 'values' as they have been called are not absolute and there are many situations 'where the uniform and effective application of Union law must, by necessity but also often for just cause, be compromised during the process of translation into each national legal order'.[72] We have discussed such qualifications to the primacy of EU law in chapter three.

Legal unity in the sense outlined above also applies to the EU's external relations law, whose instruments, be they autonomous or contractual, must be complied with by the Member States just as is the case with internal instruments. However, externally, as discussed in chapter four, unity additionally means that the European Union and the Member States must present themselves and act coherently as a 'cohesive force in international relations', as it is put in Article 24(3) TEU.

Legal unity is also the underlying rationale, it is submitted, for what is sometimes referred to as the 'convergence' or the 'coherence' of Union law and national law. The ECJ has in some instances framed the requirement to interpret Union directives in the light of EU legal principles as predicated by a principle of coherence.[73] In competition law, Article 3(2) of Regulation 1/2003 stipulates that the application of national competition law 'may not lead to the prohibition of agreements, decisions by associations of undertakings or concerted practices

[68] See Klamert, 'Einheit und Fragmentierung im Unionsrecht' (n 41) 133.

[69] See I Pernice, 'Der Europäische Verfassungsverbund und die Netzwerktheorie' (2010) *ZaöRV* 51. On the concept of unity as substantive unity as opposed to formal unity in the context of national law, see D Felix, *Einheit der Rechtsordnung: zur verfassungsrechtlichen Relevanz einer juristischen Argumentationsfigur* (Tübingen, Mohr Siebeck 1998) 162 f.

[70] *Hauer* (n 53) para 14: See also *Melloni* (n 57) para 60; Case C-206/13, *Siragusa*, ECLI:EU:C:2014:126, para 32; Opinion of AG Kokott in Case C-550/07 P, *Akzo Nobel*, ECLI:EU:C:2010:229, para 168.

[71] BVerfG, 2 BvE 2/08 et al, *Lisbon Treaty*, ECLI:DE:BVerfG:2009:es20090630.2bve000208, para 337. But see BVerfG, BvR 859/15 et al, *Public Sector Asset Purchase Programme (PSPP)*, ECLI:DE:BVerfG:2020:rs20200505.2bvr085915.

[72] See M Dougan, 'Primacy and the remedy of disapplication' (2019) 56 *CML Rev* 1459, 1488 with examples.

[73] Case C-499/04, *Werhof*, ECLI:EU:C:2006:168, para 32. See, however, Case C-673/13 P, *PAN Europe*, ECLI:EU:C:2016:889, para 64. Note that it is a different concept of coherence from that mentioned in ch 2.

which may affect trade between Member States' but are allowed under Article 101 TFEU.[74] Under this Regulation, Member States are not precluded from adopting and applying on their territory stricter national laws which prohibit or sanction unilateral conduct engaged in by undertakings. However, agreements that are not compatible with Article 101 TFEU cannot be allowed under national law. All this is about ensuring convergence in the sense of concordant individual decisions at the EU and national level, thus about a certain form of legal unity.[75]

Legal unity is thus manifested in EU law as the uniform application and the uniform interpretation of Union law, including in all Member States. The following discusses the role of structural principles in safeguarding this unity.

3. Uniform Interpretation and Structural Principles

Ensuring unity through uniform *interpretation* involves two aspects. First, an institutional aspect concerning the role of the ECJ. Secondly, it involves a substantive aspect concerning how the ECJ should interpret Union law. Both aspects are governed by several structural principles.

3.1. *The Institutional Side*

As already mentioned in chapter three in the context of autonomy, the preliminary ruling procedure is the keystone of the EU judicial system and aims at 'securing uniform interpretation of EU law'.[76] Similarly, in Opinion 2/13, the ECJ stated that the court system 'serves to ensure consistency and uniformity in the interpretation of EU law', and the preliminary ruling procedure would be a 'key element' in ensuring a uniform interpretation.[77] In *Neves*, the Court made the connection between uniform interpretation and the unity of EU law in the following words:

> That interpretation is borne out by the essential objective of Article 267 TFEU, which is to ensure that EU law is applied uniformly by the national courts and tribunals. Regarding measures of general scope for the Council to implement in a regulation under Article 215 TFEU, differences between courts or tribunals of the Member States as to the interpretation of such a measure of general scope would be liable to jeopardise the very unity of the EU legal order and to undermine the fundamental requirement of legal certainty.[78]

[74] Council Regulation (EC) 1/2003 of 16 December 2002 on the implementation of the rules on competition laid down in Articles 81 and 82 of the Treaty [2003] OJ L1/1.

[75] See Felix, *Einheit* (n 69) 159 ff on unity of the legal system as a requirement for a uniform assessment of unlawfulness.

[76] *ECHR II* (n 28) para 176. See also, eg, Case 166/73, *Rheinmühlen*, ECLI:EU:C:1974:3.

[77] *ECHR II* (n 28) para 174 ff. See K Lenaerts, 'The Unity of European Law and the Overload of the ECJ – The System of Preliminary Rulings Revisited' in I Pernice, C Saunders and J Kokott (eds), *The Future of the European Judicial System in a Comparative Perspective* (Baden-Baden, Nomos, 2011) 211.

[78] *Neves 77 Solutions* (n 36) para 50.

The requirement of uniform application in the Member States goes back to *Van Gend*, in which the ECJ assumed the power to decide on the suitability of a provision of (now) Union law for having direct application.[79] Equally, only the ECJ and not the courts of the Member States have jurisdiction to review the compatibility of EU acts with fundamental rights because allowing national courts to conduct such a review would have an 'adverse effect on the uniformity and efficacy of [Union] law'.[80] In a line of case law on the interpretation of mixed agreements, the ECJ justified the 'centralisation' of the interpretation of provisions in these agreements that can apply both to situations falling within the scope of national law and to situations falling within the scope of Union law with the claim that it 'is clearly in the Community interest that, in order to forestall future differences of interpretation, that provision should be interpreted uniformly, whatever the circumstances in which it is to apply'.[81]

The preliminary ruling procedure thus safeguards the unity of the Union's legal order.[82] On the one hand, this concerns the relation with the Member State courts, which are functional Union courts and whose organisational set-up and procedure is placed under scrutiny by the ECJ as a consequence.[83] On the other hand, safeguarding uniform interpretation means qualifying the ECJ and its jurisdiction as an essential element of Union law that must be protected against 'interference' from competing courts, such as in the *Achmea* constellation, discussed in chapter three.

The institutional side of safeguarding unity in the sense of uniform interpretation thus involves the principle of conferral, because it assigns competence and thus jurisdiction to the ECJ. Supremacy plays a role as well in policing procedural restrictions before national courts, as can be seen in cases such as *Melki*.[84] It also involves the principle of autonomy as the argument used by the Court to protect the integrity of the competences thus conferred.[85] It furthermore involves loyalty, first because the preliminary reference procedure has as such been deemed an expression of the duty of cooperation.[86] Secondly, in the *Dior* case, on the interpretation of Article 50 of the mixed Agreement on Trade-Related Aspects of

[79] Case 26/62, *Van Gend & Loos*, ECLI:EU:C:1963:1, para 3.

[80] Case 11/70, *Internationale Handelsgesellschaft*, ECLI:EU:C:1970:114, para 3. See T Lock, 'Commentary on Article 6 TEU' in Kellerbauer, Klamert and Tomkin (eds), *Commentary*, para 2 with references.

[81] See Case C-53/96, *Hermès*, ECLI:EU:C:1998:292, para 32; Case C-89/99, *Schieving-Nijstad*, ECLI:EU:C:2001:438, para 35.

[82] See Barents, *The Autonomy of Community Law* (n 49) 214.

[83] Case C-216/18 PPU, *LM*, ECLI:EU:C:2018:586; Case C-64/16, *Associação Sindical dos Juízes Portugueses*, ECLI:EU:C:2018:117.

[84] Case 103/88, *Fratelli Costanzo*, ECLI:EU:C:1989:256, para 32; Case C-409/06, *Winner Wetten*, ECLI:EU:C:2010:503, paras 55–57; Joined Cases C-188/10 & 189/10, *Melki and Abdeli*, ECLI:EU:C:2010:363, paras 43–44. See also B Schima and D Eisendle, 'Commentary on Article 267 TFEU' in Kellerbauer, Klamert and Tomkin (eds), *Commentary*, para 31.

[85] See also C Contartese, *The Principle of Autonomy in EU External Relations Law* (Milan, Wolters Kluwer, 2025) ch 4 for the link between unity and institutional autonomy.

[86] See M Klamert, *The Principle of Loyalty in EU Law* (Oxford, Oxford University Press, 2014) 212 with further references.

Intellectual Property Rights (TRIPS), it referred to the 'obligation of close cooperation in fulfilling the commitments undertaken by [the Union and the Member States] under joint competence', for which reason Article 50 TRIPS would have to be interpreted uniformly.[87]

3.2. *The Substantive Side*

The Court held as follows in a range of cases starting with *Ekro* decided in 1984:

> The need for a uniform application of Community law and the principle of equality require that the terms of a provision of Community law which makes no express reference to the law of the Member States for the purpose of determining its meaning and scope must normally be given an independent and uniform interpretation throughout the Community; that interpretation must take into account the context of the provision and the purpose of the relevant regulations.[88]

As already mentioned in chapter three, this involves a different aspect of the principle of autonomy from above, as it is the (substantive) autonomy of EU law vis-a-vis national law that is meant here. While in cases such as *Achmea* the institutional autonomy vis-a-vis competing (arbitration) courts is at issue, there can be no such institutional autonomy with national courts, which are integrated into the EU judicial system as much as possible. Substantive autonomy, by contrast, concerns *how* Union law is to be interpreted, namely in an 'independent' manner as the Court puts it above.

For this, the Court makes two arguments in the quotation above, that have become settled case law. The first seems circular: the need for uniform application of Union law would require its uniform interpretation. Arguably, uniformity is not required for the sake of uniformity alone; rather, the uniform application of Union law in all Member States is paramount for preventing the heterogeneous treatment of natural and legal persons under Union law.[89] This is expressed by the second argument relying on the principle of equality, which has already been discussed in chapter three in the context of the principle of autonomy.

4. Uniform Application and Structural Principles

Ensuring unity through uniform *application* equally involves two aspects. First, an institutional aspect concerning the role of the ECJ, and secondly a substantive

[87] Joined Cases C-300/98 & C-392/98, *Dior*, ECLI:EU:C:2000:688, paras 36-37. See M Klamert, 'Dark matter: Competence, jurisdiction and "the area largely covered by EU law". Comment on *Lesoochranárske*' (2012) 50 *EL Rev* 340.

[88] Case 327/82, *Ekro*, ECLI:EU:C:1984:11, para 11; Case C-287/98, *Linster*, ECLI:EU:C:2000:468, para 43; Case C-388/18, *Finanzamt A*, ECLI:EU:C:2019:642, para 30; Case C-373/00, *Truley*, ECLI:EU:C:2003:110, para 35.

[89] See also FC Mayer, 'Art 18 EUV' in E Grabitz, M Hilf and M Nettesheim (eds), *EU-Kommentar* (Munich, Beck, 2019) para 33.

aspect about what is required from national authorities to that end. Both aspects are again governed by several structural principles.

4.1. The Institutional Side

The Court held that it is 'the jurisdiction of the Court of Justice alone to declare an act of the European Union invalid, and in particular a directive, the purpose of that jurisdiction being to guarantee legal certainty by ensuring that EU law is applied uniformly'.[90] This closes one possible avenue for Member States to unilaterally deny Union law full application in the Member States by claiming that it is not valid.

The other possible avenue of refusing to apply Union law is shut off through supremacy. As discussed in chapter three, supremacy requires all Member State bodies including national courts to give full effect to EU law provisions.[91] Thus, concerning the safeguarding of the uniform application of EU law, it is not only the national courts that are put under obligation as is the case with the preliminary ruling procedure, but *all* authorities of a Member State.

4.2. The Substantive Side

As discussed above, when the Court in *Hauer* refers to substantive unity, this means the uniform application in the Member States (in that case) of regulations. *Hauer* is a case affirming primacy (also over national constitutional law). Uniform application is therefore primarily safeguarded by the principle of supremacy, and thereby also by all principles that have been invoked to rationalise supremacy such as effectiveness, Member State equality and solidarity.

As discussed in chapter three, the principle of loyalty has been one justification for primacy, both in *Costa* and then in *RS* as well as in the *Simmenthal* line of case law.[92] The latter role of loyalty represented also especially by the *Winner Wetten* case has moved some in the (German) literature to speak of a 'principle of uniform application' that would derive from Article 4(3) TEU.[93] Similarly, as discussed earlier in the part on effectiveness in chapter three, important voices in the literature have spoken of a 'principle of uniformity derived from procedural elements (e.g. article 177) and substantive elements (e.g. article 5) in the Treaty'.[94]

[90] *Melki and Abdeli* (n 84) para 54 with further references.

[91] Case C-573/17, *Popławski II*, ECLI:EU:C:2019:530, paras 53–54, referring to *Melloni* (n 57) para 59, and Case C-378/17, *An Garda Síochána*, ECLI:EU:C:2018:979, point 39.

[92] See *Winner Wetten* (n 84) para 55; Case -C-308/19, *Whiteland Import Export*, ECLI:EU:C:2021:47, para 31; Case C-430/21, *RS (Effet des arrêts d'une cour constitutionnelle)*, ECLI:EU:C:2022:99, para 55.

[93] See, eg, A Hatje, 'Art. 4 TEU' in J Schwarze (ed), *EU-Kommentar*, 4th edn (Baden-Baden, Nomos, 2019) paras 33 f, 44 ff. Compare M Klamert, 'Commentary on Article 4 TEU' in Kellerbauer, Klamert and Tomkin (eds), *Commentary*, para 69 with further references.

[94] See M Cappelletti, M Seccombe and JHH Weiler, 'Integration Through Law: Europe and the American Federal Experience. A General Introduction' in M Cappelletti, M Seccombe and JHH Weiler

I would hesitate to speak of a 'principle' of uniformity without explaining which normative implications such qualification would entail.[95] I would also not locate it solely in Article 4(3) TEU because uniformity, as discussed, means supremacy in particular, and supremacy is not only based on Article 4(3) TEU, as shown. While it is true that the preliminary reference procedure and Article 4(3) TEU play central roles in ensuring uniformity, the former's role is especially prominent in ensuring uniform *interpretation*. Recall that the Court in *Simmenthal* rationalised the duty to disapply national law also with 'the structure of Article 177 of the Treaty', whose effectiveness 'would be impaired if the national court were prevented from forthwith applying Community law in accordance with the decision or the case-law of the Court'.[96] However, Member State courts will less often make preliminary references doubting the validity of a provision of Union law. For uniform *application*, therefore, the duties of national courts and other authorities to apply Union law in cases before them is arguably the more impactful obligation.

Effectiveness, as mentioned, has been used to rationalise supremacy. Besides, its relevance for ensuring the uniform application of EU law is arguably more nuanced. The enforcement (even) of (directly effective) EU law mostly depends on the Member States.[97] While, under the *Rewe* and *Simmenthal* strands of case law, Member States must ensure that directly effective Union law is *actually* effective within the national legal order, this does not specify how exactly this effectiveness should be realised, thus opening the door for non-uniform applications of Union law in the Member States.

5. Unity as an Inherent Feature of EU Law

It has been claimed that unity is 'inherent' in what is now Union law.[98] While it is true that legal unity is required for any legal order as discussed above, this cannot be so easily transferred to the European Union when unity should also refer to the 'compound' unity involving the Member States. Such a view would inevitably lead to the conclusion that all the instruments and principles that safeguard this uniformity are also inherent in Union law and their existence and application would thus not require further justification.

By this logic, the Court could have simply stated that primacy is inherent in EU law and would not have to bother with the elaborate rationales it put forward, as

(eds) *Integration Through Law: Europe and the American Federal Experience*, Vol I (Berlin, de Gruyter, 1986) 3, 30.

[95] Compare also M Nettesheim, 'Grundsatz der Wirksamkeit des Gemeinschaftsrechts' in A Randelzhofer, R Scholz and D Wilke (eds), *Gedächtnisschrift für Eberhard Grabitz* (Munich, Beck, 1995) 447, 463–65.

[96] Case 106/77, *Simmenthal II*, ECLI:EU:C:1978:49, paras 19–20.

[97] See Meyer, 'The Rule of Law in the Enforcement of EU Law' (n 35).

[98] See Barents, *The Autonomy of Community Law* (n 49) 214.

discussed earlier. The Court has so far 'merely' qualified loyalty and effectiveness (and state liability) as being inherent in Union law, as discussed in chapters three and five. In the light of their roles for rationalising supremacy, it might seem only a small step to also consider supremacy as being inherent in Union law

However, it is submitted that the Court has been well advised not to argue in such a manner. Legal unity is a very unprecise and very theoretical concept. It should in my opinion not be considered a distinct, self-standing principle of Union law. It has its relevance as an explanatory (meta-)narrative, but arguably cannot substitute for a more norm-based and principles-based rationale.

6. Conclusions

We have argued in this chapter that none of the structural principles discussed in this book can claim to be more important than the others, including the principle of conferral. Autonomy might be a better descriptor for the nature of the European Union and of EU law, but other principles seem stronger normatively. The central importance of 'structural' equality, thus of the prohibition of discrimination based on nationality and Member State equality, should also not be underestimated.

We have shown that the rule of law is connected with structural principles in a number of ways beyond its more obvious link to effective judicial protection. Nothing, however, it has been submitted would be gained by also considering the rule of law a(nother) structural principle.

It has also been discussed that all structural principles (except national constitutional identity) contribute to the substantive unity of the Union legal order. This substantive unity is expressed through the uniform *interpretation* as well as the uniform *application* of EU law. Unity and uniformity are useful narratives explaining several key elements of the Union legal order. They can equally be seen as fortifications, being concepts that further support the interwoven requirements set up by the network of structural principles. However, we have submitted that they should not be considered legal (structural) principles in their own right.

Final Remarks

The structural principles discussed in this book have not been developed in a vacuum. Most structural principles have their roots in public international law. To say therefore that EU law is not unique, however, would be wrong. We have shown that all structural principles, such as conferral and loyalty, have either been framed very specifically in the founding Treaties, or have been transformed more or less radically by the European Court of Justice (ECJ). Charting this combined Otherness of EU law helps us to understand how far the European Union and its legal order have evolved compared with international organisations under public international law.

Structural principles are all intertwined and connected to actually create a network of structural principles or a 'structured network of principles' as put by the ECJ. While this network-weaving can often trace its foundations to early case law, the Court of Justice has, since the Treaty of Lisbon, been very much engaged in pushing the story that EU law is built on several foundational principles that are all connected with each other and are also linked especially to the EU's values. Autonomy has been shown to have taken on a function as a descriptor for the uniqueness the European Union is claimed to represent. While we do see that point and think that such characterisation is not only politically but also legally sound, we have shown that this endeavour of network-weaving has come with some techniques that could be considered more self-referential than would be common in international or national law.

It is not our intention to give answers to the question of whether the European Union has a constitution, is a (federal) state, or has remained an international organisation. However, it has been shown that, should one subscribe to a constitutional view of the European Union and EU law, it would be suitable to think about and discuss EU law in terms of its structural principles. Discussion in the literature has often suffered from the fact that these principles are not only heterogeneous themselves but, more importantly, and to a much greater degree, differ in many ways from general principles under Article 6 of the Treaty on European Union. Trying to theoretise all these disparate principles is futile in our opinion. We have shown that even when focusing on the principles in this book, this is not an easy task.

While structural principles do not always operate in the same manner internally and externally, their overarching and encompassing application is evidence of the existence of an 'internally' unified EU legal order. This includes the Common Foreign and Security Policy, where instruments and jurisdiction are still different, but structural principles *do* apply. We have also seen that structural principles individually and in combination contribute to the legal unity of EU law and to its uniformity in both interpretation and application. While in international law, legal unity is an aspiration and uniformity is elusive, structural principles thus bring the European Union and its law closer to national law regimes, to which such unity come much more naturally.

We therefore suggest rethinking how we look at the European Union, as an (international/supranational) *organisation* defined by its history of integration, its organs and its rule-making capacity, or as a (mature) legal *order* defined by its values, its objectives and its network of structural principles.

BIBLIOGRAPHY

Abi-Saab, G, 'Fragmentation or Unification: Some Concluding Remarks' (1999) 31 *New York University Journal of International Law and Politics* 919–33.

Accetto, M and Zleptning, S, 'The Principle of Effectiveness: Rethinking its Role in Community Law' (2005) 11 *European Public Law* 375–403.

Alexy, R, 'Zur Struktur der Rechtsprinzipien' in B Schilcher, P Koller and B-C Funk (eds), *Regeln, Prinzipien und Elemente im System des Rechts* (Vienna, Verlag Österreich, 2000) 31–52.

—— 'Formal principles: Some replies to critics' (2014) 12 *International Journal of Constitutional Law* 511–24.

Alvarez, JE, *International Organisations as Law-makers* (Oxford, Oxford University Press, 2005).

Andenas, M et al (eds), *General Principles of Law and the Coherence of International Law* (Leiden, Brill, 2019).

Arena, A, 'The Twin Doctrines of Primacy and Pre-emption' in R Schütze and T Tridimas (eds), *Oxford Principles of the European Union. Volume I: The European Union Legal Order* (Oxford, Oxford University Press, 2018) 300–49.

Arnold, R and Klamert, M, 'Außenhandelsrecht, K I. Grundlagen' in M Dauses and M Ludwigs (eds), *Handbuch des EU Wirtschaftsrechts* (Munich, Beck, 2020).

Arnull, A, 'The Principle of Effective Judicial Protection in EU Law: An Unruly Horse?' (2011) 36 *EL Rev* 51–70.

—— 'Remedies Before National Courts' in R Schütze and T Tridimas (eds), *Oxford Principles of European Union Law: The European Union Legal Order: Volume I* (Oxford, Oxford University Press, 2018) 1011–39.

Aust, A, 'Pacta Sunt Servanda' in *Max Planck Encyclopedia of Public International Law* (Oxford, Oxford University Press, 2013).

Avbelj, M, 'Supremacy or Primacy of EU Law – (Why) Does it Matter?' (2011) 17 *European Law Journal* 744–63.

Azoulai, L, 'Introduction: The Question of Competence' in L Azoulai (ed), *The Question of Competence in the European Union* (Oxford, Oxford University Press, 2014) 1–18.

—— 'Structural Principles in EU Law: Internal and External' in M Cremona (ed), *Structural Principles in EU External Relations Law* (Oxford, Oxford University Press, 2018) 31–46.

Baquero Cruz, J, *What's Left of the Law of Integration? Decay and Resistance in European Union Law* (Oxford, Oxford University Press, 2018).

Barents, R, *The Autonomy of Community Law* (The Hague, Kluwer Law International, 2004).

Basedow, J, 'General Principles of European Private Law and Interest Analysis: Some Reflections in the Light of Mangold and Audiolux' (2016) 24 *European Review of Private Law* 331–51.

—— *EU Private Law: Anatomy of a Growing Legal Order* (Cambridge, Intersentia, 2021).

—— Basedow, J et al, 'European Integration – Quo Vadis? A critical commentary on the ECB judgment of the German Federal Constitutional Court of 5 May 2020' (2021) 19 *ICON* 1–20.

Bassiouni, MC, 'A Functional Approach to "General Principles of International Law"' (1990) 11 *Michigan Journal of International Law* 768–818.

Bast, J and von Bogdandy, A, 'The constitutional core of the Union: On the CJEU's new, principled constitutionalism' (2024) 61 *CML Rev* 1471–1500.

Beck, G, *The Legal Reasoning of the Court of Justice of the EU* (Oxford, Hart Publishing, 2013).

Bélanger, ME, 'Europeanization as a Foundation of the European Construction' in R Coman, T Kostera and L Tomini (eds), *Europeanization and European Integration* (London, Palgrave Macmillan, 2014) 29–49.

Bell, M, 'The Principle of Equal Treatment: Widening and Deepening' in P Craig and G de Búrca (eds), *The Evolution of EU Law*, 2nd edn (Oxford, Oxford University Press, 2011) 611–39.

Bengoetxea, J, 'Is Direct Effect a General Principle of European Law?' in U Bernitz, J Nergelius and C Cardner (eds), *General Principles of EC Law in a Process of Development* (The Hague, Kluwer, 2008) 3–25.

—— 'General Legal Principles Navigating Space and Time' in U Bernitz, X Groussot and F Schulyok (eds), *General Principles of EU law and European Private Law* (The Hague, Kluwer Law, 2013) 45–64.

Benvenisti, E, 'The Conception of International Law as a Legal System' (2007) 50 *German Yearbook of International Law* 393–406.

Bering Liisberg, J, 'Does the EU Charter of Fundamental Rights Threaten the Supremacy of Community Law?' (2001) 38 *CML Rev* 1171–99.

Bertrand, B, 'Retour sur un classique: quelques remarques sur catégorie des principes généraux du droit de l'Union européenne' (2013) 29 *Revue française de droit administratif* 1217–30.

Besson, S, 'Sovereignty' in *Max Planck Encyclopedia of Public International Law* (Oxford, Oxford University Press, 2011).

Bingham, T, *The Rule of Law* (London, Allen Lane 2010).

Biondi, A, Dagilytė, E and Küçük, E (eds), *Solidarity in EU Law: Legal Principle in the Making* (Cheltenham, Elgar Publishing, 2018).

Bjorge, E, 'General Principles of Law Formed Within The International Legal System' (2023) 72 *ICLQ* 845–67.

Blokker, N, 'International Organisations and its Members' (2004) 1 *International Organisations Law Review* 139–61.

—— 'International Organizations or Institutions, Implied Powers' in *Max Planck Encyclopedia of Public International Law* (Oxford, Oxford University Press, 2021).

Bobek, M, 'The Effects of EU Law in the Legal Systems' in C Barnard and S Peers, *European Union Law*, 4th edn (Oxford, Oxford University Press, 2023) 140–73.

Bohme, B, 'The Future of the Energy Charter Treaty after Moldova v. Komstroy' (2022) 59 *CML Rev* 853–70.

Bosse-Platière, I, 'L'application du principe de subsidiarité dans le cadre de l'action extérieure de l'Union européenne' in E Neframi and M Gatti (eds), *Constitutional Issues of EU External Relations Law* (Baden-Baden, Nomos, 2018) 111–36.

Bosse-Platière, I and Cremona, M, 'Facultative Mixity in the Light of the Principle of Subsidiarity' in M Chamon and I Govare (eds), *EU External Relations Post-Lisbon: The Law and Practice of Facultative Mixity* (Oxford, Hart Publishing, 2020) 48–85.

Bradley, KStC, 'Legislating in the European Union' in C Barnard and S Peers (eds), *European Union Law*, 4th edn (Oxford, Oxford University Press, 2023) 100–53.

Breitler, C, 'Die unmittelbare Wirkung des Verhältnismäßigkeitsgrundsatzes zwischen Rechtsanwendung und Rechtsetzung' (2023) *Europarecht* 270–95.

Bruggeman, R and Larik, J, 'The Elusive Contours of Constitutional Identity: Taricco as a Missed Opportunity' (2020) 35 *Utrecht Journal of International and European Law* 20–34.

Burley, W and Matti, A-M, 'Europe Before the Court: A Political Theory of Legal Integration' (1993) 47 *International Organization* 41–76.

Butler, G, *Constitutional Law of the EU's Common Foreign and Security Policy* (Oxford, Hart Publishing, 2021).

Calliess C, 'Art 1 EUV' in C Calliess and M Ruffert (eds), *EUV/AEUV*, 6th edn (Munich, Beck, 2022).

—— 'Art 4 EUV' in C Calliess and M Ruffert (eds), *EUV/AEUV*, 6th edn (Munich, Beck, 2022).

—— 'Art 13 EUV' in C Calliess and M Ruffert (eds), *EUV/AEUV*, 6th edn (Munich, Beck, 2022).

Cannizzaro, E, 'Nine Theses on Autonomy: Making Sense of a Controversial Doctrine' (2023) 8 *European Papers* 1317–31.

Cappelletti, M, Seccombe, M and Weiler, J, 'Integration Through Law: Europe and the American Federal Experience. A General Introduction' in M Cappelletti, M Seccombe and J Weiler (eds), *Integration Through Law: Europe and the American Federal Experience*, Vol I (Berlin, de Gruyter, 1986) 3–68.

Casolari, F, 'Loyalty after Lisbon: An Expectation Gap to Be Filled?' in LS Rossi and F Casolari (eds), *The Principle of Equality in EU Law* (New York, Springer, 2017) 93–133.

—— 'The Acknowledgment of the Direct Effect of EU International Agreements: Does Legal Equality Still Matter?' in LS Rossi and F Casolari (eds), *The Principle of Equality in EU Law* (New York, Springer, 2017) 83–129.

Castellarin, E, 'General Principles of European Union Law and General International Law' in M Andenas, M Fitzmaurice A Tanzi and J Wouters (eds), *General Principles of Law and the Coherence of International Law* (Leiden, Brill, 2019) 131–48.

Chalmers, D et al, *European Union Law: Text and Materials*, 5th edn (Cambridge, Cambridge University Press, 2024).

Chamon, M, 'The Institutional Balance, an Ill-Fated Principle of EU Law?' (2015) 21 *European Public Law* 371–91.

—— 'Constitutional Limits to the Political Choice for Mixity' in E Neframi and M Gatti (eds), *Constitutional Issues of EU External Relations Law* (Baden-Baden, Nomos, 2018) 137–65.

Chiti, E, 'Enforcement of and Compliance with Structural Principles' in M Cremona (ed), *Structural Principles in EU External Relations Law* (Oxford, Oxford University Press, 2018) 47–68.

Claes, M, 'Negotiating Constitutional Identity or Whose Identity is it Anyway?' in M Claes et al (eds), *Constitutional Conversations in Europe: Actors, Topics and Procedures* (Cambridge, Intersentia, 2012) 205–34.

—— 'Primacy of EU Law in European and National Law' in A Arnull and D Chalmers (eds), *The Oxford Handbook of European Union Law* (Oxford, Oxford University Press, 2015) 178–211.

—— 'The equality of the Member States' in KS Ziegler, PJ Neuvonen and V Moreno-Lax (eds), *Research Handbook on General Principles in EU Law: Constructing Legal Orders in Europe* (Cheltenham, Edward Elgar, 2022) 99–117.

Cloots, E, 'The European Court of Justice and Member State Federalism: Balancing or Categorisation?' in E Cloots, G de Baere and S Scottiaux (eds), *Federalism in the European Union* (Oxford, Hart Publishing, 2012) 322–61.

—— *National Identity in EU Law* (Oxford, Oxford University Press, 2015).

Collins, R and White, N, 'International Organizations and the Idea of Autonomy: Introduction and Overview' in R Collins and N White (eds), *International Organizations and the Idea of Autonomy* (London, Routledge, 2011) 1–20.

Constantinesco, V, 'L'article CEE de la bonne foi à la loyauté communautaire' in F Capotorti et al (eds), *Du Droit International au Droit de l'Intégration: Liber Amicorum Pierre Pescatore* (Baden-Baden, Nomos, 1987) 97–114.

Contartese, C, 'The autonomy of the EU legal order in the ECJ's external relations Case law: From the "essential" to the "specific characteristics" of the Union and back again' (2017) 54 *CML Rev* 1627–71.

—— The *Principle of Autonomy in EU External Relations Law* (Milan, Wolters Kluwer, 2025).

Conway, G, *The Limits of Legal Reasoning and the European Court of Justice* (Cambridge, Cambridge University Press, 2012).

Craig, P, 'Competence: Clarity, Conferral, Containment and Consideration' (2004) 29 *EL Rev* 323–44.

—— 'The ECJ and ultra vires action: A conceptual analysis' (2011) 48 *CML Rev* 395–437.

—— 'General principles of law: treaty, historical, and normative foundations' in KS Ziegler, PJ Neuvonen and V Moreno-Lax (eds), *Research Handbook on General Principles in EU Law: Constructing Legal Orders in Europe* (Cheltenham, Edward Elgar, 2022) 25–35.

Craig, P and de Búrca, G, *EU Law: Text, Cases, and Materials*, 7th edn (Oxford, Oxford University Press 2021).

Crawford, J, *Brownlie's Principles of Public International Law*, 9th edn (Oxford, Oxford University Press, 2019).

Cremona, M, 'Neutrality or discrimination? The WTO, the EU and External Trade' in G de Búrca and J Scott (eds), *The EU and the WTO: Legal and Constitutional Issues* (Oxford, Hart Publishing, 2002) 151–84.

—— 'Defending the Community Interest: The Duties of Cooperation and Compliance' in M Cremona and B de Witte (eds), *EU Foreign Relations Law: Constitutional Fundamentals* (Oxford, Hart Publishing, 2008) 125–69.

—— 'Defining competence in EU external relations: Lessons from the Treaty reform process' in A Dashwood and M Maresceau (eds), *Law and Practice of EU external Relations: Salient Features of a Changing Landscape* (Cambridge, Cambridge University Press 2008) 34–69.
—— *Structural Principles in EU External Relations Law* (Oxford, Oxford University Press, 2018).
—— 'Structural Principles of External Relations Law' in M Cremona (ed.), *Structural Principles in EU External Relations Law* (Oxford, Oxford University Press, 2018) 3–30.
—— 'The principle of conferral and express and implied external competences' in E Neframi and M Gatti (eds), *Constitutional Issues of EU External Relations Law* (Baden-Baden, Nomos, 2018) 29–62.
D'Aspremont, J, 'The multifaceted concept of the autonomy of international organizations and international legal discourse' in R Collins and N White (eds), *International Organizations and the Idea of Autonomy* (London, Routledge, 2011) 63–86.
Daiber, B, 'Neue Hürden für den EU-Beitritt zur EMRK?' (2021) *Europarecht* 596–613.
Dashwood, A, 'Article 26 ECT and intra-EU disputes – the Case against an expansive reading of Achmea' (2021) 46 *EL Rev* 415–34.
Dashwood, A et al, *Wyatt and Dashwood's European Union Law*, 6th edn (Oxford, Hart Publishing, 2011).
De Baere, G, *Constitutional Principles of EU External Relations* (Oxford, Oxford University Press, 2008).
—— 'Subsidiarity as a Structural Principle Governing the Use of EU External Competences' in M Cremona (ed), *Structural Principles in EU External Relations Law* (Oxford, Oxford University Press, 2018) 93–116.
De Baere, G and Roes, T, 'EU Loyalty as Good Faith' (2015) 64 *ICLQ* 829–74.
De Búrca, G and Scott, J (eds), *Constitutional Change in the EU: From Uniformity to Flexibility?* (Oxford, Hart Publishing, 2000).
De Witte, B, 'Retour à "Costa" – La primauté du droit communautaire à la lumière du droit international' (1984) *Revue trimestrielle de droit européen* 425–54.
—— 'The Role of Institutional Principles in the Judicial Development of the European Union Legal Order' in F Snyder (ed), *The Europeanisation of Law: The Legal Effects of European Integration on General Institutional Principles of EU Law* (Oxford, Hart Publishing, 2000) 83–100.
—— 'European Union Law: How Autonomous is its Legal Order?' (2010) 65 *Zeitschrift fur Offentliches Recht (ZoR): Journal of Public Law* 141–55.
—— 'Direct Effect, Primacy, and the Nature of the Legal Order' in P Craig and G de Búrca (eds), *The Evolution of EU Law*, 2nd edn (Oxford, Oxford University Press, 2011) 323–62.
—— 'Sources and the subjects of international law' in S Besson and J D'Aspremont (eds), *The Oxford Handbook on The Sources of International Law* (Oxford, Oxford University Press, 2017) 769–86.
—— 'Exclusive Member State Competences – Is There Such a Thing?' in S Garben and I Govaere (eds), *The Division of Competences between the EU and the Member States: Reflections on the Past, the Present and the Future* (Oxford, Hart Publishing, 2017) 59–73.
—— 'An undivided Union? Differentiated integration in post-Brexit times' (2018) 55 *CML Rev* 227–49.
—— 'Structure and Evolution of Union Law' in PJ Kuijper et al (eds), *The Law of the European Union*, 5th edn (The Hague, Kluwer Law International, 2018) 43–67.
—— 'The Relative Autonomy of the European Union's Fundamental Rights Regime' (2019) 88 *Nordic Journal of International Law* 65–85.
—— 'Article 4(2) TEU as a Protection of the Institutional Diversity of the Member States' (2021) 27 *European Public Law* 559–70.
Dehousse, R, *The European Court of Justice: The Politics of Judicial Integration* (New York, Springer, 1998).
Delgado Casteleiro, A, 'Loyalty in External Relations Law: The Fabric of Competence, Autonomy and Institutional Balance' in in E Neframi and M Gatti (eds), *Constitutional Issues of EU External Relations Law* (Baden-Baden, Nomos, 2018) 385–408.
Delgado Casteleiro, A and Larik, J, 'The Duty to Remain Silent: Limitless Loyalty in EU External Relations?' (2011) 36 *EL Rev* 524–41.
Delledonne, G and Fabbrini, F, 'The Founding Myth of European Human Rights Law: Revisiting the Role of National Courts in the Rise of EU Human Rights Jurisprudence' (2019) 44 *EL Rev* 178–95.

Demkova, S and Hofmann, H, 'General principles of procedural justice' in KS Ziegler, PJ Neuvonen and V Moreno-Lax (eds), *Research Handbook on General Principles in EU Law: Constructing Legal Orders in Europe* (Cheltenham, Edward Elgar, 2022) 209–26.

Dobbs, M, 'Sovereignty, Article 4(2) TEU and the Respect of National Identities: Swinging the Balance of Power in Favour of the Member States?' (2014) 33 *Yearbook of European Law* 298–334.

Dougan, M, 'Primacy and the remedy of disapplication' (2019) 56 *CML Rev* 1459–1508.

—— 'The Primacy of Union Law over Incompatible National Measures: Beyond Disapplication and Towards a Remedy of Nullity?' (2022) 59 *CML Rev* 1301–32.

Dreier, H, 'Einheit und Vielfalt der Verfassungsordnungen im Bundesstaat' in K Schmidt (ed), *Vielfalt des Rechts – Einheit der Rechtsordnung? Hamburger Ringvorlesung* (Berlin, Duncker & Humblot, 1994) 113–46.

Dworkin, R, 'The Model of Rules' (1967) 35 *University of Chicago Law Review* 14–46.

—— *Taking Rights Seriously*, 2nd edn (Cambridge, MA, Harvard University Press, 1978).

Eckes, C, *EU Powers Under External Pressure: How the EU's External Actions Alter its Internal Structures* (Oxford, Oxford University Press, 2019).

—— 'Some Reflections on Achmea's Broader Consequences for Investment Arbitration' (2019) 4 *European Papers* 79–97.

—— 'The Autonomy of the EU Legal Order: The Case of the Energy Charter Treaty' (2023) 8 European Papers 1465–95.

Editorial Comments, 'The Rule of Law in the Union, the Rule of Union Law and the Rule of Law by the Union: Three interrelated problems' (2016) 53 *CML Rev* 597–605.

Eleftheriadis, P, 'The Structure of European Union Law' (2010) 12 *Cambridge Yearbook of European Legal Studies* 121–50.

Eliantonio, M and Muir, E, 'The principle of effectiveness: under strain?' (2019) 12 *Review of European Administrative Law* 255–65.

Ellis, J, 'General Principles and Comparative Law' (2011) 22 *European Journal of International Law* 949–71.

Engström, V, *Constructing the Powers of International Institutions* (Leiden, Brill, 2012).

Episcopo, F, 'The Vicissitudes of Life at the Coalface: Remedies and Procedures for Enforcing Union Law before the National Courts' in P Craig and G de Búrca (eds), *The Evolution of EU Law*, 3rd edn (Oxford, Oxford University Press, 2021) 275–306.

Erlbacher, F, 'Commentary on Article 212 TFEU' in M Kellerbauer, M Klamert and J Tomkin (eds), *The EU Treaties and the Charter of Fundamental Rights: A Commentary*, 2nd edn (Oxford, Oxford University Press, 2024).

Erlbacher, F, 'Commentary on Article 216 TFEU' in M Kellerbauer, M Klamert and J Tomkin (eds), *The EU Treaties and the Charter of Fundamental Rights: A Commentary*, 2nd edn (Oxford, Oxford University Press, 2024).

Erlbacher, F, 'Commentary on Article 217 TFEU' in M Kellerbauer, M Klamert and J Tomkin (eds), *The EU Treaties and the Charter of Fundamental Rights: A Commentary*, 2nd edn (Oxford, Oxford University Press, 2024).

Erlbacher, F and Ramopolous, T, 'Commentary on Article 205 TFEU' in M Kellerbauer, M Klamert and J Tomkin (eds), *The EU Treaties and the Charter of Fundamental Rights: A Commentary*, 2nd edn (Oxford, Oxford University Press, 2024).

Erlbacher, F and Ramopolous, T, 'Commentary on Article 215 TFEU' in M Kellerbauer, M Klamert and J Tomkin (eds), *The EU Treaties and the Charter of Fundamental Rights: A Commentary*, 2nd edn (Oxford, Oxford University Press, 2024).

Erlbacher, F and Rusche, TM, 'Commentary on Article 207 TFEU' in M Kellerbauer, M Klamert and J Tomkin (eds), *The EU Treaties and the Charter of Fundamental Rights: A Commentary*, 2nd edn (Oxford, Oxford University Press, 2024).

Esser, J, *Grundsatz und Norm in der richterlichen Fortbildung des Privatrechts* (Tübingen, Mohr, 1956).

Fabbrini, F, 'After the OMT Case: The Supremacy of EU Law as the Guarantee of the Equality of the Member States' (2015) 16 *German Law Journal* 1003–23.

Felix, D, *Einheit der Rechtsordnung: zur verfassungsrechtlichen Relevanz einer juristischen Argumentationsfigur* (Tübingen, Mohr Siebeck, 1998).

Fitzmaurice, G, 'The General Principles of International law Considered from the Standpoint of the Rule of Law' (1957) 92 *Recueil des cours* (II) 1–227.

Fromage, D, 'National Constitutional Identity and Its Regional Dimension Post-Lisbon as Part of a General Trend Towards Multilevel Governance Within the EU' (2021) 27 *European Public Law* 497–516.

Gaja, G, 'General Principles of Law' in *Max Planck Encyclopedia of Public International Law* (Oxford, Oxford University Press, 2012).

Garben, S, 'Commentary on Article 153 TFEU' in M Kellerbauer, M Klamert and J Tomkin (eds), *The EU Treaties and the Charter of Fundamental Rights: A Commentary*, 2nd edn (Oxford, Oxford University Press, 2024).

—— 'Commentary on Article 191 TFEU' in M Kellerbauer, M Klamert and J Tomkin (eds), *The EU Treaties and the Charter of Fundamental Rights: A Commentary*, 2nd edn (Oxford, Oxford University Press, 2024).

—— *The Competence Question in the (Con)Federal European Union* (Oxford, Oxford University Press, forthcoming 2025).

Gazzini, T, 'Legal Personality of International Organisations' in J Klabbers and Å Wallendahl (eds), *Research Handbook on the Law of International Organisations* (Cheltenham, Edward Elgar, 2011) 33–55.

Gorobets, K, 'Solidarity as a Practical Reason: Grounding the Authority of International Law' (2022) 69 *Netherlands International Law Review* 3–27.

Govaere, I, 'To Give or to Grab: The Principle of Full, Crippled and Split Conferral of Powers Post-Lisbon' in M Cremona (ed), *Structural Principles in EU External Relations Law* (Oxford, Oxford University Press, 2018) 71–92.

Grabitz, E, *Gemeinschaftsrecht bricht nationales Recht* (Hamburg, Appel, 1966).

Gragl, P, 'Rechtstaatlichkeit' in M Klamert (ed), *Europarecht. Jahrbuch 22* (NWV, BWV, 2022) 37–67.

—— 'Die strukturierende Wirkung der Unionsgrundrechte: Dreidimensionalität und Föderalisierung' (2024) *Europarecht*, Special Issue No 1, 89–106.

Granat, K, *The Principle of Subsidiarity and its Enforcement in the EU Legal Order: The Role of National Parliaments in the Early Warning System* (Oxford, Hart Publishing, 2018).

Griller, S, 'Judicial enforceability of WTO law in the European Union: Annotation to Case C-149/96, Portugal v. Council' (2000) 3 *Journal of International Economic Law* 441–72.

—— 'International Law, Human Rights and the European Community's Autonomous Legal Order: Notes on the European Court of Justice Decision in Kadi' (2008) 4 European Constitutional Law Review 528–53.

—— 'Der Rechtsbegriff bei Ronald Dworkin' in S Griller and H-P Rill (eds), *Rechtstheorie: Rechtsbegriff – Dynamik – Auslegung* (Vienna, Springer, 2011) 57–79.

—— 'Fragmentations in Public Law: Discourse Comparison in International and National Law' (2018) *Veröffentlichungen der Vereinigung der Deutschen Staatsrechtslehrer* (*VVDSTRL*) 238–79.

Groussot, X and Lidgard, HH, 'Are There General Principles of Community Law Affecting Private Law?' in U Bernitz and J Nergelius (eds), *General Principles of European Community Law* (The Hague, Kluwer, 2000) 155–75.

Groussot, X and Lindholm, J, 'General principles: taking rights seriously and waving the rule-of-law stick in the European Union' in KS Ziegler, PJ Neuvonen and V Moreno-Lax (eds), *Research Handbook on General Principles in EU Law: Constructing Legal Orders in Europe* (Cheltenham, Edward Elgar, 2022) 308–26.

Groussot, X, Hettne, J and Pétursson GT, 'General Principles and the Many Faces of Coherence: Between Law and Ideology in the European Union' in S Vogenauer and S Weatherill (eds), *General Principles of Law: European and Comparative Perspective* (Oxford, Hart Publishing, 2017) 77–103.

Guastaferro, B, 'Sincere cooperation and respect for national identities' in R Schütze and T Tridimas (eds), *Oxford Principles of the European Union. Volume I: The European Union Legal Order* (Oxford, Oxford University Press, 2018) 350–82.

Gutiérrez-Fons, JA and Lenaerts, K, 'The constitutional allocation of powers and general principles of EU law' (2010) 47 *CML Rev* 1629–69.

Halberstam, D, '"It's the Autonomy, Stupid!" A Modest Defense of Opinion 2/13 on EU Accession to the ECHR, and the Way Forward' (2015) 16 *German Law Journal* 105–46.

Haraldsdóttir, K, 'The Nature of Neutrality in EU Law: Article 345 TFEU' (2020) 45 *EL Rev* 3–24.
Haratsch, A, 'Nationale Identität aus europarechtlicher Sicht' (2016) 51 *Europarecht* 131–46.
Hartley, T, *Constitutional Problems of the EU* (Oxford, Hart Publishing, 1999).
Hatje, A, 'Art 4 TEU' in J Schwarze (ed), *EU-Kommentar*, 4th edn (Baden-Baden, Nomos, 2019).
Herdegen, M, 'The Origins and Development of the General Principles of Community Law' in U Bernitz and J Nergelius (eds), *General Principles of European Community Law* (The Hague, Kluwer, 2000) 3–23.
—— 'General Principles of EU Law: The Methodological Challenge' in U Bernitz, J Nergelius and C Cardner (eds), *General Principles of EC Law in a Process of Development* (The Hague, Kluwer, 2008) 343–55.
Herlin-Karnell, SEM, 'General principles and EU criminal law' in KS Ziegler, PJ Neuvonen and V Moreno-Lax (eds), *Research Handbook on General Principles in EU Law: Constructing Legal Orders in Europe* (Cheltenham, Edward Elgar, 2022) 513–29.
Herlin Karnell, SEM and Konstadinides, T, 'The Rise and Expressions of Consistency in EU Law: Legal and Strategic Implications for European Integration' (2012–13) *Cambridge Yearbook of European Legal Studies* 139–67.
Hestermeyer, HP, 'European Union Law, Autonomy of' in *Max Planck Encyclopedia of Public International Law* (Oxford, Oxford University Press, 2025).
Hilf, M and Schorkopf, F, 'Art 2 EUV' in E Grabitz, M Hilf and M Nettesheim (eds), *EU-Kommentar* (Munich, Beck, 2020).
Hillion, C, 'Mixity and Coherence in EU External Relations: The Significance of the Duty of Cooperation' in C Hillion and P Koutrakos (eds), *Mixed Agreements Revisited: The EU and its Member States in the World* (Oxford, Hart Publishing, 2010) 87–115.
—— 'A Powerless Court? The European Court of Justice and the Common Foreign and Security Policy' in M Cremona and A Thies (eds), *The European Court of Justice and External Relations Law* (Oxford, Hart Publishing, 2014) 47–70.
—— 'Conferral, Cooperation and Balance in the Institutional Framework of EU External Action' in M Cremona (ed), *Structural Principles in EU External Relations Law* (Oxford, Oxford University Press 2018) 117–74.
Hillion, C and Wessel, RA, 'Restraining External Competences of EU Member States under CFSP' in M Cremona and B de Witte (eds), *EU Foreign Relations Law: Constitutional Fundamentals* (Oxford, Oxford University Press, 2006) 79–121.
Hindelang, S, 'Conceptualisation and Application of the Principle of Autonomy of EU Law: The CJEU's Judgement in Achmea Put into Perspective' (2019) 44 *EL Rev* 383–400.
Hofmann, H, 'Conflicts and Integration: Revisiting *Costa v ENEL* and *Simmenthal II*' in MP Maduro and L Azoulai (eds), *The Past and Future of EU Law: The Classics of EU Law Revisited on the 50th Anniversary of the Rome Treaty* (Oxford, Hart Publishing, 2010) 60–68.
—— 'General Principles of EU Law and EU Administrative Law' in C Barnard and S Peers (eds), *European Union Law*, 4th edn (Oxford, Oxford University Press, 2023) 212–42.
Huber, PM and Paulus, AL, XVIth Congress of the Conference of European Constitutional Courts in 2014, Cooperation of Constitutional Courts in Europe – Current Situation and Perspectives – National Report Germany.
Hummelbrunner, S, 'The Unity and Consistency of Union Law' (2018) 73 *Zeitschrift fur Offentliches Recht (ZoR): Journal of Public Law* 295–315.
Jacqué, J-P, 'Art 3 EUV' in H von der Groeben, J Schwarze and A Hatje (eds), *Europäisches Unionsrecht*, 7th edn (Baden-Baden, Nomos, 2015).
Jakab, A, 'Re-Defining Principles as "Important Rules". A Critique of Robert Alexy' in M Borowski (ed), *On the Nature of Legal Principles*, ARSP Beiheft 119 (Stuttgart, Steiner, 2009) 145–59.
—— *European Constitutional Language* (Cambridge, Cambridge University Press, 2016).
Janssens, C, *The Principle of Mutual Recognition in EU Law* (Oxford, Oxford University Press, 2013).
Kaczorowska-Ireland, I, 'What is the European Union required to respect under Article 4(2) TEU? The uniqueness approach' (2019) 25 *European Public Law* 57–82.
Kahl, W, 'Art 4 EUV' in C Calliess and M Ruffert (eds), *EUV/AEUV*, 6th edn (Munich, Beck, 2022).

Kahn, P, *Origins of Order: Project and System in the American Legal Imagination* (New Haven, CT, Yale University Press, 2019).

Kassoti, E and Odermatt, J, 'The principle of autonomy and international investment arbitration: Reflections on Opinion 1/17' (2020) 7 *Questions of International Law* 5–20.

Kellerbauer, M, 'Commentary on Article 45 TFEU' in M Kellerbauer, M Klamert and J Tomkin (eds), *The EU Treaties and the Charter of Fundamental Rights: A Commentary*, 2nd edn (Oxford, Oxford University Press, 2024).

Kelsen, H, *Introduction to the Problems of Legal Theory* (Oxford, Clarendon Press, 1992).

Kirchmair, L, *Rethinking the Relationship between International, EU and National Law: Consent-Based Monism* (Cambridge, Cambridge University Press, 2024).

Klabbers, J, 'Straddling the Fence: The EU and International Law' in A Arnull and D Chalmers (eds), *The Oxford Handbook of European Union Law* (Oxford, Oxford University Press, 2015) 52–71.

—— 'The Transformation of International Organisations Law' (2015) 26 *European Journal of International Law* 9–82.

—— *An Introduction to International Organizations Law* (Cambridge, Cambridge University Press, 2022).

Klamert, M, Judicial Implementation of Directives and Anticipatory Indirect Effect: Connecting the Dots' (2006) 43 *CML Rev* 1251–75.

—— 'Conflicts of Legal Basis: No Legality and No Basis but a Bright Future under the Lisbon Treaty?' (2010) 35 *EL Rev* 497–515.

—— 'Dark matter: Competence, jurisdiction and "the area largely covered by EU law. Comment on *Lesoochranárske*' (2012) 50 *EL Rev* 340–50.

—— *The Principle of Loyalty in EU Law* (Oxford, Oxford University Press, 2014).

—— *Services Liberalization in the EU and WTO: Concepts, Standards and Regulatory Approaches* (Cambridge, Cambridge University Press, 2014).

—— 'What We Talk About When We Talk About Harmonisation' (2015) *Cambridge Yearbooks of European Legal Studies* 360–79.

—— 'Loyalty and Solidarity in the Euro-Crisis' (2017) *Zeitschrift fur Offentliches Recht* (*ZoR*): *Journal of Public Law* 699–715.

—— 'The Autonomy of the EU (and of EU Law): Through the Kaleidoscope' (2017) 42 *EL Rev* 815–30.

—— 'Einheit und Fragmentierung im Unionsrecht' (2019) *Europarecht*, Special Issue No 2, 133–52.

—— 'Maut, Diskriminierung und Methode', Editorial (2019) *European Journal of Business Law* 257–58.

—— 'Editorial: Vorrang, Schranken und Österreich' (2021) *European Journal of Business Law* 1057–58.

—— *EU-Recht*, 3rd edn (Vienna, Manz, 2021).

—— 'Rationalizing Supremacy: Supremacy, effectiveness, and two standards of equality in EU law' (*Verfassungsblog*, 18 October 2021).

—— 'Solidarität in der Wirtschafts- und Währungsunion' in P-C Müller-Graff, A Hatje, U Hufeld and C Ohler (eds), *Enzyklopädie Europarecht, Band 9, Europäische Wirtschafts- und Währungsunion* (Baden-Baden, Nomos, 2021).

—— 'Legal Certainty and Customary International Law: Opel Austria' in G Butler and R Wessel (eds), *EU External Relations Law: The Cases in Context* (Oxford, Hart Publishing, 2022) 367–75.

—— 'Loyalty and Solidarity as General Principles of EU Law' in KS Ziegler, PJ Neuvonen and V Moreno-Lax (eds), *Research Handbook on General Principles in EU Law: Constructing Legal Orders in Europe* (Cheltenham, Edward Elgar, 2022) 118–35.

—— 'Supremacy, the Uniformity of EU Law, and the Principle of Equality' (2022) *Austrian Law Journal* 82–92.

—— 'Commentary on Article 1 TEU' in M Kellerbauer, M Klamert and J Tomkin (eds), *The EU Treaties and the Charter of Fundamental Rights: A Commentary*, 2nd edn (Oxford, Oxford University Press, 2024).

—— 'Commentary on Article 3 TEU' in M Kellerbauer, M Klamert and J Tomkin (eds), *The EU Treaties and the Charter of Fundamental Rights: A Commentary*, 2nd edn (Oxford, Oxford University Press, 2024).

—— 'Commentary on Article 4 TEU' in M Kellerbauer, M Klamert and J Tomkin (eds), *The EU Treaties and the Charter of Fundamental Rights: A Commentary*, 2nd edn (Oxford, Oxford University Press, 2024).
—— 'Commentary on Article 5 TEU' in M Kellerbauer, M Klamert and J Tomkin (eds), *The EU Treaties and the Charter of Fundamental Rights: A Commentary*, 2nd edn (Oxford, Oxford University Press, 2024).
—— 'Commentary on Article 48 TEU' in M Kellerbauer, M Klamert and J Tomkin (eds), *The EU Treaties and the Charter of Fundamental Rights: A Commentary*, 2nd edn (Oxford, Oxford University Press, 2024).
—— 'Commentary on Article 2 TFEU' in M Kellerbauer, M Klamert, and J Tomkin (eds), *The EU Treaties and the Charter of Fundamental Rights: A Commentary*, 2nd edn (Oxford, Oxford University Press, 2024).
—— 'Commentary on Article 209 TFEU' in M Kellerbauer, M Klamert and J Tomkin (eds), *The EU Treaties and the Charter of Fundamental Rights: A Commentary*, 2nd edn (Oxford, Oxford University Press, 2024).
—— 'Was sind Strukturprinzipien des Unionsrechts?' (2024) *Europarecht*, Special Issue No 1, 9–22.
—— 'Art 215 AEUV' in T Jaeger and K Stöger (eds), *Kommentar zu EUV und AEUV* (Vienna, Manz, 2025).
Klamert, M and Bucher, S, 'Investment Screening in der EU' (2021) 8 *European Journal of Business Law* 335–42.
Klamert, M and Kochenov, D, 'Commentary on Article 2 TEU' in M Kellerbauer, M Klamert and J Tomkin (eds), *The EU Treaties and the Charter of Fundamental Rights: A Commentary*, 2nd edn (Oxford, Oxford University Press, 2024).
Klamert, M and Schima, B, 'Commentary on Article 19 TEU' in M Kellerbauer, M Klamert and J Tomkin (eds), *The EU Treaties and the Charter of Fundamental Rights: A Commentary*, 2nd edn (Oxford, Oxford University Press, 2024).
Kochenov, D, 'EU Law without the Rule of Law: Is the Veneration of Autonomy Worth It? (2015) 34 *Yearbook of European Law* 74–96.
Kochenov, D and Lavranos, N, 'Achmea versus the Rule of Law: CJEU's Dogmatic Dismissal of Investors' Rights in Backsliding Member States' (2022) 14 *Hague Journal of the Rule of Law* 195–219.
Kokott, J, 'States, Sovereign Equality' in *Max Planck Encyclopedia of Public International Law* (Oxford, Oxford University Press, 2015).
—— 'Zur unmittelbaren Wirkung des Unionsrechts (Aufgabe der Kriterien von Van Gend & Loos)' (2023) 148 *Archiv des öffentlichen Rechts* 496–520.
Kolb, R, 'Principles as Sources of International Law (With Special Reference to Good Faith)' (2006) 53 *Netherlands International Law Review* 1–36.
—— *Theory of International Law* (Oxford, Hart Publishing, 2016).
—— *Good Faith in International Law* (Oxford, Hart Publishing, 2017).
Könneke, AM, *Unionsrechtsperson – Rekonstruktion der institutionellen Autonomie der Europäischen Union* (Tübingen, Mohr Siebeck, 2024).
Konstantinidis, M, 'Demystifying Autonomy: Tracing the International Law Origins of the EU Principle of Autonomy' (2024) 25 *German Law Journal* 94–110.
Kotzur, M, 'Solidarity as a legal concept' in A Grimmel and S My Giang (eds), *Solidarity in the European Union: A fundamental value in crisis* (New York, Springer, 2017) 37–45.
Koutrakos, P, *EU International Relations Law*, 2nd edn (Oxford, Hart Publishing, 2015).
—— 'What is the principle of autonomy really about?' (2018) 43 *EL Rev* 1–2.
—— 'More on autonomy – Opinion 1/17 (CETA)' (2019) 44 *EL Rev* 293–94.
Krenn, C, 'Autonomy and Effectiveness as Common Concerns: A Path to ECHR Accession After Opinion 2/13' (2015) 16 *German Law Journal* 147–68.
—— 'Warum Unionsrecht Vorrang hat: Zur aktualisierten Begründung des Vorrangprinzips in den Urteilen Euro Box Promotion und R.S.' (2024) *Europarecht*, Special Issue No 1, 59–69.
Krieger, H, *Das Effektivitätsprinzip im Völkerrecht* (Berlin, Duncker & Humblot, 2000).

Küçük, E, 'Solidarity in EU Law – An Elusive Political Statement or a Legal Principle with Substance?' (2016) 23 *Maastricht Journal* 965–83.
Kuijper, PJ et al (eds), *The Law of the European Union*, 5th edn (The Hague, Kluwer Law International, 2018).
Kukovec, D, 'Autonomy: The Central Idea of the Reasoning of the Court of Justice' (2023) 8 *European Papers* 1403–39.
Langenbucher, K, 'Argument by Analogy in European Law' (1998) 57 *Cambridge Law Journal* 481–521.
Langenfeld, C, *Die Autonomie des Unionsrechts in der EuGH-Rechtsprechung* (Tübingen, Mohr Siebeck, 2024).
Larik, J, 'From Speciality to a Constitutional Sense of Purpose: On the Changing Role of the Objectives of the European Union' (2014) 63 *ICLQ* 935–62.
—— 'Pars Pro Toto: The Member States' Obligations of Sincere Cooperation, Solidarity and Unity' in M Cremona (ed), *Structural Principles in EU External Relations Law* (Oxford, Oxford University Press, 2018) 175–200.
Larsen, SR, *The Constitutional Theory of the Federation and the European Union* (Oxford, Oxford University Press, 2021).
Lasser, M, *Judicial Deliberations: A Comparative Analysis of Judicial Transparency and Legitimacy* (Oxford, Oxford University Press, 2009).
Lenaerts, K, 'The Unity of European Law and the Overload of the ECJ – The System of Preliminary Rulings Revisited' in I Pernice, C Saunders and J Kokott (eds), *The Future of the European Judicial System in a Comparative Perspective* (Baden-Baden, Nomos, 2011) 211–39.
—— 'La vie après l'avis: Exploring the Principle of Mutual (Yet Not Blind) Trust' (2017) 54 *CML Rev* 805–40.
—— 'No Member State is More Equal than Others: The Primacy of EU law and the Principle of the Equality of the Member States before the Treaties' (*Verfassungsblog*, 8 October 2020).
Lenaerts, K et al (eds), *Building the European Union: The Jurist's View of the Union's Evolution* (Oxford, Hart Publishing, 2021).
Lenaerts, K and Adam, S, 'La solidarité, valeur sociale commune aux États membres et principe fédératif de l' Union européenne' (2021) 58 *Cahiers de droit européen* 307–417.
—— 'Sink or Swim Together: Solidarity between the Member States as a Foundational Principle of the European Union' in C Barnard, A Łazowski and D Sarmiento (eds), *Pursuit of Legal Harmony in a Turbulent Europe: Essays in Honour of Eleanor Sharpston* (Oxford, Hart Publishing, 2024) 41–55.
Lenaerts, K and Corthaut, T, 'Of Birds and Hedges: The Role of Primacy in Invoking Norms of EU Law' (2006) 31 *EL Rev* 289–315.
Lenaerts, K and Gutiérrez-Fons, JA, 'The Role of General Principles of EU Law' in A Arnull, C Barnard, M Dougan and E Spaventa (eds), *A Constitutional Order of States: Essays in EU Law in Honour of Alan Dashwood* (Oxford, Hart Publishing, 2011) 179–98.
—— 'A Constitutional Perspective' in R Schütze and T Tridimas (eds), *Oxford Principles of European Union Law: The European Union Legal Order, Volume I* (Oxford, Oxford University Press, 2018) 103–41.
—— 'Epilogue. High Hopes: Autonomy and the Identity of the EU' (2023) 8 *European Papers* 1495–1511.
Lenaerts, K, Gutiérrez-Fons, JA and Adam, S, 'Exploring the Autonomy of the European Union Legal Order' (2021) 81 *Zeitschrift für ausländisches öffentliches Recht und Völkerrecht* 47–87.
Lenaerts, K and van Nuffel, P, *European Union Law*, 3rd edn (London, Sweet & Maxwell, 2011).
Lenaerts, K, van Nuffel, P and Corthaut, T, *EU Constitutional Law* (Oxford, Oxford University Press, 2021).
Lindeboom, J, 'Is the Primacy of EU Law Based on the Equality of the Member States? A Comment on the CJEU's Press Release Following the PSPP Judgment' (2020) *German Law Journal* 1032–44.
Lock, T, *The European Court of Justice and International Courts* (Oxford, Oxford University Press, 2015).
—— 'The future of the European Union's accession to the European Convention on Human Rights after Opinion 2/13: is it still possible and is it still desirable?' (2015) 11 *European Constitutional Law Review* 239–73.

—— 'Commentary on Article 52 CFR' in M Kellerbauer, M Klamert and J Tomkin (eds), *The EU Treaties and the Charter of Fundamental Rights: A Commentary*, 2nd edn (Oxford, Oxford University Press, 2024).

—— 'Commentary on Article 6 TEU' in M Kellerbauer, M Klamert and J Tomkin (eds), *The EU Treaties and the Charter of Fundamental Rights: A Commentary*, 2nd edn (Oxford, Oxford University Press, 2024).

—— 'Introduction to Title IV Solidarity (CFR)' in M Kellerbauer, M Klamert and J Tomkin (eds), *The EU Treaties and the Charter of Fundamental Rights: A Commentary*, 2nd edn (Oxford, Oxford University Press, 2024).

Loewenthal, PJ, 'Commentary on Article 13 TEU' in M Kellerbauer, M Klamert and J Tomkin (eds), *The EU Treaties and the Charter of Fundamental Rights: A Commentary*, 2nd edn (Oxford, Oxford University Press, 2024).

MacDonald, R, 'Solidarity in the practice and discourse of public international law' (1996) 8 *Pace International Law Review* 259–302.

Maiani, F and Migliorini, S, 'One principle to rule them all? Anatomy of mutual trust in the law of the Area of Freedom, Security and Justice' (2020) 57 *CML Rev* 7–44.

Marti, G, *Les grandes notions du droit de l'Union européenne* (Paris, PUF, 2023).

Martinico, G, 'Taming National Identity: A Systematic Understanding of Article 4.2 TEU' (2021) *European Public Law* 447–64.

Mayer, FC, 'Art 18 EUV' in E Grabitz, M Hilf and M Nettesheim (eds), *EU-Kommentar* (Munich, Beck, 2019).

Mayr, S, *EU Law and International Law: An Uneasy Relationship? The Case of Investor–State Arbitration* (forthcoming).

Mendez, M, *The Legal Effects of EU Agreements* (Oxford, Oxford University Press, 2013).

Mendez-Pinedo, E, 'The principle of effectiveness of EU law: a difficult concept in legal scholarship' (2021) 11 *Juridical Tribune* 5–29.

Meyer, F, 'The Rule of Law in the Enforcement of EU Law: Shortcomings and Future Standards' (Jean Monnet Network on EU Law Enforcement Working Paper Series 2023).

Miasik, D and Szwarc, M, 'Primacy and Direct Effect – Still Together: Popławski II' (2021) 58 *CML Rev* 571–90.

Moreno-Lax, V, 'Solidarity's Reach: Meaning, Dimensions, and Implications for EU (External) Asylum Policy' (2017) 24 *Maastricht Journal* 740–62.

—— 'The Axiological Emancipation of a (Non-)Principle: Autonomy, International Law and the EU Legal Order' in I Govaere and S Garben (eds), *The Interface Between EU and International Law* (Oxford, Hart Publishing, 2019) 45–72.

Moreno-Lax, V and Ziegler, KS, 'Autonomy of the EU Legal Order – a General Principle? On the Risks of Normative Functionalism and Selective Constitutionalisation' in KS Ziegler, PJ Neuvonen and V Moreno-Lax (eds), *Research Handbook on General Principles in EU Law: Constructing Legal Orders in Europe* (Cheltenham, Edward Elgar, 2022) 227–52.

Möstl, M, 'Preconditions and Limits of Mutual Recognition' (2010) 47 *CML Rev* 405–36.

Muir, E, 'Pursuing Equality in the EU' in A Arnull and D Chalmers (eds), *The Oxford Handbook of European Union Law* (Oxford, Oxford University Press, 2015) 919–42.

—— *An Introduction to the EU Legal Order* (Cambridge, Cambridge University Press, 2023).

Müller-Graff, P-C, 'Protectionism or reasonable national regulation?' in S Griller (ed), *At the Crossroads: The World Trading System and the Doha Round* (Vienna, Springer, 2008) 147–67.

Naert, F, 'The Use of the CFSP Legal Basis for EU International Agreements in Combination with Other Legal Bases' in J Czuczai and F Naert (eds), *The EU as a Global Actor: Bridging Legal Theory and Practice. Liber Amicorum in Honour of Ricardo Gosalbo Bono* (Leiden, Brill 2017) 394–423.

Nazzini, R, 'Potency and Act of the Principle of Effectiveness: The Development of Competition Law Remedies and Procedures in Community Law' in C Barnard and O Odudu (eds), *The Outer Limits of European Union Law* (Oxford, Hart Publishing, 2009) 401–35.

Nebbia, P, 'The Double Life of Effectiveness' (2007/08) 10 *Cambridge Yearbook of European Legal Studies* 287–302.

Neframi, E, 'The Duty of Loyalty: Rethinking its Scope Through its Application in the Field of EU External Relations' (2010) 47 *CML Rev* 323–59.
—— 'The Dynamic of the EU Objectives in the Analysis of the External Competence' in E Neframi and M Gatti (eds), *Constitutional Issues of EU External Relations Law* (Baden-Baden, Nomos, 2018) 63–88.
Nettesheim, M, 'Grundsatz der Wirksamkeit des Gemeinschaftsrechts' in A Randelzhofer, R Scholz and D Wilke (eds), *Gedächtnisschrift für Eberhard Grabitz* (Munich, Beck, 1995) 447–68.
—— 'Normenhierarchien im EU-Recht' (2006) 6 *Europarecht* 737–72.
—— 'Artikel 1 AEUV' in E Grabitz, M Hilf, and M Nettesheim (eds), *EU-Kommentar* (Munich, Beck, 2024).
Neuvonen, PJ and Ziegler, KS, 'General principles in the EU legal order: Past, present and future directions' in in KS Ziegler, PJ Neuvonen and V Moreno-Lax (eds), *Research Handbook on General Principles in EU Law: Constructing Legal Orders in Europe* (Cheltenham, Edward Elgar, 2022) 7–24.
Nic Shuibhne, N, 'Primary Laws: Judging Free Movement Restrictions after Lisbon' in P Koutrakos, N Nic Shuibhne and P Syrpis (eds), *Exceptions from EU Free Movement Law: Derogation, Justification and Proportionality* (Oxford, Hart Publishing, 2016) 297–318.
—— 'The Integrity of the EU Internal Market: Connecting Purpose and Context for Brexit – and Beyond' in F Amtenbrink et al (eds), *The Internal Market and the Future of European Integration: Essays in Honour of Laurence W Gormley* (Cambridge, Cambridge University Press, 2019) 549–60.
—— 'What is the autonomy of EU law, and why does that matter?' (2019) 88 *Nordic Journal of International Law* 9–40.
Nollkaemper, A, 'Rethinking the Supremacy of International Law' (2010) 65 *Zeitschrift fur Offentliches Recht (ZoR): Journal of Public Law* 65–86.
—— *National Courts and the International Rule of Law* (Oxford, Oxford University Press, 2012).
Öberg, M-L, 'Autonomy of the EU Legal Order: A Concept in Need of Revision?' (2020) 26 *European Public Law* 705–40.
—— *The Boundaries of the EU Internal Market* (Cambridge, Cambridge University Press, 2020).
Odermatt, J, 'The Principle of Autonomy: An Adolescent Disease of EU External Relations Law?' in M Cremona (ed), *Structural Principles in EU External Relations Law* (Oxford, Oxford University Press, 2018) 291–316.
Öhlinger, T and Eberhard, H, *Verfassungsrecht*, 13th edn (Vienna, Facultas, 2022).
Ortino, M, 'A Reading of the EU Constitutional Legal System through the Meta-Principle of Effectiveness' (2016) 52 *Cahiers de droit européen* 91–114.
Paulus, A and Leiss, JR, 'Constitutionalism and the Mechanics of Global Law Transfers' (2018) 9 *Goettingen Journal of International Law*, Special edn Holterhus 35–69.
Pauwelyn, J, 'Fragmentation of International Law' in *Max Planck Encyclopedia of Public International Law*, 2nd edn (Oxford, Oxford University Press, 2012).
Pechstein, M, 'Art 20 EUV' in R Streinz (ed), *EUV/AEUV*, 3rd edn (Munich, Beck, 2018).
Pernice, I, 'Der Europäische Verfassungsverbund und die Netzwerktheorie' (2010) *ZaöRV* 51–71.
—— 'The Autonomy of the EU Legal Order – Fifty Years After Van Gend' in A Tizzano, J Kokott and S Prechal (eds), *50ème Anniversaire de l'arrêt/50th anniversary of the judgment in Van Gend en Loos, 1963–2013* (Luxembourg, Office des publications de l'Union européenne, 2013) 55–80.
Pescatore, P, 'Das Zusammenwirken der Gemeinschaftsrechtsordnung mit den nationalen Rechtsordnungen' (1970) *Europarecht* 307–23.
—— 'Van Gend en Loos, 3 February 1963 – A View from Within' in M Poiares Maduro and L Azoulai (eds), *The Past and Future of EU Law: The Classics of EU Law Revisited on the 50th Anniversary of the Rome Treaty* (Oxford, Hart Publishing, 2010) 3–8.
—— 'The Docrine of "Direct Effect": An Infant Disease of Community Law' (2015) 40 *EL Rev* 135–53 (reprint).
Peters, A, 'Compensatory Constitutionalism: The Function and Potential of Fundamental International Norms and Structures' (2006) 19 *Leiden Journal of International Law* 579–610.
Petersmann, E-U, 'CETA, TTIP, and TiSA: New Trends in International Economic Law' in S Griller, W Obwexer and E Vranes (eds), *Mega-Regional Trade Agreements: CETA, TTIP, and TiSA* (Oxford, Oxford University Press, 2017) 17–44.

Phelan, W, 'The role of the German and Italian constitutional courts in the rise of EU human rights jurisprudence: A response to Delledonne and Fabbrini' (2021) *EL Rev* 175–93.
—— 'The Revolutionary Doctrines of European Law and the Legal Philosophy of Robert Lecourt' (2017) *European Journal of International Law* 935–57.
—— *Great Judgments of the European Court of Justice: Rethinking the Landmark Decisions of the Foundational Period* (Cambridge, Cambridge University Press, 2019).
Platon, S, 'The principle of institutional balance: rise, eclipse and revival of a general principle of EU constitutional law' in KS Ziegler, PJ Neuvonen, and V Moreno-Lax (eds), *Research Handbook on General Principles in EU Law: Constructing Legal Orders in Europe* (Cheltenham, Edward Elgar, 2022) 136–55.
Potacs, M, 'Effet utile als Auslegungsgrundsatz' (2009) *Europarecht* 465–87.
—— *Rechtstheorie*, 2nd edn (Vienna, Facultas, 2019).
Prechal, S, 'Direct Effect, Indirect Effect, Supremacy and the Evolving Constitution of the European Union' in C Barnard (ed), *The Fundamentals of EU Law Revisited: Assessing the Impact of the Constitutional Debate* (Oxford, Oxford University Press, 2007) 35–69.
—— 'Competence Creep and General Principles of Law' (2010) 3 *REALaw* 5–22.
Prechal, S and Widdershoven, R, 'Redefining the Relationship between 'Rewe-effectiveness' and Effective Judicial Protection' (2011) 4 *Review of European Administrative Law* 31–50.
Prete, L, 'The Constitutional Limits to the Choice of Mixity after EUSFTA, COTIF I, MPA Antarctic and COTIF II: Towards a More Constructive Discourse?' (2020) 45 *EL Rev* 113–27.
Ramopolous, T and Havas, L, 'Commentary on Article 23 TEU' in M Kellerbauer, M Klamert and J Tomkin (eds), *The EU Treaties and the Charter of Fundamental Rights: A Commentary*, 2nd edn (Oxford, Oxford University Press, 2024).
—— 'Commentary on Article 24 TEU' in M Kellerbauer, M Klamert and J Tomkin (eds), *The EU Treaties and the Charter of Fundamental Rights: A Commentary*, 2nd edn (Oxford, Oxford University Press, 2024).
Rasmussen, M, 'The Origins of a Legal Revolution: The Early History of the European Court of Justice' (2008) 14 *Journal of European Integration History* 77–98.
—— 'From Costa v ENEL to the Treaties of Rome: A Brief History of a Legal Revolution' in M Poiares Maduro and L Azoulai (eds), *The Past and Future of EU Law: The Classics of EU Law Revisited on the 50th Anniversary of the Rome Treaty* (Oxford, Hart Publishing, 2010) 69–86.
Rauchegger, C, 'Four functions of the principle of primacy in post-Lisbon Case law in KS Ziegler, PJ Neuvonen and V Moreno-Lax (eds), *Research Handbook on General Principles in EU Law: Constructing Legal Orders in Europe* (Cheltenham, Edward Elgar, 2022) 157–72.
Raz J, 'Legal Principles and the Limits of Law' (1972) 81 *Yale Law Journal* 823–54.
Redgwell, C, 'General Principles of International Law' in S Vogenauer and S Weatherill (eds), *General Principles of Law: European and Comparative Perspective* (Oxford, Hart Publishing, 2017) 5–19.
Reimer, F, 'Ziele und Zuständigkeiten: Die Funktionen der Unionszielbestimmungen' (2003) *Europarecht* 992–1012.
Reissner, HM, *Die Autonomie der Unionsrechtsordnung* (Tübingen, Mohr Siebeck, 2023).
Rietiker, D and Steller, S, 'The Principle of Effectiveness: And its Overarching Role in the Interpretation and Application of the ECHR' (*Völkerrechtsblog*, 10 October 2022).
Roeben, V, 'Judicial Protection as the Meta-norm in the EU Judicial Architecture' (2020) 12 *Hague Journal on the Rule of Law* 29–62.
Röhl, K and Röhl, HC, *Allgemeine Rechtslehre*, 3rd edn (Cologne, Heyman, 2008).
Rosas, A, 'EU external relations law: Time for a reality check?' (2020) 27 *Maastricht Journal* 277–83.
—— 'EU External Competence in the Absence of Internal Rules, and the Sleeping Beauty:Opinion 1/76 (Laying Up Fund for Inland Waterway Vessels)' in G Butler and RA Wessel (eds), *EU External Relations Law: The Cases in Context* (Oxford, Hart Publishing, 2022) 97–110.
Rosas, A and Armati, L, *EU Constitutional Law: An Introduction*, 3rd edn (Oxford, Hart Publishing, 2021).

Ross, M, 'Effectiveness in the European Union Legal Order(s): Beyond Supremacy to Constitutional Proportionality?' (2006) 31 *EL Rev* 476–98.
—— 'Solidarity: A New Constitutional, paradigm for the EU?' in M Ross and Y Borgmann-Prebil (eds), *Promoting Solidarity in the European Union* (Oxford, Oxford University Press, 2010) 23–45.
Rossi, LS, 'The Principle of Equality among Member States of the European Union' in LS Rossi and F Casolari (eds), *The Principle of Equality in EU Law* (New York, Springer, 2017) 3–42.
—— 'La valeur juridique des valeurs. L'article 2 TUE: relations avec d'autres dispositions de droit primaire de l'Union européenne et remèdes jurisdictionnels' (2020) *Révue trimestrielle de droit européen* 639–57.
Ruffert, M, 'Art 1 AEUV' in C Calliess and M Ruffert (eds), *EUV/AEUV*, 6th edn (Munich, Beck, 2022).
—— 'Art 3 EUV' in C Calliess and M Ruffert (eds), *EUV/AEUV*, 6th edn (Munich, Beck, 2022).
—— 'Art 20 EUV' in C Calliess and M Ruffert (eds), *EUV/AEUV*, 6th edn (Munich, Beck, 2022).
Saenz Perez, C, Mutual trust as a driver of integration: which way forward? in KS Ziegler, PJ Neuvonen and V Moreno-Lax (eds), *Research Handbook on General Principles in EU Law: Constructing Legal Orders in Europe* (Cheltenham, Edward Elgar, 2022) 530–44.
Sarmiento, D, 'Review Article – Making Sense of Constitutional Pluralism: A Review of Klemen Jaklic's *Constitutional Pluralism in the EU*' (2015) 40 *EL Rev* 110–17.
Sarooshi, D, *International Organisations and Their Exercise of Sovereign Powers* (Oxford, Oxford University Press, 2005).
Saunders, I, *General Principles as a Source of International Law: Art 38(1)(c) of the Statute of the International Court of Justice* (Oxford, Hart Publishing, 2022).
Schill, S and Krenn, C, 'Artikel 4 EUV' in E Grabitz, M Hilf and M Nettesheim (eds), *EU-Kommentar* (Munich, Beck, 2023).
Schima, B and Eisendle, D, 'Commentary on Article 267 TFEU' in M Kellerbauer, M Klamert and J Tomkin (eds), *The EU Treaties and the Charter of Fundamental Rights: A Commentary*, 2nd edn (Oxford, Oxford University Press, 2024).
Schroeder, W, Art 288 TFEU' in R Streinz (ed), *EUV/AEUV*, 3rd edn (Munich, Beck, 2018).
—— *Das Gemeinschaftsrechtssystem* (Tübingen, Mohr Siebeck, 2002).
Schroeder, W and Müller, A, 'Elements of Supranationality in the Law of International Organizations' in U Fastenrath et al (eds), *From Bilateralism to Community Interest: Essays in Honour of Judge Bruno Simma* (Oxford, Oxford University Press, 2011) 358–78.
Schütze, R, 'On "Federal" Ground: The European Union as an (Inter)national Phenomenon' (2009) 46 *CML Rev* 1069–105.
—— *European Constitutional Law*, 3rd edn (Oxford, Oxford University Press, 2021).
Schütze, R and Tridimas, T (eds), *Oxford Principles Of European Union Law: The European Union Legal Order: Volume I* (Oxford, Oxford University Press, 2018).
Semertzi, A, 'The Preclusion of Direct Effect in the Recently Concluded EU Free Trade Agreements' (2014) 51 *CML Rev* 1125–58.
Semmelmann, C, 'General Principles of EU Law: The Ghost in the Platonic Heaven in Need of Conceptual Clarification' (2013) 2 *Pittsburgh Papers on the European Union* 1.
Serghides, GA, 'The Principle of Effectiveness in the European Convention on Human Rights, in Particular its Relationship to the other Convention Principles' (2017) 30 *Hague Yearbook of International Law / Annuaire de La Haye de droit international* 1–15.
Seyr S, *Der effet utile in der Rechtsprechung des Europäischen Gerichtshofs* (Berlin, Duncker & Humblot, 2008).
Shao, X, 'What We Talk about When We Talk about General Principles of Law' (2021) 20 *Chinese Journal of International Law* 219–55.
Shaw, M, *International Law*, 9th edn (Cambridge, Cambridge University Press, 2021).
Shelton, D (ed), *The Oxford Handbook of International Human Rights Law* (Oxford, Oxford University Press, 2013).

Södersten, A, 'The Birth of the Principle of Close Cooperation, Declaration of Competences, and the Ruling Procedure: Ruling 1/78 (Convention on Nuclear Protection)' in G Butler and RA Wessel (eds), *EU External Relations Law: The Cases in Context* (Oxford, Hart Publishing, 2022) 111–22.
Somek, A, 'On Supranationality' (2001) 5 *European Integration Online Papers* 1.
—— *Individualism: An Essay on the Authority of the European Union* (Oxford, Oxford University Press, 2008).
—— 'Is Legality a Principle of EU Law?' in S Vogenauer and S Weatherill (eds), *General Principles of Law: European and Comparative Perspectives* (Oxford, Hart Publishing, 2017) 53–75.
Sommermann, K-P, 'Art 3 TEU' in H-J Blanke and S Mangiameli (eds), *The Treaty on European Union (TEU): A Commentary* (New York, Springer, 2013).
Spaventa, E, 'A Very Fearful Court? The Protection of Fundamental Rights in the European Union after Opinion 2/13' (2015) 22 *Maastricht Journal* 35–56.
Spieker, LD, 'Framing and Managing Constitutional Identity Conflicts: How to Stabilize the Modus Vivendi between the Court of Justice and National Constitutional Courts' (2020) 57 *CML Rev* 361–98.
—— 'The Conflict over the Polish Disciplinary Regime for Judges – An Acid Test for Judicial Independence, Union Values and the Primacy of EU Law: Commission v Poland' (2022) 59 *CML Rev* 777–812.
—— 'Werte, Vorrang, Identität: Der Dreiklang europäischer Justizkonflikte vor dem EuGH' (2022) 33 *European Journal of Business Law* 305–13.
—— *EU Values Before the Court of Justice: Foundations, Potential, Risks* (Oxford, Oxford University Press, 2023).
Stöger, K, 'Art 4 EUV' in T Jaeger and K Stöger (eds), *Kommentar zu EUV und AEUV* (Vienna, Manz, 2024).
Streinz, R, 'Art 4 EUV' in R Streinz (ed), *EUV/AEUV*, 3rd edn (Munich, Beck, 2018).
—— 'Art 6 EUV' in R Streinz (ed), *EUV/AEUV*, 3rd edn (Munich, Beck, 2018).
Syrpis, P, 'Theorising the Relationship' in P Syrpis (ed), *The Judiciary, the Legislature and the EU Internal Market* (Cambridge, Cambridge University Press, 2012) 3–24.
Temple Lang, J, 'The ERTA Judgment and the Court's Case-law on Competence and Conflict' (1986) 6 *Yearbook of European Law* 183–218.
—— 'The Duties of Cooperation of National Authorities and Courts under Article 10 EC: Two More Reflections' (2001) 26 *EL Rev* 84–89.
Terhechte, JP, '§ 14 Prinzipienordnung der Europäischen Union' in A Hatje and P Müller-Graff (eds), *Europäisches Organisations- und Verfassungsrecht*, 2nd edn (Baden-Baden, Nomos, 2022) 773–812.
Teubner, G and Fischer-Lescano, A, 'Regime-Collisions: The Vain Search for Legal Unity in the Fragmentation of Global Law' (2004) 25 *Michigan Journal of International Law* 999–1046.
Thies, A, 'Shared Competence and the EU Member States' Obligations to Refrain from Unilateral External Action: PFOS and Beyond' in J Diez-Hochleitner et al (eds), *Recent Trends in the Case Law of the Court of Justice of the European Union (2008–2011)* (Madrid, La Ley, 2012) 703–28.
—— 'The Search for Effectiveness and the Need for Loyalty in EU External Action' in M Cremona (ed), *Structural Principles in EU External Relations Law* (Oxford, Oxford University Press, 2018) 263–90.
Tomkin, J, 'Commentary on Article 18 TFEU' in M Kellerbauer, M Klamert and J Tomkin (eds), *The EU Treaties and the Charter of Fundamental Rights: A Commentary*, 2nd edn (Oxford, Oxford University Press, 2019).
—— 'Commentary on Article 20 CFR' in M Kellerbauer, M Klamert and J Tomkin (eds), *The EU Treaties and the Charter of Fundamental Rights: A Commentary*, 2nd edn (Oxford, Oxford University Press, 2024).
Tridimas, T, *General Principles of EU Law*, 2nd edn (Oxford, Oxford University Press, 2006).
Tuominen, T, 'Reconceptualizing the Primacy–Supremacy Debate in EU Law' (2020) 47 *Legal Issues of Economic Integration* 245–66.
Usher, JA, *General Principles of EC Law* (London, Longman, 1998).
Van Damme, I, 'Treaty Interpretation by the WTO Appellate Body' (2010) 21 *European Journal of International Law* 605–48.

Van de Beeten, J, 'On Metaphor and Meaning: The Autonomy of EU Legal Order Through the Lens of Project and System' (2023) 8 *European Papers* 1441–64.

Van Elsuwege, P, 'The potential for inter-institutional conflicts before the Court of Justice: Impact of the Lisbon Treaty' in M Cremona and A Thies, *The European Court of Justice and external relations law: constitutional challenges* (Oxford, Hart Publishing, 2014) 115–36.

—— 'Exporting the Internal Market Beyond the EU's Borders: Between Political Ambition and Legal Reality' in F Amtenbrink et al (eds), *The Internal Market and the Future of European Integration: Essays in Honour of Laurence W Gormley* (Cambridge, Cambridge University Press, 2019) 637–50.

—— 'The Duty of Sincere Cooperation and its Implications for Autonomous Member State Action in the Field of External Relations' in M Varju (ed), *Between Compliance and Particularism. Member State Interests and European Union Law* (New York, Springer, 2019) 283–98.

—— 'Judicial Review and the Common Foreign and Security Policy: Limits to the Gap-Filling Role of the Court of Justice' (2021) 58 *CML Rev* 1731–60.

Van Elsuwege, P and Merket, H, 'The Role of the Court of Justice in Ensuring the Unity of the EU's External Representation' in S Blockmans and RA Wessel (eds), *Principles and Practices of EU External Representation* (CLEER Working Paper 5, 2012) 37–58.

Van Rossem, JWC, 'The Autonomy of EU Law: More is Less?' in RA Wessel and S Blockmans (eds), *Between Autonomy and Dependence: The EU Legal Order under the Influence of International Organisations* (The Hague, Springer, 2013) 13–46.

—— 'Pushing Limits: The Principle of Autonomy in the External Relations Case Law of the European Court of Justice' in M Andenas et al (eds), *EU External Action in International Economic Law* (The Hague, Springer, 2020) 35–68.

Verellen, T, 'On hybrid decisions, mixed agreements and the limits of the new legal order: Commission v. Council ("US Air Transport Agreement")' (2016) 53 *CML Rev* 741–61.

Vianello, I, 'The Rule of Law as a Relational Principle Structuring the Union's Action Towards its External Partners' in M Cremona (ed), *Structural Principles in EU External Relations Law* (Oxford, Oxford University Press, 2018) 225–40.

Vogenauer, S, *Die Auslegung von Gesetzen in England und auf dem Kontinent* (Tübingen, Mohr Siebeck, 2001).

Von Arnauld, A, 'Harmonisation through general principles of law' in KS Ziegler, PJ Neuvonen and V Moreno-Lax (eds), *Research Handbook on General Principles in EU Law: Constructing Legal Orders in Europe* (Cheltenham, Edward Elgar, 2022) 40–61.

Von Bogdandy, A, 'Grundprinzipien des Unionsrechts – eine verfassungstheoretische und -dogmatische Skizze' (2009) *Europarecht* 749–69.

—— 'Founding Principles of EU Law: A Theoretical and Doctrinal Sketch' (2010) 12 *European Law Journal* 95–111.

—— *The Emergence of European Society through Public Law: A Hegelian and Anti-Schmittian Approach*, Collected Courses of the Academy of European Law (Oxford, Oxford University Press, 2024).

Von Bogdandy, A and Bast, J, 'The Federal Order of Competences' in A von Bogdandy and J Bast (eds), *Principles of European Constitutional Law*, 2nd edn (Oxford, Hart Publishing, 2009) 275–307.

—— 'Die Systematik des Verfassungsrechts der europäischen Gesellschaft' in A von Bogdandy and J Bast (eds), *Unionsverfassungsrecht – Eine Neubestimmung anhand der Grundlagen im EU-Vertrag* (Baden-Baden, Nomos, 2025) 39–66.

—— *Unionsverfassungsrecht – Eine Neubestimmung anhand der Grundlagen im EU-Vertrag* (Baden-Baden, Nomos, 2025).

Von Bogdandy, A and Schill, S, 'Overcoming absolute primacy: Respect for national identity under the Lisbon Treaty' (2011) 48 *CML Rev* 1417–53.

Von Danwitz, L, *Föderale Verhältnismäßigkeit Bedeutung und Funktion von Art. 5 Abs. 4 EUV im Föderalismus der Europäischen Union* (Tübingen, Mohr Siebeck, 2024).

Von Danwitz, T, 'B. II. Rechtsetzung und Rechtsangleichung' in M Dauses and M Ludwigs (eds), *Handbuch des EU Wirtschaftsrechts* (Munich, Beck, 2023).
Vranes, E, 'Lex Superior, Lex Specialis, Lex Posterior – Rechtsnatur der "Konfliktlösungsregeln"' (2005) 65 *ZaöRV* 391–405.
Wagner, L-J, 'Competence in Common Foreign and Security Policy' in S Garben and L Gormley (eds), *The Oxford Encylopedia of EU Law* (Oxford, Oxford University Press, 2024).
Walker, N, 'The Philosophy of European Union Law' in D Chalmers and A Arnull, *The Oxford Handbook of European Union Law* (Oxford, Oxford University Press, 2015) 3–27.
Wallerman Ghavanini, A, 'Remedies for Non-Material Damages: Striking Out in a New Direction? Braathens' (2022) 59 *CML Rev* 151–70.
Weatherill, S, 'From Myth to Reality: The EU's "New Legal Order" and the Place of General Principles Within It' in S Vogenauer and S Weatherill (eds), *General Principles of Law: European and Comparative Perspectives* (Oxford, Hart Publishing, 2017) 21–38.
—— *The Internal Market as a Legal Concept* (Oxford, Oxford University Press, 2017).
Weatherill, S and Vogenauer, S, 'Introduction' in S Weatherill and S Vogenauer (eds), *General Principles of Law: European and Comparative Perspectives* (Oxford, Hart Publishing, 2017) 1–4.
Weber, T, *Bundesstaatliche Identitäten und ihre Achtung im Unionsrecht* (Baden-Baden, Nomos, 2022).
Wegener, B, 'Art 267 TFEU' in C Calliess and M Ruffert (eds), *EUV/AEUV*, 6th edn (Munich, Beck, 2022).
Weiler, J, 'The Transformation of Europe' (1991) *Yale Law Journal* 2403–83.
Wendel, M, 'Artikel 18 AEUV' in E Grabitz, M Hilf and M Nettesheim (eds), *EU-Kommentar* (Munich, Beck, 2024).
Wessel, RA, 'Legality in EU Common Foreign and Security Policy: The Choice of the Appropriate Legal Basis' in C Kilpatrick, J Scott (eds), *Contemporary Challenges to EU Legality* (Oxford, Oxford University Press, 2021) 71–99.
—— 'General Principles in EU Common Foreign and Security Policy' in KS Ziegler, PJ Neuvonen and V Moreno-Lax (eds), *Research Handbook on General Principles in EU Law: Constructing Legal Orders in Europe* (Cheltenham, Edward Elgar, 2022) 607–24.
Wessel, RA and Łazowski, A, 'When Caveats Turn into Locks: Opinion 2/13 on Accession of the European Union to the ECHR' (2015) 16 *German Law Journal* 179–212.
Westerman, P, 'Weaving the Threads of a European Legal Order' (2023) 8 *European Papers* 1308–15.
White, ND, 'Separate but Connected: Inter-Governmental Organizations and International Law' (2008) 5 *International Organisations Law Review* 175–95.
Wimmer, M, 'The Dinghy's Rudder: General Principles of European Union Law through the Lens of Proportionality' (2014) 20 *European Public Law* 331–53.
Wolfrum, R, 'Solidarity Amongst states: an emerging structural principle of international law' (2009) 49 *Indian Journal of International Law* 8–20.
—— 'Solidarity' in D Shelton (ed), *The Oxford Handbook of International Human Rights Law* (Oxford, Oxford University Press, 2013) 401–19.
Wouters, J, 'National Constitutions and the European Union' (2000) 27 *Legal Issues of Economic Integration* 25–92.
Wouters, J et al, *The Law of EU External Relations: Cases, Materials, and Commentary on the EU as an International Legal Actor*, 3rd edn (Oxford, Oxford University Press, 2021).
Wouters J, Coppens D and Geraets D, 'The Influence of General Principles of Law' in SE Gaines, B Egelund Olsen, and K Engsig Sørensen (eds), *Liberalising Trade in the EU and the WTO: A Legal Comparison* (Cambridge, Cambridge University Press, 2012) 43–74.
Wouters, J and Schmitt, P, 'Equality Among Member States and Differentiated Integration in the EU' in LS Rossi and F Casolari (eds), *The Principle of Equality in EU Law* (New York, Springer, 2017) 43–82.
Ziegler, KS, Neuvonen, PJ and Moreno-Lax, V (eds), *Research Handbook on General Principles in EU Law: Constructing Legal Orders in Europe* (Cheltenham, Edward Elgar, 2022).

INDEX

www.ingramcontent.com/pod-product-compliance
Ingram Content Group UK Ltd.
Pitfield, Milton Keynes, MK11 3LW, UK
UKHW020251290926
15470UKWH00002B/863

9 781509 97952